THE TROUBLE BEGINS AT EIGHT

MARK TWAIN'S LECTURE TOURS

Maguire's Academy of Music

THE SANDWICH ISLANDS!

MARK TWAIN

(Honolulu Correspondent of the Sacramento Union)

will deliver a
Lecture on the Sandwich Islands,
at the Academy of Music
On Tuesday Evening, October 2

❧

*In which mention will be made of Harris, Bishop Staley, the
American Missionaries, etc., and the absurb Customs and
Characteristics of the Natives duly discussed and described.
the great VOLCANO OF KILAUEA
will also receive proper attention.*

❧

A SPLENDID ORCHESTRA
Is in town, but has not been engaged.

Also,

A DEN OF FEROCIOUS WILD BEASTS
Will be on exhibition in the next block.

MAGNIFICENT FIRE WORKS
were in contemplation for this occasion, but the
idea has been abandoned.

A GRAND TORCHLIGHT PROCESSION
May be expected; in fact, the public are privileged
to expect whatever they please.

❧

Dress Circle—$1.00   *Family Circle*—50 cts.

DOORS OPEN AT 7 O'CLOCK

THE TROUBLE BEGINS AT 8 O'CLOCK

THE TROUBLE BEGINS AT EIGHT

MARK TWAIN'S LECTURE TOURS

FRED W. LORCH

IOWA STATE UNIVERSITY PRESS, AMES, IOWA

WINNER, 1966,
*Iowa State University Press Annual Award
for the most outstanding book manuscript
by an Iowa author*

THE LATE FRED W. LORCH joined the faculty of Iowa State University in 1921 where he was head of the Department of English and Speech from 1942 to 1959. His articles on Mark Twain have appeared in many of the leading scholarly journals in the field of American literature. The manuscript to this book was submitted to the Iowa State University Press in 1966 but, regrettably, Professor Lorch did not learn of its award of excellence by the Press prior to his death in Sherman, Texas, in January 1967. The author editorial tasks associated with its subsequent publication were taken over by his son, Robert S. Lorch, professor of political science, California State College, Long Beach, California.

© 1968 The Iowa State University Press
Ames, Iowa, U.S.A. All rights reserved

Stock #1709

First edition, 1968

Library of Congress Catalog Card Number: 68–17493

FOR RUTH

PREFACE

During his early years as lecturer Mark Twain spoke of lecturing as his alternate career—alternate, that is, to journalism and the writing of books. For long periods of time, lecturing was indeed a parallel career, and its influence upon him as a writer still remains to be fully examined. It is not without significance that Mark Twain once declared the ability to talk invaluable—far superior to the ability to put thoughts on paper.

This book tells the story of Mark Twain on the lecture circuit—the story of his tours. It deals only incidentally with the occasional lectures he gave from time to time; it deals not at all with his after-dinner speeches, for which he was widely noted. The focus is upon the famous humorist's rise to platform celebrity; upon various elements that contributed to his successes and failures; and upon his attitudes toward himself as a humorist-lecturer. It directs attention to his growing interest in the art of reading and his eventual preference for reading performances. It presents assessments of his lecture techniques, critical reaction to his performances, and the financial successes and failures of his lecture tours. It offers an analysis of the factors which eventually led Mark Twain to retire from paid public performances, and, finally, it presents in composited form extended portions of five of his major tour lectures, abstracted largely from the local newspapers which reported them.

It should be kept in mind that the word "lecture" has been applied indiscriminately to both lectures and reading performances, for the reason that Mark Twain himself used that term with reference to each.

In speaking of Mark Twain's career on the public platform, the author should like to suggest that no circumstance contributed more powerfully to the transformation of Mark Twain, "Wild Humorist of the Pacific Slope," to Mark Twain, celebrated American and world humorist and cultivated gentleman, than did his platform career. The transformation manifested itself mainly in his changing estimate of himself from a regional journalist-lecturer who had thoroughly adopted the fairly crude but widely accepted and indeed widely admired social mores of Far West communities during the 1860's to that of a cultivated personality who could feel at home on many levels of society, including the most cultured, both at home and abroad.

No other experience, not even his marriage to the daughter of an affluent and cultivated eastern family, was able to produce the transformation more rapidly and effectively. Facing audiences all across the country, attending social affairs inevitably associated with lecture engagements, talking to reporters and others who constantly sought to interview him or to make his acquaintance, meeting people of local and national prominence wherever he went, being constantly in the public eye, seeking to create the image of a popular yet respected humorist on the platform—all these, rather than authorship, provided the opportunities and means to effect that transformation and played a major role in developing Mark Twain into a distinguished American personality.

IN ASSEMBLING the materials for this book, I am indebted to a great many people, but chiefly to a multitude of librarians in large towns and small in the United States and around the world. Almost without complaint they searched their files of local newspapers for evidence that Mark Twain had lectured in their town or had passed through it to lecture engagements elsewhere. They supplied me with copies of reviews of his lectures along with other items concerning him that often appeared either before or following his performance. Some of the copies were photostats, some were on microfilm, but a great many were typescripts made at the cost of the librarians' precious time. I should like to thank them all for their generosity to a stranger.

I would also like thank Henry Nash Smith, former editor of the Mark Twain Papers at the University of California Library, Berkeley, for permitting me to examine the papers, and also Frederick Anderson, then his assistant (and now editor) for generous help on the occasion of my visit to Berkeley.

I am indebted to these publishers for permission to reprint copyrighted material: the Henry E. Huntington Library and Art Gallery, San Marino, California; Harper and Row, Publishers, Inc., New York, N.Y.; and to the Mark Twain Company, Thomas G. Chamberlain, President.

Finally I should like to acknowledge the patient help of Miss Lois Thomas of Iowa State University, who, during spare moments of busy days, did most of the typing.

FRED W. LORCH

CONTENTS

xiii

LIST OF ILLUSTRATIONS

THE TROUBLE BEGINS AT EIGHT

MARK TWAIN'S LECTURE TOURS

CHAPTER ONE

APPRENTICESHIP

There is an unwritten law about human successes. . . . No occupation without an apprenticeship. —ECCENTRICITIES OF GENIUS, P. 229.

I N MARCH, 1878, Mark Twain wrote to his brother Orion Clemens, then living in Keokuk, Iowa, about the importance of apprenticeship for anyone who aspired to success in literature. Orion, then fifty-three years old and a failure in a variety of ventures,[1] had finally decided to try his hand at fiction. He had written a burlesque of Jules Verne in which he had sent his hero adventuring into the regions of Hell, and he wanted his distinguished brother's opinion of his accomplishment. As Mark Twain read the manuscript he was not pleased. In the first place, it contained matters which in his judgment ought not to be printed. They would be sure to give serious offense. He himself, he informed Orion, had tried for a number of years to think up an appropriate way of "doing" Hell, and he had always had to give it up. One had to approach such matters with care. But Mark Twain pointed up another objection, equally serious. Orion's writing was incompetent—too crude to offer to any prominent periodical. Writing, like any other craft or trade, he argued, had to be *learned*. It required a skill which could only be won by slow and painful processes. "The apprentice-hand, in blacksmithing, in medicine, in literature, in everything," he declared, "is a thing that can't be hidden. It always shows."[2]

A year later, still hopeful of finding a quick road to financial success and celebrity which his younger brother Sam was enjoying, Orion decided to abandon literature for lecturing. About literature, he concluded, Sam was probably correct. Writing was was not a craft that could be acquired by merely "picking it up." It had to be learned. But what about lecturing? Here was an activity in which Sam had also won wealth and distinction without that slow and painful apprenticeship which appeared to be the inescapable prerequisite for literary success. Or so, at least, it must have seemed to Orion, who in the fall of 1866 had watched his brother's sudden emergence into platform celebrity in San Francisco with pleasurable surprise. Perhaps public speaking was different, for in that area, certainly, Sam's apprenticeship appeared sketchy. In looking back over his brother's early career he could recall a few beginnings, of course, but little that could be described as a slow and painful process toward its perfection as an art. Perhaps lecturing, unlike literature, was like pocket mining, an activity which sometimes produced quick and rich rewards by an accidental or fortunate strike.[3]

Whether Orion sought his brother's advice about lecturing is not a matter of record, but the fact of Mark Twain's sudden rise to platform popularity and his subsequent world-wide celebrity as a lecturer and reader give the question of his apprenticeship in the activity frequently referred to as his "parallel career" considerable importance. What, precisely, were the beginnings, the circumstances, and the influences which helped to produce one of the most popular platform personalities of the last half of the nineteenth century? Was there an apprenticeship, a background, a preparation? And if there was, what was it like? Were there any awkward, fumbling starts where the apprentice-hand showed through, or any evidences of uncertain gropings concerning his artistic purposes? Did he derive his platform manners, devices, and techniques mainly from others; or were they largely the native and original products of his own personality and imagination? All these questions deserve attention in contemplating Mark Twain's emergence as a public lecturer and his later success.

An examination of Mark Twain's early childhood, it must be confessed, offers little evidence that any of his dreams and aspirations included eminence, or even a desire for proficiency, in the field of public speaking. If at any time he professed an interest in it the record is lost. At the grammar school he attended up to the age of about twelve, little attention was paid to elocution, as it was called in that day, except incidentally as it related to the declamation of literary materials which had been committed to memory for recitation in class, or for special occasions when relatives and friends were invited to watch the children perform. And it is quite apparent that such instruction as might have been given could have had little or no influence in preparing him for the style and manner of speaking and reading which later distinguished his platform performances. In 1864, for example, he observed during a visit to Miss Clapp's school in Carson City, Nevada, that the manner in which children read poetry and prose had not changed since his Hannibal school days. He gave as an example the well-known stanza of Mrs. Heman's poem:

> The boy stood on the burning deck,
> Whence all but he had fled;
> The flames that lit the battle's wreck
> Shone round him o'er the dead.

He noted the same tendency to place the rising and falling inflections "at measured intervals, as if they had learned the lesson on a 'see saw.'" It was, he declared, "the old-fashioned *impressive* style—stately, slow-moving and solemn."[4] That he was conscious of differences in reading styles during his own school days in Hannibal, however, appears unlikely. Certainly, there is no indication that he liked to read before his assembled classmates.

Nor can it be determined with any degree of certainty what opportunities Mark Twain availed himself of as a boy to hear effective public speaking. Though Hannibal was on the frontier, it must not be supposed that it was without pretensions to culture. Local organizations, some in which Orion was prominent, frequently engaged lecturers to bring enlightenment to their fellow townsmen. In the autumn of 1851, for example, young Sam Clemens might have heard Colonel Z. C. Judson, better known to the public as "Ned Buntline," lecture impassionately on Cuba and Its Martyrs. Newspapers of the time reveal that there were lectures on religious topics, witchcraft and demonology, phrenology, mesmerism and human magnetism, moral philosophy, temperance, and national affairs. Each year, of course, there were the rousing Fourth of July speeches which he may have listened to; though it is more likely when the day was hot and humid that he succumbed to the enticements of swimming in Bear Creek or at the riverfront. There is a probability that during the fall of 1849 he heard Senator Benton of Missouri orate in Hannibal, though the only evidence to support it is to be found in *The Adventures of Tom Sawyer*, where Tom reports having heard Benton speak and describes his disappointment in discovering that the great Senator fell far short of being twenty-five feet tall.[5]

While Mark Twain is disappointingly silent about his attendance at speech-making occasions during his boyhood in Hannibal, it is probable that he attended some of them. His mother was notably fond of attending lectures and all sorts of public performances,[6] and had a remarkable facility for reporting to her family what she saw and heard. Furthermore, it must be remembered that Orion, editor of the Hannibal *Journal* and always civic minded, had a lively personal interest in bringing speakers to town. Under such strong influences at home, it is inconceivable that Mark Twain should have escaped all attendance at lectures.

One kind of performance which he reported attending with great pleasure during these early Hannibal days, probably without his family's approval, was the minstrel shows. The courtly, artificial, and painfully correct speech of the middleman, contrasted with the broad Negro dialect and the clever repartee of Bones and Banjo, the end men, gave him immeasurable delight. He was too young to know that the minstrel shows were the product of a studied art. He knew only that these performances kept him alert and pleased him, whereas the stilted, overblown manner of classroom declamation and pulpit oratory bored him. It was from the minstrels, also, that he derived his lifelong love for the Negro jubilee songs, and for the more rudely comic songs popular at that time, like "Buffalo Gals" and "Camptown Races."[7]

In dealing with Mark Twain's early years, both at Hannibal and later at Keokuk, Iowa, biographers and critics customarily allude to his interest in the ministry. It is occasionally suggested that this interest was prompted by a desire to see himself in the pulpit, a focal point of attention, addressing the congregation. The implication is that this ambition revealed an early interest in public address. That for a brief time, at least, young Sam Clemens seriously considered the ministry as a career has some measure of support. Albert Bigelow Paine, deriving his information from the autobiographical papers of Orion Clemens, reports Orion as saying that the ministry was an ambition "which Sam shared with him for a time."[8] He further reports Mark Twain himself as saying that the ministry was "the most earnest ambition" he had ever had.[9] And in 1902, eight years before his death, during a nostalgic visit to Hannibal, Mark Twain told a graduating class there that when he was a boy he had earnestly desired "to stand in the Presbyterian pulpit and give instruction, but had never been asked. . . ."[10]

Despite these utterances there yet remains considerable doubt that Mark Twain's ambition to be a minister was in any conscious way prompted by a desire to speak in public. Indeed his statement to Paine that the ministry was the most earnest ambition he had ever had was followed by the declaration that his reason for wanting to be a preacher was the fact that it never occurred to him "that a preacher could be damned. It looked like a safe job."[11] Nor does the circumstance, often reported, that Mark Twain liked the association of clergymen and sometimes referred to his lectures as sermons and to lecturing as preaching supply convincing evidence that a desire to be a public speaker played any significant role in his early ambitions.

Another ambition which Mark Twain may have shared with Orion for a time, and which was popularly regarded as requiring skill in public address, was the law. Orion himself eventually became a lawyer, though he rarely practiced it; and there are indications that he and other members of the Clemens family, and friends, tried to persuade Sam at various times to consider law as a career. An event which probably gave rise to this hope occurred in Keokuk in 1856 when Mark Twain was in his twentieth year. After leaving Hannibal, and after a brief interlude at Muscatine, Iowa, Orion had bought the "Ben Franklin" book and job printing office in Keokuk and had hired Sam, who was now a journeyman printer, to take charge of the job work. One evening in January, when Mark Twain had been in the city only a few months, he was invited to attend a banquet given by the printers of the city in honor of the 150th anniversary of the birth of Benjamin Franklin, their patron saint. Judging from the report which appeared two days later in the Keokuk *Gate City*, and written by none other than Orion Clemens himself, the dinner was an elaborate affair. A considerable number of locally prominent guests had been invited, completely filling the banquet hall of the Ivens House, then Keokuk's best hotel. After the dinner, prominent members of the printers' fraternity were called upon to speak, and when they had concluded their remarks, shouts arose in the audience for Sam Clemens to rise and speak. Whether the request was entirely unexpected is difficult to say, At any rate, a young printer's apprentice who sat next to him that evening reports that Sam rose, blushing, and began his remarks in an embarrassed, stammering fashion; that he presently rallied his powers as he went along, and before he sat down had convulsed his hearers with a remarkable production of wit and humor.[12] So successful was Sam's speech at the banquet that evening that Orion had no hesitation in describing it in his report to the *Gate City* as "replete with wit and humor," adding that it had been interrupted by long and continuous bursts of applause.[13]

What Sam Clemens said at the printers' banquet that January evening in Keokuk has not been recorded, but as a prelude to his later career on the platform the event was of signal importance. It marked the first definite beginning in a direction which later led to incomparable success. Paine (again probably deriving information about the occasion from Orion's autobiographical papers) reports that the humor of the speech was of a primitive type, and that whatever its shortcomings, it delighted his audience. As a consequence, Sam's prestige in Keokuk rose by several degrees and it is reported that he was persuaded to join a debating society.[14]

It was probably Sam Clemens' success at the printers' banquet and his subsequent activity in the debating society which led his family and friends to suggest the law as a promising career. But it was the river and a career as pilot on Mississippi steamboats that presently called him. Yet from time to time the idea of the law cropped up. In February, 1861, for example, Mark Twain went to visit a well-known fortune teller in New Orleans by the name of Madame Caprelle. A few days later he reported that visit in a long letter to Orion. Among the many things the Madame had told him was that he "should have been a lawyer—that is where your talents lie; you might have distinguished yourself as an orator."[15] Whether Madame Caprelle made the assertion because she was impressed with her visitor's verbal facility cannot be known. It is likely, however, that when he stepped into her parlors, she was far better acquainted with Sam Clemens' background than he ever suspected. He had been urged to visit Madame Caprelle by Mrs. Holliday (The Widow Douglas in *The Adventures of Tom Sawyer*), a family friend of the Clemenses, who made frequent trips down to New Orleans, occasionally rode on Sam's boat, and was well acquainted with the Madame. The probability is strong that word of Sam's success as a speaker at the printers' banquet had reached Mrs. Holliday, together with the family's hope he might study for the law, and that she relayed this information to Madame Caprelle.[16]

When the river closed in the spring of 1861, as the war broke out, and Sam Clemens suddenly found himself without an occupation, the question of preparing for the law appears again to have been suggested by members of his family. But he was not persuaded. An opportunity had presented itself to go adventuring to the Far West with Orion who had recently been appointed Secretary of Nevada Territory. Not long after his arrival in Carson City, the territorial capital, he wrote his mother, asking her to inform his Aunt Mary that he was sorry she thought he intended to study law. He did not love the law and had no intention whatever of preparing for it.[17] Thereafter there was no further mention of the law or any indication that his ambitions were in any way rooted in an attraction for public address.

The fact is that, during his early years, the most effective preparation for Mark Twain's career as a public speaker came in ways so subtle and undetected that at the time neither he nor his family and friends ever suspected them of possessing any influence at all. This preparation came primarily through his exposure to a number of exceptionally able raconteurs and his own gradual absorption of their skills. The importance of this has long been recognized in the development of Mark Twain as a writer, but has not been sufficiently emphasized in his development as a public lecturer and reader. It was Orion's inability to perceive the importance of this exposure which led him to suppose that his brother's platform success had been achieved without the slow processes of apprenticeship.

Nor did Albert Bigelow Paine sufficiently perceive its importance to Mark Twain's platform career. His assertion that most of Mark Twain's attainments came as a natural gift has dubious validity.[18] It certainly does not account adequately for Mark Twain's skill as a storyteller. The truth is that few American platform celebrities preceding Mark Twain experienced a more extensive and impressive apprenticeship in the art of storytelling than he.

Fortunately, his association with masterful raconteurs came at a very early age. Most influential of all, probably, was his mother. As a child and as a growing boy he was not consciously aware of the moving power of her speech, but years later he remembered it and paid it a warm tribute. "There was something moving in her voice and manner," he recalled, "that was irresistibly pathetic. . . . I know now that she was the most eloquent person whom I have met in all my days, but I did not know it then. . . . I had been abroad in the world for twenty years and known and listened to many of the best talkers before it at last dawned upon me that in the matter of moving and pathetic eloquence none of them was the equal of that untrained and artless talker . . . that obscure little woman with . . . the great heart and the enchanted tongue."[19]

But in those early years Mark Twain had the high fortune of listening to other masterful raconteurs besides his mother. One of the earliest and most impressive was his father's slave, Uncle Ned. It was from him that Mark Twain heard, and never forgot, the ghost story, The Golden Arm, with its startling climax which later became one of his most successful readings on the public platform.[20] It was during these early years, also, that he heard and never forgot the stories told at his Uncle John Quarles' farm, near Florida, Missouri, where, up to the age of twelve, he spent most of his summers.

According to local tradition, John Quarles possessed a ready and hilarious wit, was brilliant in repartee, and a born storyteller. Sam Clemens greatly admired his mirth-loving uncle, who contrasted so pleasantly with his silent and stern-faced father, and listened to his stories with rapt attention. It was probably from John Quarles that Mark Twain first heard the Jumping Frog story, an ancestral version of the one he later heard in the barroom at Angel's Camp in California. But no less influential were the old spirituals and stories of mystery, magic, and imagination which he encountered in the slave quarters—stories by Aunt Hanner and Uncle Dan'l, the latter known to readers of *The Adventures of Huckleberry Finn* as Jim—both wonderful storytellers.[21] Some of these yarns were so vivid and delightful, or hair-raising, that they stayed in his memory throughout his life and served him often and well both in his books and on the platform. There can be little doubt that during these early and formative years Mark Twain's imagination was shaped not so much by books as by talkers—by storytellers whose untutored and seemingly simple art brought life and magic to their recitals and stamped them forever upon his memory.

By the time the farm days were over and the death of his father in 1847 made it necessary for him to go to work, his love and respect for accomplished storytellers were deeply rooted. Thereafter, whenever he met good raconteurs, he listened to their yarns with absorbed interest. In Ament's print shop in Hannibal, for instance, where Sam was an apprentice for a time, there was Pet McMurray, a journeyman printer in his twenties who was full of stories. Typical of journeymen at the time, he was a carefree drifter who had been many places and seen many things. If he failed to find work in his own profession, he turned to lecturing on temperance. All McMurray wanted, Mark Twain later recalled, was a plate, a bed, and enough money to get drunk on.[22] In some respects he resembled the Duke in *The Adventures of Huckleberry Finn,* though there is nothing to indicate that he was quite so disreputable a character. In Ament's shop, also, was Wales McCormick, a large lad of eighteen whose hilarious sense of humor, practical jokes, and stories amused and sometimes irritated Sam. But both McMurray and McCormick were excellent storytellers, and Mark Twain never forgot them.

In the years that followed, Mark Twain's wanderings and his various employments brought him in contact with an ever widening circle of raconteurs. There were the endless stories he heard in the pilot houses of Mississippi steamboats, in the ships' bars, and in the Pilots' Association rooms in St. Louis, Memphis, Baton Rouge, and New Orleans. And after the war had closed the river and he had gone west with Orion, he encountered a whole new world of storytellers—in the mining camps, in the saloons, and in the newspaper offices of Virginia City, Carson City, and San Francisco.

One of the richest bonanzas Mark Twain struck in oral literature occurred in the winter of 1864–65, when a series of circumstances took him down to the Twolumne district of California to spend an indefinite period with his old friend Jim Gillis, a pocket miner and gambler who lived in a cabin on Jackass Hill. Sharing the cabin with Gillis were his younger brother William, Dick Stoker (Dick Baker in *Roughing It*), and Dick's cat, Tom Quartz. When bad weather stopped mining activities, the long days and nights were often spent in storytelling. Years later he remembered those scenes, especially the rainy days when they all gathered about the fireplace and listened to Jim, with his back to the warmth, tell stories of his own creation, "forged as he went along." For the most part, as Mark Twain recalled, Gillis' stories usually consisted of the wonderful adventures of his companion Dick Stoker, "portrayed with humor and that serene and vagrant fancy which builds as it goes, careless as to whither it is proceeding and whether the story shall end well or ill, soon or late, if ever."[23]

It was from Jim Gillis, that winter in the Twolumne Hills, that he heard the delightful story of Dick Baker's cat (Tom Quartz), the Jay Bird and the Acorn, and the Burning Shame (which later found its way into *The Adventures of Huckleberry Finn*). That same winter in a saloon at Angel's Camp, he heard Ben Coon, a solemn and drowsy-witted old ex-Illinois river pilot, tell in a slow monotonous way the story of the Jumping Frog. What caught Mark Twain's fancy on this occasion was not so much the substance of the tale (he had probably heard other versions of it, as we have seen), but the exquisite absurdity of Coon's manner of telling the story without betraying a single hint that he regarded it as humorous.[24]

As a result of his long and impressive tutelage under master raconteurs it is inevitable that Mark Twain should himself have become a talker and a skilled storyteller. No better example of his ability as a raconteur, before he ever became famous on the platform, could be offered than an incident that occurred one evening in San Francisco, in 1864 or 1865, when he was working as a reporter for the *Morning Call*. A group of his associates had planned to attend the theater and had met in one of their rooms. Presently Mark Twain drifted in, sat down on the end of a bed, and began telling stories. They listened with such absorbed interest that the theater was entirely forgotten, and it was near midnight before the storytelling had ended.[25]

The most evident beginning in Mark Twain's career as a public speaker, however, took place in Carson City in the winter of 1863–64. Mark Twain had gone west in the summer of 1861, when the outbreak of war had closed the Mississippi. For a time he had worked with Orion, serving in an unofficial capacity as secretary to the Secretary. Then, after a brief, unsuccessful try at silver mining in various Nevada communities, he became a reporter on the Virginia City *Enterprise*. It was while working for this paper that he reported the sessions of the Nevada Territorial Legislature sitting at Carson City. His popularity among the legislators soon became so great that on the evening of December 11, 1863, immediately after the close of the Constitutional Convention held in Nevada that year, Mark Twain was elected President of the Third House, and given the honorary title of "Governor." A unique institution in the American scene, the Third House was a mock legislature organized for the purpose of burlesquing the issues, debates, and personalities of the regular legislative sessions. It elected its own slate of "state officials," and made fun of the legislative processes in general.[26]

Mark Twain's delightfully dead-pan report of the procedures of the meeting on the night of December 11 appeared in the *Enterprise* a few days later. Concerning his remarks in acknowledgment of his election as "Governor" he reported himself merely as saying: "Gentlemen: This is the proudest moment of my life. I shall always think so. I shall ponder over it with unspeakable emotion down to the latest syllable of recorded time. It shall be my earnest endeavor to give entire satisfaction in the high and bully position to which you have elevated me."[27]

Thereupon the real fun of the evening began with Mark Twain presiding as President of the House and revealing his awareness of the mannerisms of the various legislators who had risen to speak by burlesquing the "I . . . ah, I . . . ah" manner of Legislator Youngs and the annoying habit of buttoning and unbuttoning his coat by Mr. Ralston.

The Third House was to have its opening meeting toward the end of January, 1864, while the regular legislative session was still in progress. At that time "Governor" Mark Twain was scheduled to deliver the annual message. In the meantime, the Constitutional Convention having ended, he returned to Virginia City to resume his routine reporting of local news for the *Enterprise*. But the events that took place during the next few weeks were anything but routine. In fact, for his future career as a public lecturer they were momentous.

The excitement which presently developed in Virginia City was caused by the appearance of Artemus Ward, celebrated humorist, writer, and lecturer, who had speaking engagements in Virginia City, Carson City, and other towns in the district. Artemus Ward, then in his thirtieth year, was at the pinnacle of his career and tremendously popular. He had just arrived from San Francisco where he had lectured to enthusiastic houses. He had planned to stay only a few days in Virginia City, but he was so captivated by the genial companions he found there, particularly in the office of the *Enterprise,* that he could not bear to leave till the end of the month.

The story of Artemus Ward's bibulous visit in Virginia City and his fondness for the company of Mark Twain, who was a year younger, has been frequently told and need not be repeated here. But the influence which Ward exerted upon the writing career of the popular young reporter for the *Enterprise,* and more especially upon his career as a public lecturer during the three-week visit in Virginia City deserves attention.

That Artemus Ward quickly recognized in Mark Twain not only a kindred humorous personality but also a gifted journalist is abundantly clear. In their quieter moments together, Ward praised his friend's writings and urged him strongly to seek an outlet for them in eastern journals. He especially recommended the New York *Sunday Mercury* and promised to write a letter to its editor introducing him and his work.[28] It was precisely the kind of advice and encouragement which Mark Twain needed at the moment. Though eminently successful as a Washoe journalist and already well known in San Francisco where many of his articles were appearing in some of the leading newspapers, his outlook was still provincial. He needed wider horizons, a national rather than a regional view; and Ward, an Easterner of distinction, was the person best suited to point the direction. Indeed, so powerfully moved was Mark Twain to follow Ward's advice about publication in eastern journals that he sent two articles to the *Sunday Mercury* within two weeks after Ward's departure from Virginia City. Both were immediately accepted.[29] Thus Ward's influence upon Mark Twain as a writer, during the Virginia City visit, is clear and easily definable. He did not, so far as can be determined, however, offer Mark Twain any advice about writing style or technique. Nor is there anything in the record to show that Mark Twain either sought or felt that he needed such advice.

Ward's influence upon Mark Twain as a lecturer, on the

other hand, is far more difficult to assess. Conclusions concerning it can be based only upon inference and supposition. Though it is highly probable that Ward may have narrated some of his lecturing experiences to Mark Twain, there are no indications that he offered advice about lecturing or that he even suspected his journalist friend of having ambitions for platform success. Had he stayed in Nevada long enough to hear Mark Twain deliver his "Governor's" message to the Third House, the story might have been different. At the moment, however, he was merely aware that the *Enterprise* reporter was a most engaging talker and a splendid storyteller.

Nor is there any evidence that Mark Twain consciously examined Ward's platform manners and techniques, at this time, for the purpose of employing them himself at some future occasion. As a reporter, however, whose duty it was to cover Ward's lecture Babes in the Wood for the *Enterprise,* it must be assumed that he listened to the great showman's performance with absorbed interest, and observed his platform art. It is probable, also, after the lecture, especially after Mark Twain's report of it appeared in the *Enterprise,* that the two men found an opportunity to discuss briefly, at least, the art of a humorous lecture and the most effective means of making an audience laugh.

Unfortunately, Mark Twain's review of Ward's lecture in Virginia City has not been preserved since the files of the *Enterprise* for the years when Mark Twain worked for the paper are no longer extant. The only glimpse we get of it is from an item in the Virginia City *Evening Bulletin* of December 28, 1863, which quotes Mark Twain as follows:

> There are perhaps fifty subjects treated in it [Babes in the Wood], and there is a passable point in every one of them, and a healthy laugh, also, for any of God's creatures who hath committed no crime, the ghastly memory of which debars him from ever smiling again while he lives. The man who is capable of listening to "Babes in the Wood" from beginning to end without laughing either inwardly or outwardly must have done murder, or at least meditated it at some time during his life.

Whether or not Mark Twain offered an extended analysis of Ward's platform manner and technique for the benefit of his readers cannot now be established. They could scarcely, however, have escaped his attention—the dead-pan facial expression even at the most humor-provoking passages, the casualness of his manner, the simulated unconsciousness that anything funny had been said, the feigned look of surprise when the audience laughed, the pause and the use of anticlimax by "dropping a studied remark, apparently without knowing it, as if one were thinking aloud."[30] That he was deeply impressed by the performance is evident. Eight years later, during the season of 1871–72, he included Artemus Ward in his lecture Reminiscences of Some Uncommonplace Characters I Have Chanced to Meet. And when that lecture failed, he prepared a new one devoted entirely to Ward, as the most compelling and important uncommonplace character in his repertoire.[31] In that lecture Mark Twain drew heavily upon his observations of the man he had admired so much during the Virginia City days.

The time came years later when Mark Twain's early admiration for Ward's platform technique diminished somewhat, as he realized that there had been too much technique about his lectures. There were too many tricks, too often repeated. Though delightfully humorous on first hearing, they did not stand repetition well. People learned the tricks. They could anticipate them, see them coming. One of the perfections of Mark Twain's mature artistry, on the other hand, was to prevent the artistry from "showing through." His humor, compared with Ward's, seemed natural, rather than contrived. In 1863, however, his admiration for Ward's artistry on the platform appears to have been unqualified, nor does he appear at this time to have questioned the propriety of Ward's use of the content of his lecture merely for the purpose of extracting humor.

Nevertheless, one must conclude that during his Virginia City visit, Artemus Ward did exert a powerful influence upon Mark Twain's later platform career. Never before had Mark Twain had the opportunity to observe a humorist perform with such consummate skill on the platform. If the devices and techniques which produced such floods of laughter were not new to him, the finesse with which they were employed, and the studied artistry behind the seeming casualness and simplicity of Ward's manner, were impressive. Beyond anything he had ever observed or imagined possible, Ward's lecture showed him how a master performer completely captured an audience with humor by a clever manipulation of techniques and an exploitation of manner. Whether or not the impact of observing Ward's artistry at the time set him dreaming of seeing himself on the platform, capturing audiences with humorous lectures in a similar way, cannot be determined. More important is the fact that he absorbed what he saw, and when the time came to face his own paying audiences a few years later, he consciously attempted to adapt them to his own platform personality, materials, and purposes.[32]

Within a week or two after Ward's departure from Virginia City, Mark Twain was back in Carson City reporting the new session of the territorial legislature. Also he was now busy preparing his Governor's Message to the Third House, scheduled for January 27. As this date neared, the trustees of the Presbyterian Church in Carson City, to which Orion belonged, addressed a letter to Mark Twain, asking him to help them raise funds for their unfinished church building. They suggested an admission charge of one dollar each for the privilege of listening to his "communication."

The request appeared in the Carson City *Daily Independent* on January 23, 1864, and Mark Twain's reply appeared in the same paper on the same day.

GENTLEMEN:
Certainly. If the public can find anything in a grave state paper worth paying a dollar for, I am willing they should pay that amount or any other. And although I am not a very dusty Christian myself, I take an absorbing interest in religious affairs, and would willingly inflict my annual message upon the church itself if it derive benefit thereby. You can charge what you please, and I promise the public no amusement, but I do promise a reasonable amount of instruction. I am responsible to the Third House only and I hope to be permitted to make it exceedingly hot for that body, without caring whether the sympathies of the public and the church be enlisted in their favor and against me or not.

According to Clement Rice, a reporter for Virginia City *Daily Union,* who had attended the lecture, "a large and fashionable audience" turned out to watch the fun and to hear Mark

Twain orate, and when the evening was over, two hundred dollars had been collected toward the completion of the church.[33] Concerning the substance of the lecture and Mark Twain's manner of speaking, Rice was silent. Not so charitable, however, was a writer for the *Daily Union* who called himself "Meriden," an unidentified critic who disliked burlesques in general and the Third House burlesque in particular. Whether or not Meriden heard Mark Twain's speech is a matter of doubt, but the occasion offered him an opportunity to voice his unflattering opinion of Mark Twain's satire. He was not amused when the reporter for the *Enterprise* "ornamented" a church item by referring to "dusty old Christians," or, in a description of a public school, introduced a juvenile who wiped his nose so audibly with his fingers as to require castigation by his teacher. "The humor and the wit thus exhibited," he concluded, "partake wholly of the characteristic of the monkey as he climbs."[34] These criticisms, however, and the comparison with Ward, appear to have been based upon Mark Twain's newspaper writings rather than upon his message to the Third House. Concerning that message, Meriden, unfortunately, offered no direct comment.

Mark Twain's report of his speech appeared in the *Enterprise* the next day. It throws further light on his performance and offers a bit of self-criticism.

> I delivered that Message last night, but I didn't talk loud enough—people in the far end of the hall could not hear me. They said "Louder—louder" occasionally, but I thought that was a way they had—a joke, as it were. I had never talked to a crowd before, and knew none of the tactics of the public speaker. I suppose I spoke loud enough for some houses, but not for that District Court-room, which is about seventy-five feet from floor to roof, and has no ceiling. I hope the people will deal as mildly with me, as I did with the public officers in the Annual Message. Some folks heard the entire document, though— there is some comfort in that. Hon. Mr. Claggett, Speaker Simmons of the inferior House, Hon. Hal Clayton, Speaker of the Third House, Judge Haydon, Dr. Alban, and others whose opinions are entitled to weight, said they would travel several miles to hear that message again. It affords me a good deal of satisfaction to mention it. It serves to show that if the audience could have heard me distinctly, they would have appreciated the wisdom thus conferred

upon them. They seemed to appreciate what they did hear though, pretty thoroughly. After the first quarter of an hour I ceased to whisper, and became audible. One of these days when I get time, I will correct, amend, and publish the message, in accordance with a resolution of the Third House ordering 300,000 copies in the various languages spoken at the present day.

P.S. Sandy Baldwin and Theodore Winters heard that message, anyhow, and by thunder they appreciated it, too. They have sent a hundred dollars apiece to San Francisco this morning, to purchase a watch [and] chain for His Excellency Governor Twain. I guess that is a pretty good result for an incipient oratorical slouch like me, isn't it? I don't know that anybody tendered the other Governor a testimonial of any kind.

Since Albert Bigelow Paine declared the Governor's Message to be Mark Twain's first public appearance in a field in which he was later to achieve very great fame, a brief examination of Mark Twain's comments about it, virtually the only ones still extant, and of the circumstances under which he made the speech, is in order. It will raise into prominence, if nothing more, certain aspects of this first public appearance which had a bearing upon Mark Twain's later development on the public platform.

His assertion, first of all, that he had never talked to a crowd before is only approximately correct. He had certainly talked to an assembly of legislators on the night of December 11, when he went to the speaker's rostrum to acknowledge his election as Governor of the Third House. And in the meeting that immediately followed that election, where he presided as president, he talked to a crowd. But he apparently did not consider his remarks at that occasion as a talk, that is to say, a connected discourse; nor was the assembly of legislators at all comparable, in his mind, to the packed house which heard him on January 27.

Furthermore, his statement that he did not know the tactics of the public speaker must be taken with a grain of salt. As a reporter for the *Enterprise* he was often required to summarize or comment on the lectures that were given in Virginia City, which, because of its prominence and its splendid Opera House, received much of the good talent of all kinds that came to San Francisco. It is furthermore inconceivable that he was ignorant of the techniques of a public speaker after just having listened to Artemus Ward, one of the most accomplished tacticians on the public platform. It would have been nearer the truth to say that he had never before had an opportunity to try out the tactics of a public speaker. Actually, what Mark Twain meant to say, however, was that if he had had experience as a public speaker he would have talked loud enough for everyone in his audience to hear him. His remark was an explanation, an apology. Its importance lies in the fact that Mark Twain early recognized a weakness in his platform performance which then and later gave him trouble. It took time for him to learn to gauge the size of the hall and the audience properly so as to be heard everywhere.

Notable, too, is Mark Twain's frank pride in the fact that more people had turned out to hear him than had turned out for Artemus Ward. He must have been aware, of course, that his message had a peculiarly local appeal, since everybody in town knew that the public officials of Nevada would be put on the gridiron and satirized. People flocked in to hear what the speaker had to say, not only about themselves but particularly about their friends and neighbors. And when the occasion was turned into a benefit for the Presbyterian Church, probably the entire congregation came to see the fun. Nevertheless, Artemus Ward was a nationally celebrated speaker and had drawn large audiences all over the country. He had also drawn well in Virginia City and Carson City. To have packed in a bigger house than Ward, therefore, was no small accomplishment. It afforded Mark Twain particular satisfaction because it gave him something of a means, at least, of measuring himself against a very high standard.

Another aspect of Mark Twain's speech that deserves comment is the courage he demonstrated in his severe satire of Governor Nye at the risk of losing a coveted notarial appointment.[35] The opportunity to demonstrate courage in public utterance came to him during this period primarily through newspaper reporting, but then and later, both in print and on platform, he spoke out courageously against shams, pretenses, abuses of arbitrary power, and public corruption.

A most significant comment about the Governor's Message, however, appeared in a letter which Mark Twain wrote to his sister Pamela in St. Louis. Replying to her request for a copy of the speech, he explained that he couldn't send the Message because "It was written to be *spoken*—to write it so that it would *read* well, would be too much trouble. . . ."[36] The significance of the statement lies in the fact that a large measure of the success of his first public appearance obviously lay in the *manner* of his delivery, and that he was, at this early time, at the very beginning of his career as a public speaker, aware of the importance of platform manner and the difficulty of communicating manner through the mere medium of words. Later, during his tour lectures, newspaper reporters commonly confessed their inability to report his lectures satisfactorily because the text itself gave no adequate notion of the nature and quality of the performance. To know what a Mark Twain lecture was like, they claimed, one had to see him and hear him.

To what extent Mark Twain, either consciously or unconsciously employed the manners and techniques in the Governor's Message which characterized his later performances on the lecture platform is impossible to say. So far as is known, no one who was present in the Presbyterian Church that evening later described it in written form with sufficient particularity to make a firm judgment about the matter. It is highly probable, however, that in personality, manner, and technique he was entirely himself and that no one felt that he was well known in the Washoe area. Everyone knew that his slow drawling manner of speech was genuine. And if, during the Message, he employed such devices as dead-pan humor, an assumption of casualness, veiled shrewdness, and the pause, one may be sure that all of them were techniques he had long been familiar with and had long ago absorbed in his own art of storytelling.

Finally, in speaking of the Governor's Message to the Third House, it is worth noting that in later years Mark Twain never referred to it as his first public lecture. That description was reserved for his Sandwich Islands lecture, given in San Francisco in the fall of 1866. His reasons for ignoring the Governor's Message may easily be conjectured. The lecture was not the product of his own initiation. It was something required of him in consequence of his election as Governor of the Third House. Though admission had been charged to hear him, he had no hand in determining what it should be; nor did he receive, or expect to receive, a fee. Consequently, he felt under no money obligation to amuse the public or care "whether the sympathies of the public and the church" were with him or not.[37] Only a paid lecturer was obligated to satisfy the demands of audiences who expected to get their money's worth.

In fact, the entire occasion, including the lecture was a special one. The audience was made up of legislators, public officials, prominent citizens of the Territory of Nevada, and members of the Presbyterian Church in Carson City. Most of these people knew each other personally. Their presence was motivated by the expectation of having fun at their neighbors' expense. Mark Twain's role as chief speaker was that of gadfly, spokesman for the public conscience and public good, satirist, and jester. While his Message provided hilarious amusement, its import was serious. There was a message. It was a role he reveled in then and later, both as a writer and speaker.

With the Governor's Message behind him, the major phases of Mark Twain's apprenticeship for a career on the public platform came to an end. His actual experience on the platform during the formative years had been brief though impressive. On the other hand his long exposure to expert raconteurs had been exceptionally rich and rewarding, and his love for talking and storytelling had spurred him on. Artemus Ward had shown him what a professional could do on the platform. Twain had not, as Orion mistakenly believed, leapt into platform celebrity without apprenticeship.[38]

FIRST PUBLIC LECTURE

In October, 1866, I broke out as a lecturer, and from that day to this I have always been able to gain my living without doing any work. —MARK TWAIN IN ERUPTION, PP. *304–5.*

DURING the next year and a half, except for an interval of about three months when he went down to Jackass Hill and Angel's Camp to engage in pocket mining, Mark Twain remained in San Francisco and worked for a number of newspapers. At first he took a regular reporting job with the *Morning Call,* but the daily routines became such a fearful drudgery that after six months he resigned. Even while working on the *Morning Call,* however, he had been supplying articles to the *Golden Era* and the *Californian.* Later he began to correspond regularly with his former newspaper, the Virginia City *Enterprise.* But his chief claim to distinction during this period came from the publication of the Jumping Frog story in the New York *Saturday Press,* November 18, 1865, and its appearance in the *Californian* about a month later.

It may have been the remarkable success of that story in an eastern journal that fired anew Mark Twain's ambition to seek a wider field for his endeavors and that made his life in San Francisco seem unendurably irksome. Looking about for a more adventuresome occupation, he finally managed to persuade the publishers of the Sacramento *Union* to send him to the Sandwich Islands as a traveling correspondent to report on the Islands' agriculture and commerce, and on such aspects of its life and natural characteristics as commended themselves to his interest.[1]

For Mark Twain's future career, the *Union* assignment was extremely important. It constituted a major turning point in his development as a literary personality, for it led directly not only to his emergence as a writer of books but also as a public lecturer.

Mark Twain's stay in the Islands lasted about five months. When he returned to San Francisco on August 13, he wrote in his notebook: "Home again. No *not* home again—in prison again and all the wide sense of freedom gone. The city seems so cramped and so dreary with toil and care and business anxiety. God help me, I wish I were at sea again."[2] Paine reports that for a period of time after his return from the Sandwich Islands Mark Twain was so depressed in spirit that only the lack of courage prevented him from committing suicide.[3] But so severe an attack of depression, if it occurred at all, which is doubtful, must have been very brief, for immediately upon his return he found himself busily engaged in a ferment of activities and plans. He still had some Sandwich Islands letters to finish for the *Union*. As soon as he could manage, he made a trip to Sacramento to call upon the managers of that paper to collect pay for recent letters and for his "scoop" story of the "Hornet" disaster, which the *Union* had featured on its front page. To his mother he proudly reported that the *Union* people had paid him a great deal more than they had promised him.[4]

There were a number of other projects. He rewrote the Hornet article for *Harper's Magazine* and was delighted when it was immediately accepted. A far more ambitious plan was to write a series of articles about the Sandwich Islands and his observations there for eastern journals, and to follow it up with a book on the subject.[5] Indeed, he had probably conceived such a plan even before he left the Islands, a supposition which might explain why he carried away with him a copy of Jarves' *History of the Sandwich Islands* which he had borrowed from Father Damon's Mission Library in Honolulu.[6] But the plan which seems to have fired his imagination most at this time was to undertake a round-the-world tour as correspondent for a metropolitan newspaper. The project appeared especially attractive in view of an invitation from Anson Burlingame, United States

Minister to China, whom Mark Twain had met in Honolulu, to visit him in Peking and to make his house there a base for learning about China and the Far East, and for meeting important people.[7] How soon after his return to San Francisco Mark Twain ventured to propose his plan to any of the San Francisco or Sacramento papers is uncertain, though it is apparent that he began pressing the matter whenever and wherever opportunities presented themselves.

In the meantime, however, another plan was occupying his attention. As mentioned, he hoped to bring out a book about the Sandwich Islands based upon his letters to the *Union*.[8] That project, like some of his others, required cash, at least enough to pay his living expenses while he was preparing the manuscript. It is evident that the need for money now prompted Mark Twain to consider public lecturing as the most promising means of solving his financial difficulties. It is probable, in view of his character and personality, that in time he would have taken up lecturing out of sheer love of talking, regardless of his need for money; but there is no question that the present urgent need served as the immediate prod. As he himself reported, he returned from the Islands empty of cash but full of information proper for delivery from a lecture platform.[9] And why should he not try? He was not without experience. Had he not successfully lectured to a good-sized audience in Carson City? Had he not carefully observed Artemus Ward's techniques and manners when the showman had lectured in Virginia City? And had he not, as a newspaperman, frequently reported the successes and failures of other lectures? In his favor, too, was the fact that his letters about the Islands had given him a good deal of reputation in San Francisco, Sacramento, and in all the back country of California and Nevada. Why shouldn't he capitalize on these favorable circumstances by taking to the platform? To offer himself as a public lecturer, however, required a good deal of courage. Also it involved considerable financial risk. The rental of a hall and the cost of advertising all added up to more than he could muster.

In *Roughing It* Mark Twain tells the story of how he wrote a first draft of the Sandwich Islands lecture, and of the reaction of some of his friends when he showed it to them. All shook their heads in doubt. Some were fearful that he could not talk nearly as well as he could write, and that he might break down when making his first appearance.[10] They could not foresee the fact, well recognized by later critics, that Mark Twain's lecture manuscripts revealed scarcely a hint of the success of his platform performance, and that the secret of that success lay in his manner and style of speaking rather than in the substance of his lecture or in the words themselves. Almost persuaded that the lecture would fail and that nobody would come to hear him, he was on the verge of abandoning the idea when Colonel John McComb, one of the managers of the *Alta California,* came forward with encouragement. Take the largest hall in town, he urged, and charge a dollar a head. It was probably also McComb who suggested that Mark Twain approach Tom Maguire, manager of the big new opera house, about sharing the risk with him. Maguire had known Mark Twain in Virginia City by reputation, if not personally, (he also managed the opera house there), and with McComb's endorsement agreed to let the popular young journalist have it at half price—fifty dollars.[11]

The decision made, Mark Twain proceeded at once with the advertising. With characteristic foresight he made up an announcement designed to set the tone for the humorous lecture he had prepared and to stir up interest. It appeared both as a handbill which was circulated through the city and as an advertisement in the newspapers, and is shown on the facing page as it appeared in the *Alta California,* on Tuesday, October 2, 1866, the day of the lecture.

News of Mark Twain's intention to lecture had filtered into the newspaper offices as early as September 29, and from that day to the date of the performance local reporters had fun with their humorist friend. The *Californian* promised that the lecture would refute some of the extravagant stories which had recently been circulating through the city, particularly the story of his romantic adventures with the mermaids on the beach at Honolulu.[12] The *Alta California,* in imitation of some of the absurdities of the handbill, expressed doubt that Mark Twain would include in his program the Hawaiian Hornpipe, but that his friend Brown (Mark Twain's alter ego in the Sandwich Islands letters) would "sing a refrain in the Kanaka tongue."[13] It also declared, facetiously, that the lecture would be "high-toned" if he spoke loud enough.

There were also serious comments about the forthcoming lecture. The *Alta California* obviously predisposed in Mark Twain's favor, predicted that a big audience would appear to hear him, and that everybody expected a rare treat.[14] The *Morn-*

MAGUIRE'S ACADEMY OF MUSIC
THE SANDWICH ISLANDS!
MARK TWAIN
(Honolulu Correspondent of the Sacramento Union)
will deliver a
Lecture on the Sandwich Islands,
at the Academy of Music
On Tuesday Evening, October 2,

❧

*In which mention will be made of Harris, Bishop Staley, the
American Missionaries, etc., and the absurd Customs and
Characteristics of the Natives duly discussed and described.
The great VOLCANO OF KILAUEA
will also receive proper attention.*

❧

A SPLENDID ORCHESTRA
Is in town, but has not been engaged.
Also,
A DEN OF FEROCIOUS WILD BEASTS
Will be on exhibition in the next block.
MAGNIFICENT FIRE WORKS
were in contemplation for this occasion, but the
idea has been abandoned.
A GRAND TORCHLIGHT PROCESSION
May be expected; in fact, the public are privileged
to expect whatever they please.

Dress Circle—$1.00   *Family Circle—50 cts.*
DOORS OPEN AT 7 O'CLOCK   THE TROUBLE BEGINS AT 8 O'CLOCK

❧

---

ing Call and the *Evening Bulletin* also predicted success, assuring
their readers that the lecture would be a good one, and advised
all who planned to attend to come early if they wanted seats.

But the sentence in the handbill that attracted most comment was the closing one, "The trouble begins at 8 o'clock."
Mark Twain himself was so greatly impressed with it that he
included it with delightful variations in all later advertisements
of the lecture during the season of 1866–67. Sometimes the
announcement read "The Wisdom will flow at 8"; at other times,
"The Orgies will commence at 8," "The Inspiration will begin

to gush at 8," or "The Insurrection will start at 8." Indeed, so popular did the legend become that other performers borrowed it frequently, and Mark Twain once claimed having seen it in a newspaper advertisement reminding school children in summertime when the next term would begin.[15] The only part of the sentence in the advertisement of the San Francisco lecture that was original with Mark Twain, however, was the word "trouble." The general pattern of the legend announcing the time of the beginning of the program had long been used in the advertisements of lectures and other public performances and usually read "The program will begin at 8," or, as was common in the advertisement of Artemus Ward's lectures, "Entertainment to commence at 8."[16] At any rate, Mark Twain's inspired variations of the old pattern greatly amused the public and not only aroused their interest in his lecture, but what was even more important, put them in a proper frame of mind for the sort of lecture he had prepared for them.

There is little question that Mark Twain's first San Francisco performance on the evening of October 2, 1866, was a momentous landmark in his career, a turning point of major importance. Albert Bigelow Paine, his official biographer, has dealt with it at length. Later biographers, particularly Ivan Benson and Walter F. Frear, have supplied detailed accounts of it. Mark Twain himself has told the story with dramatic flourish in *Roughing It.*[17] All these accounts, especially Mark Twain's own, describe the mounting fear that gripped him as lecture time approached— fear that few people would pay money to come to hear him, and fear that his lecture, which he obviously conceived as a humorous performance, would not be well received. In his trepidation, Mark Twain tells us that he resorted to a number of devices to avoid failure. First he persuaded three old friends, large of stature and "stormy-voiced," to seat themselves in the parquet and help him through. "This thing," he told them, "is going to be a failure; the jokes in it are so dim that nobody will ever see them." The three men were to bring heavy canes and pound the floor "whenever the feeblest joke might show its head."[18]

Next he sought the support of the wife of a popular citizen with whom he had some acquaintance and persuaded her and her husband to occupy a prominent seat in the left hand stage box where the whole house could see them. He explained that whenever in the course of the lecture he turned to her and smiled, that was to be a signal that he had delivered an obscure joke and that she should not then stop to investigate, but immediately *respond*.[19]

On the day of the lecture—the day the box office was open for the sale of reserved seats—Mark Twain reports that he could no longer restrain his excitement. Late in the afternoon he crept down to the theater to see what the ticket sales had been like, but found the ticket seller gone, and the box office locked up. "I had to swallow suddenly or my heart would have got out. 'No sales,' I said to myself; 'I might have known it.' I thought of suicide, pretended illness, flight. I thought of these things in earnest, for I was very miserable and scared. But of course I had to drive them away, and prepare to meet my fate. I could not wait for half past seven—I wanted to face the horror and end it. . . . I went down back streets at six o'clock, and entered the theater by the back door. I stumbled my way in the dark among the ranks of canvas scenery, and stood on the stage. The house was gloomy and silent, and its emphasis depressing. I went down among the scenes again, and for an hour and a half gave myself up to the horrors, wholly unconscious of anything else."[20]

Despite this moving account of his trepidation, it is inconceivable that Mark Twain could have restrained himself from prying into the true situation at the box office, or of reading the optimistic predictions in the newspapers. The fact was, of course, that the house had been completely sold out long before opening time, and that many who came late had been turned away.[21]

When curtain time arrived, the audience began stomping its feet, the customary signal that it wanted the program to begin. As Mark Twain appeared in the wings, there was a sudden roar of applause, for many in the audience were personally acquainted with the popular young journalist, and nearly all felt they knew him through his newspaper reporting. The roar continued as he sauntered bashfully and awkwardly toward the lectern, his hands shoved carelessly into his trousers pockets,[22] and a look on his face that registered a mixture of surprise, perplexity, and fear.

Turning then and facing the audience, he gazed silently for a few moments at that vast hall packed from pit to dome, all standing room occupied.[23] Even before he began speaking, some of the fear that had all but paralyzed him drained away as he saw about him a sea of friendly, laughing, and encouraging faces. Many years later, recalling the agonizing moments when he first faced the audience, he said that the memory of it was indestructible, but that "it had its compensations, for it made him immune from timidity before audiences for all time to come."[24]

He began by apologizing for the absence of an orchestra, declaring he wasn't accustomed to getting up operas of this sort. "He had engaged a musician to come and play the trombone, but after the bargain was closed, the trombone player insisted upon having some other musicians help him. He had hired the man to work, and wouldn't stand for any such nonsense, and so discharged him on the spot."[25] He then proceeded with his lecture, opening with the familiar phrase "When in the course of human events. . . ."[26] After explaining the location of the Sandwich Islands, their size and number, he described the traits of character, customs, and habits of the Islanders with such detail as only a close observer could supply and which could not adequately be gotten out of books. With the virtues of the natives he dealt generously. Their vices he set forth in such humorous style that the audience was kept in almost a constant state of merriment. Interspersed throughout the lecture, however, were important facts concerning the economic life of the Islands of special interest to the businessmen of San Francisco; and these, together with frequent references to Hawaiian history, traditions, religion, and political and social structure, richly provided the instructional element of the lecture.[27] It was noted with pleasure that Mark Twain praised the labor of the missionaries in bringing culture and enlightenment to the natives. Noted also was his observation that since these Islands were especially valuable to American business, and in time had to "fall to some heir," why shouldn't they fall to the United States?[28] What particularly surprised the audience that evening, however, was Mark Twain's eloquent description of the volcano Kilauea, a magnificent piece of word painting that especially delighted the hearers, and that came quite unexpectedly from a man whose reputation among them derived chiefly from his wild humor.[29]

So warmly was Mark Twain's lecture received that the services of the clacquers he had placed in the parquet proved quite unnecessary. The lady in the box at left stage, who had agreed to respond when Mark Twain smiled at her, played her part almost too well by responding at the wrong time. "Presently," said Mark Twain in reporting the incident, "I delivered a bit of serious matter with impressive unction (it was my pet), and the

audience listened with an absorbed hush . . . and as I dropped
the last word of the clause, I happened to turn and catch Mrs.
_____['s] intent and waiting eye; my conversation with her flashed
upon me, and in spite of all I could do I smiled. She took it for
the signal, and promptly delivered a mellow laugh that touched
off the whole audience; and the explosion that followed was the
triumph of the evening. . . . But my poor little morsel of pathos
was ruined. It was taken in good faith as an intentional joke, and
the prize one of the entertainment, and I wisely let it go at
that."[30]

At the close of the lecture, and after many in the audience
had risen to leave, a new burst of applause brought Mark Twain
out from the wings again. He apologized for inflicting his lecture
upon them, giving as an excuse that he was engaged in writing a
book about the Sandwich Islands and needed money for its
publication.[31]

With minor reservations, the newspaper reports following
the lecture were uniformly complimentary, hailing it as superior
to Artemus Ward's Babes in the Wood in point of humor, especially since it revealed none of Ward's straining after effect, yet
contained solid qualities lacking in the great showman's lecture.[32]
"From here on," declared the *Golden Era* pridefully, "Artemus
can hide his diminished luminary under several bushels; he is as
a penn'orth of tallow to a mammoth circus chandelier."[33] The
Alta California declared that Mark Twain has established himself as the most humorous and piquant lecturer on the coast
since the days of the lamented John Phoenix.[34] But the heartiest
and most soul-satisfying praise came from the *Golden Era,* despite the fact that it chided the other San Francisco newspapers
for being too uniform in their praise and suggested as a reason
that all were afraid of his pen. In the reporter's opinion, Mark
Twain had made some remarks in his lecture which were not hits
at all. Nevertheless, he declared, "We regard this subject with
mingled admiration and awe, and approach him with hesitation.
Nature must have been in one of her funniest moods when she
fashioned this mixture of the sublime and the ridiculous. . . .
Never did an aspirant for public favor take more rapid strides
than did the future historian of the Sandwich Islands on that
momentous evening. Quote Artemus Ward no more; our Pacific
slopes can discount him. True, he displayed not the polish of the
finished lecturer—nor did he need it; the crude, quaint delivery
was infinitely preferable."[35]

What the *Golden Era* reporter took for a lack of polish appears in retrospect, however, to have been far more conscious art on Mark Twain's part than either he or his audience guessed. Noah Brooks, who was present at the lecture, dimly perceived this fact when he said of Mark Twain's performance that his "method as a lecturer was distinctly unique and novel. His slow, deliberate drawl, the anxious and perturbed expression of his visage, the apparently painful effort with which he framed his sentences, and above all, the surprise that spread over his face when the audience roared with delight or rapturously applauded the finer passages of his word-painting, were unlike anything of the kind they had ever known. All this was original; it was Mark Twain."[36]

Brook's appraisal of Mark Twain's platform style during the first San Francisco lecture was unusually perceptive; for it is now clear that from the very beginning Mark Twain's style was not awkward, but original. It bears out Albert Bigelow Paine's statement that Mark Twain's manner of delivery did not change with the years except to become more finished, and that his naturalness and apparent lack of art was his greatest charm.[37]

No less perceptive and wider ranging, was the comment Bret Harte made of the opening performance, which he heralded as a brilliant success. Mark Twain's humor, he ventured to affirm, surpassed that of Artemus Ward because it was more legitimate. It had "the Western character of ludicrous exaggeration and audacious statement," which he found even more thoroughly national and American than the Yankee delineations of Lowell. There was more motive in his humor than in Ward's, more shrewdness and abhorrence of shams. "His faults," he observed, were "crudeness, coarseness, and an occasional Panurge-like plainness of statement."[38] Except for the charge of coarseness, Bret Harte's appraisal, if it ever came to his attention, must have greatly pleased Mark Twain. Though he probably had little acquaintance with the Yankee delineations of James Russell Lowell, it is likely that he was well aware, at least, of Lowell's high distinction as a man of letters.

Paine reports that Mark Twain wrote the first San Francisco lecture on sheets of manila paper, in a large hand, in order that it might be read in dim light, and that Mark Twain carried it under his arm, like a ruffled hen, to the rostrum.[39] It is likely, however, that on this occasion, as was true at later times, Mark

Twain had committed his lecture to memory and that he carried the manuscript with him more for reassurance than for reference.

Nothing is said in the newspaper accounts of Mark Twain's dress or appearance on the evening of his first lecture. On later occasions, in the East and the Middle West, he always dressed formally for the platform and felt uncomfortable when circumstances forced him to appear in a bobtailed coat. On this night, however, he probably dressed in a business suit. Even if he owned formal attire at this time, which is doubtful, it is likely that it would have been inappropriate in view of the burlesque tone of the advertising which had preceded the lecture.

Perhaps the best description of Mark Twain during these early days in San Francisco comes from Bret Harte, whom the young humorist had met through George Barnes, editor of the San Francisco *Morning Call:* "His head was striking. He had the curly hair, the aquiline nose, and even the aquiline eye—an eye so eagle-like that a second lid would not have surprised me—of an unusual and dominant nature. His eyebrows were thick and bushy."[40] There can be little question that Mark Twain's piercing eyes, bushy brows, and other facial features contributed notably to his platform effectiveness.

Since one of Mark Twain's chief motives for undertaking the first San Francisco lecture was money, a word about profits is in order. The gross box office receipts ran to something over $1,200. By agreement, as we have seen, he paid Maguire fifty dollars for the Opera House, and then divided the remainder with him. Out of his half Mark Twain still had the advertising costs to pay. When all debts had been settled he had about $400 clear; not as much as a more cautious bargain with Maguire would have netted him, but still a very handsome sum for a man desperately in need of cash. Thus, lecturing opened up for him a pleasingly quick and lucrative way of earning a living, and since he soon came to love the hour he spent on the platform, he had some justification for saying in later years that from that day on he had always been able to gain his living without doing any work.[41]

The most important question about the first San Francisco lecture has to do with its significance to Mark Twain's future career. He himself declared it to be a turning point in his life, but nowhere did he ever attempt to set down an analysis of the new directions it led to. Was it merely, as he sometimes suggested, an easy and rapid way of making money—a lucrative parallel activity which he turned to only when necessity demanded? Or did it contribute in any significant way to his celebrity as an American literary personality and to his technique and art as a writer? Certainly it increased importantly the dimension of his understanding about the art of public address. It brought forcibly home to him the fact that a lecturer enjoyed compensations not afforded to a writer of newspaper articles, no matter how enthusiastic the reaction of his readers might be. A writer did not see his reader's response. The lecturer, on the other hand, not only saw it but felt it when facing his audience. It was immediate and visible. Their laughter acted like a subtle intoxicant which produced a feeling of closeness and harmony between him and his auditors, warming him and giving him a sense of power. He discovered how much his audiences appreciated good descriptive passages offered in a more elevated diction than that which characterized the main body of his speech, and the importance of contrast in style. He discovered also the value of naturalness and simplicity of platform manner and the appearance of unstudied art and improvisation. And whether or not he realized it at the time, his lecturing experience probably influenced his writing in at least two important ways. It contributed to the colloquialization of his writing style, and it tended to tone down his extravagant exaggerations and burlesques and bring them within more acceptable bounds.[42]

--»⟨⟨ CHAPTER THREE ⟩⟩«--

THE JUBILANT TOUR

. . . I have made the most sweeping success of any man he knows of. —MARK
TWAIN'S LETTERS, I, *121*.

I T WOULD APPEAR from the accounts of Mark Twain's biographers and from Mark Twain's own account in *Roughing It* and elsewhere that the San Francisco lecture of October 2, 1866, was planned as an isolated event, and that the interval between the decision to lecture and the lecture itself was a matter of only a few days.[1] It would also appear from these accounts that the lecture was planned without reference to any tour following it, and that it was only after the impressive success of that lecture that Mark Twain decided to go on tour. By thus focusing the spotlight upon his first appearance as a public lecturer, a truly momentous turning point in his career, the importance of the event could be dramatically highlighted. The probability is, however, that the decision to lecture in various California and Nevada towns was made in advance of October 2, and that by this date at least some of the arrangements had already been made or were in progress.

The schedule of engagements for the first phase of the tour, which presently developed, was as follows: October 11, Sacramento; October 15, Marysville; October 20, Grass Valley; October 23, Nevada City; October 24, Red Dog; October 25, You Bet; October 31, Virginia City; November 3, Carson City; November 10, Gold Hill. In addition to these he planned to include Silver City, Dayton, and Washoe,[2] but for reasons which appear later these towns were dropped. While this schedule can scarcely be called a tight one, it would have been very difficult in the week's interval between the San Francisco lecture and the one at Sacramento to have made the necessary arrangements for so extensive a tour, without some previous preparations, especially at a time when California mails were still moving by stagecoach, the telephone had not yet made its appearance, and the only means of rapid communication was by telegraph, which cost money.

As business manager for the tour and as companion, Mark Twain chose his old friend Denis McCarthy, who was in San Francisco at the time and apparently without fixed employment. Mark Twain had known McCarthy in Virginia City and was fond of him. In fact it was to McCarthy that Sam Clemens had first introduced himself, in the spring of 1862, when he stepped into the *Enterprise* office to report for work.[3] At that time McCarthy was co-proprietor with Joseph Goodman of the *Enterprise,* and acted as shop foreman. Good-natured, tall, strong, and something of a boxer, he had been one of Mark Twain's companions, along with Dan DeQuille and Joe Goodman, who helped entertain Artemus Ward so bibulously during the three hilarious weeks the famous showman had spent in Virginia City in December of 1863. Now, with McCarthy as his companion and with the enthusiastic reports of his platform success in San Francisco preceding him, Mark Twain's progress from town to town turned into a jubilant triumphal procession.

The trip from San Francisco to Sacramento was made by river boat, Mark Twain choosing this type of transportation rather than stagecoach not only for nostalgic reasons, remembering his Mississippi steamboat days, but because it was more comfortable, more scenic, and because the boat had a bar. At Sacramento he visited again with the proprietors of the *Union,* the newspaper which had sent him to the Sandwich Islands, and perhaps discussed with them his plan to undertake a reporting trip around the world for some metropolitan newspaper. Indeed, arrangements for such a trip were presently made, as we shall see, but with the *Alta California* rather than with the *Union.*

The popularity of his Sandwich Islands letters in the *Union* should have assured Mark Twain that he would have a large audience in Sacramento, but he took no chances. To insure success he again resorted to the kind of circus advertising which had so greatly amused the people of San Francisco and had lured them into the theater. Mark Twain, the announcement proclaimed, would deliver a lecture on the Sandwich Islands for one night only, and for only a portion of that. "THE CELEBRATED BEARDED WOMAN! Is not with this Circus. THE WONDERFUL COW WITH SIX LEGS! Is not attached to this Menagerie. That Curious and Unaccountable Freak of Nature, THE IRISH GIANT! Who stands 9 feet 6 inches in height and has a breadth of beam in proportion . . . will not be present and need not be expected. THE KING OF THE ISLANDS! failed to arrive in season for the Lecture in San Francisco, but may confidently be expected on this Occasion. Doors open at 7 P.M.— The Trouble to begin at 8.⁴

Whether because of the advertising or of his reputation, a good house assembled in the Metropolitan Theater to hear Mark Twain mix "amusement with instruction." Next day the Sacramento *Union* and the *Bee* reported the lecture only briefly but favorably. The *Union* praised his easy colloquial style, his magnificent descriptions of Hawaii's great volcanos, and his just tribute to the labors of the missionaries.⁵ The *Bee* complimented him for his wise mixing of the pathetic with the humorous, though it acknowledged that there was more of the humorous than the pathetic. The transitions from one to the other were so sudden "that before a tear had time to gather head enough to fall, the laughing came in. Occasionally it was just the other way—the tears came from the overflow of laughter."⁶

From Sacramento the tour led to the old mining towns of Marysville and Grass Valley. For the latter town Mark Twain concocted another circus type of announcement in which he promised, after his lecture, to perform a series of "wonderful feats of SLEIGHT OF HAND, if desired to do so." At a given signal he would go out with any gentleman and take a drink. Also, if desired, he would repeat "this unique and interesting feat" until everyone was satisfied that there was no deception about it. Next he promised, at a moment's warning, that he would depart from town and leave his hotel bill unsettled. He had performed this ludicrous trick many times, in San Francisco and elsewhere, and it had always elicited the most enthusiastic comments. For an additional feat he promised "at any hour of the night, after 10, he would go through any house in the city, no matter how dark it may be, and take an inventory of its contents, and not miss as many of the articles as the owner will in the morning."[7]

An amusing incident occurred in Grass Valley when Mark Twain learned that a husband and wife team was scheduled to put on a tightrope walking act on the evening of his lecture. The husband, fearing that both performances might suffer by competition in so small a town, proposed that they put on their act just outside the theater preceding the lecture. By this arrangement, he believed, one performance might profitably support the other.[8] He may have been emboldened to make this unusual proposal after reading some of the humorous advertisements of Mark Twain's lecture which had appeared in the newspapers and in handbills posted throughout the town and which had more of the appearance of a circus advertisement than a lecture announcement. McCarthy, enchanted by the novelty of the idea, or perhaps seeing an opportunity to have some fun at Mark Twain's expense, was willing to give it a try; but Mark Twain wisely refused. He had formerly known the husband in Virginia City as a compositor on the *Enterprise* and disliked him. At any rate, he rightly sensed the unwisdom of tying his lecture to an act commonly associated with street carnivals and circuses.

It was at Grass Valley, too, where Mark Twain encountered one of the many amusing introductions that delighted him over the years. The introducer was an unprepared person selected at the last moment. Obviously ill-at-ease, he said, "Ladies and Gentlemen, this is the celebrated Mark Twain from the celebrated city of San Francisco, with his celebrated lecture about the celebrated Sandwich Islands."[9]

At Red Dog, Mark Twain experienced another amusing introduction. The person who was to introduce him had failed to appear. Much against his will a big awkward miner was selected from the audience to make the introduction. This gentleman, Mark Twain reported later, had a good head, and said he supposed I didn't want any compliments. I said he was exactly right, I *didn't* want any compliments. And when he introduced me he said, "Ladies and Gentlemen, I shall not waste any unnecessary time in the introduction. I don't know anything about this man; at least I know only two things about him; one is that he has never been in the Penitentiary, and another is that I can't imagine why."[10] The novelty of this introduction pleased Mark

Twain so much that on later tours in the East and the Midwest he often shared it with his audiences, always to their delight.

By far the most exciting part of the tour came with Mark Twain's return to Virginia City and Carson City. It was at Virginia City where he had acquired fame and notoriety as a reporter on the *Enterprise*. Here he had first used the pseudonym "Mark Twain" and had given it currency throughout Nevada and California. And here he had perpetrated a number of literary hoaxes, especially The Empire City Massacre, the story of an incredibly bloody murder and suicide that was supposed to have occurred in the neighborhood of Virginia City. Though he had assumed that the hoax would easily be detected by people acquainted with the general neighborhood of the supposed massacre, so bloody and revolting were the reported details that it immediately aroused a storm of angry protest against its author when the deception was discovered. It was also at Virginia City where he had become involved in a duel with a rival editor, and had become embroiled with the ladies of Carson City whom he had grievously offended. These latter incidents had stirred up so many animosities against him and had so damaged his reputation that he decided to leave Virginia City and take up residence in San Francisco. The Gold Hill *Evening News,* commenting on his departure, declared that it was not surprised, for "Mark Twain's beard is full of dirt, and his face is black before the people of Washoe."[11]

That Mark Twain now entertained a good deal of misgiving about returning to Nevada to lecture can well be imagined. Nevertheless he had reason to hope that he would be well received, for during the two and a half years of his absence he not only had become a West Coast celebrity but was also getting some attention in the East. Variously referred to as the "Washoe Giant" and the "Wild Humorist of the Pacific Slope," his articles had appeared in such big San Francisco newspapers as the *Morning Call,* the *Californian,* the *Golden Era,* and the *Dramatic Chronicle.* He had even contributed a series of articles to the Virginia City *Enterprise.* Some of his articles had appeared in the New York *Sunday Mercury.* And in November of 1865, the New York *Saturday Press* had published his Jumping Frog story, which was still circulating in the American exchanges and gaining popularity with every passing month. His immediate claim to celebrity, however, were the Sandwich Islands letters to the

Sacramento *Union*. Indeed, these were still appearing in the *Union* while the lecture tour was in progress, and were well known to readers in the Virginia City and Carson City area.

As he had hoped, the welcome at Virginia City was warm. Joe Goodman and Dan DeQuille, his old friends at the *Enterprise*, were there to greet him and to give him friendly and free publicity. Even the Gold Hill *Evening News* promoted his lecture at Virginia City, scheduled for Wednesday evening, October 31, by informing its readers that it "would be very amusing and well worth hearing, as Mark has few equals as a humorist any place."[12]

As might be expected it was the *Enterprise* which gave him the most extended attention. It heralded the enthusiasm with which the lecture had everywhere been greeted. "Our state," it proudly declared, "can justify its claim of Mark Twain as its own peculiar production. It was while in residence here and associated with the *Enterprise* that he assumed the name 'Mark Twain' and developed that rich and inexhaustible vein of humor which has made the title famous. True, he has since . . . expanded his thought by ocean pilgrimages, and heated his eloquence in volcanic fires; but all these rest upon the solid foundation which was originally laid in our native alkali and sagebrush."[13]

On the evening of the lecture it continued its panegyric. Those who planned to attend the lecture, it promised, would not be entertained solely by humor but would also be instructed. The lecturer's reputation, it acknowledged, was chiefly that of a humorist, but "his description of the great volcano of Kilauea is . . . sublime. Mark Twain is an original. He . . . succeeds in placing the realities and comicalities of life in such strange juxtaposition that no stoic, however stubborn, can resist him."[14]

With such fulsome though well-founded praise the lecture went off extremely well. A large and "most fashionable" audience of about eight hundred persons attended, filling all seats and standing room. In reporting the lecture the following day, the newspapers refrained, probably at Mark Twain's request, from reprinting portions of his lecture. The *Enterprise* described the large attendance as a magnificent tribute to Mark Twain from his old friends, and again praised the lecture as a splendid combination of statistical and general information with passages of the drollest humor—"an entertainment of rare excellence and

interest."[15] No less pleasing to Mark Twain was praise from
Sandy Baldwin, one of his old Virginia City friends and now a
leading attorney in the Territory, who told him that he had
made the most sweeping success of any man he knew of.[16] Mark
Twain's jubilation led him next day to report the success of his
lecture to his family in St. Louis. "You know," he proudly informed them, "the flush times are past, and it has long been impossible to more than half fill the theatre here, with any sort of
attraction, but they filled it for me, night before last—full—dollar
all over the house."[17]

Mark Twain now turned his attention to Carson City where
he hoped next to lecture. He was "mighty dubious" about Carson,[18] in view of the hornet's nest he had stirred up there with
his miscegenation joke two years earlier, and he had taken pains
to sound out the situation before proceeding with arrangements.[19]
Only when a number of cards and telegrams from Carson City
friends, including Governor H. G. Blaisdel, invited him to come
and assured him of a cordial reception, did he accept. Deeply
pleased, he immediately inserted a card in the *Enterprise* addressed to the Governor and to others in Carson City who had invited him, thanking them for their generous invitation and
promising to do his level best to please them. Expressing the
hope that they would be more indulgent toward his shortcomings than toward those of a stranger, he promised to appear Saturday evening, November 3, and "disgorge . . . as much truth
as I can pump out without damaging my constitution."[20]

The lecture at Carson City proved highly successful, and
his old offenses against the ladies of that city were forgiven, if
not forgotten, in his week-long stay there and in the neighboring
towns. At Gold Hill, where he lectured next, he also seems to
have had a splendid audience. But now occurred an event which
so thoroughly upset Mark Twain that he apparently canceled
any further lectures in the area and returned in a huff to San
Francisco. The story of the fake holdup that was perpetrated
upon him by his old Virginia City friends has been told so often
that it deserves only brief mention here.[21] After the lecture at
Gold Hill he and McCarthy were making their way over the Divide on their way to Virginia City. They were on foot and were
carrying the proceeds of the evening's lecture in their pockets.
Presently, out of the darkness, a group of men appeared, flour-
ishing pistols and demanding their money and valuables. The

valuables included a gold watch which Sandy Baldwin and Theodore Winters had given Mark Twain during his Virginia City days and which he prized very much. The next day, prematurely, the news of the fake holdup leaked out. By evening most of the town knew it. The friends had hoped to keep the matter secret for a time in order to enjoy their joke while listening to Mark Twain's version of the robbery. They fully expected, after they *had* told him of their friendly conspiracy, that he would enjoy the humor of it as much as they. But Mark Twain was deeply offended and angry. Perhaps he had shown more trepidation at the holdup than he liked to remember, and consequently felt a measure of shame.[22] He was especially incensed when he discovered that Denis McCarthy was a member of the conspirators. In his fury he sought McCarthy out, paid him off, and told him he wanted no more of his services. Thereafter, canceling a repeat performance in Virginia City the next evening, he immediately left for San Francisco from where some days later, he sent the following notice to the *Enterprise:*

> Now I want to say to you road agents as follows:
> My watch was given me by Judge Sandy Baldwin and Theodore Winters, and I value it above anything else I own. If you will send that to me (to the *Enterprise* office, or to any prominent man in San Francisco), you may keep the money and welcome. You know, you got all the money Mac had—and Mac is an orphan—and besides, the money he had belonged to me. Adieu, my romantic young friends.

Though Mark Twain later professed to have forgiven the conspirators, the very thought of the fake holdup continued to rankle him. On the eve of his departure from California, about six weeks later, he still smarted from the recollection of it and couldn't resist including in a farewell letter to the *Alta California* a final thrust at his conspirator friends.

> Good-bye felons—goodbye. I bear you no malice. And I sincerely pray that when your cheerful career is closing, and you appear finally before a delighted and appreciative audience to be hanged, that you will be prepared to go. . . . So-long, brigands.[23]

Inevitably it occurred to some of Mark Twain's acquaintances, especially to those who had observed with interest his audacity in publicizing his lectures, that the holdup on the Divide was a pure fake got up by Mark Twain himself for publicity purposes. Thus a reporter for the San Francisco *Golden Era*, a skeptic who called himself "Sans Souci," advanced the theory that the robbery had been deliberately staged to get free publicity for a second lecture in San Francisco. In need of money to get back east and to cover other expenses—whiskey on a steamship being "two-bits a glass"—and finding paid advertising to be costly, Mark Twain had contrived a friendly holdup for the purpose of creating a sensation. And when it was successfully accomplished he "turned his face toward San Francisco, where a golden harvest awaited him."[24]

Though Sans Souci's theory is both plausible and ingenious, there is no real evidence to support it. In view of the splendid successes of his performances in San Francisco, Sacramento, Virginia City, Carson City, and elsewhere, it is unlikely that Mark Twain felt the need to resort to the manufactured sensationalism of a highway robbery in order to win another good house in San Francisco, no matter how urgently he needed money. It is much more probable that Mark Twain's friends in Virginia City, remembering his love for practical jokes and hoaxes, simply decided to enliven his homecoming by paying him back in kind.

Mark Twain's second lecture in San Francisco on Friday evening, September 16, attracted an unusually large audience.[25] It was advertised not only as a new lecture on the Sandwich Islands but also, facetiously, as a Farewell Benefit (that is, for his private benefit), since he planned to sail for New York the following Monday. As matters turned out, he did not sail till nearly a month later. The advertisement included the appealing announcement that he would conclude his talk with "the only true and reliable history of the late revolting highway robbery perpetrated upon the lecturer at dead of night. . . ."[26] Since the local newspapers had carried stories of the robbery a few days previously, citizens of San Francisco were eager to hear Mark Twain's side of the story.

Nevertheless, despite this added attraction, the second San Francisco lecture proved distinctly less successful than that of October 2, a fact which the *Golden Era* pointed out, saying: "The lecture . . . bore no comparison to his first effort. It is evident that being robbed even in a joke doesn't agree with Mark's constitution. Mark can do better, and . . . he ought, in consideration of the generous support he has received, to have done his level best."[27]

Indeed, the second San Francisco lecture proved less satisfactory than the first for a number of reasons. It was charged that he was too familiar with his audience, that the quality of some of his humor was too audacious, and that some of the jokes were so nearly improper and verging on coarseness that ladies in the audience could not laugh at them. A more cynical appraisal of its value was the observation that Mark Twain had fulfilled his promise of perpetrating a robbery upon the people of San Francisco, and after the lecture had returned to his lodgings in the Occidental with his pocket filled with cash. Only the *Alta California* pointed out some of its praiseworthy elements, paying tribute to the "gorgeous word-painting" in two eloquent descriptive passages; and, perceptively, to a platform device which Mark Twain skillfully employed, perhaps for the first time, that of pretending with "unexampled diffidence . . . to forget a word so as to break the spell in which he held the audience. . . ."[28]

There were, however, other and more serious objections to the lecture. As a reporter for the *Morning Call* pointed out, a select audience had come to be edified, to hear what Mark Twain had to say about life in the Sandwich Islands; but, as the lecture developed, the "facts and the facetiae" became so intermixed that the audience had difficulty in distinguishing one from the other.[29] Certainly the lecture contained a considerable amount of informative material; yet it is well known that during these beginning days of his platform career his chief aim was not actually to inform but to amuse, to get a laugh. He had yet fully to understand that audiences not only expected to be informed but desired to be informed, and that while they were greatly delighted with his humor, they had at least to feel that they had been instructed in order to believe they had received their money's worth. No other problem was to give Mark Twain more concern in the tours that followed than precisely this one: how to satisfy his own desire to make his audiences laugh while at the same time satisfying them that they had been instructed.

There was, however, another cause for the sense of confusion which the audience experienced. The unmistakable fact is that Mark Twain erred seriously in this lecture by twice diverting the attention of his audience away from his main subject by including two extensive passages which had nothing whatever to do with it. While it is true that his remarks at the close of the lecture about the highway robbery had been expected, because of the announcement in the advertisments, their inclusion could not fail to distract the audience and allow them to leave the lecture hall with their minds focused more upon the highway robbery incident than upon life in the Sandwich Islands.

But to make matters worse, there was still another diversion, and an extended one, at the beginning of the performance when Mark Twain attempted an experiment which he hoped would give his lecture a humorous start. The experiment was based upon a conviction, as he reported many years later in his *Autobiography* when recalling the second San Francisco lecture, that any precisely worded and unchanging formula, if frequently and gravely repeated, would compel laughter.[30]

The anecdote he had selected for the experiment was the Horace Greeley–Hank Monk story, a silly and pointless yarn which had been circulating in San Francisco for half a dozen years and had long ago become boring and mouldy. In Mark Twain's audience that night were many reporters and old friends who knew him well and admired him, and who would become sick at heart when they heard him bring out that old shopworn story and offer it up as if it were something new and good. He led up to the anecdote by describing his first day on an overland stage coach, five years earlier, when he had first come west. He then launched upon the narrative:

"At a little 'dobie station out on the plains, next day, a man got in and after chatting along pleasantly for a while he said, 'I can tell you a most laughable thing indeed, if you would like to listen to it. Horace Greeley went over this road once. When he was leaving Carson City he told the driver, Hank Monk, that he had an engagement to lecture at Placerville and was very anxious to go through quick. Hank Monk cracked his whip and started off at an awful pace. The coach bounced up and down in such a terrific way that it jolted the buttons all off of Horace's coat and finally shot his head clean through the roof of the stage, and then he yelled at Hank Monk and begged him to go easier—said he warn't in as much of a hurry as he was a while ago. But Hank Monk said, "Keep your seat, Horace, I'll get you there on time!" . . . and you bet he did, too, what was left of him!'"

Mark Twain reports that he told the story in a level voice

and in such a colorless and monotonous way, that he succeeded in making it utterly dreary and stupid. Then, looking pleased with himself, he paused for a moment as if expecting laughter. But only a dead silence met him. His "friends and acquaintances looked ashamed, and the house, as a body, looked as if it had taken an emetic." He could see that some of his friends were pitying him, but that others were "thirsting for blood." Pretending embarrassment, he stammered through some new features of the overland trip and then worked his way toward the anecdote again with the air of a man who had not told it well the first time but now hoped to tell it with better art.

It was necessary to repeat the anecdote at least twice more, he reports, before the audience perceived the "sell" and broke into a laugh. Then the whole house burst into a tumultuous roar of applause, a heavenly sound, for he was nearly exhausted from apprehension that he would never make them understand that he was attempting a delicate piece of satire.

While the hazardous experiment in compelling laughter by repetition succeeded, its inclusion in the Sandwich Islands lecture was a mistake. The anecdote was not only entirely extraneous to the subject, but in view of his slow rate of speech, it must have consumed a great deal of time that should have been allowed for the main theme. It is not at all surprising, therefore, that most reporters regarded the second lecture as far inferior to his first effort, and that he owed it to the friends who had so generously supported him to do better.

Mark Twain had announced in advertising the second San Francisco lecture that he planned to sail for New York the following Monday, November 19. But the date came and he did not sail. The precise circumstances which caused the delay are somewhat obscure, but a brief item in the Washoe *Evening Slope,* supplies a likely clue. It declared flatly that the proceeds of Mark Twain's "benefit" lecture in San Francisco had been attached for the benefit of one of his creditors.[31] The Gold Hill *Evening News* referred to the matter more guardedly, attributing Mark Twain's delay to a "severe attack of impecuniosity. . . ."[32] Since San Francisco papers remained silent, one may conjecture that the attachment proceedings were initiated in Nevada, probably for unpaid bills in Virginia City or Carson City.

At any rate Mark Twain changed his plans and scheduled

additional lectures in San Jose, Petaluma, Oakland, and a third and final lecture in San Francisco. It may be that "impecuniosity," which followed payment of the bills, made the extension of his platform activity necessary; yet there may have been another reason. Planning to continue his lecturing career in the East, he did not relish the thought of having the unfavorable criticism of his second San Francisco lecture stand as a final judgment of his platform appearance there, especially since San Francisco news items filtered widely through eastern exchanges.

The lecture at San Jose on November 21 deserves special mention because of one incident. It was there that Mark Twain introduced in his lecture for the first time an offer to demonstrate cannibalism as practiced in the Sandwich Islands if a mother in the audience would bring her child to the platform. This announcement, made with a perfectly straight face and in a grave manner, followed by a brief pause as if waiting for a mother to come forward, was so successful as a humorous device that Mark Twain used it frequently thereafter. Only occasionally did it become the target of criticism as an offense to good taste.

Whether the lecture at Petaluma two days later pleased the audience is difficult to say. It obviously did not please the editor of the Petaluma *Journal* and *Argus,* who took the San Francisco newspapers to task for their fulsome praise of Mark Twain. It revealed their lack of appreciation, he asserted, between stars of the first and ninth magnitude. It raised people's expectations of something fine and then doomed them to disappointment. Of the lecture at Petaluma it offered no specific criticism other than to say that as a lecturer Mark Twain "fell below mediocrity."[33]

On November 27, Mark Twain lectured in Oakland, where he expected a large audience. Unfortunately, because of a misunderstanding about the time at which the lecture was to take place, only a small house of about two hundred people assembled in College Hall to hear him. Attending the lecture, however, were all the members of the City Council, who canceled a regularly scheduled meeting that evening and proceeded in a body to the lecture hall. But even their presence did not serve to make Mark Twain happy about the Oakland lecture. Years later he recalled his acute suffering there, as he stood in the wings impatiently waiting for the school band to get through with its interminable concert before he could come on.[34]

Mark Twain's third and final lecture in San Francisco took place on Monday evening, December 10, at Congress Hall. Ostensibly, the decision to lecture was made in response to an invitation he received in the form of a letter signed by twenty prominent citizens of San Francisco. Several of the undersigned, it stated, had not heard his first lecture on the Sandwich Islands. The others wished to hear it again. For these reasons, they declared, "and also as a testimony to the strangers among whom you are going, of the esteem in which your abilities are held among your friends here at home, we invite you to repeat that lecture. . . ."[35] Charitably, nothing was said of the second lecture. Whether Mark Twain arranged this invitation, as he certainly had arranged earlier ones, may never be known, but it must be confessed that the phrasing of this one has the earmarks of being genuine.

Mark Twain replied by letter the very next day. Expressing his appreciation, he accepted the invitation and named the date, December 10.[36] The announcement of the lecture specifically stated that it would be a repetition of his first Sandwich Islands lecture, and that it would include a description of the great volcano Kilauea and the extinct volcano of Haleakala, a mention of Bishops Staley and Harris, and a description of the peculiarities of the Islanders, plus many "uncommonly bad jokes." It was positively his last "farewell benefit." He would conclude his performance with an impromptu farewell address got up "especially for this occasion." The doors would open at 7 and the inspiration would begin to gush at 8.[37]

The December 10 lecture was well attended and well received. Respecting Mark Twain's request that his lecture not be reported in detail, the newspaper comments which followed were brief but favorable. The *Alta California* pronounced it a success in every respect.[38] Never before, the San Francisco *Times* reported, was "so much actual information imparted in such an agreeable manner. . . ."[39] The *Evening Bulletin,* inclined to be friendly to Mark Twain, declared that men of his sort never overstocked the market and predicted that he would "find room for an honorable career in the field to which he is going."[40] The "impromptu" address which he had prepared for the occasion was especially well received, partly because it predicted a great and prosperous future for the city of San Francisco, but also because it revealed Mark Twain's genuine love of the city and his gratitude for the generous treatment he had received there. A verbatim report of the impromptu farewell address appeared in the *Alta California,* December 15, as follows:

My Friends and Fellow-Citizens: I have been treated with extreme kindness and cordiality by San Francisco, and I wish to return my sincerest thanks and acknowledgements. I have also been treated with marked and unusual generosity, forbearance and good-fellowship, by my ancient comrades, my brethren of the Press—a thing which has peculiarly touched me, because long experience in the service has taught me that we of the Press are slow to praise but quick to censure each other, as a general thing—therefore, in thanking them I am anxious to convince them, at the same time, that they have not lavished their kind offices upon one who cannot appreciate or is insensible to them.

I am now about to bid farewell to San Francisco for a season, and to go back to that common home we all tenderly remember in our waking hours and fondly revisit in dreams of the night—a home which is familiar to my recollection, but will be an unknown land to my unaccustomed eyes. I shall share the fate of many another longing exile who wanders back to his early home to find gray hairs where he expected youth, graves where he looked for firesides, grief where he had pictured joy—everywhere change! Remorseless change where he had heedlessly dreamed that desolating Time had stood still!—to find his cherished anticipations a mockery, and to drink the lees of disappointment instead of the beaded wine of a hope that is crowned with its fruition!

And while I linger here upon the threshold of this, my new home, to say to you, my kindest and my truest friends, a warm good-bye and an honest peace and prosperity attend you, I accept the warning that mighty changes will have come over this home also when my returning feet shall walk these streets again.

I read the signs of the times, and I, that am no prophet, behold the things that are in store for you. Over slumbering California is stealing the dawn of a radiant future! The great China Mail Line is established, the Pacific Railroad is creeping across the continent, the commerce of the world is about to be revolutionized. California is Crown Princess of the new dispensation! She stands in the center of the grand highway of the nations; she stands midway between the Old World and the New, and both shall pay her tribute. From the far East and from Europe, multitudes of stout hearts and willing hands are preparing to flock hither; to throng her hamlets and villages; to till her fruitful soil; to unveil the riches of her countless mines; to build up an empire on these distant shores that shall shame the bravest dreams of her visionaries. From the opulent lands of the Orient, from India, from China, Japan, the Amoor; from tributary regions that stretch from the Arctic circle to the equator, is about to pour in upon her the princely commerce of a teeming population of 450,000,000 souls. Half the world stands ready to lay its contributions at her feet! Has any other State so brilliant a future? Has any other city a future like San Francisco?

The straggling town shall be a vast metropolis; this sparsely populated land shall become a crowded hive of busy men; your waste places shall blossom like the rose, and your deserted hills and valleys shall yield bread and wine for unnumbered thousands; railroads shall be spread hither and thither and carry the invigorating blood of commerce to regions that are languishing now; mills and workshops, yea, and *factories* shall spring up everywhere, and mines that have neither name nor place today shall dazzle the world with their affluence. The time is drawing on apace when the clouds shall pass away from your firmament, and a splendid prosperity shall descend like a glory upon the whole land!

I am bidding the old city and my old friends a kind, but not a sad farewell, for I know that when I see this home again, the changes that will have been wrought upon it will suggest no sentiment of sadness; its estate will be brighter, happier and prouder a hundred fold than it is this day. This is its destiny, and in all sincerity I can say, So mote it be!

It was appropriate and in the self-interest of the *Alta California* to print the farewell address in full and to follow it with the announcement that Mark Twain was about to start upon a long journey around the world as its traveling correspondent. It further took occasion to explain that it was giving the brilliant young journalist a free rein as to time, place, and direction. He would write his weekly letters on such subjects and from such places as would suit him best. "That his letters will be read with interest needs no assurance from us—his reputation has been made here in California, and his great ability is well known; but he has been known principally as a humorist, while he really has no superior as a descriptive writer—a keen observer of men and their surrounding—and we feel confident his letters to the *Alta*, from his new field of observation, will give him a world-wide reputation."[41]

With this splendid tribute to his abilities and the prophecy of far wider successes ringing in his ears, Mark Twain left San Francisco on December 15. The world tour he dreamed of did not materialize, but his letters to the *Alta California* on the "Quaker City" Holy Land Excursion the following summer, which eventually became the basis for *Innocents Abroad,* amply fulfilled the prophecy of his world-wide reputation.

ON HOME GROUND

His are not the worn out jests and hack-
neyed phrases. . . . —KEOKUK « GATE
CITY, » APR. *6, 1867.*

O N HIS WAY HOME from San Francisco, Mark Twain spent
nearly seven weeks in New York City—from January 12 to
March 3, 1867.[1] Although Albert Bigelow Paine reports
that he stayed only long enough to assure himself that publication of the Jumping Frog story in book form was making satisfactory progress,[2] he did find time for other activities. It was indeed a very busy seven weeks, given over to visiting the theaters,
attending the leading churches, going to lectures, observing wom-
en's fashions, taking note of Californians who were currently in
New York, and snooping out anything of interest that would
make good copy for his San Francisco paper, the *Alta California.*
While he reported at some length the scanty costumes of the famous "girlie" show of the time, "The Black Crook," he gave equal
space to the sermons of Henry Ward Beecher and the public lectures of Anna Dickinson. In view of his own recent experience as
a public lecturer, the platform art of both these speakers impressed him tremendously.

Another item of New York news that had special interest for
him at the moment were arrangements being made by a group of
prominent Brooklynites who were getting up a great European
and Holy Land pleasure excursion for the coming summer. The
excursion was especially exciting because it paralleled in part his

plans for a world tour, and also because it promised to offer exceptional news reporting opportunities. In a letter to the *Alta California* he described the plans in detail and expressed the hope that the newspaper would send him on the excursion and pay his passage.[3] When the *Alta* printed his letter in San Francisco, it informed its readers that they would not veto his plans and that they had telegraphed Mark Twain to "go ahead."[4]

With the Jumping Frog book now in the press, and arrangements well under way for the Holy Land trip, he left New York on March 3 and arrived in St. Louis about two days later, after an absence of more than five years. There to greet him were his mother, his sister Pamela Moffett, and Pamela's pretty young daughter Annie (later Mrs. Charles L. Webster). Perhaps Orion and Molly had also come down from Keokuk to be present at the homecoming, for by this time Orion had left Nevada and returned to Iowa. Understandably, the family was immensely proud of Sam. In 1861, when he had left St. Louis to go west with Orion, he had been obscure and greatly troubled about a career. Now he was something of a celebrity, both as a journalist and lecturer. The pseudonym "Mark Twain" was known from coast to coast, and while his mother probably lacked enthusiasm about his fame as the Wild Humorist of the Pacific Slope, she no longer feared for her son's future.

For Annie Moffett, now in her fifteenth year, the return of her Uncle Sam was particularly exciting, for he not only brought her gifts from the Sandwich Islands but seemed to find special pleasure in her company. It is from Annie that we get a glimpse of Mark Twain while visiting with his family in St. Louis. He had been invited, she recalled many years later, to give a lecture on the Sandwich Islands for the benefit of a mission school. As an introduction to the lecture, he had been asked to speak at the school on the Sunday preceding the lecture. The Clemenses made up a small party and started out to look for the Sunday school which they knew to be somewhere in the southern part of the city, in Carondelet. There they found a large mission school which they supposed was the right one. They all went in and were politely given seats. After waiting in vain for someone to announce Mark Twain's presence, they discovered that they were in the wrong Sunday school. They filed out and eventually found the right place. Annie Moffett couldn't remember just what Uncle Sam said to the boys, but she remembered distinctly that he said he intended to talk on the importance of always telling the truth, using as an example the story of the man who had been blown into the sky by an explosion and the mean corporation that had docked his wages for being absent fifteen minutes.[5]

While Annie Moffett's memory of what Uncle Sam said to the Sunday school boys that afternoon may be accurate, it is somewhat at variance with Mark Twain's own account of the talk as he reported it a day or two later in his letter to the *Alta California*. There he wrote that the superintendent of the school came around to his pew and asked him if he had ever had any experience in instructing the young. "I said, 'My son, it is my strong suit.' . . . So I got up there and told that admiring multitude all about Jim Smiley's Jumping Frog; and I will do myself the credit to say that my efforts were received with the most rapturous applause, and that those of the Deacon's to stop it were entirely unheeded by the audience. I honestly intended to draw an instructive moral from that story, but when I got to the end of it I couldn't discover that there was any particular moral sticking around it any where, and so I just let it slide."[6]

According to Mark Twain, he had not really intended to give a public lecture in St. Louis, but when he was asked to do so for the benefit of a Sunday school mission, he consented. "So," he tells his *Alta California* readers, "I preached twice in the Mercantile Library Hall."[7] These lectures, both on the Sandwich Islands, were well received by large and appreciative audiences who were attracted in part, no doubt, by the humorous advertisement of the lecture which appeared in the *Missouri Republican* of March 24, and by an equally amusing letter in the same issue. The advertisement repeated the promise he had first made in his lecture at Petaluma, California, to illustrate the customs of the ancient Sandwich Islands cannibals by devouring a child in the presence of the audience if some lady would kindly volunteer an infant for the occasion.

The letter, also an advertising puff for his lecture, explained his fitness to lecture for the benefit of Sunday schools, and offered a number of farcical prizes for those who attended. Typical of one of a number of devices which Mark used to lure people to his lectures, especially during the first year of his public lecturing, it is offered here in full:

EDITOR, Sunday *Republican:* You may not know that I am going to lecture at Mercantile Hall tomorrow night for the benefit of the South St. Louis Mission Sunday School, but I am. I do not consider any apology necessary. I would like to have a Sunday School of my own, but I would not be competent to run it, you know, because I have not had experience, and so I have thought that the next most gratifying thing I could do would be to give somebody else's Sunday School a lift. I used to go to Sunday School myself, a long time ago, and it is on that account that I have always taken a powerful interest in such institutions since. I even rose to be a teacher in one once, but they discharged me because they said the information I imparted was of too general a character.

I have done some good in my time though. When I was elected to the Chief Magistry of the Burlesque Government of the territory of Nevada, I delivered my annual message to the Legislature for the benefit of a church, and charged double admission. The proceeds enabled them to put a new roof on that church, and everybody said that that roof would cave in, some time or other, and mash the congregation, because I was one of those sinful newspaper men, but it never did. Ever since that I have been ambitious to put a roof on a Sunday School and see if it could stand it, and now I got a chance. I feel a little proud about it, and I wish you would mention it in your paper that I am going to lecture for the benefit of a Sunday School, so that they will see it in California, because, you know, if I were merely to say it myself, without any endorsement, they would copper it. (That is a Californian poetical simile; when they don't believe a statement there, they say copper it.)

I want this Sunday School experiment of mine to be a success, now that I have got this opening, and so I offer the following splendid prizes to encourage an interest among the public. (One has got to turn everything into a lottery now-a-days, to make it popular. However, there is no harm in it maybe, because even the church festivals have their little lottery arrangements, you know.)

For the best conundrum, first prize, a beautiful elephant. *N.B.* He is a little cadaverous, now, but a few tons of hay and confectionery would soon feed him up to a condition of symmetry and vivacity that would render him a favorite at the fireside, and the pet of the household. It is far better to have an elephant around than a cat, because cats sleep on the bed, but an elephant never.

For the best poem on Summer or Summer Complaint (option with the author), the second prize, consisting of eighteen hundred Auger Holes, will be awarded. These auger holes are really magnificent specimens of the carpenter's beautiful art, and have elicited the wildest burst of admiration wherever they have been exhibited, both in America and among the crowned heads of Europe. Queen Victoria observed of them that she only wanted to see these auger holes once more and then die. Competitors for this prize may crawl around and look through them free of charge, if they desire it. They will be found to possess as many virtues as any auger holes.[8]

For the most plausible Essay on Female Suffrage the Third prize, consisting of that splendid piece of property known as Lafayette Park, is offered.[9] This beautiful park lies out toward Compton Hill, and is tastefully laid out in walks, and bridges, and holes in the ground, and piles of dirt, and has neat legible signs to tell you where the grass is when there is any there.

The iron fence around it is a gem in itself. Few people can contemplate it without emotion, and nobody can climb it without stilts. Lafayette Park would cut up handsomely for city lots, and bring enormous prices. The winner of the Third prize will be awarded it. The diversion he will experience in trying to get possession of the property, must be a fortune in itself, and will afford him the liveliest entertain- as long as he lives.

How's that?

N.B. This moral lecture on the Sandwich Islands, which I am going to deliver, is a separate institution all by itself, and is not connected with any other circus.

MARK TWAIN

A reporter for the *Missouri Republican,* who was in the audience at the Mercantile Library during one of the lectures, took much of it down in shorthand. It was a fortunate circumstance, for his report of the lecture preserved for posterity the most accurate and extensive text of the earliest version of the Sandwich Islands lecture. In after years, Mark Twain liked to recall that that reporter was no other than Henry M. Stanley, later famed for his search for the lost David Livingstone.[10]

If Mark Twain's account of the manner in which he undertook the lectures at St. Louis may be trusted, it appears that his

engagements at Hannibal, Keokuk, and Quincy may also have
resulted from invitations rather than from any direct efforts of
scheduling on his part. Certainly such invitations might easily
have come from old friends in Hannibal where he grew up, and
also from Keokuk where he had worked in Orion's printing shop
for two years, and was well known. It is a little more difficult
to account for the lecture in Quincy, Illinois, though relatives
of the family were living there in 1867 who may have arranged
an invitation.[11]

Of the lecture in Hannibal on April 2, and of Mark Twain's
visit at his old home, unfortunately little is known. Hannibal
files for the period are no longer extant. One can well imagine,
however, that the opportunity to lecture in the town where he
had grown up gave him exceptional delight, for here he was
among boyhood friends, people who had known him most of
his life and who were proud of his success and curious to see him
after so many years of absence. His visit in Hannibal lasted
about a week, after which he left for Keokuk.

It was on Thursday, April 4, that the people of Keokuk
were informed by posters stuck about on street corners that
"Sam Clemens, the greatest Humorist in America," was coming
to lecture to them. Whether this self-appraisal was intended as
a piece of humorous exaggeration to amuse his old friends is hard
to say. Whatever the motive, the newspapers extended him an
immediate and friendly welcome, and congratulated the people
of Keokuk for the opportunity of hearing his lecture. "His are
not the worn-out jests, and hackneyed phrases . . . he is fresh
and vigorous, full of life and spirit. . . . Years ago, before the
war, Mark Twain . . . was one of the cleverest and most popular 'printer boys' in Keokuk. He returns to us now, a famous
man, and proverbs or scripture to the contrary, we trust that our
citizens will honor him with a rousing house. . . ."[12]

If the house was not a rousing one, at least a "respectable
audience" was in attendance, large enough to net the Library
Association an amount considerably above that which Ralph
Waldo Emerson's lecture had brought in a few months earlier.
That the lecture was also a platform success is indicated by the
comment which appeared in the Keokuk *Constitution* the next
day. "It has been many a day since our ribs were tickled so
much as at listening to Sam Clemens' lecture last evening upon
the Sandwich Islands. . . . Those of our citizens who did not

hear the lecture missed one of the richest treats of their lives"[13]
The following day Mark Twain left for Quincy to give the
last lecture before returning to New York. There he again resorted to the device of puffing his lecture by means of a letter
which appeared in the Quincy *Herald* on April 9. He offered
the letter as a reply to one signed "John Smith," inviting Mark
Twain, as a traveling correspondent for New York and San Francisco newspapers, to deliver one of his lectures for the instruction
and amusement of the citizens of Quincy. John Smith, of course,
was Mark Twain himself, or to be more specific, a fictional traveling companion he frequently used in his newspaper correspondence during this period, and invented as a means to air his
opinions and to give vigor and immediacy to his writing.

JOHN SMITH, ESQ.—Dear Sir: It gratifies me, more than
tongue can express, to receive this kind attention at your
hand, and I hasten to reply to your flattering note. I am
filled with astonishment to find you here, John Smith. I
am astonished, because I thought you were in San Francisco.
I am almost certain I left you there. I am almost certain it
was you, and I know if it was not you, it was a man whose
name is similar.

I am surprised to find you here, John Smith. And yet I
ought not to be, either, because I found you in New York,
most unexpectedly; and I stumbled on you in Boston; and
was amazed to discover you in New Orleans; and thunder-
struck to run across you in St. Louis. You must certainly
be a sort of roving disposition, John Smith. You certainly
are, John, and you know that a rolling stone gathers no
moss. And a rolling Smith never gathers any moss. There
is no real use in anybody's gathering moss, John, because it
isn't worth any more in the market than sawdust is, and
hardly even as much—but then, if we want to get along
pleasantly with the world, we must respect the world's little
whims and caprices; and you know that the world has a
foolish prejudice in favor of a man's gathering moss. So
you had better locate, John, and go to gathering some. It is
no credit to you, anyhow, John Smith, that you are always
sure to turn up wherever a man goes. It may be—no, it cannot be possible—that there are two John Smiths. The idea
is absurd.

However, I always liked you, Smith, and I am right
glad to come across you again, moss or no moss. I am proud
to be asked to lecture for you and shall always treasure the

recollection of that compliment with peculiar fondness; but you see I have already agreed to lecture for the Encore Club, and so of course I have to decline your kind offer. But do not let this provoke a coolness, John; on the contrary, let it bind us together more tenderly than ever in the common bonds of our rolling and mossless good fellowship. Come to National Hall Tuesday night, 9th inst., John, and bring some of your relations. I would say bring all of them, John, and say it with all my heart, too, but the hall covers only one acre of ground, and your Smith family is a large one, John.

Yours tenderly
MARK TWAIN[14]

Whether Mark Twain immediately proceeded to New York after the lecture at Quincy or returned to St. Louis for a farewell visit is uncertain. It is clear, however, from a news item in the Louisiana, Missouri, weekly *Journal* of April 12, that his reputation as writer and lecturer had spread widely through the Mississippi river towns, and that, had he desired, he could easily have arranged an extensive lecture tour in the Middle West.

"Sam Clemens," the *Journal* reported, "better known as Mark Twain . . . has returned home. . . . Mark Twain has a national reputation as a humorist and lecturer; we hope he can be induced to visit our city. Our people are near starved for a humorous treat and we assure Mark Twain that our largest hall would fill to overflowing if it were announced that his inspiration was going to 'gush' there on a certain evening." There is no evidence, however, that an invitation to lecture in the town ever reached Mark Twain or that he would have accepted it had he received one. New York and the Holy Land excursion were again fully occupying his attention. The sense of drifting that had so long troubled him had passed away. At the moment, the future seemed bright and full of promise.

CHAPTER FIVE

NEW YORK AND BROOKLYN

For an hour and fifteen minutes I was in Paradise. —MARK TWAIN'S AUTOBIOGRA-PHY, II, *355.*

ACK IN NEW YORK again by April 16, Mark Twain immediately found himself involved in a demanding round of activity. He continued his correspondence with the *Alta California,* at the rate of $20 a letter, and contributed a number of articles to the New York *Weekly* on the Sandwich Islands. Furthermore, the Jumping Frog book was now in press and scheduled to appear April 30. Anticipation of the appearance of his first book kept him in a simmer of excitement, added to which was the unrest caused by his preparations for the "Quaker City" excursion to the Holy Land, scheduled to begin June 8.

Despite all these activities, flushed with the success of his Sandwich Islands lecture in the Far and Middle West, he lost little time in making arrangements to speak in New York; and the first performance was presently scheduled for May 6 in Cooper Institute. In later years Mark Twain claimed that the Institute lecture had been suggested, engineered, and successfully carried out by a group of old West Coast friends, including ex-Governor Frank Fuller of Utah, who was now a New York businessman.[1] This claim appears to be supported by a statement in the prospectus of the lecture, that Mark Twain was speaking by "Invitation of a large number of prominent Californians and

Citizens of New York."² On the basis of these statements, Albert Bigelow Paine asserted that Mark Twain agreed to the Cooper Institute lecture with considerable reluctance on the grounds that he had no reputation with the general public in New York and that he couldn't get a baker's dozen to hear him.³

Despite these statements, it is highly improbable that Mark Twain waited for an invitation before deciding to lecture at Cooper Institute. The truth is that here, as on previous occasions, he preferred to make it appear that he was lecturing by invitation rather than offering to do so. It can easily be imagined that he feared he might have a small audience in view of his relative obscurity in New York; but that his fears were great enough to deter him from initiating the lecture is difficult to believe. Lack of confidence and shrinking modesty were never prominent traits in Mark Twain's character. Furthermore, the possibility of lecturing in New York had been a subject of discussion with his friends while he was still in San Francisco. They had warned him that if he ever should lecture there, he should be "very choice" in his language, lest he might offend the easterners.⁴

Besides the fact that Mark Twain loved to talk to audiences, the decision to lecture in the New York area was based upon a number of considerations. First of all, he faced a pressing need for money for the Holy Land trip beyond the amount the *Alta California* had agreed to pay him for correspondence. He dreaded the thought of being pinched for funds on so ambitious a venture. Hardly less important was the prospect of a greatly increased reputation; for should the lecture at Cooper Institute, and others he might undertake, prove successful, they would not only give added prestige to his *Alta* correspondence but considerably enhance his status aboard the "Quaker City." That they did, in fact, have precisely this effect soon became evident from the attention he received from such discerning shipmates as Mary Mason Fairbanks, writing for her husband's newspaper, the Cleveland *Herald;* the Solon Severances, also of Cleveland; Moses S. Beach of the New York *Sun;* Julia Newell, who contributed to the Janesville, Wisconsin, *Gazette;* and other prominent passengers.

According to Frank Fuller, whom Mark Twain acknowledged as a chief promoter of the lecture at Cooper Institute, the events leading up to it proceeded as follows. One day, while

he was sitting in his office at 57 Broadway, Mark Twain walked
in and said, "Frank, I want to preach right here in New York
and I must have the biggest hall to be found. It is Cooper
Union . . . it costs $70 for one evening, and I have got just
$7."⁵
   Fuller promised to help. He secured the hall at his own
risk and immediately began to devise ways (with Mark Twain's
help, no doubt), to advertise the lecture and stir up public interest. Through notices in the newspapers he first called up all
Pacific Coast people then in the city to attend a meeting at the
Metropolitan Hotel for the purpose of drumming up a rousing
audience for the lecture. At this meeting, which was well attended and appears to have been a rollicking affair, Mark Twain
was called upon to speak. What he said was not recorded, but
that it added to the general hilarity of the occasion and won
support for the venture at Cooper Institute is apparent.
   During the evening it was suggested that someone go to
Washington, D.C., to persuade Senator James W. Nye, former
governor of Nevada Territory and well known to the Californians, to come up to New York to introduce Mark Twain and sit
on the platform during the performance. Fuller was selected to
make the trip. In Washington, Nye received him graciously, appeared to enter wholeheartedly into the spirit of the occasion,
and promised to be on hand to make the introduction.⁶ To confirm his intention, he wrote Mark Twain a letter which was obviously intended for use in advertising the performance. He
stated that he had heard Mark Twain give the Sandwich Islands
lecture in San Francisco to delighted audiences some months
earlier, and praised it for its array of facts, its splendid descriptions of life, manners and customs among the natives, and especially for its sparkling wit and genial humor.⁷
   Heartened by Nye's letter, Fuller proceeded with the publicity. He supplied the New York newspapers with selected clippings reporting the San Francisco lectures and released the information that Senator Nye would make the introduction. It
was from Fuller, perhaps, that a reporter learned that Mark
Twain was "handsome, single, and rich," with a future altogether fair and promising, and that the Senator was also a good
deal of a humorist. Indeed, if the Senator did his level best in
the introductory speech, he would force Mark Twain to look to
his laurels.⁸ An elaborate prospectus of the lecture, got up much

in the fashion of those devised by Artemus Ward, listed thirty-eight topics which would receive "marked attention" during the evening's performance. It also reproduced the complimentary letter from Senator Nye.[9]

With these preliminaries attended to, Mark Twain began seriously to revise and perfect his lecture. At every opportunity he also dropped in on Fuller to see how business matters stood and to listen to his friend's assurances that all would go well. Unfortunately, expenses were running higher than expected. What gave them most concern, however, was the fact that a number of strongly competing attractions were billed in the city for the same evening. Schuyler Colfax, an able speaker with a good following, was scheduled to appear at Irving Hall; Adelaide Ristori, a famous singer, was performing at the French Theater; Thomas Maguire, who had rented Mark Twain the Academy of Music in San Francisco on the occasion of his maiden performance on the public platform several months earlier, was presenting his "Imperial Troupe of Wonderful Japanese Jugglers" at the New York Academy of Music; and "The Black Crook," the most daring girlie show of the time, was playing at Niblo's Garden. He voiced his concern about the competition in a letter to his family in St. Louis. They must not expect to hear from him for a time, since he was full of business about the lecture. At the moment, he confided, everything looked shady, if not dark. He had a good agent (referring to Fuller), but they had rented Cooper Institute and had gone to the expense of $500 before discovering how many competing attractions were booked for the same evening. And with all this against him, he wrote, "I have taken the largest house in New York, and cannot back water. Let her slide! If nobody else cares I don't."[10]

According to Fuller, as lecture day neared, a question arose concerning the manner in which Mark Twain should dress for the platform. Mark Twain contended that an ordinary dress suit was good enough, but Fuller insisted upon evening dress and ordered a first class New York tailor to make it. He then invited Mark Twain to come to his office and rehearse the lecture in full attire. Mark Twain complied, but he was not happy. He railed at the "damned tailor who had sewed up the button-holes" of his coat, despite Fuller's assurances that dress coats weren't buttoned. Nevertheless, Mark Twain insisted upon buttoning his, and had the stitches cut.[11]

As the day of the lecture approached, his fear of facing a vast emptiness in Cooper Institute mounted. Ticket sales had been alarmingly slow. Fuller, too, became concerned. He had already flooded the city with handbills and had advertised extensively in the newspapers. There was one last thing to do—to "paper" the house by sending hundreds of complimentary tickets to the schoolteachers and other professional people of the city. By this means they hoped they might at least secure a fair audience even though they would sustain a financial loss.[12]

At 7:30 on the evening of the lecture Mark Twain and Fuller waited impatiently at the Westminster Hotel for Nye to join them. But Nye never showed up. In a fever of anxiety and disappointment, they took a carriage and proceeded to the Institute. Fully convinced that Nye had failed him and would not be waiting at the hall, Mark Twain begged Fuller to take Nye's place. But Fuller flatly refused. He did, however, make a helpful suggestion. "You get up," he said, "and begin by demeaning Nye for not being here. That will be better anyway."[13]

As they approached the lecture hall, they were surprised to see the streets all blocked with people. The traffic had stopped. "I couldn't believe," Mark Twain recalled later, "that those people were trying to get into Cooper Institute; yet that was just what was happening." He managed to work his way backstage, and when he finally stood on the platform facing the audience, there "wasn't room enough left for a child. I was happy, and I was excited beyond expression."[14]

Advancing to the edge of the platform, he gazed intently down into the pit as if anxiously looking for somebody. Then, addressing himself to the audience, he announced, with a troubled expression, that Senator Nye had agreed to introduce him, but had failed to appear. Perhaps the Senator was lost in the audience somewhere. The Californians who were present and who had greeted Mark Twain's appearance with a loud yell suspected that the man they knew as the Wild Humorist of the Pacific Slope would not let Nye escape as a target for satire; and they were not disappointed. To their screaming delight he told stories about Nye as governor of Nevada Territory that set the whole house roaring.[15] Then, in complete rapport with his audience, he launched out upon his lecture, entertaining them with descriptions of the manners and customs of the Sandwich Islands natives, and with graphic and eloquent word pictures of the scenic beauties of the Islands and their spectacular volcanic eruptions. Never before had he experienced so profound an exhilaration before an audience. "They laughed and shouted," he recalled many years later, "to my entire content. For an hour and fifteen minutes I was in Paradise. From every pore I exuded a divine delight. . . ."[16]

In his next letter to the *Alta California* Mark Twain reported his success at Cooper Institute only briefly, but he could not deny himself the pleasure of expressing his feelings about Nye's conduct. "Governor Nye promised to introduce me," he declared, ". . . and I published it; but he was not at his hotel when a carriage went for him, has not been seen since, and has never sent a word of explanation. However, it is of no consequence. I introduced myself as well as he could have done it—that is, without straining myself."[17]

Though Mark Twain was in no mood to appreciate it then, Nye's failure to appear turned out to be a true blessing. It taught him that self-introductions had special advantages, especially for a humorous lecture. They not only protected him from various sorts of embarrassments and annoyances, but what was far more important, they provided him with valuable opportunities for achieving surprise, humor, and rapport with his audiences before the lecture proper ever began. Thereafter, during most of the tours that followed, he customarily insisted upon the privilege of introducing himself.

Years later, in a letter to Albert Bigelow Paine shortly after Mark Twain's death, Fuller reported that he had once asked Senator Nye why he hadn't kept his promise to introduce Mark Twain. Nye's reply was that he had never intended to introduce him because Mark Twain was nothing but a "damned secessionist."[18] In view of the circumstances, however, it is hard to believe that Nye made the promise without intending to keep it. To have done so deliberately, if known, might have cost him the friendship not only of Fuller, who was not without influence in the West, but also of the people from Nevada and California in the audience. While it is possible that Nye was aware of Mark Twain's wavering sympathy for the Northern cause during his Virginia City days, when Nye was governor of Nevada Territory, in the absence of knowledge to the contrary, it appears more probable that the charge of secessionism, as a justifiable excuse, occurred to him later when he read The Private

History of a Campaign that Failed, Mark Twain's account of his brief service with the confederates in Missouri.[19] According to Fuller, Nye was a fat, vulgar, and profane person, but witty, and an effective speaker.[20] It was for the latter qualities, no doubt, as well as for his political prominence that the Californians had considered his services on the platform as particularly desirable.

Brief complimentary reports of Mark Twain's lecture appeared the next day in all the leading newspapers. The most extensive and perceptive was that in the New York *Tribune,* written by Edward H. House, whom Mark Twain had met soon after his arrival in New York, and whose company he enjoyed.[21] Singled out for praise was his easy, lounging manner on the platform, his quaint, pleasing speech, and his eloquent description of the great volcanic eruption of 1840.

Fuller reports that the expenses of the lecture at Cooper Institute ran to something over three hundred dollars (not five hundred, as Mark Twain reported to his family), and that the receipts amounted to a little less than that. A number of years later, when the two men met again, Fuller asked Mark Twain if he remembered the time he wanted to preach at Cooper Institute and had only seven dollars to his name. "Seven dollars!" Mark Twain exclaimed. "I had $700 in gold in the hotel safe." And when Fuller replied he had not understood that, Mark Twain countered, "Well, maybe I didn't bring out the second syllable quite plainly."[22]

The unquestioned platform success of the Cooper Institute lecture and the complimentary news reports that followed, especially in the *Tribune,* all but insured success for the two remaining lectures Mark Twain had arranged, the first in Brooklyn, on May 10, and the last in Irving Hall, New York, May 16. For the Brooklyn lecture he stated in his printed announcements that he considered it the best lecture he ever wrote, and added that it was also the only one he ever wrote. It was, he declared, an infallible cure for all bronchial afflictions, sore eyes, fever and ague, and warts.[23]

Both the Brooklyn lecture and the one in Irving Hall were well attended. In general the newspapers were complimentary, especially about the humor if not about the substance of the lecture. As a result, Mark Twain reports, "a flattering lot of invitations to appear before various and sundry literary societies" poured in upon him.[24] These he was forced to decline in order to catch up with his *Alta California* correspondence and to complete his preparations for the Holy Land trip, which was now imminent. Among the invitations he declined was one from Thomas Nast, the rising young cartoonist. Nast proposed a joint tour on which Mark Twain was to lecture and he was to illustrate it with "lightning" sketches.[25] It was such an interesting proposal that Mark Twain kept it in mind, and years later tried to resurrect it.

If Mark Twain ever tried to assess the value of his New York and Brooklyn lectures in his career on the public platform there is no record of it. Yet their importance was enormous. Aside from the celebrity they provided him among the "Quaker City" passengers and in the New York area generally, their chief value lay in the assurance they gave him that his humor, style of speaking, and platform manner were as pleasing to eastern as to western audiences, and that his fear of the greater sophistication of eastern audiences greatly diminished.

CHAPTER SIX

RETURN TO THE FAR WEST

I put together a lecture on the Quaker City *trip and delivered it in San Francisco at great and satisfactory pecuniary profit; then I branched out into the country.* . . . —MARK TWAIN'S AUTO-BIOGRAPHY, I, 242–43.

I N AN ARTICLE called "The Turning Point of My Life," written about a year before his death, Mark Twain reported an episode which explained how he became a member of the "literary guild," that is to say, something more than a mere journalist. On his return to America from his "Quaker City" excursion to the Holy Land he reported: "Circumstance was waiting on the pier. . . . I was asked to *write a book,* and I did it, and called it *Innocents Abroad.*"[1] The episode which Mark Twain referred to was Elisha Bliss's proposal that the "Quaker City" journalist supply his publishing house, The American Publishing Company of Hartford, Connecticut, with a book based upon his past letters.[2] What Mark Twain failed to report was that Bliss's proposal also had the significant effect of promoting his career as a public lecturer.

If circumstance was not quite at the pier on November 19 when the "Quaker City" docked at New York, it did arrive soon enough thereafter to justify Mark Twain's slight telescoping of events. Bliss's letter, dated November 21, might have reached him a day or two later had Mark Twain stayed in New York, but he had almost immediately left for Washington, D.C., and the letter did not reach him till December 1. Mark Twain replied at once, but a further delay in negotiations occurred because Bliss was ill when the letter reached him and he did not reply till a month later.

In the meantime Mark Twain was in Washington employed as private secretary to Senator William M. Stewart whom he had known during his Virginia City days. He had accepted the position partly because he liked the Senator, partly because it solved the immediate problem of earning a living, but even more because it promised not to interfere with his primary objective, that of writing for the newspapers and magazines. The success of the "Quaker City" letters in the *Alta California,* and his friendly reception at the offices of the New York *Herald* and the *Tribune* after his return from the Holy Land, convinced him that he could become a regular correspondent for big metropolitan newspapers in the East.

There may, however, have been another motive for accepting the position with Stewart. It gave him an excellent opportunity to acquaint himself with politics in the national capital, and with the operations and concerns of the national government, in order to become more knowledgeable for his contemplated trip to China. But now, amid a flood of new interests and particularly because of Bliss's letter, the China plans, though not abandoned, receded momentarily into the background. The prospect of bringing out another book began to occupy his attention to such a degree that his secretarial duties under Stewart soon grew irksome.[3]

While waiting for a reply from Bliss about the proposed book, Mark Twain made occasional trips to New York to visit his old "Quaker City" companions, Jack Van Nostrand, Charles Langdon, the Beaches, and others. It was during one of these trips that an incident occurred which came to have signal importance both for his personal life and for his later development as a public lecturer and reader. On January 2 or 3 he went to Steinway Hall to hear the visiting Englishman, Charles Dickens, read from his books.[4] Albert Bigelow Paine makes much of the fact that at Mark Twain's side that evening sat Olivia Langdon, sister of his "Quaker City" cabin mate, the girl who later became his wife.[5] The Langdons had come to New York to attend the Dickens reading and incidentally to meet the rising young journalist from the West whom Charlie so greatly admired. That Mark Twain was excited by the presence of the beautiful young lady at his side is obvious from the relationship which followed, yet there is little reason to believe that she completely engrossed his attention that evening. It is evident that the readings by the celebrated English novelist also commanded his deep interest and that they suggested to him the possibilities of a platform artistry which he had never before imagined.

In 1868 Dickens was, of course, at the very peak of his enormous popularity. Many came to Steinway Hall merely to see the man; and Mark Twain shared the popular veneration, for he had been a lover of Dickens' novels from boyhood.[6] As he listened and watched the great novelist as he stood in a spot of light behind a lectern on which lay his manuscript,[7] a conviction formed in Mark Twain's mind—a conviction that the basic ingredient of the success of public reading of this nature was dramatic skill, the ability to act, and that with this skill a writer of reputation could provide his audience with a moving and a rewarding experience. Mark Twain's attendance at the Dickens reading that memorable night provided the initial stimulus which led later to his own decision to engage in public readings, and which subsequently led also to his participation in authors' readings programs which flourished in the 1880's and later. Particularly, of course, it led to his famous reading tour with George Washington Cable during the season of 1884–85 and to the reading tour around the world in 1895.

On his return to Washington, late in the evening of January 8, a surprise awaited him. He learned that during his absence an old "theatrical friend" of his had got drunk, and while in that condition had made arrangements for him to lecture at Metzerott Hall the following evening, and had also sent notices of the lecture to the newspapers. What was he to do? He decided he could not back out by telling people he was unprepared, and "that my friend was intoxicated when he made the arrangements."[8] As a result, he was forced to stay up all night, "working like sin," as he later wrote his mother, hastily putting together a lecture based upon his "Quaker City" trip to the Holy Land. For this lecture he selected the title Frozen Truth, frankly acknowledging that there was more truth in the title than in the lecture.[9]

For a good part of the next day he was in panic. Though

the lecture had been announced, it had not been properly advertised in the newspapers or by handbills; as a consequence, he greatly feared that he might be talking to an empty house. To add to his troubles, word reached him in the early afternoon that the manager at Metzerott Hall had taken ill and that he must find his own doorkeeper. That evening, when he came upon the stage, the events of the day had so muddled him that he scarcely knew what he was to talk about. Fortunately, a "tolerably good house" had assembled and according to his own report the lecture "went off in splendid style."[10] Next day, newspaper reports of the lecture were on the whole favorable, though it is apparent that some people in the audience, in view of the possible implications of the title Frozen Truth, had expected Mark Twain to say more than he had in exposure of the more secret and less savory aspects of the Holy Land excursion.

Whether the inebriated friend was also responsible for a lecture scheduled in Metzerott Hall two nights later, on January 11, is not revealed. At any rate, Mark Twain declined because the manager was still sick, and he was expected to take care of all the details himself. To account for the manager's illness, Mark Twain humorously explained that he had read his lecture to that individual, never suspecting that "it would be so severe on him. . . ." He would certainly never do that again.[11]

It is a misfortune that the full text of the Frozen Truth lecture has not been preserved, or that the Washington reporters failed to offer their readers verbatim extracts of it. Fortunately, a reporter for the Washington *Star* did summarize it for the issue of January 10 and thus provided us with the only information known to exist concerning its content. In view of its importance the Washington *Star* report is offered in full.

> Almost everybody who fancies he knows a good thing, in the humorous way, when he sees or hears it, was on hand last night to assist at the debut of Mr. Clemens, otherwise known as "Mark Twain," as a lecturer.
>
> The subject announced was "Frozen Truth," but as in the case of the well-remembered "discursive" lecture of the lamented "Artemus Ward" upon the "Babes in the Wood," in which the audience were favored with only a single allusion to the babes, to the effect that they were the children of poor, but respectable parents, and died young, so in this discourse of last night, the promised gelid facts never made

their appearance, though anxiously looked for by literal sort of hearers.

The thread of the lecture was a running review of the renowned excursion of the New English pilgrims, per steamer "Quaker City," to the Holy Land, and this trip, illustrated from the "Mark Twain" point of view, afforded matter for the most successful attack upon the risibles. His description of the sea-sick pilgrims (the pilgrims he liked, but didn't dote on); of the aggravating doctor, who was continually making himself disagreeable by having the toothache and the heart disease, though remonstrated with; of the fellow traveller who sat up all night, on the watch for Scylla and Charybdis; of the breakfast with the emperor of Russia; his personal description of the Emperor, who treated him so kindly and frankly, telling him he "could leave whenever he wanted to"; his rough experience in Syria, the only pleasing reminiscence of which was the time he had the cholera in Damascus; his mathematical comparison of the proportion of arable land to desert in Syria, to that of the absolute lemon in the pies known as lemon pies, at his Washington Hotel; his warmly expressed detestation of the villainous camels "that were always trying to bite you when you hadn't done anything to 'em"; his unanswerable argument against matrimony found in the fact that the Sultan "has 900 wives and isn't happy"; his adcaptandum appeal to his bachelor auditors apropos to this muchness of matrimony, "How would *you* like your sleeping apartment lumbered up with a bed six feet long and thirteen hundred feet wide?"; his comparison of the public institutions, buildings and monuments of the U.S. to those of the Old World; his proud claim that no quarter of the Old World has *such* a monument as the Washington Monument; and that no officials are more efficient and patriotic, or collect their salaries more promptly than our members of Congress—these and a thousand other kindred touches and points, served to give pungency to the lecture. In the didactive portions he was not so effective, his voice and style not being favorable to the expression of sentiment or pathos.

"Mark Twain" in a certain grotesque fanciful humor reminds one of "Artemus Ward," and though not in any sense an imitator, his humorous description of the inconveniences and perplexities experienced by the Sultan with his surplusage of wives, was much in the same vein as "A. Ward's" description of the kindred tribulations of Brigham Young.

In person Mr. Clemens is not the kind of man the spectator "expected to see." Of medium size, a cast-iron inflexibility of feature, grave face, eyes that lack expression from their neutral hue, and the light color of the brows, a drawling speech, and a general air of being about half-asleep, "Mark Twain" has a very unpromising look for humor. Many of the audience last night supposed that his slowness of speech and movement was stage mannerism, but that was a mistake. That imperturbable drawl is habitual to him; and he is probably the laziest walker that ever stepped. In his most fluent and vivacious moods he has never been known to disgorge more than ten words per minute; and the saunter of Walt Whitman is a race-horse pace compared with his snail-like progress over the ground.

On February 22, Washington's birthday, he was again on the platform, this time in Forrest Hall, Georgetown, lecturing for the benefit of the Ladies' Union Benevolent Society. For this occasion Mark Twain switched to the Sandwich Islands lecture, on the assumption, perhaps, that it might be more acceptable to a predominately female audience than his Frozen Truth lecture. Coming on stage without an introducer, he explained that the young man who had promised to do the job had met with an accident—had fallen down and broken his heart or his neck—he didn't know which. Since he had been requested by the Ladies' Union to lecture in behalf of the poor, he embraced the opportunity since he had always had a grudge against the poor and was therefore happy to inflict a lecture upon them. Before beginning the lecture itself, he declared, he considered it appropriate to the occasion of Washington's birthday to repeat a new anecdote he had recently heard about George. The new anecdote, however, proved to be the familiar one about the cherry tree, but ending with a slightly new twist.[12]

The newspapers reported the lecture a pleasing success. Many of the most prominent persons of Georgetown had come out to hear him, and throughout the lecture the audience was in "almost continuous roars of laughter." A new anecdote, not noted in previous reports of the Sandwich Islands lecture, was the story of the Honolulu gas company which had lost a good deal of money during a particular month because everybody in the city had gone to bed at nine o'clock.[13]

By the time Bliss had recovered from his illness, and nego-

tiations for a book had proceeded to a satisfactory stage, Mark
Twain had made up his mind to use only the "Quaker City"
correspondence as a basis for it, never doubting that the *Alta
California* people would grant immediate permission. When he
was informed by Joe Goodman that they had copyrighted the
letters and that they themselves intended to publish them in
book form,[14] Mark Twain became alarmed and decided at once
to go to California to deal with the managers of the *Alta* in
person.

He arrived in San Francisco on April 2. In urgent need of
money to pay for the trip and to support himself during his stay
in California, he committed himself to a program of work so
grueling that a man of less stamina and driving ambition might
have suffered a breakdown. He kept up his journalistic commit-
ments by writing for the Virginia City *Enterprise* and the *Alta
California* each week. Twice a week he supplied the New York
Herald with an article, and sent occasional letters to the New
York *Tribune* and the *Galaxy*. And when the Chicago *Republican* begged him to supply them with correspondence, he somewhere found the energy to comply with a total of six long letters.
Fortunately, the *Alta* soon agreed to release the "Quaker City"
letters for his use in book form, and he set to work immediately
to adapt them to his purpose.

Despite the heavy burden of work that faced him, it is
nevertheless clear that Mark Twain had determined, even before
his arrival, to lecture in California and Nevada, covering, in
general, the same itinerary as his 1866 tour. He needed money,
and he knew that no other activity promised so lucrative and
quick a financial return as the platform. He lost no time in
making his plans known. In reporting his arrival in San Francisco, the *Alta California* announced on April 3 that the genial
and jolly humorist proposed to lecture in a few days.

Actually, it was April 14 before the first lecture took place.
The interval gave him time to contact by mail and telegraph
the lecture committees or hall managers in the communities he
hoped to visit and to write some advertising blurbs and announcements. He was, of course, well known in the entire area.
Although the *Alta California* had copyrighted the "Quaker
City" letters and had thus prevented other newspapers from reprinting them without permission, its fairly wide circulation
through northern California and Nevada had served to keep his

name before the public. Furthermore, the fact that his letters were still running in the *Alta* during the period of the tour, the last one appearing as late as May 17, was also in his favor.

San Francisco newspapers announced that the opening lecture would take place in Platt's Hall and that Mark Twain would speak on Pilgrim Life. The lecture would provide a sketch of "his notorious voyage to Europe, Palestine, etc." According to *Golden Era,* "The High Muck-a-Muck of . . . fun and fancy," had promised to expose the scandal of the "Quaker City" and its male passengers and to explain "how his innate morality was unsuccessfully assailed during his perilous career."[15] Whether because of statements of this provocative nature, or because of the interest aroused by his "notorious" letters in the *Alta California,* Platt's Hall was quickly sold out. That evening, when he emerged from the wings, he faced a laughing, stamping audience ready for an evening of hilarious fun.

It was not his intention, he began, to say much about the Holy Land. He had already been scolded for the remarks he had made on that subject in his *Alta California* letters. He would speak, rather, of his own experiences. What those experiences were, however, the newspapers reported only briefly. There was the story of how Mark Twain had fallen in love with a Russian girl who weighed 252 pounds, and his remark afterward that she became no burden on his conscience because it could bear the weight. There was also the story of the inquiry which had been conducted into the moral character of the excursionists before admitting them to the passenger list on the "Quaker City." He had given as references, he told his audience, General Grant, President Johnson, and Emperor Norton. (Everyone in Platt's Hall knew Emperor Norton, an amusing derelict, an ex-gold miner who had gone mad and who spent his days wandering about the streets of San Francisco imagining himself to be ruler of California and Mexico.)

In the main, the Pilgrim Life lecture covered much the same ground as the Frozen Truth, dwelling chiefly upon the idiosyncrasies of Mark Twain's shipmates, the visit to Russia, the Sultan's difficulties with his many wives, the ancient cities along the Mediterranean, and the scenery and people of the Holy Land.

While the lecture provoked a great deal of laughter and for that reason provided Mark Twain with a measure of satisfaction, the fact remains that the newspaper reports which followed were not, on the whole, favorable. As the *Evening Bulletin* judiciously pointed out, the Pilgrim Life lecture was not as completely prepared or as warmly received as his first Sandwich Islands lecture had been two years earlier. It was not as well organized. It further regretted that he had not said more about Palestine and other places of historic interest and less about the bald-headed, spectacled, and sedate old pilgrims on the "Quaker City."[16] The comment reveals that in adapting the Frozen Truth lecture to his West Coast audience, Mark Twain had made little if any effort to improve upon the loose organization evident in the Washington *Star* summary of that lecture, and that he was still devoting too much time to personal satire, not realizing, perhaps, that the personalities he satirized commanded less interest in California than in the East.

And there were other criticisms more important in some particulars than those concerning structure. The *Morning Call*, for example, informed its readers that Mark Twain had worked himself into a grotesque rage over dullness, and had "made it lively for respectability." Harsher criticism appeared in the San Raphael *Marin County Journal,* which castigated him as a "miserable scribbler whose letters in the *Alta* had sickened everyone who had read them. . . ." This man now had the "audacity and impudence to attempt to lecture to an intelligent people."[17] What apparently had sickened the *Journal* reporter, as well as others, had been such impious passages in the *Alta California* letters as, for example, the assertion that there would never be a Second Advent because the Savior would never think of returning to so dismal and dirty a country as Palestine. Such remarks had also incensed the local clergy, provoking one of them to speak of "this son of the devil, Mark Twain." Equally harsh was a blast from the *California Weekly Mercury* which bitterly took the *Alta* and the *Times* to task for praising Mark Twain's performance. In its opinion the lecture was "foul with sacrilegious allusion" and "malignant distortions of history and truth." A man so lost to every sense of decency and shame should be allowed to expire in obscurity.[18] The criticism was a double-barreled one—first, that Mark Twain was irreverent, and second, that his statements about art and historical matters were deliberately false.

That Mark Twain was sufficiently disturbed by the charge

of irreverence to guard himself against it in the future is indicated by the fact that later, when he faced eastern audiences, this charge was rarely leveled against him. The claim that he distorted history, on the other hand, appears to have concerned him very little. His aim, frankly, was to amuse by reporting personal experiences on the "Quaker City" trip, not to impart historical fact; and if his statements of history departed slightly from the perpendicular of truth, no harm was done if they tended to heighten the effect of his presentation. A certain amount of exaggeration and distortion, he felt, was allowable.

The criticism that gave him most concern, it appears, was the charge that he had given insufficient attention to Palestine and to other scenes of Old World interest, and that consequently he had amused but had not instructed. This criticism may have surprised Mark Twain, for he no doubt thought he had said enough about the Old World to satisfy his hearers, especially since some of the newspapers had commended him for his eloquent description of Rome's gray ruins and the dreary desolation of Palestine. At any rate, when he arrived at Sacramento, he made a point of defending himself against the charge. He wished, he declared, to correct a misstatement about the subject of his lecture. It had never been his intention, he emphasized, to speak much about the Holy Land, but rather about the voyage of the "Quaker City" and the company aboard her.[19] This defense, in effect, was an implied petition that his lecture be regarded as a humorous and satiric performance rather than one primarily instructive. Nevertheless, the criticism troubled him, since it indicated that so matter what his intention was, the desire of the audience for instruction could not be laughed off.

Mark Twain's own judgment about his first Pilgrim Life lecture in San Francisco was harsh, though the financial rewards had been unusually gratifying. In a letter to Mrs. Abel Fairbanks, a fellow passenger on the "Quaker City" in whom he confided a great deal during these days, he reported that the house had brought in over $1,600 in gold and silver. Hours before the doors had opened, the seats had all been taken and he had stopped the sale of tickets. This had made a "large number of people mad . . . but I couldn't help that. I didn't want them standing up & bothering me." Nevertheless, he declared, the lecture had been miserably poor. The next time he came to San Francisco, he intended to prepare a better one.[20]

It may be, however, that the reception of the lecture proved to be unsatisfactory not only because of its irreverence and lack of substance, but because of Mark Twain's use of an unfortunate attention-getting device. Curiously, he had appeared on stage in what a reporter for the *Evening Bulletin* called a "singular disguise," though the voice and the comments had quickly betrayed his identity. In explanation of the costume he reported that he was dressed "for a masquerade," but offered no hint concerning the occasion for which it was intended, nor did he identify the disguise.[21] That Mark Twain's appearance on stage in masquerade dress was a deliberate device employed in the hope that it might arouse interest and laughter and provide a proper tone for the reception of a humorous lecture must be taken for granted. Perhaps the costume was intended in some manner to suggest the native dress of one of the countries he was describing, or, what appears more probable, the dress of a "Quaker City" pilgrim as modified by the adoption of certain foreign items of dress. However it may have been intended, its use was a blunder, for it tended to distract the audience not only from the substance of the lecture but also perhaps from the quality of its humor. The incident represents one of the few instances of mistaken art in Mark Twain's rapid rise to platform popularity.

The next evening, April 15, Mark Twain gave a repeat performance in Platt's Hall. This time there was no disguise, and there was less obvious straining after effect. According to the *Alta California* he had now "got the hang of the sermon and delivered it with more non-chalance" than on the preceding evening. His confidential conversational tone had broken down "all barriers between the man on the stage and the people occupying the seats."[22]

From San Francisco the tour led to Sacramento where he lectured on April 17 in the Metropolitan Theater. There he greatly amused many by apologizing for the absence of Elder Knapp, a well-known local revivalist who had distinguished himself recently in his campaigns against theaters and dancing. There were some, however, who were displeased by the "extremely frivolous" remarks Mark Twain had made during the opening minutes of the lecture, probably because they respected the energetic revivalist and were not amused by Mark Twain's obvious satire.

The Sacramento *Union,* the newspaper in whose columns the Sandwich Islands letters had appeared, commented upon the lecture at length. It confessed its "partiality for this California humorist." At the bottom of his intellectual character there seemed to lie a vast deal of good sense, which his humor dressed up in a most presentable style. As a lecturer and humorist he was far superior to Artemus Ward. In an obvious attempt to answer the objections of the critics who had found Mark Twain's sentiments about the Holy Land irreverent, the *Union* freely acknowledged that his picture of Palestine was "greatly at variance with the customary sentimentalities and grandiloquent musings of the popular travellers" who had in recent years written on the subject. But no two men, it pointed out, were impressed alike with any scene. "Renan dreamed out some of his finest thoughts on the sad shores of the Sea of Galilee, and Lamartine took some of his loftiest flights in Judea. Twain did not behold these scenes through their glasses. He saw them through the eyes of a practical American, keenly alive to progress and the present."[23] The observation of the *Union* reporter was unusually perceptive. It also appears to have been persuasive, for during the remainder of the tour Mark Twain's critics reported his lecture with greater charity.

The schedule of lectures now proceeded as follows: Marysville, April 18; Nevada City (where he announced that the "doors will be surrounded at 7 o'clock and the insurrection will begin at 8")[24] April 20; Grass Valley, April 21; Virginia City, April 27 and 28; and Carson City, April 29 and 30. Bouncing about from one small mining camp to another it is likely that he missed the company of Denis McCarthy, his genial Irish traveling companion of two years earlier, who, though he had mistaken the tour for a spree, had done so much to make the journey delightful. This time, traveling alone and acting as his own manager, the trip seemed much more exhausting. From San Francisco to Sacramento, as before, he had taken the steamboat. It had a splendid bar. Besides, the ride was more comfortable than by stage. Here the weather was warm and pleasant, and the countryside beautiful with peach and rose blooms. From Sacramento he proceeded by rail to the summit of the Sierras where the snow lay thirty feet deep on level ground and one hundred feet deep in drifts. Then came the arduous ride down the eastern slope of the mountain, first by six-horse sleigh down to Donner Lake, then mail coach to

Coburn's Station, and then railway and stagecoaches to Virginia City. It was the hardest trip over the Sierras he had ever made, but in his report of it there is no hint of unhappiness. He knew the country and loved it, and had deep joy in seeing it again.[25]

Of Mark Twain's reception at Virginia City the record has little to offer. The *Daily Trespass* reported that he looked "a little lean to what he used to," and that he still talked as rapidly as ever—"gets out a word every three minutes"—but was silent about the lectures and any social attention paid to the returning pilgrim. Nor was there any reference to the highway robbery on the Divide which had so upset Mark Twain two years earlier. There were, however, here and there sly allusions to his bibulous tendencies during his reportorial days in Virginia City. The *Daily Trespass,* for example, conjectured that he looked lean because he had joined the "Eye Owe Gee Tease," (The Independent Order of Good Templars), a temperance organization.[26] And when a local resident presented him with a forty-dollar bar of silver with the inscription: "Mark Twain—Matthew, V:41— Pilgrim" ("Whosoever shall compel thee to go a mile, go with him twain"), the *Enterprise* implied that Mark Twain would gladly go even further where a bar was concerned.[27]

On April 29 he proceeded to Carson City. Here he was also on familiar ground and was warmly received. It is reported that on the night of his first lecture there Mark Twain sauntered on stage with a big roll of brown wrapping paper under his arm. At first the audience supposed it was a map, but it turned out to be his lecture, written in a very large hand. To the immense amusement of the audience he held the roll aloft, adjusted his position to get full advantage of the light, and began his opening remarks.[28] Whether the audience recognized the incident as a deliberate attempt to satirize the poor lighting of the hall, as it probably was, is not revealed.

The next evening he lectured again in Carson City, this time on the Sandwich Islands, to a small audience of about a hundred. The lecture had been requested for the benefit of the school children who had missed the opportunity of hearing it two years previously.[29] He was happy to comply, though it meant two or three hours of hasty brushing up which might have been spent more enjoyably with friends. This performance, Mark Twain declared, was his "last Will and Testament" of the

Sandwich Islands lecture. In this judgment, however, he was greatly mistaken, for in the years that followed he gave it often. Indeed, it became his favorite lecture.

The tour completed, Mark Twain returned to San Francisco and at once reestablished himself at an old favorite haunt, the Occidental Hotel, which he once referred to as "heaven on the half-shell."[30] There, for two full months, he settled down and worked on *Innocents Abroad* and on his newspaper correspondence. He had planned to leave California near the end of June, but finally set July 6 as the day of departure. Before saying farewell to the city he loved, he decided to give a final lecture and set the date, July 2. Though he was no doubt again in need of money, he also remembered the promise he had made himself to give the San Francisco audience a better lecture than the one on Pilgrim Life. The subject he selected this time was The Oldest of the Republics—Venice, Past and Present. As might be surmised from the title, the lecture was obviously to be more informative than the earlier one, less personal, less satiric, though humorous. And he intended to do all he could to insure a full house.

The advertising for the farewell lecture developed into the kind of horseplay Mark Twain thoroughly enjoyed and which at that time was excitingly novel. It was just the sort of technique, nevertheless, which the people of San Francisco regarded as typical of the man they knew as the Wild Humorist of the Pacific Slope. The first announcement for the lecture was a handbill, dated June 30, which circulated through the city, protesting a proposal that before his departure Mark Twain read a few chapters from his forthcoming book. The protest, in the form of a letter, bore the signatures of many leading citizens of San Francisco, all of whose names Mark Twain had made free use of. Listed also were a number of local organizations, benevolent societies, and "1,500 in the steerage."

Below this, in a long, mockingly serious letter, Mark Twain declared he would ignore all protests and go on with the lecture as planned. He felt free to torment the people if he wanted to. After giving them peace and quiet for nearly two years was he going to be denied the privilege of lecturing them once more? He wanted to tell them all he knew about Venice. The new lecture would "furnish a deal of pleasant information, somewhat highly spiced, but still palatable, digestible, and eminently fitted for the intellectual stomach." He admitted that his Pilgrim Life lecture was not as good as he had at first imagined it was, but this one was better. He had submitted it to several able critics and they had pronounced it good. Why, therefore, should he withhold it? "Let me talk only just this once, and I will sail positively on the 6th of July, and stay away until I return from China—two years."

On the same handbill, following Mark Twain's reply, came a series of additional remonstrances to his lecture, one from a local association of brokers, another from the clergy, a third from the proprietors of the leading newspapers, and a final one from the chief of police. All urged him to leave San Francisco without delay. Following these notices, at the bottom of the handbill came the formal announcement of Mark Twain's farewell lecture in the New Mercantile Library on Bush Street on July 2, the admission price a dollar all over the house. The doors would open at 7 and the "orgies" were to commence at 8 P.M.[31]

The immense audience that greeted Mark Twain that evening was a heartwarming spectacle. As he walked out from a side door of the stage, he looked about anxiously for a few moments, as though wondering what his reception would be like, and then in a serious vein made the following remarks before beginning his lecture:

> LADIES AND GENTLEMEN: If anyone in San Francisco has a just right this evening to feel gratified—more, to feel proud—it is I. I, who stand before you. The compliment of your attendance here I thoroughly appreciate. It is a greater compliment than I really deserve perhaps—but for that matter I have always been rather better treated in San Francisco than I actually deserved. I am willing to say that. I appreciate your attendance here tonight all the more because there was such a widespread and such a furious, such a determined opposition to my lecturing upon this occasion. Pretty much the entire community wrote petitions imploring me *not* to lecture—to forebear—to have compassion upon a persecuted people. I have never had such a unanimous call to-to-to leave, before. But I resisted, and am here; and I am glad that I am privileged to address a full house, instead of having to pour out this cataract of wisdom upon empty benches. I do not exactly propose to *instruct* you this evening, but rather to tell you a good many

things which you have known very well before, no doubt, but which may have grown dim in your memories—for the multifarious duties and annoyances of daily life are apt to drive from our minds a large part of what we learn, and that knowledge is of little use which we cannot recall. So I simply propose to refresh your memories. I trust this will be considered sufficient apology for making this lecture somewhat didactic. I don't know what didactic means, but it is a good, high-sounding word, and I wish to use it, meaning no harm whatever.[32]

In reporting the lecture the next day the local newspapers again respected Mark Twain's wishes not to reproduce portions of it, and offered only brief summaries of his remarks. The report in the *Alta California,* however, gives us a good idea of the content of the lecture and of its humor. After a few preliminary remarks he

> . . . gave a sort of compressed history of Venice, the youngest of the Italian cities, and contrasted it in its palmy times with the Venice of today, as seen in the glare of sunlight, and not in the charitable rays of the moon—likened it to Sacramento when overflowed; stripped the romance from the gondola (a canoe with a hearse body) and the gondolier; pictured the ladies going shopping; the lover slyly stealing up to the old man's house; the merchant to the counting room—all in gondolas, making the place a paradise for cripples. The lecture was interspersed with humorous allusions to the Americans abroad who affect foreign airs but wound up with a burst of glowing rhetoric to the city which is yearly wedded to the sea by solemn ceremonies. The applause was frequent and appreciative throughout the lecture, which lasted one hour and fifty minutes, though it was not a minute too long. Mr. Clemens leaves for the East on Monday, and may be proud to leave with such a tribute to his popularity as his attendance last night.[33]

A brief note in the *Daily Examiner* also spoke of the lecture as a perfect success, both from a literary and financial point of view, adding that it deserved and would no doubt have, a successful run in the Atlantic States.[34] The latter suggestion supplies the first hint that even before leaving California Mark Twain was already contemplating an eastern lecture tour, based

upon the materials of his forthcoming book. To Mrs. Fairbanks
he reported the success of his Venice lecture with becoming
modesty. He confessed, however, that a lecture which his West
Coast friends might "pronounce very fine," would probably
prove "a shameful failure before an unbiased audience such as I
would find in an eastern city. . . . I only claim that these citizens *here* call this a good lecture—I do *not* claim, myself, that it
is. I am satisfied it would be pretty roughly criticized in an
eastern town. . . ."[35]

Concerning the financial success of his California and
Nevada tour he made no comment at this time, either to Mrs.
Fairbanks or to his family in St. Louis. The truth was, however, that it turned out to be less profitable than he had expected. Recalling the experience for his autobiography many
years later, he blamed the *Alta California* for his modest earnings
on the score that that "prodigiously rich" newspaper had copyrighted "all those poor little twenty-dollar" "Quaker City" letters and had threatened to prosecute any journal which ventured
to reprint any portion of them without permission. As a consequence, he claimed, he had been entirely forgotten in the back
country, and when he came to lecture there, he never had
enough people in his houses "to sit as a jury of inquest" on his
lost reputation.[36] Actually, the damage to his reputation was
not nearly so great as Mark Twain assumed. The *Alta,* as reported earlier, enjoyed a substantial circulation in the back
country, and through its columns kept the readers well informed
of Mark Twain's activities, as did other prominent papers like
the Sacramento *Union.*

The Venice lecture marked an important step in the evo-
lution of what eventually became Mark Twain's first lecture on
the lyceum circuit, The American Vandal Abroad. The Frozen
Truth lecture, as we have seen, was the first step in that evolu-
tion. In it he had satirized the idiosyncrasies of his "Quaker
City" shipmates, poked fun at foreign customs, manners, and
dress, and presented a disparaging picture of life and scenery in
the Holy Land. At San Francisco he repeated the Frozen Truth
lecture, with minor modifications but changed the title to Pilgrim Life. His experiences at Washington, D.C., had indicated
that the old title was misleading, since it appeared to imply that
the whole truth about the excursion had not been told and that

he now proposed to uncover it in his lecture. That the reporters who heard him in Washington, D.C., had expected such a revelation was apparent from their charge that "the promised gelid facts never made their appearance." Actually, he had probably never intended, when he prepared the Frozen Truth lecture, to do much more than to elaborate upon the things he had written in his New York *Herald* letter the night the "Quaker City" had slid into port.[37] And if in the Pilgrim Life lecture he promised to "expose the scandal of the 'Quaker City' and its male passengers," as the *Golden Era* reported, the promise was probably made only in jest to attract an audience.

But the Pilgrim Life lecture satisfied neither the San Francisco audiences nor Mark Twain himself. Critics had been quick and emphatic in pointing out what they regarded as shortcomings. Here and there its humor had threatened to offend because it bordered on bad taste. To others it was unduly irreverent, and careless about its treatment of historic fact. The main objection appeared to be, however, that it merely amused —it did not instruct. Many had paid their money, expecting to learn something worthwhile about Europe and the Holy Land and had come away empty. Didn't a person who lectured for pay owe his audiences something more than mere humor?

The Venice lecture was clearly designed to meet the objections of his critics. Though humor still played a dominant role, the new lecture contained a considerable amount of information about Venice and its history, and offered the audience a number of splendid descriptive passages concerning the beauties of the city that was wedded to the sea. The lecture appears to have been carefully organized, and if there were any jokes of dubious taste, or allusions sufficiently irreverent to give offense, the newspapers were charitably silent.

The success of the Venice lecture marked an important turning point in Mark Twain's career on the public platform. It taught him how to combine informative material with humor in such a manner as to give a high degree of pleasure and satisfaction. And though he had difficulty in remembering that lesson at times, he no longer entertained any doubts concerning its value to a paid lecturer.

Two months later, back east, Mark Twain framed a new lecture on this "Quaker City" trip. Combining the best materials and humor of the Frozen Truth, Pilgrim Life, and Venice lectures, and keeping in mind the need of giving proper attention to instruction, he produced The American Vandal Abroad, the lecture which first established his reputation on the American lyceum circuit.

CHAPTER SEVEN

ON THE LYCEUM CIRCUIT

---

*. . . a man may be a humorist without
being a clown.* —CLEVELAND « HERALD, »
NOV. *18, 1868.*

ARK TWAIN arrived in New York about July 28, and
after a few days there, proceeded to Hartford, Connecticut, to talk with Elisha Bliss about his forthcoming
book, *Innocents Abroad.* There was still work to do on the manuscript, and since Bliss hoped to bring the book out in December,
he remained in Hartford to finish it. There were also other
matters that engaged his attention. Probably at the suggestion of
Anson Burlingame, who was sponsoring a Chinese treaty in the
Congress at this time, he supplied the New York *Tribune* with an
article on the subject.[1] He also maintained his connection with
the Chicago *Republican* by sending them a promised travel
letter.[2] But his primary concerns during the weeks that followed
were the courtship of Olivia Langdon of Elmira, New York, and
the growing necessity of replenishing his rapidly diminishing
funds.

Of the courtship of Livy Langdon little need be said here
other than to point out that the hope of marriage with the
daughter of a wealthy coal baron made the necessity of acquiring
funds quickly all the more urgent. Though he no doubt hoped
that the publication of *Innocents Abroad* would bring in royalties, he could not count on them; and even if the book were successful, it would be several months before any cash actually

reached him, since publication date had been postponed till the following March.[3] The most promising remedy, of course, was to take to the platform. Even before leaving California, he had planned to lecture in the Middle West, if not in the East, and the time for putting that plan into effect was rapidly approaching. Consequently, during the summer of 1868 it appears Mark Twain sought to get lecture engagements by whatever means he could. It is likely that he offered himself to a number of local Y.M.C.A.'s and lyceum committees, announcing his lecture subject and supplying clippings from newspaper reports of his lectures in the Far West, New York, Missouri, Iowa, and other places were he had lectured. But he also sought and apparently received most of his engagements through the Associated Western Library Associations at Dubuque, Iowa, which, for a number of years, had served as a lecture bureau for the lyceums in the Middle West area.[4]

The lecture he tentatively decided upon was The American Vandal Abroad, based upon his *Innocents Abroad* materials. The choice of this subject, however, gave him considerable misgiving, since he feared that his satirical treatment of the venerable memorials of Europe and the Old Masters in that book might give offense to people whose respect and good will he needed for success on the lyceum circuit. Indeed, his concern about the wisdom of offering this lecture was so great that for a time he seriously considered using the Sandwich Islands lecture instead. That lecture, certainly, would involve fewer risks. Furthermore, it had met with more public approbation than the Frozen Truth, Pilgrim Life, and Venice lectures based upon *Innocents Abroad*. Nevertheless, these materials were more freshly at hand and offered splendid opportunities for humor. They had been reasonably well received by all his audiences, and with judicious reworking would, he believed, prove as popular as the Sandwich Islands lecture.

Mark Twain's dilemma about which lecture to choose deserves an explanation, for its solution was extremely important and marked a turning point in his development as a literary personality and creative artist. The dilemma appears to have been based in part on his fear that midwestern and eastern audiences were far more sophisticated and critical than those in the Far West. The Venice lecture, for example, had given much satisfaction to his San Francisco audience, he reported to Mrs.

Abel Fairbanks, but he knew that it would likely "prove a shameful failure before an unbiased audience . . . in an Eastern city. . . ."[5] Primarily, however, his concern derived from the role Mrs. Fairbanks was playing with regard to the lecture. Wife of the publisher of the Cleveland *Herald,* she had joined the "Quaker City" group as a correspondent for her husband's newspaper.[6] Strongly attracted to the Wild Humorist of the Pacific Slope, as he was frequently advertised when she first met him, she quickly became his friend and literary mentor. As a matter of fact, it was presently Mrs. Fairbanks' hope that the rising young journalist would buy an interest in her husband's newspaper and write for its colunms. Partly with this hope in mind, and partly because she had a strong personal liking for her young protege and recognized his exceptional talent, she set out to polish his literary manners and to tame some of his verbal wildness. She earnestly admonished him against profanity, slang, and other inelegancies of speech, and strongly voiced her disapproval of the indelicacies and improprieties which appeared in his conversations, writings, and speeches. She chided him, for example, for the unkind and ill-natured remarks he had made in a letter to the New York *Herald* about his fellow passengers on the "Quaker City" the day after the boat docked.[7] She was even more unhappy about the impropriety of a remark he had more recently made in a toast to "Woman," given at a stag dinner of the Correspondents Club in Washington, D.C. The offending passage, which ennumerated woman's usefulness to man, ended with the statement, "She bears our children," and then after a pause, "ours as a general thing."[8] The speech was reprinted in a number of papers and presently came to Mrs. Fairbanks' attention. Aware that the remark would provoke a protest, Mark Twain immediately wrote Mrs. Fairbanks, asking her not to abuse him on account of the speech. He had not expected to be quoted *"so verbatimly."*[9] But she wrote him "a Scorcher" nevertheless; and when he replied, he humbly confessed that he deserved the censure, and promised, in the future to "eschew slang and vulgarity, even in foolish dinner speeches. . . ."[10]

That Mark Twain was sincerely grateful for Mrs. Fairbanks' advice and for her concern for his literary future is apparent. Under her tutelage, he began to perceive that if he wished to win the approbation of cultivated eastern audiences, whether in the press or on the platform, it would be necessary to guard against the offenses she had admonished him about. He began to realize also that his California reputation as Wild Humorist carried a deserved implication of crudeness and irresponsibility which he no longer wished his pseudonym Mark Twain to convey. His letters to Mrs. Fairbanks during this period, variously signed "Yr. Improving Prodigal," "Cub," and "The Reformed Prodigal," reveal unmistakably his sincere acceptance of her forthright criticism.[11]

If Mrs. Fairbanks had limited her advice to slang, profanity, and vulgarities, her role as literary mentor would not have troubled the "Cub." His need for reform in these matters was patent. But when in October of 1868 she undertook to advise him about the *kind* of a lecture he should prepare for the lyceum circuit (on the assumption that he would lecture on the "Quaker City" excursion), he took alarm. What Mrs. Fairbanks apparently feared was that he might make ill-natured and satiric attacks upon some of their "Quaker City" associates as he had done in the New York *Herald* article and in the Frozen Truth lecture in Washington, D.C.[12] Perhaps news that he was considering giving his lecture a title like The American Vandal Abroad also troubled her. Furthermore, she feared that he might alienate his audiences by irreverences and by his uninstructed treatment of the Old Masters. She expected the lecture to contain humor, coming from Mark Twain, but she hoped that it would be mainly informative, in keeping with her notion of the purposes of the lyceum courses, and that it would deal respectfully with the memorials of European art and culture. She wished it to be a dignified performance, free from slang and other inelegancies, and if satiric here and there, at least good-natured. To clarify for him the sort of lecture she considered appropriate she prepared and sent him an outline containing a list of the main headings.

But even before he received the outline, he realized that he could never construct the sort of lecture she was planning for him. In the first place, he was well aware of his ignorance of art and culture and had no intention of giving up his time to a study of it now, as Mrs. Fairbanks had suggested.[13] "Blame the fine arts & the Old Masters, mother mine," he wrote her. "That is forbidden ground to me."[14] Yet there was a far more fundamental objection to her plan. It required an emphasis upon substance and a formality of treatment that were completely alien to his thought and personality. He simply could not follow her plan and be true to his own genius. Though the lecture he planned contained informative matter, it was interlaced with all sorts of "preposterous yarns." "I *must not* preach to a select few in my audience," he warned her, "lest I have only a select few to listen, next time. . . ." What the societies were asking of him was something in the nature of entertainment "to *relieve* the heaviness of their didactic courses. . . ."[15]

Having made up his mind to reject her advice about the kind of lecture he was to give, he wrote her that he had tried hard to follow her plan, but finally concluded that it was futile. He could never weave it into a web that would suit him. So he altered the title to The American Vandal Abroad and began again. After outlining the lecture as he had now written it, he asked her placatingly, "Now that isn't ill-natured is it?"[16] In thus freeing himself gently but decisively from the confining influence of Mrs. Fairbanks concerning the nature and tone of his lecture, Mark Twain asserted his literary independence. It was a significant step. Never again did he consult her, or for that matter anyone else unless now and then Livy, concerning the subject of his lectures and his manner of dealing with his materials.

The lecture which he finally constructed was, he acknowledged, "smouched" from the manuscript of *Innocents Abroad*. After instructing his audience what he meant by the term "vandal" he satirized the vandal gently for aping foreign ways, gathering specimens from various memorials, and gravely seeking information from guides. He followed him through Genoa and Milan, where in the Cathedral was the hideous statue of a skinned man. Then to Venice with its gondolas and famous waterways, to the coliseum at Rome, the picture galleries of Florence, the Leaning Tower of Pisa, the ruins of Herculaneum and Pompeii, and, of course, Greece, Egypt, and the Holy Land. Interspersed here and there, Mark Twain treated his audience to what he jokingly reported to Mrs. Fairbanks were "starchy & high-toned" glimpses of places of particular note like St. Peter's, Venice, the Pyramids, and Damascus. These portions of the lectures proved in fact to be eloquent and moving descriptive passages that gave universal delight. And the lecture had a moral—not that it needed one or that it proceeded necessarily from the text. He simply offered it gratuitously. The moral was that the American Vandal should continue to travel, for it liberalized him and made a better man of him.[17]

The tour began in Cleveland on November 17. The reason for choosing that city for the opening lecture was obvious. While Mark Twain was unwilling to subordinate his literary personality to Mrs. Fairbanks, he was eager to secure her help, through the columns of the Cleveland *Herald,* in giving his first lecture on the lyceum circuit favorable press notices. When the invitation to lecture at Cleveland came through Colonel Herrick, a "Quaker City" companion, he immediately wrote Mrs. Fairbanks and asked her to write a critique after the lecture. It would not then, he declared, "be *slurred over* carelessly, anyhow."[18]

Mrs. Fairbanks did more. About nine days prior to the date of the lecture she began to prepare the people of Cleveland for Mark Twain's appearance in the city by printing in the *Herald* a series of notices concerning the lecture, together with numerous brief reminders. In addition, the *Herald* reprinted three of his articles—an essay on Horace Greeley, The Jumping Frog, and a letter to the editor of the *Herald* under the title A Mystery. The letter had to do with an unidentified individual who had impersonated Mark Twain in Cleveland some months earlier.

On November 18, the day after the lecture, she complied with Mark Twain's request for a critique by supplying the *Herald* with the following report:

> The course of lectures before the Library Association was inaugurated last evening by the brilliant entertainment of the humorist "Mark Twain." Notwithstanding the unpropitious weather, and strong competition of counter attractions in the way of amusements, Case Hall was early filled with an assembly who were prepared to criticize closely this new candidate for their favor. A few moments sufficed to put him and his audience on the best of terms, and to warm him up with the pleasant consciousness of their approval. For nearly two hours he held them by the magnetism of his varied talent.
>
> We shall attempt no transcript of his lecture, lest with unskillful hands we mar its beauty, for beauty and poetry it certainly possessed, though the production of a profound humorist.
>
> We know not which to commend, the quaint utterances, the funny incidents, the good-natured recital of the

characteristics of the harmless "Vandal," or the gems of beautiful descriptions which sparkled all through his lecture. We expected to be amused, but we were taken by surprise when he carried us on the wings of his redundant fancy, away to the ruins, the cathedrals, and the monuments of the Old World. There are some passages of gorgeous word painting which haunt us like a remembered picture.

We congratulate Mr. Twain upon having taken the tide of public favor "at the flood" in the lecture field, and having conclusively proved that a man may be a humorist without being a clown. He has elevated his profession by his graceful delivery and by recognizing in his audience something higher than merely a desire to laugh. We can assure the cities who await his coming, that a rich feast is in store for them and Cleveland is proud to offer him the first laurel leaf, in his role as lecturer this side of the "Rocky-slope."

The next day, after reading Mrs. Fairbanks' critique in the *Herald* and listening to the praises of other friends in the audience whose judgment he respected, Mark Twain was jubilant. To his family in St. Louis he wrote, "Made a *splendid* hit last night, & am the 'lion' to-day. . . . I *captured* them, if I *do* say it myself."[19]

While Mrs. Fairbanks refrained, in her critique, from transcribing any portion of the lecture, the same issue of the *Herald* on another page, offered verbatim his Apostrophe to the Sphynx as one of the gems of the lecture.[20] This eloquent passage, together with her splendid report of the lecture, was of immense value to Mark Twain, for it brought his name to the favorable attention of local committee chairmen who were still trying to fill out their season's programs. Especially valuable was her comment that he was a humorist without being a clown and that he recognized in his audience something higher than a mere desire to laugh. It was true, as Mark Twain was beginning to discover, that many societies welcomed at least one humorous program to relieve the heaviness of their didactic courses; yet it was no less true that they tended to shy away from mere humor as incompatible with the purposes of a lyceum course. To be acceptable, a humorous lecture must contain instructional matter and a clearly recognized moral. Mere clownishness or buffoonery would bring the committee into disrepute and injure the course. The enthusiastic but dignified critique in the *Herald* was thus precisely the sort of statement most calculated to bring Mark Twain's lecture favorably to the attention of the committees and to allay their fears about booking such a lecture. And the Apostrophe to the Sphynx offered an excellent specimen of its moments of high seriousness.

It took time, of course, for Mrs. Fairbanks' critique to filter through the exchanges. This fact, along with the circumstance that he had entered the field late in the season, accounts in some measure for the small number of lecture engagements which Mark Twain secured during the last half of November and much of December. A more important factor, however, for the slow start was his relative obscurity in 1868. Despite his rapidly growing reputation through the publication of The Jumping Frog and his articles in various metropolitan newspapers, he was not well known. *Innocents Abroad* had not yet made its appearance. At best, in so far as he was known at all in midwestern communities, he was still a mere newspaper humorist—fresh, vigorous, and promising, a man with an interesting pseudonym, but with nothing really substantial to recommend him to the local lyceum committees.

After Cleveland, there appear to have been only two other lectures during the remainder of the month, one at Pittsburgh on November 19, and another at Elmira, New York, November 23. At Elmira he felt he had failed a bit by relying too much upon notes,[21] but this fact apparently escaped the notice of Olivia Langdon who sat in the audience that evening with her family. Indeed, she was so greatly impressed by the success of his performance and its obviously favorable reception that before his departure from the city she and her family had tentatively, at least, accepted him as her suitor. Perhaps the news of his success at Pittsburgh had also impressed the Langdons. There he had attracted an audience of fifteen hundred against Fanny Kemble, a famous actress of the day, who, according to Mark Twain's report, played to only two hundred.[22]

The engagements in December numbered only about eight and were geographically spotty, taking him through New York, New Jersey, Michigan, and Ohio. In January, however, business flourished. News of his successful performances was circulating widely. That month there were twenty bookings which took him on an itinerary that criss-crossed Indiana, Illinois, Iowa, Wisconsin, Michigan, and Ohio. The long journeys in poorly lighted, poorly ventilated, and poorly heated coaches, together with frequent poor rail connections and hotel accommodations exhausted him. By January 14 he acknowledged to his sister Pamela that the pace of the lecture circuit was a hard one and that he was "getting awful tired of it."[23] It constitutes the first record of Mark Twain's disenchantment with tour lecturing, a disenchantment which grew rapidly in succeeding tours and which caused him so often, in the years that followed, to declare his hatred for the platform.

But there were rewarding moments on the platform, as well as business matters to attend to, which made him forget at times the weariness and the irritations of travel. From Chicago, where he lectured on January 7, he wrote Bliss, his publisher in Hartford, urging him to do more to synchronize the advertising of *Innocents Abroad* with his lecturing engagements. "Why don't you issue prospectuses & startling advertisements now that I am stirring the bowels of these communities?" he asked.[24] On January 20 he was jubilant about his success at Toledo, Ohio, where his friend Petroleum V. Nasby had worked on the *Blade*. "I swept Nasby's dunghill like a Besom of Destruction," he wrote Livy, forgetting momentarily, in his exuberance, her distaste for inelegancies of expression.[25] Two days later he was back in Cleveland, a city that had become dear to him, for a repeat performance. He had accepted an invitation to lecture for the benefit of the Protestant orphan asylum.

Again he drew a large audience in Case Hall, "the best humored audience we ever saw," as one reporter declared.[26] In a brief peroration he explained the worthiness of the cause, and then pictured the sixty little parentless children that inhabited the institution.

> LADIES AND GENTLEMEN: I am well aware of the fact that it would be a most gigantic fraud for you to pay a dollar each to hear my lecture. But you pay your dollar to an orphan asylum, and have the lecture thrown in! So if it is not worth anything it does not cost you anything! There is no expense connected with this lecture. Everything is done gratuitously, and you have the satisfaction of knowing that all you have paid goes for the benefit of the orphans. I understand that there are to be other entertainments given week after next for the same object, the asylum

being several thousand dollars in debt, and I earnestly recommend to you to attend them and not let your benevolence stop with this lecture. There will be eating to be done. Go there and eat and eat and keep on eating and *pay as you go.* The proprietors of the skating rink have generously offered to donate the asylum the proceeds of one evening, to the amount of a thousand dollars, and when that evening comes, go and skate. I do not know whether you can all skate or not, but go and try! If you break your necks it will be no matter; it will be to help the orphans.

Don't be afraid of giving too much to the orphans, for however much you give, you have the easiest end of the bargain. Some persons have to take care of these sixty orphans, and they have to *wash* them. Orphans have to be washed! And it's no small job, either, for they have only one wash tub and it's slow business. They can't wash but one orphan at a time. They have to be washed in the most elaborate detail, and by the time they get through with the sixty, the original orphan has to be washed again. Orphans won't stay washed. I've been an orphan myself for twenty-five years and I know this to be true. There is a suspicion of impurity and imposition about many ostensibly benevolent enterprises, but there is no taint of reproach upon this for the benefit of these little waifs upon the sea of life, and I hope your benevolence will not stop here. In conclusion I thank you for the patience and fortitude with which you have listened to me.[27]

During February the engagements grew spotty again, though they took him erratically through Illinois, Ohio, Pennsylvania, and New York. But the time between some of the engagements was not wasted, for whenever the opportunity offered he hurried to Elmira to be with Livy and to read proof on *Innocents Abroad.*[28] The tour finally came to an end on March 3 in Lockport, New York, after which he hurried off to a longer visit at Elmira before proceeding to Hartford to take care of last minute matters in connection with the book, which was now in press.

Financially, the tour did not pan out as well as he might have expected. Paine asserts that Mark Twain lectured between fifty and sixty times during the season of 1868–69, and that he earned "something more than $8,000."[29] The estimate appears too high. On February 1 Mark Twain wrote Bliss that he had "now lectured thirty-five or forty times. . . ."[30] It is doubtful that he lectured more than a dozen times thereafter.[31] But even if he lectured as often as Paine indicates, $8,000 is still too high, since it is well known that Mark Twain's fee during the tour of 1868–69 was a hundred dollars "a pop," as he wrote his mother[32] and that he sometimes received less. The net earnings were, of course, much lower. The discursiveness of the itinerary had made travel costs exceptionally high. And when he added to these the costs of his frequent unscheduled trips to Elmira, it is understandable that for all his work he scarcely had two thousand dollars left to show for it. Nevertheless it had been a splendid season. He had won public acclaim all along the circuit, and his courtship of Livy had prospered. What he now looked forward to was the success of *Innocents Abroad*.

Despite the fact that The American Vandal Abroad was a successful lecture, well received all along the western circuit, it is interesting to note that after the tour of 1868–69, Mark Twain abandoned it. (During the season of 1871–72 he made use of anecdotal parts of it in his Reminiscences lecture, but this lecture proved so disappointing that he gave it up after four performances.) The reasons for not keeping it in his repertoire of lectures are perhaps not hard to find. In the first place, after the publication of *Innocents Abroad*, there was really no further need to lecture about it. The book told the story. There was, however, a more likely reason. As time passed and his acquaintance with the memorials of European culture increased, he was no longer willing, especially before New England audiences, to make light of them from the platform. While he could safely confide to Mrs. Fairbanks in 1868 that the Old Masters were forbidden ground to him, he no longer felt it expedient to exploit them for the purposes of humor in the period that followed. The change in attitude was part of the transformation that took place in Mark Twain during the late 1860's and early 1870's— from Wild Humorist of the Pacific Slope to Mark Twain, humorist, a man who could be humorous without being a clown.

CHAPTER EIGHT

UNDER REDPATH'S MANAGEMENT

. . . guard me against the injury of a synopsis. —GLIMPSES OF THE PAST, OCTOBER, *1935.*

MARK TWAIN had hardly finished the long tour of 1868–69 through the Middle West when he began making plans for another tour the following winter. After only one season on the lyceum circuit the young humorist from the Pacific slope had become a leading star on the platform and invitations for him to accept engagements came from every side.

The precise circumstances which now led to his important association with James Redpath of the newly established Boston Lyceum Bureau are somewhat obscure. Albert Bigelow Paine may be correct in his claim that Redpath had become interested in Mark Twain following the humorist's success at Cooper Institute in 1867,[1] but he is in error when he states that early in the fall of 1868 Mark Twain "began a lecture engagement with James Redpath."[2] Redpath did not establish his bureau till the spring of 1869.

Which of the two men made the first advance is not clear. It may well be that Mark Twain, somewhere along the circuit, had heard of the new lecture bureau being organized in Boston and had written to Redpath to make inquiries; or that after the tour had come to an end, he had, on his own initiation, visited the bureau office. There is an equal probability that Redpath, having heard of Mark Twain's platform popularity the preceding season, had sought to add the humorist's name to the roster of speakers he was preparing during the spring of 1869.

At any rate, on April 24, 1869, Redpath wrote to Mark Twain, expressed his regrets for having been out of the office when he called, and immediately proceeded to make a number of proposals about lecturing under his management. Since the letter is important in establishing the initial business association of the two men, the following sections of it have special interest.

> Now about lecturing, let me use your name, say from the 1st of November . . . ; tell me your terms; send me regularly all *your most humorous pieces* so that I may get them republished and so keep up and increase your reputation in N.E. I think you would do well in this section; although you are not so widely known here as you are in the Middle and Western States. However by sending me a lot of your newspaper scraps, that can be remedied.
>
> What I purpose to do—is to advertise my whole list in the leading papers, send circulars to every "Post" (G.A.R.), Y.M.C.A. & Lyceum newspaper editors in N.Y., and when the lecturers furnish me with special circulars scatter them at my own expense.
>
> I enclose the two last that have come to hand for me. Can't you get up something similar and let me have 500 copies?[3]

That Mark Twain responded to Redpath's request and supplied him with humorous pieces, newspaper reports of his lectures, and other items is evident from the appearance of such materials in the newspapers of towns where Redpath later booked him. Whether he sent the five hundred circulars is not known.

Still mindful of the hardships and fatigues of the preceding season, however, Mark Twain was now resolved to commit himself to a briefer and less far-ranging tour. He promised Redpath he would lecture ten nights in the state of New York, provided the towns were close together, but for the most part intended to accept engagements only in the six New England states. And if he were to "get located in a newspaper," he had no intention of lecturing at all the following winter.[4]

Actually, by early June, he was already negotiating to buy an interest in the Cleveland *Herald*, but when that paper raised the purchase price and informed him that he would be expected

The Lyceum.

NUMBER I.   BOSTON, AUGUST, 1869.   QUARTERLY.

LYCEUMS AND THEIR WANTS.

THE need of an intermediate agency between Lyceums and Lecturers has been felt for a long time in New England and elsewhere.

Committees find constant difficulty in reaching lecturers; and lecturers in putting themselves in communication with committees.

The Boston Lyceum Bureau supplies this want of a common centre of communication.

It is already the agent of more than two hundred Lecturers, Readers, and Musicians, and its list is not yet completed.

It is prepared to supply any demand that may be made on it for Lyceum Lectures, Commencement Orations, Occasional Speeches, Vocal or Instrumental Musicians, Elocutionary Readers or Dramatic Personators.

Any committee that has already engaged its full list of lecturers, in case of a failure on their part during the course of the coming season, can be supplied with a substitute at the shortest notice, by telegraphing or addressing the Boston Lyceum Bureau.

For nearly all the Lecturers and Readers on this list, no engagement can be made, either by themselves or others, excepting through the agency of this Bureau.

Although $50 is the lowest sum named on the list, Lyceums that are struggling under difficulties, or Lyceums that are willing to take "off nights," can be supplied at even lower rates.

"Modifications," as used in the list, means both more and less,—in a city, "$50 with modifications," may mean $60 or $75, and in a village $30 or $40. But the rates will always be stated in advance.

The Bureau will furnish several different lists, of ten lectures and entertainments each, for the aggregate sums of $350, $400, $450, $300, $600, $700, and upwards, on receipt of a fee of five dollars, which, if any course shall be engaged through the Bureau, will be refunded to the Lyceum.

Committees in applying for any Lecturer, should name several dates that will suit them, and we will then fix the first day of the number that is left at our disposal, and that can be arranged into a convenient route for the Lecturer.

The list herewith submitted is the best and most varied, both as regards names and subjects, that has ever been offered in this country for the consideration of committees.

We guarantee that every engagement made by us shall be promptly met, or that the name of the Lecturer who fails, unless a satisfactory explanation is made to the committee, shall be promptly erased from our list.

No charge whatever will be made to Lyceums for any engagements that we may make for them.

Address:

JAMES REDPATH,
Boston Lyceum Bureau,
No. 20 Bromfield Street,
BOSTON, MASS.

(Office hour from 12, M. to 1, P. M.)

— The second number of this Journal, greatly enlarged, will be issued a few weeks in advance of the regular date of publication.

BOSTON LYCEUM BUREAU.

JAMES REDPATH, - - - GEORGE L. FALL,
Managers.

BOSTON, AUGUST 2, 1869.

In consequence of the increasing demands made on us for a fuller list than we issued in May last, we subjoin the names of such Lecturers, Readers and Musicians as have completed their arrangements with this Bureau.

We are prepared to make arrangements for them in New England, New York, New Jersey, Pennsylvania, Maryland, and all the British North American Provinces.

LECTURERS.

ABBOTT, REV. JOHN S. C.
Subjects.—"France and her Emperor." "Romance of Spanish History."
TERMS.—$100, with modifications.

ALGER, REV. WM. R.
Subjects.—"Patriotism as a Principle, as a Sentiment, and as a Passion." "Human Life as a Fine Art." "The Nature and Value of Music." "The Knights of the XIXth Century." "The Origin, Essence and Influence of Chivalry." "The Origin and Uses of Poetry."
TERMS.—$100, with modifications.

AMES, MRS. NELLIE.
Subject.—"Working Women of New York." Mrs. Ames is the author of the serial, "Up Broadway," published in the "Revolution." Recommended by a distinguished N. Y. author; as "a lady of great talent, a fine speaker, and has the magnetism necessary to enchain an audience."
TERMS.—$100.

ATKINSON, EDWARD.
Subject.—"Hands off"; a lecture on Political Science.
TERMS.—$50, with modifications.

ATKINSON, PROF. W. P.
Subjects.—"What Constitutes a Liberal Education?" "English Poetry and How to Study it." "Language and the Study of Language." "Revolutions in History." "The Boyhood of Scott and his Contemporaries." "The Manhood of Scott and his Contemporaries." "Wit and Humor."
TERMS.—$50, with modifications.

BARNARD, CHARLES, 2d.
Subjects.—"My Jack-knife, and how to use it." A lecture on the theory and practice of pruning, illustrated on the blackboard. "Glass-farming." A lecture on the forcing of plants.
TERMS.—$80 with modifications.
(Mr. Barnard is better known by his newspaper name of Jane Kingsford, and his recent books, "Farming by Inches," and "My Ten Rod Farm.")

BELDEN, REV. WM. W.
Subjects.—"Value of Character to the Young." "Heroic Thinkers." "Manliness." "Books and Reading." "Washington and Lincoln." "Youth, the Season of Strength." "Positive Forces of our Age."
TERMS.—From $50 to $100.

BILLINGS, JOSH.
Subjects.—"Milk." "A Plaintive Discourse on Natral His'r'y." The last lecture is "warranted for 60 days."
TERMS.—Outside of New England, Mr. Billings' average terms are $90.40, "with the privilege of throwing off the $90 if I was a mind to, but never to discount the 40 cents." In New England, his terms range from $75.40 to $100.40. Time.—All December. Lyceums who desire to secure him should apply soon.

BRACKETT, J. Q. A.
Subject.—"Work and Play."
TERMS.—$50, with modifications.

BRAINARD, CHARLES H.
Subjects.—"Whittier and his Poetry." "Life in Washington." "Walter Raleigh." "Readings in Prose and Verse."
TERMS.—$50, with modifications.

BRIGHAM, W. L.
Subject.—"Personal Reminiscences of Gov. Andrew." Mr. Brigham was Gov. Andrew's Military Secretary during the war.
TERMS.—$50, with modifications.

BROWN, REV. OLYMPIA.
Subjects.—"The Almighty Dollar." "The Coming Woman." "Diversity of Gifts."
TERMS.—$50 and expenses, with modifications.

BROWN, REV. SELAH W.
Subject.—"From New York to Jerusalem, with pictures of European and Oriental Life."
TERMS.—$50, with modifications.

BROWN, WM. WELLS.
Subject.—"Hannibal, the Carthagenian Hero."
TERMS.—$50, with modifications.

BUCKLEY, REV. J. M.
Subjects.—"Switzerland." "Six Weeks in London." "Extraordinary Phenomena of Human Nature." "Trance." "Personal Magnetism."
TERMS.—$50 and expenses, with modifications. Cannot lecture on Wednesday or Saturday.

BURLEIGH, WM. H.
Subjects.—Various poem-lectures.
TERMS.—$75, with modifications.

BURLEIGH, MRS. CELIA.
Subjects.—"Womanhood." "Values."
(Mrs. Burleigh is Secretary of the N. Y. Sorosis, and is highly recommended.)
TERMS.—$75, with modifications.

BURNHAM, SAMUEL.
Subjects.—"Live while we Live." (A humorous and didactic poem.) "The Huguenots in America." (An historical lecture.) "The Early New England Clergy." (Historical and Anecdotal.)
TERMS.—$50, with modifications.

BURNS, ROBT. FERRIER, (of Illinois).
Subjects.—"Sketches of the Middle Ages." "The Book and its Influence." "An Evening with the Poets of England." "Modern Infidelity." "Russia." "Plea for the Classics." "Abraham Lincoln." Two Lectures on Temperance. "Principles, Practices, Institutions and Missions of the Jesuits; four lectures." "Mahommed."
TERMS.—$30.

CHASE, PLINY E.
Subject.—"Astronomy."
TERMS.—$75.

CLARKE, REV. JAMES FREEMAN.
Subjects.—"What for?" "Why should not Women Vote?" "The Teacher who Leads, and the Teacher who Drives." "Our Dumb Relations."
TERMS.—$50, with modifications.

COLLIER, REV. ROBERT LAIRD.
Subjects.—"The Personality and Blunders of a great Genius." "Woman's Place." Also, a new lecture on his European trip.
TERMS.—$100. Time.—Mr. Collier can lecture in New England during the first weeks of December only.

COLLYER, REV. ROBERT.
Subject.—Not stated. Will be given by letter.
TERMS.—$100. Time.—Mr. Collyer can lecture in the last half of November only.

LOGAN, MISS OLIVE.
Subjects. — "Paris; City of Luxury," and "Girls."
TERMS. — $100 to $200.

LORD, DR. JOHN.
Subjects. — Historical Lectures on Representative Men. Dr. Lord has devoted twenty-five years to Historical Subjects, and has upwards of fifty lectures. Send for circular.
TERMS. — $100, with modifications.

LORING, DR. GEO. B.
Subjects. — "The Value of Classical Culture." "Female Education and rights." "Jefferson and Lincoln." "Chief Justice Parsons." "Martial Statesmanship as Illustrated by Washington and Grant."
TERMS. — $75 and $50, with modifications.

MALLALIEU, REV. W. F.
Subjects. — "The American Idea, or the Philosophy of American Politics." "The Hope and Glory of the Republic." "The English Aristocracy." "The Blues." "Self-Culture." "The Huguenots." "The Yankee, his Home and Habits."
TERMS. — $50, with modifications.

MANNING, JEROME F.
Subjects. — "Power of Culture." "Leaders." "Lord Brougham."
TERMS. — $50 to $100, with modifications.

McKEOWN, REV. ANDREW.
Subjects. — "Oratory and Orators." "Self Surrender." "Nova Scotia and the Nova Scotians."
TERMS. — $50, with modifications.

MERWIN, MAJOR J. B.
Subjects. — "Heroism." "Elements of Power."
TERMS. — $150.

MONTGOMERY, REV. DAVID H.
Subjects. — "Our Debt to the Past." "Nothing Lost." "Natural History of a Drop of Blood."
TERMS. — $50, with modifications.

MOORE, REV. JAMES B.
Subject. — "Fore."
TERMS. — $50, with modifications.

MORGAN, REV. HENRY.
Subject. — "Agitators and Come-Outers."
TERMS. — $50, with modifications.

MORTON, EDWIN.
Subject. — "Personal Reminiscences of John Brown."
TERMS. — $30, with modifications.

OSCANYAN, HON. C. (Ottoman Consul General in New York.)
Subjects. — Mr. Oscanyan has six separate Lectures. Three on "Social Life in Turkey," one on "Persia," and two on "Palestine." These Lectures are illustrated with appropriate costumes; the speaker chants the cry of the Muezzin and performs the genuflexions of Mussulman worship, etc. Mr. Oscanyan can be engaged either for a course or a single lecture.
TERMS. — $150, $125 and $100, according to the place; local expenses in all instances required.

PARSONS, HON. WILLIAM (of Ireland).
Subjects. — "Columbus." "Peter the Great." "Wm. Caxton." "Michael Angelo." "Napoleon." "Richard Brinsley." "Edmund Burke." "Cicero." "Oliver Goldsmith." "Dante." "Samuel Johnson." "George Stephenson." "Paris and the Parisians." "Orators and Wits" "The Romance of the Law Courts." "Don Quixote." "Old Homer and His Days." "Curran." "Ireland." "An Evening with Thackeray." For syllabus, see circular.
TERMS. — $100, with modifications. Time. — From November 17th to December 31st, in New England.

PECK, REV. J. O.
Subjects. — "Golden Opportunities and Golden Men." "The Coronation of Labor." "Young Blood." "An Old Enemy Rampant."
TERMS. — $50 to $100.

PIERCE, S. E.
Subject. — "Hewers and Workers." Mr. Pierce is the political editor of the Watchman and Reflector, and is well known from his war-correspondence, signed "Ranger."
TERMS. — $50, with modifications.

POTTER, REV. HENRY C. (D.D.)
Subjects. — "Growth." "The Tyranny of Respectability." "The New Era of Chivalry." "Travel and Travellers."
TERMS. — $75.

QUINCEY, JOSIAH PHILLIPS.
Subjects. — "The Comedy of the Boarding-House." "American Ideals, or Good Yankees in Paris."
TERMS. — $50 to $100.

RICHARDS, PROF. WM. C.
Subjects. — "1. The Matter King." 2. "The Matter Queen." 3. "Castles in the Air." 4. "Electron, or the Modern Puck." 5. "Science in Soap Bubbles." 6. "Lung Work." 7. "Wealth from Waste." 8. "Science is King."
TERMS. — $75 for Nos. 7 and 8; $100 for Nos. 1, 2, 3, 5 and 6; $125 to $150 for No. 4.

ROCKWELL, MRS. E. F.
Subjects. — "A Yankee Girl's Thoughts." "Young America."
TERMS. — $50, with modifications.

RUSSELL, JUDGE THOMAS.
Subjects. — "The Scholar's Place in the World." "The Lessons of War." "The Duties of Peace." "The Wars of England for Two Hundred Years." "National Greatness Dependent on National Character." A new Lecture to be announced hereafter.
TERMS. — $50, with modifications.

ST. JOHN, C. HENRY F.
Subjects. — "Among the Fogs; or, Life in Newfoundland." "Sea Kings." "Lamartine." "Henry Kirke White." "Hooks and Eyes." "Our Educators."
TERMS. — $50, with modifications.

SARGEANT, REV. JOHN T.
Subjects. — "The Interests of Labor and the Mechanic Arts." "The Issues and Prospects of a Radical Philosophy." "The Relation of Fine Art to the Growth and Morals of a Community."
TERMS. — $50, with modifications.

SAXE, JOHN G.
Subjects. — "Yankee Land." "Love." "Poetry and Poets." Also, a new Lecture.
TERMS. — $75 to $100.

SEELYE, PROF. J. H.
Subject. — "The State of the Nation."
TERMS. — $100.

SIKES, WIRT.
Subjects. — "After Dark in New York." "Assassins."
TERMS. — $75 to $100.

STANTON, MRS. ELIZABETH CADY.
Subject. — "The Woman Question."
TERMS. — $75, with modifications.

SPOFFARD, RICHARD.
Subject. — "Romance of our National Growth."
TERMS. — $50, with modifications.

STEBBINS, DR. RUFUS P.
Subjects. — "Labor, its Blessings and Achievements." "Rights; is not this a Free Country?" "The New Education; Stones or Bread." "The Laws and Phenomena of Progress."
TERMS. — $50, with modifications.

STOCKBRIDGE, DR. J. C.
Subjects. — "A Week in Athens." "Rambles in and Around Rome."
TERMS. — $50, with modifications.

SUMNER, HON. CHARLES.
(Senator Sumner, if his other engagements permit, will lecture during October and November. All applications must be made to this Bureau, and a route will be arranged as early as possible. Lyceums that desire to secure Senator Sumner should name a series of dates from which a selection can be made. It is hardly necessary to add that early applications will be necessary.)

SWEET, REV. JOHN DAVIS.
Subjects. — "Pompeii and Herculaneum." "The Cities of the Dead." "Neapolitan Life." "The Old and the New." "Beautiful Women; a contemplation from the standpoint of the XIX. Century of the Rights, in her appropriate sphere, to advancing position in the forefront of civil and Christianity."
TERMS. — $50, with modifications.

TALMAGE, T. DE WITT.
Subjects. — "Gramber & Co." "The Things." "Rocks on which People New Home; or, Pleasures of Hous."
TERMS. — $160.

TAYLOR, BENJ. F.
Subjects. — "English Words, their Use, and Beauty." "Thought and its Chu." "Horizon Breakers and Makers." "Fa the Alphabet of Success."
(Mr. Taylor is a popular Western Lecturer; h never appeared in New England Lyceums; is willing to lecture here if a route of twenty engagements can be made at $80 each, between November 15th and December 12th.)

THOMPSON, JAMES T.
Subjects. — "A Visit to Moscow, with Glimpses of Russian Life." "Manliness." "Pictures of Spanish Scenery." "Life and History."
TERMS. — $100.

THWING, EDWARD P.
Subjects. — "Reminiscences of Scotland." "The Circean Cup."
TERMS. — $50 and expenses.

TIMMINS, REV. THOMAS.
Subject. — "Life in England, by an Englishman." (Mr. Timmins is lately from England, where he has been one of the most successful of those engaged in the "Penny-Reading Movement." The papers speak of him as an accomplished elocutionist, and his lectures are described as being "eloquent and full of interest."
TERMS. — $50, with modifications.

TOWNLEY, REV. H. C.
Subjects. — "Woman and the Ballot." Also, a new Lecture.
TERMS. — $50 to $100.

TOWNSEND, REV. L. T.
Subject. — "In and out of Place."
(Mr. Townsend is the author of the popular book lately issued, entitled "Credo.")
TERMS. — $50, with modifications.

TWAIN, MARK.
Subject. — "Curiosities of California."
TERMS. — $100, with modifications.
(This celebrated humorist has been a very successful Lecturer in the West. This is his first season in New England. Lyceums must apply for him an early date, unless they can secure their hall for any evening.)

TYLER, PROF. MOSES COIT.
Subjects. — "Castes." Also, a new Lecture.
TERMS. — $75 to $100.

UPSON, PROF. ANSON, (of HAMILTON COLLEGE, Clinton, N. Y.)
Subjects. — "The Child-like Spirit." "American Life from the Inside." "The Poetry of Life." "Dr. Samuel Johnson." "The Glory and Shame of Actors and Acting." "English Words in this Country." "The truth about Physiology."
TERMS. — $50 to $100.

VINCENT, REV. J. H.
Subjects. — "From Chicago to Jerusalem." "The Model Husband."
TERMS. — $50 and expenses.

WARREN, REV. HENRY W.
Subjects. — "The Forces in a Sunbeam." "Crises of Liberty." "Personal Beauty and Power." Also, a new Lecture on the "Early History of Christian Art."
TERMS. — $75 and $50.

WEISS, REV. JOHN.
Subject. — Not stated.
TERMS. — $50, with modifications.

WHIPPLE, E. P.
Subjects. — "Joan of Arc." "Courage." "Shoddy." "Loafing and Laboring."
TERMS. — $75 and $50.

WHITTLESY, COL. CHARLES.
Subject. — "The Geological Evidence of the Antiquity of Man."
TERMS. — $75.

WHEDON, REV. D. A.
Subjects. — "The forces of American Progress."
TERMS. — $50, with modifications.

WILLARD, JOHN B.
Subject. — "The Marriage Theory of Novels."
TERMS. — $50, with modifications.

to assume the duties of political editor, Mark Twain withdrew.[5] Thereafter there were brief skirmishes for positions with the Hartford *Post* and the Springfield *Republican*, but these prospects also failed to materialize. In August, however, when an opportunity presented itself to acquire a third interest in the Buffalo, New York, *Express* for $25,000, he decided to buy, accepting financial assistance from his prospective father-in-law, Jervis Langdon.

But even before the purchase was made Mark Twain's resolve not to lecture at all if he "got located" in a newspaper had rapidly faded away.[6] The debt which would result from such a purchase and his impending marriage to Olivia required cash— quickly, and in considerable amounts. It was true that *Innocents Abroad*, which was to appear late in July, might prove profitable, but how could one be sure? The only *sure* way of getting money was by lecturing. As a consequence, much of July found him in Elmira at the Langdon house, busily writing a lecture. "It takes me every day to do it," he confided to Mrs. Fairbanks, "and it isn't finished yet. I write on top of the house where it is cool & solitary."[7]

The lecture he was working on during those hot July days was not the Vandal lecture (which by this time he had abandoned, as we have already noted, fearing that his irreverent treatment of the memorials of Europe might offend the cultivated audiences of New England), but a brand new one which Redpath began advertising around the lecture circuit some weeks later in his new magazine *The Lyceum*. The first issue, dated Boston, August, 1869, listed all the lecturers under his management for the coming season, together with the lecture topics and the terms for each lecturer. Mark Twain was announced as follows:

> Subject., "Curiosities of California."
> Terms.—$100, with modifications.
> (This celebrated humorist has been a very successful lecturer in the West. This is his first season in New England. The lyceums must apply for him at an early date, unless they can secure their hall for any evening.)

In examining Redpath's long list of names, it is interesting to note that Mark Twain was the only one referred to as "celebrated," an indication of the bureau chief's exceptionally high regard of Mark Twain's platform success the preceding year. The terms, $100, were good—as high, indeed, for the season of 1869–70, as those specified for such a well-known platform favorite as Josh Billings who was also on Redpath's list. At least they came within forty cents of those terms, advertised at $100.40 in New England, with the facetious announcement that Billings reserved the privilege of throwing off the $100, if he "was of a mind to, but never to discount the 40 cents."

On August 14, however, a few days after purchasing the partnership in the *Express,* and about the time that the bureau was advertising the California lecture along the entire lyceum circuit, Mark Twain wrote Redpath that he was canceling all of next season's lecture engagements and intended, after his assumption of duties in Buffalo, to establish housekeeping there.[8] Jervis Langdon's generous financial aid, which had made the *Express* purchase possible, together with Olivia's desire for a home life uninterrupted by absences when her husband lectured, obviously prompted the change in plans.

But Redpath refused to be put off. Arrangements with some of the local committees, he felt, had proceeded too far for Mark Twain to pull out altogether. Besides, he knew that "good phools are skarse," to use Josh Billings' phrase,[9] and that he could not satisfy the clamor for his most celebrated humorist by supplying a substitute. Under Redpath's continued pressure, Mark Twain capitulated. "He can't get me free from Boston & 2 or 3 other places," Mark Twain wrote Livy somewhat fearfully, anticipating her displeasure. And since it wasn't worthwhile to write a lecture and go to all the labor of memorizing it for the sake of a half-dozen performances, he had instructed the bureau to go ahead and book him for the season. Also, after considering the matter well, he had concluded that he ought to have "some money to commence married life with. . . . When I once start lecturing I might as well consent to be banged about from town to town while the lecture season lasts."[10] Besides, he informed her, his associates on the *Express* wanted him to lecture some during the winter.[11]

In his letter to Redpath, informing him that he would lecture, Mark Twain insisted upon certain conditions. He would not accept lecture engagements on Saturdays and Sundays; the bookings should be confined chiefly to New England and New York—in any event, within easy reach of Boston and Elmira;

The Boston Lyceum Bureau

"MARK TWAIN,"

[SAMUEL L. CLEMENS.]

MARK TWAIN is widely known as one of the most humorous writers in the country. He has made very successful lecturing tours in the West, but has never, we believe, appeared before in a New England Lyceum. His lecture on the " American Vandal Abroad " was everywhere spoken of by the Press, in the highest terms of commendation.

From a large number of flattering notices, we extract a few sentences only, in order to show that his fame as a writer does not suffer by his appearance as a lecturer

THE *Cleveland Herald* says : " No written description can do justice to the lecture. It must be heard to be fully appreciated. After hearing it the second time we do not wonder that "The Vandal" met with the unbounded enthusiasm that has attended it at every place where it has been heard. The humor of the lecture is peculiar and irresistible, the descriptive portions brilliant and eloquent, and the whole tone humanitarian and elevating."

Another Cleveland journalist says : — " The course of lectures before the Library Association was inaugurated last evening by the brilliant entertainment of the humorist, "Mark Twain." Notwithstanding the unpropitious weather, and strong counter attractions in the way of amusements, Case Hall was early filled with an assembly who were prepared to criticise closely this new candidate for their favor. A few moments sufficed to put him and his audience on the best of terms, and to warm him up with the pleasant consciousness of their approval. For nearly two hours he held them by the magnetism of his varied talent.

" We shall attempt no transcript of his lecture, lest with unskilful hands we mar its beauty, for beauty and poetry it certainly possessed, though the production of a professed humorist.

" We know not which most to commend, the quaint utterances, the funny incidents, the good-natured recital of the characteristics of his harmless "Vandal," or the gems of beautiful descriptions which sparkled all through his lecture. We expected to be amused, but we were taken by surprise when he carried us on the wings of his redundant fancy, away to the ruins, the cathedrals, and the monuments of the Old World. There are some passages of gorgeous word-painting which haunt us like a remembered picture.

" We congratulate Mr. Twain upon having taken the tide of public favor ." at the flood " in the lecture field, and having conclusively proved that a man may be a humorist without being a clown. He has elevated the profession by his graceful delivery and by recognizing in his audience something higher than merely a desire to laugh. We can assure the cities who are awaiting his coming, that a rich feast is in store for them, and Cleveland is proud to offer him the first laurel leaf in his *role* as lecturer, this side the " Rocky slope."

Boston Lyceum Bureau (Redpath) Circular advertising its services as agent for Mark Twain.

and that he would accept no engagements after January 22. Since the date of his wedding had been set for the first week in February, he needed time to attend to personal matters.[12]

Redpath worked hard to please his young star in all particulars, though after the first month, with Mark Twain's consent, he began Saturday bookings. The tour he contrived was agreeable. It ranged up and down the coast from Maine to Washington, D.C., and throughout New York State and eastern Pennsylvania. And since Redpath had managed to book many of the lectures with Boston as a hub, Mark Twain was able to maintain his room at Young's Hotel and return there almost nightly to be with friends and spend pleasant hours visiting in Redpath's bureau. What pleased him no less was the fact that the tour included nearly all the large cities in the entire area.

At what point and for what reasons Mark Twain now decided to give up the lecture on California in favor of the old Sandwich Islands lecture is not clear, but the time must have been late September or early October. In a letter to Mrs. Fairbanks dated September 27, he claimed he was still fidgeting and fuming and sweating, trying to whip a lecture into shape (presumably the California lecture), but finding that he couldn't "write serenely."[13] And so, perhaps, as the moment arrived when he had to make a final decision in order to allow Redpath time to inform the committees what his subject would be, he turned to the Sandwich Islands lecture out of sheer desperation. Whatever the circumstances, the choice was a wise one. It was a lecture he loved to give, and, with the exception of New York and Brooklyn, where he had given it in 1867, it was new to eastern audiences. With some reworking here and there (which he immediately undertook), he was confident that it would not only please his eastern audiences but provide the instruction which they would expect.

The tour began in Pittsburgh on Monday, November 1. Arriving in the city on the preceding Saturday, Mark Twain was met by a group of reporters and members of the lecture committee, about twenty in all, who conducted him to a private restaurant where an oyster supper had been prepared.[14] It turned out to be just the kind of an evening that Mark Twain enjoyed. "No wine, no toasts, no speeches," he wrote Livy happily, "nothing but conversation."[15]

The next day was a pleasantly busy one. He received a number of callers, people he had known in California and Nevada, some casual visitors, and a number of local newspaper reporters. Among the latter was O. T. Bennett of the *Commercial* whom Mark Twain found particularly agreeable—"a good fellow, modest, & pleasant."[16] At an appropriate moment during the visit, Bennett was polite enough to ask Mark Twain if he might make a synopsis of his lecture the following evening for his newspaper, or report it in full. He obviously believed that by doing so he would be complimenting the celebrated humorist.

But the question touched on one of Mark Twain's raw spots and might have thrown him into a rage had not Bennett's gentle and polite manner disarmed him. Carefully and at length he gave Bennett a full outline of his objections to such practices.

A synopsis of a lecture such as his, he explained, held up all the jokes "in a crippled condition for all the world to remember," and to hate when they subsequently heard them repeated on the platform. Furthermore, extracting jokes from a humorous lecture was the same as "taking the raisins out of a fruit cake," leaving the lecture and the cake but a *"pretense* of a something it was *not,* for such as came after." In addition, the charm of humorous remarks, he insisted, cannot be expressed upon paper. A verbatim report of a humorous lecture leaves out its soul, and no more represents "that lecture to the reader than a person represents a *man* to you when he ships you a corpse." Synopses injure and harm, he added, because they travel ahead of the lecturer and give people a despicable opinion of him and his production.

But Mark Twain's objection to a verbatim reporting of his lecture was rooted in still another conviction—that his lecture was his private property and that a man had no more right to take it from him by printing it without his consent, than he had to take any of his other property. "I showed you what time it was by my watch a while ago," he told Bennett, "and it never occurred to me that you might pull the hands off it so that it would be only a stupid blank to the next man that wanted the time—but yet I see you meditate pulling the hands off my lecture with your synopsis and making it a blank to future audiences." Bennett would not think of walking off with Mark Twain's valise because it is property. But, urged Mark Twain *"do* take the valise and let my lecture alone. I own both of them—I *alone.* Take the valise—it is only worth a hundred dollars—the lecture is worth ten thousand."[17]

In reporting his conversation with Bennett to Livy he acknowledged that if Bennett's boss ordered him to report the lecture, Bennett couldn't help himself; for though "the law protects rigidly the property a shoemaker contrives with his hands, it will not protect the property I create with my brain."[18]

But the boss apparently gave no order. As a consequence, Bennett commented favorably on Mark Twain's lecture the following evening but reproduced very little of it in the *Commercial*. A reporter for the Pittsburgh *Post* who probably listened in as Mark Twain outlined his objections to Bennett merely informed his readers that the rules of the craft did not permit publication of a public lecture or of a private conversation.[19]

Mark Twain's objections to the synopsizing of his lectures deserves attention. In general he respected the responsibilities of reporters and refrained from criticizing them or their craft openly. His own early experience as a reporter had made him familiar with their duties and their ways of thinking and had given him a sense of comradeship with them. It is true that at times he felt that certain newspapers and reporters were hostile to him and that they unjustly abused him.[20] There was, for example, the occasion in a Michigan town where he had declined to dine with a local editor who was drunk, and the editor later reported in his paper that Mark Twain's lecture was profane, indecent, and calculated to encourage intemperance.[21] But in the main, he believed, newspapermen were his friends and were fair in their treatment of his performances. He read their reviews of his lectures regularly, kept a file of clippings, and made a point of meeting briefly with all the reporters in the areas in which he lectured. Often, after the evening's performance was over, he joined them for an hour's talk and refreshments, and felt perfectly at home in their company.[22]

The injuries which Mark Twain suffered from extensive verbatim reporting of his lectures began early in his career. In 1867, for example, Henry M. Stanley, later celebrated for his search for the lost Livingstone in Africa, synopsized his lecture in St. Louis so "verbatimly" that Mark Twain claimed he could never use it in that city again. The next time he went there expecting to give the same lecture, he claimed, "I was told to give them something fresh," as they had already read his lecture in the newspapers.[23] In 1868, while he was lecturing in California, he revealed his concern about the practice of verbatim reporting in a letter to a "friend Williams," obviously a newspaper reporter but not otherwise identified. "Please," he begged, "see that no reports or synopses (even the most meagre one) are made of my lecture. . . . I ask this as a particular personal favor, and beg that you will guard me against the injury of a synopsis."[24]

In the tours that lay ahead, it may be pointed out by way of anticipation, he was still to suffer cruelly from the practice. At Lansing, Michigan, in December, 1871, for example, a reporter for the *State Republican* printed his entire Roughing It lecture word for word. When the Chicago *Tribune*, a few days later provided its wide reader area with extensive excerpts from the same lecture, Mark Twain exploded to Livy, "If these devils incarnate only appreciated the suffering they inflict with their infernal synopses, maybe they would try to have humanity enough to refrain."[25]

It is noteworthy to observe that his resentment toward the practice of synopses and his arguments against it as outlined to Bennett at Pittsburgh, especially his contention that his lectures were as much his property as his material possessions, later became the fundamental basis for his vigorous espousal of the international copyright of books.

But to return to the opening lecture at Pittsburgh—the hall scheduled for the performance was the Academy of Music. According to the Pittsburgh *Post* the largest audience that had ever assembled in that building since it was built gathered to hear their "modest fellow-citizen" lecture. It was, indeed, an overflow crowd, with hundreds of people unable to find seats. When the newspapermen arrived in a body, together with the lecture committee, they found all the seats taken. The only unoccupied area left was the vast expanse of the stage behind the speaker. Here they were provided seats "in close proximity to the savage Twain," who proved to be a "tolerable civilized savage notwithstanding his reputation."[26] Of the lecture itself the reporters had little to say except to praise Mark Twain's graphic description of a volcanic eruption.

From Pittsburgh the tour led eastward. On November 9 he was at Providence, and November 10 at Boston. Boston at this time was the cultural capital of the country, and for that reason widely regarded as the test town for lecturers hoping for success with eastern audiences. A failure at Boston was disastrous, success an assurance of general acceptance throughout New England. Despite Mark Twain's claim in a letter to his mother on the eve of his lecture that he was not all distressed at the thought of meeting an audience of "4000 critics" in old Music Hall,[27] it appears that he was not altogether without apprehension. "Warrington," the well-known Boston correspondent for the Springfield *Republican,* had heard, he declared, that the young humorist from the West was nervous at the idea of facing a Boston audience. What there was in a Boston audience, however, to frighten anybody he couldn't imagine. In his opinion Boston audiences were moved by the same appeals, laughed at the same jokes, yawned at the same dullness, and wondered at the same platitudes as other people. He was sure there was no reason for Mark Twain's anxiety.[28]

When Mark Twain stepped out on the platform of the large and somewhat dimly lighted hall, the greeting he received was heartwarming and reassuring. The house was not filled—he could hardly have expected that—but he could see at a glance that the audience was larger than usual. Redpath, anxious to get his young star off to a good start, came on stage with him and introduced him. Whether Mark Twain had invited the impresario in the hope that his presence would lend prestige to his performance is uncertain. That it did lend prestige there can be little doubt, but generally Mark Twain much preferred, as we have seen, to make his own introductions.

It did not take Mark Twain long that evening in Boston to know that he had nothing to fear from the genial upturned faces that greeted him. Almost from the opening remark of the lecture to its close they paid him the tribute he most desired of audiences anywhere—laughter, more laughter, waves of it. The next day, when he had an opportunity to scan the newspaper accounts of his performance, he was not boasting when he wrote Livy, who was anxiously awaiting word in Elmira, that he had scored "a handsome success."[29] New England audiences no longer had any terrors for him and he knew he could look forward to a successful tour.

In his perceptive review of Mark Twain's lecture, Warrington refrained from synopsizing its "plums." He alluded briefly to its best humorous passages, and finished by praising Mark Twain as not only a genuine humorist (as, in his opinion, De Cordova and Nasby were not) but a most enjoyable and successful lecturer.[30]

Many years later, in 1898, while reminiscing about his early lecturing experiences, Mark Twain vividly recalled the ordeal which lecturers experienced in exposing their performances in

Boston's old Music Hall for a first verdict. It was by that verdict, he recalled, that "all the lyceums in the country determined the lecture's commercial value." The tours did not begin in Boston, he explained, but in the neighboring towns where the lecturers rehearsed their performances and made all the necessary corrections. "This system," he added with a touch of nostalgia, "gathered the whole tribe together in the city in early October, and we had a lazy and sociable time there for several weeks. . . . We spent the days in Redpath's bureau, smoking and talking shop; and early in the evenings we scattered out among the towns and made them indicate the good and poor things in the new lectures."[31]

From Boston the tour proceeded through a number of nearby towns in Massachusetts and Connecticut, swung into Vermont and back again into Connecticut. During all of December and the first three weeks of January he lectured every night, except Sundays, filling engagements in nearly all the large cities of the East—New York, Brooklyn, Philadelphia, Washington, D.C., Albany, Troy, and Utica, to mention only the chief ones.

So popular was his lecture that he found it impossible to take nearly all the engagements that were offered in the East, to say nothing of those that came pouring in from farther west, saying, "Charge all you please, but *come*."[32] Nevertheless, he was not too busy, when in the vicinity of Elmira, to pay Livy a number of quick visits and to spend three or four days with her during the New Year's weekend.

On January 13, when he arrived at Cambridge, New York, an incident occurred which threw him into a rage. A member of the lyceum committee informed him that the Troy *Times* had published his Sandwich Islands lecture entirely and had gone so far as to use dashes in an attempt to imitate his drawling manner of speech. And when his informant added that the *Times* had a wide circulation in the Cambridge area, Mark Twain completely lost his temper, and abused the man for the stupidity of not knowing better than to *tell* him he was about to talk to an audience that had already read his lecture.[33]

The tour finally came to a close on the evening of January 21 at Jamestown, New York, and ended, unfortunately, on a sour note. When he faced his audience that evening he did not sense, from the reception he received, that anything was amiss, though he felt that the lecture had not gone well. When the newspaper reports reached him a day or two later, he discovered that he had become the subject of a bitter dispute between local groups who disagreed about the quality of the lectures provided by the local lyceum committee, about the appropriateness of humorous lectures in the winter's course, and about his own performance in particular.

The attack on his lecture appeared the next day in the Jamestown *Journal* over the signature of a person who signed himself "Many Citizens," implying that he was speaking for others besides himself. He charged that the lecture lacked valuable substance, that much of it was irrelevant, that the entire performance was in disgustingly bad taste, that it was an affront to the noble missionaries who had worked so devotedly in the Sandwich Islands, and that the entire lecture was worthless.[34]

At the time, Mark Twain was too engrossed in his wedding plans to worry about "Many Citizens." But some years later the extent of his injured feelings became manifest in a letter he wrote but never sent to the author of the newspaper attack who was now asking a favor of Mark Twain. Admitting that the lecture at Jamestown had been poorly delivered because he was "fagged with railroad travel," he bitterly denied the request for help. "And you want a consulship," he raged,—"what you want is a rope. I will send you one—the thing you want is a burial permit. You have only to speak, I will see that you get it."[35]

That the tour had been a pronounced success, despite the affair at Jamestown, was quite apparent. Nearly everywhere he had had large audiences. At Hartford, as at Pittsburgh, all seats were filled and large numbers sat on the stage. Utica reported an enormous house; Newark the largest lecture gathering of the season. Poughkeepsie, Newtonville, Mt. Vernon, Hornelville, and many others reported large audiences.

The reports of the lecture were also, on the whole, gratifying. Here and there a dissident note appeared, as at Pawtucket, New York, where it was observed that his lecture "was intensely interesting to those who were intensely interested," but in the main the audiences went away happy and pleased, and Mark Twain knew it.

According to Albert Bigelow Paine, when Mark Twain received an invitation to lecture on the night of February 2, he replied that he was sorry to disappoint the applicant. He could not lecture because he "was going to marry a young lady on that evening, and he would rather marry that young lady than deliver all the lectures in the world."[36]

CHAPTER NINE

THE MOST DETESTABLE CAMPAIGN

> *. . . the most detestable lecture campaign that ever was. . . .* —MARK TWAIN
> TO MRS. FAIRBANKS, P. *158.*

A S A CONSEQUENCE of his outstanding popularity on the platform during the season of 1869–70, Mark Twain was in great demand for immediate engagements to finish out the season interrupted by his marriage. So great was the demand, indeed, that on March 1, less than a month after his marriage, he felt compelled to print a circular, from his office at the Buffalo *Express,* declining all requests:

> DEAR SIR: In answer, I am obliged to say that it will not be possible for me to accept your kind invitation. I shall not be able to lecture again during the present season.
>
> Thanking you kindly for the compliment of your invitation, I am,
>
> > Yours truly,
> > SAM'L L. CLEMENS
> > *(Mark Twain)*[1]

Will Clemens, writing for *Ainslee's Magazine,* August, 1900, claimed that Mark Twain finally relented and made lecture trips to towns in New York State during April and May, but there is no evidence at hand for this statement.

In the meantime, requests for Mark Twain lectures for the

following season were pouring into James Redpath's office. The bureau manager hopefully passed them along to Elmira where Mark Twain was spending the summer. The brilliant young humorist had become one of his leading stars, and he wanted very much to be able to list him as early as possible in *The Lyceum* bulletin, in order that local committees, in planning their winter series, could relieve their ordinarily heavy didactic course with at least one light entertainment program. Furthermore, Mark Twain had become commercially valuable to the bureau, and Redpath was not one to forego profit through lack of persistence.

But Mark Twain's situation had altered in a way to put all thoughts of lecturing into the background. Early in the spring of 1870 he asked Redpath to count him out for the season. He had decided, he said, to give up lecturing forever. He had ciphered things down to a fraction; knew just what it would cost to live and could make enough money without resorting to the platform.[2]

A little later, on May 10, he informed Redpath that he guessed he was out of the field permanently, and was sending his circular declining invitations to all applicants. He now had, he declared, "a lovely wife; a lovely house, bewitchingly furnished; a lovely carriage, and a coachman whose style and dignity are simply awe-inspiring—nothing less—and I am making more money than necessary—by considerable, and therefore why crucify myself nightly on the platform."[3]

Redpath did not give up easily, but in July he regretfully informed the readers of *The Lyceum* that Mark Twain would probably not lecture the coming season. If he changed his mind the bureau would announce the fact early in the autumn.[4] Further along in the same issue he inserted a brief statement explaining why, for a season, a star of the lyceum firmament was being lost. "The fate of Midas has overtaken this brilliant but unfortunate lecturer. He lectured—and made money; he edited —and made money; he wrote a book—and made money; and when a relative under the guise of friendship, perpetrated 'a first class swindle' on him, he made a great deal of money by that. Even the income-tax collector has failed to soften the rigor of his fate. Under these disheartening circumstances he cannot be made to see the necessity of lecturing: 'Just for a vault full of silver he left us!' R. & F."[5]

As matters turned out, however, it was not so much affluence that took Mark Twain out of lecturing during the season of 1870–71 as a series of tragic circumstances and duties which made all thoughts of lecturing impossible. First of all, his editorial activity for the Buffalo *Express* occupied much of his time. In addition he had assumed the editorship of a department in the *Galaxy* magazine and had contracted to furnish ten pages a month for its columns.[6] Furthermore, the publishers of *Innocents Abroad,* and other publishers, were clamoring for another book. In response to these requests he was considering a trip west "to rub up old California memories."[7] While such a trip never materialized, he immediately began putting his memories on paper and planning the book which eventually became *Roughing It.*

In the meantime, on August 6, after several weeks of painful illness from cancer of the stomach, his wife's father, Jervis Langdon, died, leaving the whole family, including Mark Twain, exhausted from his care. A few weeks later another tragic circumstance developed. Emma Nye, a friend of Livy, who had come to Buffalo to visit with the Clemenses, took sick and died. The burden of Emma Nye's care and death, coming so soon after Jervis Langdon's lingering death, left the Clemenses physically all but prostrate. Then, on November 7, Langdon Clemens, Mark Twain's first child, was born prematurely. It was clearly no summer to give any thought to lecturing.

By late fall and winter of 1870 it became apparent to Mark Twain that for a number of reasons his connection with the Buffalo *Express* was failing to give him the satisfaction he had looked for. For one thing, he had paid too much for his share of the stock. Nor did he any longer enjoy living in Buffalo.[8] He had found more stimulating friends and literary companions in Hartford, Connecticut, and was much attracted to that city. As soon as matters could be arranged, he sold his interest in the *Express* at a considerable loss and moved his family to Hartford.

Once more in debt and needing quick income, Mark Twain was again ready by the early summer of 1871 to accept lecture engagements. Informing Redpath of his intention, he immediately began work on a subject that had recently occupied a good deal of his attention and one that he considered suitable for the lyceum circuit. It had to do with the rights of boys, and for a few days at least he was convinced that this would be his principal lecture for the season. Redpath advertised it in the July issue of *The Lyceum* under the title An Appeal in Behalf of the Extended Sufferage to Boys.[9] But by the time that issue had gone to press, Mark Twain had abandoned the Boy lecture in favor of others. On July 27 he informed Redpath, with an air of exuberance, "Wrote another lecture—a third one—today. *It* is the one I am going to deliver. I think I shall call it 'Reminiscenses of Some Pleasant Characters Whom I Have Met,' (or should the 'Whom' be left out?). It covers my whole acquaintance—kings, lunatics, idiots, and all. Suppose you give the item a start in the Boston papers. If I write fifty lectures, I shall only choose one and talk that only."[10] Before the day was over, however, he was less sure. He again wrote Redpath: "Don't be in a hurry about announcing the title of my lecture. Just say: 'To be announced.' Because I wrote a new lecture today, called simply 'D. L. H.' During July I'll decide which one I like best."[11]

In the meantime, remembering the hardships of earlier tours—the long train rides between engagements, the miserable hotel accommodations, the poor halls to speak in—he wrote Redpath a detailed letter in which he laid down a number of conditions to guide the bureau manager in making up the schedule of engagements. So far as possible, he wanted lecture stops only along main lines, and reservations only in the best hotels. He wanted to open in Boston and not go farther west than St. Louis.[12] He did not want to lecture in churches,[13] and he didn't want to lecture in Buffalo or Jamestown.

He mortally hated Buffalo society. He had filled the house there on an earlier occasion and they hadn't even the politeness to thank him.[14] As for Jamestown, all lecturers hated it, and after his experience there in the spring of 1870, he wanted no more of that place.[15]

Redpath knew by this time that the popular humorist had some of the characteristics of a prima donna, and may have written Mark Twain that it would be extremely difficult, if not impossible, to make up a schedule that observed all the conditions imposed upon him. At any rate, on August 8 Mark Twain acknowledged to Redpath that he was "different from other women; my mind changes oftener. People who have no mind can easily be steadfast and firm, but when a man is loaded down to the guards with it, as I am, every heavy sea of foreboding or inclination, maybe of indolence, shifts the cargo. See? Therefore,

if you will notice, one week I am likely to give rigid instructions
to confine me to New England; the next week send me to Arizona;
the next week withdraw my name; the next week give you full,
untrammeled swing; and the week following modify it. You must
try to keep the run of my mind, Redpath; it is your business,
being the agent, and it always was too many for me. . . . Now
about the West this week, I am willing that you shall retain all
the Western engagements. But what I shall want next week is
still with God."[16]

While Mark Twain was struggling to make up his mind
about what he wanted and didn't want, the local committees in
various parts of the country had no difficulty in making up their
minds that they wanted Mark Twain. As summer advanced to
fall so many requests for him had reached the bureau that Redpath, wondering what he should do with them all, conceived a
plan which he ventured to hope might relieve the difficulty. Why
couldn't Mark Twain write a lecture and have some other person
deliver it (presumably before audiences Mark Twain would not
face)? And since women lecturers were currently in great demand,
why not a woman?

None of Redpath's suggestions ever fell flatter. "The idea
of a *woman* reading a *humorous* lecture," Mark Twain emphatically informed the bureau manager, "is perhaps the ghastliest
conception to which the human mind has yet given birth." It
was a depressing thought. He doubted that any "woman ever
lived who could read a densely humorous passage as it should be
read." They can do tenderness well, and pathos, and tragedy;
but they fail in humor, *"except in the sparkling vivacious kind—
high and brilliant comedy."*[17] In fact, except for Anna Dickinson, who had pleased him mightily when he had heard her lecture in New York in 1867,[18] Mark Twain was not favorably impressed by women lecturers. Kate Field, who had achieved brief
celebrity during his early tour years with her highly lauditory
lecture on Dickens, and Olive Logan, vigorous defender of
women's rights, both came under his critical scrutiny.[19] Even
Anna Dickinson did not entirely escape. Like most women, he
observed, she flubbed her climaxes by dragging toward it instead
of exploding it on her audience.[20] Now if Redpath had a competent man whom Mark Twain could take home and drill for a
week or two, the scheme might work. But it probably wouldn't
work anyway, because no satisfactory financial agreement could

be arranged in the event the substitute were successful. Obviously, the scheme was completely impractical.[21]

But let us return to the lectures. What the initials D. L. H. stood for remains a mystery. Mark Twain never again alluded to it. After some correspondence, a title for the Reminiscences lecture was agreed upon. Redpath advertised it as Reminiscences of Some Uncommonplace Characters I Have Chanced to Meet. According to Dixon Wecter, it featured Artemus Ward; Dick Baker the quartz miner; Riley the journalist; the king of the Sandwich Islands; and others.[22] In the original plan it no doubt included all these, but by the time Mark Twain brought it to the platform it appears to have undergone considerable change. A reporter for the Bethlehem, Pennsylvania, *Daily Times* claimed that the lecture was made up almost entirely of humorous incidents from *Innocents Abroad,* including the Roman mummy and the Christopher Columbus stories having to do with the Roman guides.[23] After only three disappointing performances in eastern Pennsylvania (Allentown, Wilkes-Barre, and Scranton), he abandoned it. At the close of the Scranton lecture he apologized for his poor performance on account of sad news from home.[24] Telegraphing the committees at Easton and Reading, he asked them to allow a postponement of his lectures there until November. Again, his reason for making the request was that sad news from home made it impossible for him to give his remarks their wanted pungency. To his wife he confided the real reason: "This lecture *will never* do. I *hate* it and won't keep it."[25]

From Reading, Mark Twain hurried at once to Washington, D.C., where he was booked to lecture on Monday, October 23. He spent the weekend furiously writing a new lecture, confining himself this time to only one of the uncommonplace characters he had met, Artemus Ward. This lecture was usually advertised in the papers as Artemus Ward, Humorist, or The Life and Sayings of Artemus Ward. Actually, however, the lecture contained so many of Mark Twain's own anecdotes that the Washington reporters were puzzled about how to classify it. The audience was puzzled, too, for it had come to hear the Reminiscences lecture and wasn't aware of a change in program until Mark Twain announced it from the platform. Next day, under the facetious title, Mark Ward on Artemus Twain, the Washington *Evening Star* said of the lecture, "Mark Twain talked about 'Artemus Ward' last night to the largest audience ever assembled at Lincoln Hall. Very pleasant talk it was, characteristically droll and full of humor, but many of his audience seemed to be in the same condition of painful doubt and uncertainty as the audience described by him who attended the first lecture of A. Ward on The Babes in the Wood. They didn't know whether he was lecturing on uncommonplace characters, or only one uncommonplace character. . . . 'Artemus Ward' aforesaid . . . in fact, they couldn't get the hang of it all. Then again, when they came to study it all out today they have A. Twain's jokes so mixed up with M. Ward's . . . no, M. Twain's with A. Ward's . . . and get so confused trying to separate Clemens from Browne that their mental condition is pitiable. No lecturer has the right to trifle with his audience in that kind of style."[26]

At later lecture stops, in a facetious attempt to explain his shift from the advertised Reminiscences lecture to that on Ward, Mark Twain declared that when he had started out with the idea of lecturing about some people he had chanced to meet, he had intended to include Josephus, John Bunyan, Martin Luther, John Knox, Oliver Cromwell, and others but concluded he couldn't get them all within the scope of a single lecture. Therefore, he had selected only one uncommonplace character, Artemus Ward.[27] But even this piece of humor often failed to satisfy his audiences, especially if they were displeased with the Artemus Ward lecture on other accounts.

Criticisms of the new lecture caused Mark Twain some uneasiness. To Livy he confided that his lecture needed considerable patching and that he was trying to weed Artemus Ward out, and work himself in. "What I say *fetches* 'em—but what *he* says don't."[28] Yet, despite all his patching, the Artemus Ward lecture was not particularly well received especially in smaller communities. A number of criticisms were leveled against it. It was nothing more than a desultory and incoherent biography of the great showman, in which Mark Twain merely retold some of Ward's old jokes, but doing Ward the disservice of mutilating them so as to be hardly recognizable. In speaking of Ward's ancestors, he alluded to the Pilgrim fathers with disrespect. At Norristown it was particularly noted as evidence of poor taste that Mark Twain twice pointedly mentioned on the platform that Artemus Ward had received $500 an hour when he lectured, with the obvious implication that his own fee was too small.[29]

The most damaging charge, however, as the following extract from the Erie, *Weekly Observer* reveals, had to do with the propriety of the lecture. "The impropriety of discussing the life and character of a dead popular favorite in a burlesque vein is manifest to every person of refined taste, and it comes with peculiarly bad grace from a brother humorist who aspires to rank among the first class talent of his profession."[30]

The criticisms, however, were by no means all unfavorable. At Philadelphia, Boston, Worcester, Lowell, and elsewhere, his lecture was praised for its rich humor, for his illustrations of the difference between wit and humor, for the amusing self-introductions, and for the touching poem about the death of the great showman with which Mark Twain frequently closed his lecture and which he apparently read with skill and effect.

Nevertheless, the Artemus Ward lecture lasted only about seven weeks. For a number of reasons it failed to satisfy Mark Twain. In the first place, as he discovered, the life and writings of Ward were so well known in the East that he could say little that was new; and when he introduced variations of Ward's stories for greater effect, the audience detected them and were often not pleased. Then, too, he sensed a danger, reflected in criticisms of his lectures, in speaking humorously about Ward before audiences that loved him and remembered his sparkling wit with admiration. And wasn't he inviting unfavorable comparison with a most distinguished fellow humorist? His critics were probably right—Artemus Ward was too beloved, too admired, and too recently dead to be treated humorously.

It is possible, of course, that none of these considerations played a major role in causing him to abandon the lecture. During the early part of the tour he was reading proof on his new book *Roughing It,* and it is highly probable that he saw in its material far more promise of a good lecture than in Artemus Ward. At any rate, by December 8 Mark Twain was again ready to make a change. "Notify all hands," he instructed Redpath, "that from this time I shall talk nothing but selections from my forthcoming book, 'Roughing It.' Tried it last night. Suits me tip top."[31] Nevertheless he did give the Artemus Ward lecture about three times more, probably to avoid criticism from audiences who had not yet been notified of the change.

The Roughing It lecture was unquestionably the most successful in Mark Twain's repertoire for the season 1871–72, and

Lyceum Circular.

January 1, 1872.]   BOSTON LYCEUM BUREAU.   [Redpath & Fall.

"MARK TWAIN."

(S. L. CLEMENS.)

MARK TWAIN will not repeat his lecture on "Artemus Ward, the humorist," this season, but will deliver, instead of it, a new lecture, entitled

"ROUGHING IT,"

which he first gave in Chicago, Dec. 19.

To enable our correspondents to advertise it properly, we reprint the subjoined notices of the Chicago press.

The Chicago Times said: —

"MARK TWAIN'S LECTURE.— The brilliant and successful conclusion of the first season of the South-Side Star Lecture Course, on last evening, must have been as gratifying to the managers as it was flattering to 'Mark Twain,' whose genius drew together one of the largest as well as the most intelligent audiences, that have ever gathered in this city to hear a lecture. Over a week ago, nearly all the seats were taken ; and it became apparent, that, in order to provide for the crowd that would throng the Michigan-avenue Baptist Church, arrangements more extensive than usual would have to be made. Accordingly, on last evening, the transepts of the church, which open into the main auditorium by means of hanging-doors, were thrown open, thus adding nearly a thousand seats, — every one of which, as well as those in the body of the church, was filled. In the presence of this vast audience, at the appointed time, came strolling on the platform, in the most indifferent and careless manner, the 'hero of the hour.' As he repeats the lecture to-night on the West Side, and we have been requested to restrain our desire to tell some of the good things he said, so that they will be enjoyed the more by those who have had the good fortune to secure seats, we do not give any detailed report of his lecture.

"It consisted chiefly of reminiscences of 'roughing it' in California, with accounts of new discoveries in the animal, vegetable, and mineral kingdoms, glowing descriptions of exquisite scenery, droll yarns of life in the bush, which convulsed the audience with laughter during the entire evening. Nothing could have been more quaint than the unconscious manner in which he related his stories, and the half-surprised look he assumes when his audience laughs at some of the serious things he says."

The Chicago Evening Post said: —

"The entertainment of the season, thus far, was the curious, disjointed, delightful talk of Mark Twain (Clemens is his married name), last evening, in the Michigan-avenue Baptist Church, below Twenty-second Street.

"Every seat in the house, four hundred chairs in the aisles, and standing-room for two or three hundred, were crowded full, when the lank, lantern-jawed, and impudent Californian bestrode the stage as if it were the deck of a steamboat, and, getting to the middle of the front, rubbed his bony hands, and gazed around. A thin man of five feet ten, thirty-five, or so, eyes that penetrate like a new gimlet, nasal prow projecting and pendulous, carrotty, curly hair, and mustache, arms that are always in the way, expression dreadfully melancholy, he stares inquisitively here and there, and cranes his long neck around the house like a bereaved Vermonter who has just come from the death-bed of his mother-in-law, and is looking for a sexton. For something like a minute, he says not a word, but rubs his hands awkwardly, and continues the search. Finally, just as the spectators are about to break into giggles, he opens his capacious mouth, and begins in a slow draw, — about three words a minute by the watch.

"Mr. Twain took his auditors on a flying trip to California and the mountain mining-regions ; giving alternate glimpses of sense and nonsense, of humor, burlesque, sentiment, and satire, that kept the audience in the most sympathetic mood. He dipped into pathos, rose into eloquence, kept sledding right along in a fascinating nasal snarl, looking and speaking like an embarrassed deacon telling his experience, and punctuating his tardy fun with the most complicated awkwardness of gesture. Now he snapped his fingers ; now he rubbed his hands softly, like the catcher of the he continued it without change through February, despite his fear for a time that he would have to abandon it in the general area of Chicago after the Chicago *Tribune* published large portions of it verbatim.[32]

Writing from Champaign, Illinois, a few days later, he reported his unhappiness about the Chicago paper to Livy, revealing that he had written another lecture and was in the process of committing it to memory. He declared he would "begin talking it the moment I get out of range of the cursed Chicago *Tribune* which printed my new lecture [Roughing It] and so made it impossible for me to talk it with any spirit in Illinois."[33]

During the closing weeks of the tour Mark Twain begged Redpath not to make further bookings and was apparently happy when local committees canceled their enagagements.[34] He even refused an invitation from Boston, telling Redpath he would rather rot than fill another engagement.[35] The "most detestable campaign that ever was" came to an end late in February at Amherst. While it turned out to be quite rewarding financially, in other ways it was probably the most troublesome and least satisfying of all his tours, filled with worries about contriving new lectures and being satisfied with few of them.[36] To Mrs. Fairbanks he confided, "I think I built and delivered 6 different lectures during the season—and as I lectured 6 nights in the week and never used notes, you may fancy what a fatiguing, sleepy crusade it was."[37]

A puzzling fact about the 1871–72 tour is that Mark Twain delayed so long before deciding to use passages from his manuscript of the book *Roughing It*. Since he was reading proof of the book on tour, his mind was full of these materials. Why, then, did he delay, and burden himself with the less ready materials of the Reminiscences, Artemus Ward, and other lectures which he claims he wrote and delivered? Did he or his publishers question the advisability of using portions of the manuscript for lecture purposes prior to publication? It hardly seems plausible that Mark Twain should have questioned it, since he must have known that his lectures on The American Vandal Abroad had helped tremendously in advertising *Innocents Abroad*. The fact is that when he did start giving the Roughing It lecture, he advertised the book quite openly from the platform. At Grand

Circular advertising Roughing It.

Rapids, Michigan, for example, he informed his audience that he had a book in press, a book of six hundred pages, the style the same as in *Innocents Abroad,* "splendidly illustrated, and costing only . . . " but he wasn't canvassing for the book. No; only if they wished it, he could read them thirty or forty pages of it from memory, or indeed the whole 600 pages.[38] But of course he *was* advertising the book, if not canvassing for it, and the unanswered question remains: Why didn't he start with the lecture much earlier and thus extend through the entire tour the opportunity of bringing his book before the public?

CHAPTER TEN

LIFE ON THE LECTURE CIRCUIT

*I made an ass of myself leaving a mean
hotel at midnight to hunt up a good one
twenty miles away.* —MY FATHER, MARK
TWAIN, P. *48.*

ONE EVENING in July of 1869, some months after he had
closed his first big tour, Mark Twain had a long visit with
a famous fellow lecturere and humorist, Petroleum V.
Nasby. They sat up till daylight reading Bret Harte and laughing over their recent western lecture experiences. What a wonderful magazine article one could make of them, Mark Twain
thought, and regretted that they could only be told in private.[1]
The truth is that during the long midwestern tour many of
his experiences had been anything but jolly. Now, in retrospect,
they took on a fairer light because in the meantime high fortune
had come to him. His difficult courtship of Olivia Langdon had
finally succeeded, and a formal engagement had been announced
on the preceding February 4. Furthermore, he was reading the
final proof sheets of *Innocents Abroad* and was elatedly awaiting
its publication. Forgotten, or at least pushed into the background now, were the long rides in smoky, gas-lit coaches, the
inconvenient schedules, the missed connections, the poor hotels,
the snow, the cold, the fatigue, the thousand and one petty
annoyances, and above all, the loneliness.
During the early lecture tours in California and Nevada,
the hardships of travel and the difficulties encountered (if one

excepts the mock robbery on the Divide between Gold Hill and Virginia City in 1866) do not seem to have troubled Mark Twain. On the contrary, as we have seen, he made these tours in a spirit of high anticipation and exuberance, pleased with the public acclaim which followed him from town to town, and extremely gratified with the newly discovered source of income from an alternate career which public lecturing brought him. Fortunately, these tours were brief ones over familiar and loved territory. Furthermore, moving about day by day satisfied his restless spirit and gave him a sense of accomplishment which allayed, to a degree at least, his uncertainty about the future which had oppressed him, especially after his return from the Sandwich Islands. Also during these tours he reveled in the excitement of facing audiences which responded so appreciatively to his humor, and in the warm receptions he received from old friends and acquaintances. Nowhere in his letters is there any suggestion of fatigue, loneliness, or irritation about the hardships of travel. That was to come in the later tours, and to increase in volume and vehemence until the very thought of tour lecturing made him shudder and resolve to quit the public platform forever.

The difficulties and annoyances that assailed him during the long tours on the lecture circuit were, in the main, those that every tour lecturer of his day had to contend with. There were times, for example, when he became separated from his baggage. As a consequence he was without clean linen for a number of days and had to lecture in his "bob-tail" coat, which made him feel awkward and uncomfortable on the platform.[2]

Frequently there was difficulty about getting his mail, usually because of poor train connections or because the chairman of the local lyceum committee was carrying it in his pockets and forgetting to give it to him. One such incident occurred at Lockport, New York, in 1869, about three weeks after his engagement to Olivia Langdon, when he was eagerly expecting letters from her at every stop. "I have raced my feet off in the storm," he raged in his next letter to her, "trying to find the villain [of the committee] who has got your letter. If it were not wicked, I could cordially wish his funeral might occur tomorrow."[3] The trains were, of course, a never-ending source of complaint. In the winter they were cold and drafty; always they were dirty, smoke-filled, and poorly lighted. Worst of all, they did not run on schedule, causing him at times to miss important connections and to go as much as thirty-six hours without sleep. There were times when he had to ride the cabooses of coal trains to keep an engagement, and on one occasion he hired a locomotive at $75 to keep from having to rise at two o'clock in the morning in order to get to his next stop.[4]

Typical of the sort of difficulties he sometimes encountered was a series of incidents that took place one cold December night in 1871. He had gone to bed considerably after midnight. At four o'clock he had got up again and had gone breakfastless down to the train station. There, to his surprise and delight, was a sleeping car which he might have been occupying all night had a member of the lecture committee or anyone at the hotel informed him about it. He took a berth and the train left at once. It was due in Chicago in two hours, hardly enough time to settle down comfortably, but because of a number of unexpected delays it did not arrive till three o'clock in the afternoon—nine hours late. In all that time he had had nothing to eat. To add to the irritation and fatigue, at the Chicago station there was neither a cab nor anyone to help him with his baggage. As a result, he had to carry two heavy bags half a mile to Robert Law's house where he was to stay for the night. Now, he hoped, he could go to his room and get a few hours of rest.

But Law had other plans. He wanted to show his guest the ravages of the recent great Chicago fire. So, for two whole hours of a bitter cold day they "capered among the solemn ruins" in an open buggy. Dog tired by now, he nevertheless felt compelled for courtesy's sake to sit up and talk with his host till nearly ten o'clock. Thereafter, in his room, he worked till after midnight amending his lecture for the following evening. When he finally turned in, he wrote Livy, he slept like a log—"I don't mean a fresh, *green* log, but an old dead, soggy, *rotten* one, that never turns over or gives a yelp."[5]

Mark Twain soon learned to be cautious about accepting invitations for overnight entertainment in the homes of members of the local lyceum committees or of other citizens who wished to entertain him. Usually these invitations were prompted by the desire for social prestige. There were exceptions, of course, and Mr. Law of Chicago appears to have been one of them, since he speaks of him without irritation. Always he enjoyed being a guest in the home of "Mother" Fairbanks in Cleveland, of Dr. A. A. Jackson of Chicago, whom he had celebrated as the guide-destroying doctor in *Innocents Abroad,* and of his old California and Nevada friends. In Norwich, New York, there was a family by the name of Mason he enjoyed staying with. "I am here, the guest of Judge Mason," he wrote Mrs. Fairbanks, "—& happy. Mrs. Mason is *so* good, & so kind, so thoughtful, so untiring in her genuine hospitality, & lets me be just as troublesome as I want to, and I just love her. . . . She lets me smoke in the house, & bring in snow on my boots, & sleep late, & eat at unseasonable hours, & leave my valise wide open on the floor, & my soiled linen scattered about it just exactly as I leave it and as it *ought* to be to make life truly happy."[6]

But these exceptions were rare. A lecturer, he once declared, dreads a private house more than he dreads two hundred miles of travel. In spite of himself he can't respect their unholy breakfast hours. Then he feels drowsy and miserable for two days and gives two audiences a poor lecture.[7] In Canton, Massachusetts, at the home of Mr. Ames, the son of Oakes Ames, the railroad magnate, Mark Twain was especially incensed because no smoking was allowed on the premises. It was the last time, he declared, that he would ever again stop in a New England private house. "Their idea of hospitality is to make *themselves* comfortable *first,* and leave the guest to get along *if he can.* . . ."[8] A few nights later he had a worse experience in the home of Dr. Sanborn in Rockport, Massachusetts. He vented his wrath by reporting to Livy that the "dog at whose house I staid" had taken advantage of his hospitality and had asked him to knock ten dollars off the price of the lecture in order to keep the local lyceum society alive so that they could hear him again next year. Mark Twain bluntly refused and declined the next morning to have breakfast with his host. On leaving, he offered Sanborn ten dollars for his night's lodging. And when the doctor accepted it and said he would hand it to the committee, Mark Twain insisted he would do nothing of the kind—that he "must accept the ten dollars for his New England hospitality or not take it at all." Sanborn took it, Mark Twain reports, with a world of servile thanks.[9]

That Mark Twain's insistence upon privacy and the freedom to do as he pleased often made him a difficult guest is revealed not only in his letters to Livy, but in a comment Josh Billings once made about the unwisdom of those who invited Mark Twain to stay overnight at their house. "Think ov asking

Mark Twain home with yu. . . . Yure good wife has put her house in apple-pie order for the okashun; everything is just in the right place. Yu don't smoke in yure house, *never*. Yu don't put yure feet on the center-table, yu don't skatter the nuzepapers all over the room. . . . But if yu expeckt Mark Twain to be happy, or even kumfortable, yu hav got to buy a box of cigars . . . and yu hav got to move all the tender things out ov yure parlor. . . . Yu hav got to ketch and tie all yure yung ones . . . for Mark luvs babys only in theory;[10] yu hav got to send yure favorite kat over to the nabors and hide yure poodle. These are things that hav to be done, or Mark will pak hiz valise . . . and travel around yure streets . . . until lektur time begins."[11]

Fortunately, Mark Twain's private hosts were usually kind and generous people. Indeed, their fault, from his point of view, was their very generosity. They wanted to entertain him, and in so doing, invaded his privacy, and kept him up late when he wanted to go to bed. He felt he had to fit into their domestic routines when he wanted nothing better than to be left alone and do as he pleased. For these reasons he preferred to stay in hotels. They were the only proper places for lecturers. There he could be absolutely free. And if he felt ill-natured, he could ring up a domestic and give him a quarter and then break the furniture over his head. Thereafter he could go to bed "calmed and soothed and sleep peacefully as a child."[12]

But if the hotels gave him freedom they frequently gave him no comfort, no conveniences. "Here I am in a hotel—The Clinton House—& a villainous one it is, shabby bed, shabby room, shabby furniture, dim lights—everything shabby & disagreeable."[13] On another occasion he said, "I made an ass of myself leaving a mean hotel at midnight to hunt up a good one twenty miles away. The train was behind time and didn't get me here till 2:30 A.M.—and wasn't it bitter cold—the coldest night of the season. No one at the depot. Hunted up the hotel myself and carried my own baggage. Found every bed in the house occupied—so I had to sit up in a fireless office the rest of the night. My splendid overcoat earned its cost—every cent of it. My body was not cold for a moment—but all the shirts and things I could find in my valise wouldn't keep my legs warm. I wouldn't tell who I was, or I could have fared better—I was too savage."[14]

The splendid overcoat was a huge sealskin with the hair on

the outside. He had bought it especially for protection against the rigors of winter encountered on his lecture tours. A sealskin cap matched it. He did not, he claimed, wear it for grandeur;[15] yet he was proud of it and found it wonderfully comfortable. "All days are alike to my sealskin coat—I can only tell it is cold by my nose & by seeing other people's actions."[16]

It is easy to understand that with all the fatigue of traveling and the necessity of being physically and mentally fit during his hour and a half on the platform that Mark Twain was often irritable and at times savagely unreasonable in his conduct. An incident which occurred at the new Clinton House in Iowa City, Iowa, in January of 1869, and reported in the Iowa City *Republican* the next day serves as a case in point.

"The morning after the lecture nothing was seen of him up to nine o'clock, and the landlord in his kindness, went to his room to see if he might not be in want of something, but received a storm of curses and abuse for disturbing him. Of course the landlord retreated and left him. After a while a terrible racket was heard and unearthly screams, which frightened the women of the house. The landlord rushed to the room and there found a splendid specimen of the vandal and his works. There, before him, was the veritable animal, with his skin on at least, but not much else, and in a towering rage. He had kicked the fastenings from the door, not deigning to open it in the usual way—that would have been too much like other folks. He poured upon the landlord another torrent of curses, impudence and abuse. He demanded to know where the bell pull was. The landlord told him they were not yet up, as they had not yet got the house fully completed. His kicking the door open and his lung performance were his substitute for a bell. At two o'clock P.M. he had not dressed, and whether he did before he left on the five o'clock train we did not learn."[17]

If the landlord *had* watched Mark Twain leave the hotel and try to board an omnibus for the depot, he would have seen him slip and fall with all his weight on his left hip, causing him to be stiff and sore for days.

Mark Twain reported the incident at the Clinton House in his next letter to Livy; consequently we get a glimpse at his side of it.

"I have just been doing that thing which is sometimes so hard to do—making an apology. Yesterday morning, at the hotel in Iowa City, the landlord called me at 9 o'clock, & made me so mad I stormed at him with some little violence. I tried for an hour to go to sleep again & couldn't—I wanted that sleep particularly, because I wanted to write a certain thing that would require a clear head & choice language. Finally I thought a cup of coffee might help the matter, & was going to ring for it—no *bell.* I was mad again. When I *did* get the landlord up there at last, by slamming the door till I annoyed everybody on my floor, I showed temper again—*& he didn't.* See the advantage it gave him. His mild replies shamed me into silence, but I was still too obstinate, too proud, to ask his pardon. But last night, in the cars, the more I thought of it the more I repented & the more ashamed I was; & so resolved to make the repentance good by apologizing—which I have done, in the most ample & unmincing form, by letter, this morning. I feel satisfied and jolly, now."[18]

Unfortunately, the landlord either failed to show Mark Twain's letter of apology to the editor of the Iowa City *Republican,* or what is more likely, the editor decided not to print it because he hadn't liked Mark Twain's lecture anyway. In his opinion it was a humbug and he wouldn't give two cents to hear him again.[19]

To escape any interference with his privacy Mark Twain sometimes deliberately chose obscure hotels and occasionally employed the pseudonym "Samuel Langhorne" while on tour.[20] He especially disliked being disturbed before lecture time and often took his meals in his room. At the St. James Hotel in Danville, Illinois, in 1872, he had so many visitors calling on him that he told a local reporter he might have made some money if he had posted a doorkeeper and charged 25¢ for admission.[21] Sometimes, however, he relented and allowed visits, as during a thirty-hour layover at Geneseo, New York, where a group of about a half dozen young men, twenty to twenty-five years of age, received him at the depot with a handsome open sleigh and drove him to his hotel. They accompanied him to his room, invited a number of others in, ordered cigars, and made themselves entirely at home. But Mark Twain found them hard to entertain, for they wanted primarily to hear him talk. After dinner they asked him to join them in a sleigh ride, but he begged off and told them he was tired and wanted to go to bed. Later in the evening they came up to his room again. Again he spoke of retiring, but without effect. "Then I rose & said, 'Boys, I shall have to bid you a good-afternoon, for I am stupid and sleepy—& you must pardon my bluntness, but I *must* go to bed.' " "Poor fellows," he wrote Livy, "they were stricken speechless . . . & went blundering out like a flock of sheep, treading on each other's heels in their confusion." He went to bed and tried to sleep; but as he lay there and thought about how ungrateful he had been after all their wholehearted friendliness and youthful enthusiasm to entertain him, he got up again and dressed "and gave the boys *all* of my time till midnight & also from this noon till I left at four this afternoon."[22]

Nothing exasperated Mark Twain more on cold winter days than to be driven around a town in a freezing open buggy to see the places of local interest. When he was staying at a hotel and paying for his accommodations, he could refuse without suffering any pangs of conscience; but when he was an overnight guest in a private home he felt obligated to repay his host's hospitality by accepting the invitation. Once, in a Massachusetts town, after his host had taken him on a freezing tour about the city, Mark Twain described the pattern which these tours usually took and his reaction to them. The places of interest always consisted of the mayor's house; the ex-mayor's house; the house of the state senator; house of an ex-governor; house of a former member of Congress; the public school; the female seminary; the paper mill or factory of some kind or other; the cemetery; the court house; the plaza; and the place where the park was going to be—"& I must sit & shiver & stare at a melancholy grove of skeleton trees & listen while my friend gushes enthusiastic statistics & dimensions." All towns appeared to him to be alike, with the same stupid trivialities, all demanding an impossible interest at the suffering stranger's hands. Why wouldn't they believe him when he pleadingly protested that he wished to remain quietly at his room. And then, after all the principal places of interest had been visited, they had to call on the prominent citizens of the community—the mayor, the richest man, the village wit with his stale jokes and humorous profanity, the village editor, and a lot of other people he didn't wish to see. What a fervent prayer of thankfulness rose up in his heart when by accident some of them were not at home.[23]

Mark Twain's exasperation at being disturbed by people who wished to entertain him or merely to visit with him at the hotels or on the railway cars by no means indicated a wish to be solitary. He was by nature a very sociable person and loved the company of friends. But during each of the great lecture tours in the late 1860's and the early 1870's he was always engaged in concurrent enterprises which constantly occupied his attention, or was beset by personal problems which needed his care. During the tour of 1869–70, for example, he was courting Livy, and much of the courtship was carried on by mail. On the cars, in the hotels, in private homes where he was a guest, in depots—wherever he found an opportunity he wrote letters to Livy. Furthermore, he was reading proof on his book *Innocents Abroad,* and when a batch of it reached him at some town en route, he worked on it as opportunity offered, often staying up till the early hours of the morning to finish it. Under such circumstances it is understandable that he resented interruption or interference with sleep. Each succeeding tour found him similarly burdened. There were books in preparation, articles to write, lectures to revise, and business matters to attend to. As a matter of fact, Mark Twain was customarily under so much tension from matters totally unconnected with lecturing during each of the tours that one can readily believe that the hour and a half on the platform was, except for his correspondence with Livy, the happiest part of his day.

Though he was too busy to be lonely, loneliness was nevertheless one of his chief charges against the hardships of lecturing. It was not that he was lonesome for company, that is, just *any* company, but at times he so desperately missed Livy and home that he found excuses for canceling engagements and caught the first train back to Elmira or Hartford. Sometimes, when stranded in a small town over Sunday, he walked, out of sheer boredom, through the local cemeteries, idly deciphering old weather-worn inscriptions and contemplating the Great Leveler which wipes out all distinctions of life on earth.[24] The lonesomest times, of course, were such holidays as Thanksgiving, Christmas, and New Year's Day, which families want most to celebrate together. Then the very essence of loneliness sank into his soul, and the only way he could find relief was to stay in his room and pour out his thoughts and feelings in letters to his loved ones.

To relieve the tedium of long train rides he always carried with him literary classics that had come to his attention, books by prominent literary contemporaries, and such things as Livy wanted him to read. During the courtship days the books she sent him were usually chosen with the hope that they might influence him to become a cultivated Christian gentleman; for her image of him at that period was that of a talented, generous, and well-meaning man whose manners and habits, unfortunately, were unregenerate, who was indifferent to sacred things, and unstable—a diamond in the rough. She sent him religious tracts and sermons and marked passages for his special attention. On one occasion she sent him a sermon by Henry Ward Beecher on self-culture and self-denial, which Mark Twain knew was sent for his sober contemplation and improvement. "I like the sermon," he wrote her, "not withstanding it was below Mr. Beecher's average. You found little in it to mark, but what there was, was Truth, & came home to me."[25] Under her strong influence he himself occasionally bought a few books of sermons and read them with care. A volume by the Reverend George Collyer of Chicago pleased him especially. Collyer's sermons, he believed, lacked the profundity and insight into the secret springs and impulses of the human heart, and the penetrating analysis which distinguished Beecher's sermons, but they were more poetical, polished, and felicitously worded, and he promised to send them to her soon.[26]

The best record available of Mark Twain's reading while on tour is to be found in his letters to Livy, for it appears that he was as much concerned to cultivate his wife's reading habits and her critical ability as she was to improve his personal habits and manners. Though there is never the slightest hint of conscious intention discoverable in any of these letters of guiding her into the role of an author's wife, the unconscious intention was unquestionably there. Often when he read a book he marked it and sent it to her, knowing that she would read it and ponder the passages marked. "I am glad I marked those books for you, since the marking gives you pleasure. . . . I have marked many a book for you, in the cars, & thrown them away afterward, not appreciating that I was taking a pleasure of any great moment from you."[27]

Some of the books he read, however, he did not mark—deliberately. There was *Tristram Shandy*, for instance. He liked the "Recording Angel" passage, but declared that the book, on the whole, was coarse and "I would not have you soil your pure mind with it."[28] Nor did he mark *Gil Blas*. "If you have not read it you need not. It would sadly offend your delicacy, and

I prefer not to have that dulled in you. It is a woman's chief ornament."[29]

He read *Gulliver's Travels* and was charmed with it; and reread *Don Quixote,* an early favorite, and sent Livy the marked copy.[30] He found Elizabeth Barrett Browning's *Aurora Leigh* a trifle obscure and asked Livy to help him interpret it. He tried to read *Hypatia,* a book his friend Twichel had given him. He considered it one of Kingsley's most tiresome books. But Charles Reade's *The Cloister and the Hearth* enchanted him. "I read it with a pencil by me, sweet-heart, but the book is so uniformly good that I find nothing to mark."[31] He promised to send her one of Lowell's books but hated to mark it and mar the dainty pages.[32] And there were a host of other books, among them a French political novel called, *A Member From Paris, The Golden Legend* by Jacobus de Voragine, Alexander Smith's *Edwin of Deira,* Ballentine's *Erling the Bold,* and Longfellow's *The New England Tragedies.*[33] These, with the magazines and the metropolitan newspapers which he read regularly, helped ease the boredom of travel and the lonesomeness when these oppressed him.

Perhaps it is well that during the early tours Mark Twain gave up, at Livy's request, the drinking of liquor, and was persuaded, for a time, that he was the better off for it.[34] This act of self-denial kept him out of the taverns when loneliness or boredom oppressed him. But her attempt to make him give up smoking was a different matter. He was an inveterate smoker and found infinite solace and pleasure in it at all times, and especially while on tour. And no amount of logic convinced him that it was either socially objectionable or physically harmful. Had she been able to imagine the tortures her husband would have been subjected to by giving up smoking, it is doubtful that she would have suggested it even as a possibility. There was only one thing, he declared, that would make him give it up. "I will lay down this habit which is so filled with harmless pleasure, just as soon as you write me or say to me that *you desire it.* . . . I stopped chewing tobacco because it was a mean habit, partly, and partly because my mother desired it. I ceased from profanity because Mrs. Fairbanks desired it. I stopped drinking strong liquors because you desired it. . . . I did what I could to learn to leave my hands out of my pantaloon pockets and quit lolling at full length in easy chairs, because you desired it. . . .

Discarding these habits curtailed none of my liberties—on the contrary the doing it released me from various forms of slavery. With smoking it is different. No argument against it is valid—and so to quit it I must do without other reason than that *you* desire it."[35] Fortunately Olivia Langdon had the good sense to drop the matter and thus allow her harrassed husband to continue his tours indulging a pleasure which gave him unmeasured solace and contentment, and which no doubt often provided a much needed safety valve when the pressures of life threatened to become unendurable.

Out of the deep well of his long experience with the vicissitudes of tour lecturing Mark Twain was in no measure facetious when he once advised his friend Thomas Nast to be piously grateful that he was permitted to spend his days quietly at home. "Do all your praying now," he said, "for a time is coming when you will have to go railroading and platforming, and then you will find that you cannot pray anymore, because you will have just time to swear enough."[36]

LECTURES IN ENGLAND

*. . . it is something magnificent for a
stranger to come to the metropolis of the
world and be received so handsomely as
I have been.* —LONDON « TIMES, » OCT. *19,
1873.*

IF REDPATH was aware of Mark Twain's utter disgust with the
tour of 1871–72 and of his resolve never to return to the platform again, that knowledge did not deter him in the slightest
from trying to book the popular humorist for the season just
ahead. He well knew from previous experience that Mark
Twain's resolves were not to be taken too seriously, that they expressed a hope or a momentary mood rather than an irrevocable
purpose, and that in the end financial circumstances determined
whether or not he would accept further lyceum engagements.
By July 12 Redpath had already received requests for Mark
Twain from over twenty cities, most of them large, ranging all
the way from Boston to Lawrence, Kansas. It was a heavy list
for so early in the season, and he was sure it could be greatly extended as soon as he could positively announce that Mark Twain
would lecture and could supply a title. "Will you? Or won't you?"
he wrote Mark Twain hopefully. "When will you decide?"[1]

Mark Twain's reply is not preserved, but it is apparent that
he had no intention whatever of lecturing during the season of
1872–73. As a matter of fact, by the time Redpath's letter had
reached him he was already making arrangements for a trip to

England and had set August 21 as the date of departure. His plan was to travel through various parts of the British Isles to collect material for a book that would do for that country what *Innocents Abroad* had done for Europe and the Holy Land. A second objective was to secure a British copyright for *Roughing It*.[2]

He arrived in England in early September, and from that time until November 12, when he returned home, he was so frequently entertained by the literary and civic leaders of London that he scarcely had time for anything else. Among the visitors who came to his rooms to call on him was George Dolby, the well-known British impresario who had managed Dickens' reading tour in the United States in 1867. The purpose of Dolby's visit was soon clear. He wanted to win Mark Twain's consent to give a brief series of lectures in London, and, if the English liked the American humorist's colloquialized fun, to book him for an extended tour in the provinces.[3] But, for the present at least, Mark Twain declined. There was too much business to attend to, and too much sociability, to take on the burdens of lecturing.[4] He promised, however, through the pages of the London *Times,* that he would return the following year and lecture a month during the autumn upon "such scientific topics as I know least about and consequently feel least trammelled in dilating upon."[5]

In the meantime Redpath had not given up hope that Mark Twain would return home in time to lecture for at least part of the season of 1872–73. His urgent letters reached the humorist in London, full of news about the large number of requests that had come in for him from all along the lecture circuit, and of attractive fee offers from some of the larger cites. By way of trade gossip which Redpath thought might interest his friend, he reported that Henry M. Stanley, the African explorer, was getting $50,000 for one hundred nights. But Mark Twain was not encouraging. As a matter of fact, the report of Stanley's earnings only served to stir up again his smoldering discontent about his own fees on the lyceum circuit. From London he wrote Redpath it cost two dollars to hear Parepa, a popular Scottish operatic soprano, sing two pieces that took only fifteen minutes. If people in America were required to pay a single dollar to "hear one of us fellows squeak, it would become the fashion to hear us . . . we would always have a full house. When I yell again for less than $500 I'll be pretty hungry. But I haven't any intention of yelling at any price."[6] In the same letter, however, he reported that he was polishing up his Roughing It lecture "just for fun." The phrase "just for fun" was obviously ironic. He certainly had no intention of lecturing free of charge. He simply meant to convey to Redpath that when he lectured in London, he expected to receive substantially higher fees than he had been receiving in the United States.

Mark Twain returned to New York on November 26. In December, news of the death of King Kamehameha V was flashed across the country. The New York *Tribune*, aware of Mark Twain's familiarity with Hawaii, hastened to invite him to furnish them with correspondence relating to the affairs of the Islands. He immediately complied with two long letters which appeared in the *Tribune* January 6 and 9, and concluded with a plea for the eventual annexation of the Sandwich Islands by the United States.[7]

As might have been expected, work on the *Tribune* correspondence had the effect of reviving his interest in the Sandwich Islands lecture, which had long been his favorite. Consequently, when urgent invitations reached him to take it to the platform again, some of them at higher fees than he had ever before received, he consented to accept a limited number of engagements. The first lecture took place on January 31, 1873, in Hartford. He gave it free for the benefit of Father Hawley's missionary work among the city's poor. On February 5 he lectured in New York, February 7 in Brooklyn, and February 10 in New York again. He might have accepted other invitations, some of them tantalizingly lucrative (for example, an offer of $500 for a lecture at Philadelphia), had Livy approved. But she and the family were making plans to return to England in a matter of weeks; and preparation for departure, business matters in connection with the building of their new house in Hartford, and Mark Twain's collaboration with Charles Dudley Warner on *The Gilded Age*, needed immediate attention.

By early June the Clemenses were in London, comfortably housed in the Langham Hotel, Portland Place and Regent Street, where their apartment soon became a gathering place for London's literary notables. During July and August they toured Scotland and Ireland. Then, in September, after two weeks of busy sightseeing and shopping in Paris, they returned again to their rooms at the Langham. By this time Mrs. Clemens had become so homesick that she wanted to return to Hartford at

BROOKLYN ACADEMY OF MUSIC, FEB. 7th

Tickets at 244 Fulton St. and
172 Montague St.

Advertisement of lecture at the Brooklyn Academy of Music, February 7, 1873.

once. Furthermore she had grown weary of sitting through interminable dinners, often in the company of ladies who seemed to take pleasure in snubbing each other. Added to this was the fact that the hotel fare was making her ill.[8] Nevertheless, there were compelling reasons which made an immediate return seem unwise. Matters concerning the copyright of *Roughing It* had not yet been satisfactorily concluded. There was also the promise to Dolby that he would lecture before finally returning to America. It was Livy's opinion that the extra money the British copyright of *Roughing It* would bring in hardly seemed worth another month's absence from home. Only when it was argued that her husband's reputation in England would greatly be enhanced by staying on and lecturing did she withdraw her objections.[9]

Dolby proceeded at once to set up a schedule of lectures to begin the second week of October in the Queen's Concert Rooms in Hanover Square. The choice of this hall, the most fashionable in London, instead of the more popular Egyptian Hall where Artemus Ward had lectured, was unquestionably made at Mark Twain's request. He meant to lecture to the elite of London and to charge high prices for admission. If there was reputation to be won in England he wanted to win it from its leading citizens.[10]

About a week before the opening lecture, he resorted to a publicity device which he had found effective at home. He informed the public through a humorous letter in the *Standard* that he intended to lecture in London on the subject of the Sandwich Islands. In view of the current frenzy in England about these Islands, he declared, he felt called upon to supply information about them and to allay the unwholesome excitement that had arisen among the British people. He had always, he said, been able to paralyze the public interest in any topic he chose to lecture on; therefore he had chosen this one.[11] The next day an extended announcement appeared, informing the public that Mark Twain would deliver a lecture of a humorous character entitled Our Fellow Savages of the Sandwich Islands, beginning Monday evening, October 13, and continuing each evening through the following Friday. On Saturday there would be a matinee performance beginning at three o'clock. It further informed the public that Mark Twain had spent several months in the Islands and was well acquainted with his subject. The lecture might be expected, therefore, to furnish considerable matter of interest. The latter part of the announcement was no doubt introduced by Dolby, with Mark Twain's endorsement, to dispel the notion which some Londoners might entertain that the lecture would consist chiefly of humor and would be unrewarding as to substance. The price of admission was advertised at five shillings for reserved seats, and three for the unreserved, or approximately $1.25 and 75 cents respectively in American money.[12] While this did not match the admission price to hear Parepa sing, it was apparently sufficient to satisfy Mark Twain's ego, especially in view of the fact that he was lecturing to a highly cultivated audience in the world's leading metropolis.

Mark Twain's decision to use the Sandwich Islands lecture for the opening series in London, instead of Roughing It, which he had planned to use prior to the death of Kamehameha, was in every way a wise one. The British public was well informed about Hawaii from the reports of Captain Cook, their famous fellow countryman who had explored the Islands and who had later met his death there in a shore fight with the natives. Furthermore, the British carried on a brisk trade with the Islands, and still entertained the hope of eventually gaining political control over them, if not their outright annexation. Now that the whole Hawaiian matter had again been brought into focus by the death of the king, Mark Twain recognized the timeliness of the Sandwich Islands lecture and the importance of the strong current of public interest flowing through the British press.

The decision was also wise for another reason. In preparing the lecture for his American audience during the past winter, he had carefully revised it, deleting passages which had no direct bearing upon the subject, and removing certain indelicacies. For example, he no longer offered to illustrate cannibalism on the platform. He also eliminated the reference to the cannibal who wanted to see "how a white man would go with onions."[13] What revisions he made later for the purpose of pleasing his London auditors cannot be determined from the newspaper reports of the lecture, since few attempts were made to synopsize it or to reproduce the anecdotes. In any event, it appears that he considerably improved it and felt confident that the British would like it.

As the evening of the opening lecture drew near, the leading newspapers and some of the magazines noted his presence in the city and announced the lecture. *Punch*, the magazine of humor, took especial delight in publicizing Mark Twain's appearance by means of puns upon the American humorist's pen name suggested by various passages in the works of Shakespeare. In the issue of October 18, it printed the ingenious though somewhat laborious lines:

> 'Tis time we Twain did show ourselves. 'Twas said
> By Caesar, when one Mark had lost his head:
> By Mark, whose head's quite bright, 'tis said again;
> Therefore, "go with me, friends, to bless this Twain."

In a later issue, borrowing somewhat loosely from *A Midsummer Night's Dream* and from *A Winter's Tale*, it continued its punning by speaking of "Twain, at large discourse," and by referring to his brief stay in the city with the line "Mark, a little while." It announced its confidence in his ability to please, with "Twain Can Do't."[14]

If Mark Twain was in any measure overawed by the fashionable London audience that faced him on the evening of October 13 in the Queen's Concert Hall, the newspapers betrayed no hint of it. On the contrary, it appeared obvious from his complete self-possession that he had long familiarity on the platform. As he emerged from the wings and lounged onto the stage (there was a little table with a water tumbler and glass, but no lectern) he was greeted with "a storm of welcome."[15] He came on alone, in full evening dress. There was no one to introduce him. He carried no manuscript, and not once, it was observed, did he refer to a note.[16] After standing for a moment gazing quizzically at his audience, he proceeded to introduce himself in the same humorous fashion as was his custom before American audiences. He then began his lecture and talked about an hour and twenty minutes. At the close, to the delight of his audience, he launched upon a description of the scenic beauties of the Islands, which proved so "singularly eloquent," that the hearty and prolonged applause which greeted it recalled him to the platform twice.[17]

Except for one particular, the newspaper reports of the lecture were gratifyingly favorable. The humorous self-introduction, one critic noted, made the audience too prone, subsequently, to regard the performance only from a comic point of view, thus doing the lecturer an injustice.[18] It was a perceptive observation which pointed to a dilemma that constantly faced Mark Twain, whose comic treatment and manner tended to obscure the fact that his lecture had substance.

While it was observed that his platform manner was not particularly graceful, his easy sort of awkwardness nevertheless made his audience feel remarkably at home.[19] And if the quality of his voice was not particularly pleasing, the "delicious" California dialect made up for it by adding a delightful piquancy to his speech.[20] One critic declared he spoke slower than any other man he had ever heard.[21] As for the lecture itself "a more genuine intellectual treat" had not been presented to the public in years. It was useless to quote good things from it, however, for "like butterflies they could not be netted without losing their sheen."[22] The lecture was also praised for its remarkably shrewd observations about men and events, revealing that the American humorist had a reflective mind. Unlike the kind of treatment that Artemus Ward would have given the Sandwich Islands, it was observed, Mark Twain's lecture contained a considerable amount of information. Even the most serious in the audience, the reporter declared, could profit from it. While it was admitted that the humorous outweighed the serious, it was nevertheless clear the American deeply appreciated the pathos of life which lay at the base of all true humor.[23] It was further observed that though the lecture gave an impression of artlessness, behind Mark Twain's colloquial style of speaking and his unusually plain manner of storytelling lay a calculated and studied art.[24]

At the close of the matinee lecture on Saturday, October 18, loud applause recalled Mark Twain to the platform. The audience knew that he was making a hurried trip to America and that it would be a month before he would return to resume his lectures. As he faced them now, and sensed the warmth of their appreciation of his performances, he was deeply moved. His voice faltered as he acknowledged his gratitude. "I do not wish to appear pathetic," he said, "but it is something magnificent for a stranger to come to the metropolis of the world and be received so handsomely as I have been. I simply thank you."[25]

Whatever doubts Mark Twain may previously have entertained about his ability to amuse and satisfy the sophisticated and fashionable London audiences at the Queen's Concert Hall, they had now entirely evaporated. There had been a splendid first night with an audience any author might have been proud of. The response had been hearty and warm. Congratulations, many from London's leading men of letters, had come to cheer him. Fearing that on the second night attendance might fall off, Dolby had judiciously "papered" the house on the assumption that many Britishers were unacquainted with American humor and that only skillful management could draw them out. The precaution hardly proved necessary. Attendance, good from the start, had steadily increased to the point where extra seats had to be brought in and the stage itself had become crowded.[26] The *Daily News,* the *Morning Post,* the *Times,* the *Saturday Review, Once A Week,* the *Standard*—all had given his lectures fairly extended and flattering attention. Mrs. Clemens, homesick as she was, was deeply impressed. She could no longer doubt that her husband's brilliant success had been worth staying over for.

The next day the Clemenses started for home. They proceeded to Liverpool where Mark Twain had accepted a lecture engagement for the evening of October 20, prior to his departure on the "Batavia" the next day. A packed house assembled to hear him, and when he emerged from the wings, the audience gave him a splendid ovation. The passages that apparently gave the most delight were the character sketches of Morgan the trader, Harris the legislator, and of one of the recent kings. The Stammering Story, with its intermingled whistling, was reported as one of the funniest features of the lecture. High praise was also accorded to his eloquent discription of the soft, dreamy beauty of the far-off "toy kingdom" of Hawaii.

Nevertheless, the Liverpool reporters found some aspects of the lecture not entirely to their liking. His humor was tricky rather than delicate, and the suddenness of his hits disarmed the audience from criticizing their clumsiness. His jokes were sometimes "laboriously ambushed to provoke the sudden roar," and his mannerism was one which would soon pall because it would not bear repetition. As for his speech, it proceeded in a "low, rather droning monotone, except when poetical and descriptive passages were introduced. Then his voice gathered force and became increasingly earnest.[27]

After only six days in the United States Mark Twain returned alone to London, arriving there about November 20, and again took up residence at the Langham. About twelve days later, on December 1, he resumed his Sandwich Islands lectures, appearing each evening through December 5, with two matinees, one on Wednesday, December 3, the other on Saturday, December 6. Here came a two-day break. For various reasons he decided it was time to give up the Sandwich Islands lecture in favor of Roughing It. Perhaps he felt he had sufficiently drained public interest in the Islands and wished, before leaving England, to share with his London audiences the humor of his experiences on the silver frontier in Nevada. He had, as we have seen, begun the revision of Roughing It several months earlier, with the specific purpose of presenting it to English audiences. On the other hand, it simply may be, as Livy reported to Mrs. Fairbanks, that he had grown weary of the Sandwich Islands lecture and wanted a change.[28] In any event, he was quite aware that a new lecture would serve to enhance his reputation by manifesting his versatility.

Roughing It on the Silver Frontier, as the new lecture was called, opened on the evening of December 9 and continued each evening through December 20. In addition, there were four matinees, one each Wednesday and Saturday during the two-week period, bringing the total number of lectures in the new series to sixteen.

To arouse public interest in the Roughing It lectures, Mark Twain again resorted to an advertising device he had frequently used at home. He supplied the London *Morning Post* with a delightfully amusing letter in which he apologized for the fact that his earlier lectures had failed to attract prominent members of the government whose presence would have given distinction to his entertainment. The owner of a waxworks had offered to remedy this circumstance by supplying him with a couple of kings and some members of the nobility, and had assured him that they would not only sit out his lecture, but would still be sitting there after he left. As a consequence, Mark Twain declared, he had considered advertising that on a particular evening His Majesty King Henry VIII would honor his entertainment, on another evening William the Conqueror, and so on during the series. Unfortunately, a porter had fallen down the stairs and smashed Henry VIII, and something had let go inside William the Conqueror and he lost all his sawdust. He had given up the idea advertising the presence of Moses and Aaron when he discovered that the waxworks owner had been fraudulently exhibiting the Siamese Twins to represent these characters. If he could manage to get hold of a king for just a little while, he concluded, "I would take good care of him and pay the tab myself."[29]

If newspaper reports may be trusted, the new lecture was extremely well attended, the large room often filling long before the performance began. Many people asked each other where the silver frontier was which Mark Twain proposed to talk about. Some had the notion it was in Mexico. But even the explanation that it was in Nevada left many in the dark concerning its precise location. Almost all Britishers knew where the Sandwich Islands were, but few had ever heard of Nevada. And those who had heard of it had only the foggiest notions concerning its location and its significance in the general economy of things.

On opening night, with many new faces before him, Mark Twain sought to put his audience on the alert and to set the tone for his lecture by resorting to impersonation. Stepping out upon the platform in full evening dress, he assumed the air of a manager with a disappointing announcement to make. "Mr. Clemens," he began apologetically, "has landed at Liverpool, and had fully expected to reach London in time, but"—here he paused long enough for murmurs of disappointment to arise. Then, assuming his own identity, he announced he was happy he had been able to reach London in time for the lecture after all and that he was now ready to proceed.[30]

He began by explaining where the silver frontier was. He had lived in that portion of the world three years. It was inhabited by editors, thieves, miners, gamblers, and desperadoes of all sorts. On the way there he had assisted at a Mormon marriage, but did not wait to see it all finished. The weather and scenery was quite unlike that of England. During eleven months of the year there was no rain, no thunder, no lightning, no dew. There was no twilight. There were three kinds of birds in the district, the magpie, the raven, and the sage hen. The region was so dry that birds crossing it had to carry their own provisions. Hay for draft animals was so scarce it cost $150 a ton. The six thousand Indians who inhabited the territory fed chiefly upon grasshoppers, which are not popularly regarded as nourishing diet. He described the dust storms whipped up by the Washoe Zephyrs, the villainous rivers of Nevada, the wretched Indians that inhabited the area, and, in contrast, the wondrous beauty of Lake Tahoe in the nearby mountains, and the imposing Mount Davidson at whose base lay Virginia City.[31] By means of humorous anecdotes he told of some of his own experiences on the silver frontier—his efforts at silver mining, riding a bucking Mexican plug, a duel with a rival editor, the wild games of poker at the mines, and others. After describing some of his own poker-playing escapades there, which hugely delighted the audience, he suddenly became unctuous and declared, "All that was long ago. I never gamble *now.*" And then, after a pause, "Unless I can make something by it." The story of the duel appears also to have been a favorite, winning prolonged applause as Mark Twain concluded the anecdote by saying, "But I never fight duels now. If a man insults me now, do I challenge that man? Oh, no! I take him by the hand, and with soft persuasive words lead him to a dimly lighted apartment and—kill him!"[32]

Like the Sandwich Islands lecture, Roughing It on the Silver Frontier was praised for its eloquent description of scenery—the desert, the mountains, the grand beauty of Lake Tahoe—and for the fact that it contained a substantial amount of informative matter. It was admitted, however, that the tendency was toward the droll rather than toward the didactic. It was noted too that if his humor here and there was of the broadest kind, it never offended by going beyond the line.[33] In closing, Mark Twain amused the audience by expressing the hope that he had said nothing in his lecture which might provoke a massive depopulation of England by causing a flood of emigration to set in toward the strange county he had described.[34]

A few days after beginning the Roughing It lectures, and only three weeks after his return to London, Mark Twain was already complaining of loneliness and wishing he were back home. To Livy he confided that while he found great pleasure in his hour on the platform, and in seeing the splendidly dressed and bejeweled men and women in his audiences, the long daylight hours leading up to those moment of pleasure were boring.[35]

Actually, if Mark Twain's later recollections of the occasion may be accepted at face value, the hours of boredom appear to have been relatively short. Certainly he had little opportunity to be lonesome, though with Livy no longer with him, the hotel and the view out the windows looked less cheerful. The fact is that he had been in London scarcely a day or two when an old California friend, Charles Warren Stoddard, dropped in on him. He had met the California poet in San Francisco in 1864, probably in the office of the *Golden Era,* which from time to time printed some of Stoddard's pieces. Mark Twain was fond of the Californian despite the fact that he was somewhat effeminate, unworldly, and given to religious enthusiasms. Stoddard had come to London to supervise the publication of the British edition of his *South Sea Idylls*. To maintain himself abroad he had made arrangements to provide the San Francisco *Chronicle* with a series of travel articles.[36] When he arrived in England and discovered that Mark Twain was lecturing in London, he immediately called on him at the Langham. Mark Twain was delighted to see him, and not only invited him to share his rooms, but hired him as a secretary, primarily in order to have his company.

Different as the two men were in character and personality, the arrangement proved mutually agreeable. Speaking of their association afterward, Mark Twain explained that he paid Stoddard fifteen dollars a week and board and lodging to sit up nights with him and dissipate.[37] It was the Californian's duty to amuse him from the close of one lecture to the beginning of the next. He was to "listen to the wise and instructive conversation between Dolby and me, and to laugh in the proper places." More seriously, it was Stoddard's duty to reply to all correspondence concerning lecture engagements, and to some of the social invitations. He kept a file of newspaper clippings relating to Mark Twain's lectures and presence in England, and also of the Tichbourne trial which was then prominently featured in the British press and which interested Mark Twain greatly. Some of these duties, Mark Twain later reported facetiously, Stoddard did not perform well. He did not laugh boisterously enough at some of the stories (the off-color ones, presumably) which Mark Twain and Dolby exchanged in the evenings after the lecture when the three men gathered in Mark Twain's rooms to go over the events of the day. "Neither did he always keep awake when Dolby and I were talking," he continued. "He would lie down on a couch and sleep and interrupt the conversation with a species of snores which he had acquired in some foreign land."[38] Aside from these minor defects, he acknowledged, he found Stoddard a most delightful companion.

Fortunately, Stoddard also recorded his association with Mark Twain during the final series of the London lectures, and it is through his account that we get delightfully intimate glimpses at the manner in which the long hours between lectures were spent, and of Mark Twain on the platform. Breakfast, he reported, was served at 12:30, and usually consisted of toasted muffins, chops, and coffee. After breakfast, cigars were brought in, along with the day's leading newspapers, mail, messages from friends, and invitations to dinners and to various social functions. After these had been attended to, and Stoddard had filed the newspaper clippings and the correspondence, the two men usually went out for a slow walk through nearby parks or shopping areas, or attended some social affair.

If there were no other demands upon their time, the hour before dinner was spent quietly in their rooms talking. At this time Mark Twain sometimes sat down at the piano and lustily sang jubilee songs or old favorites like "Ben Bowline," rolling the vowels. He sang fairly well, and his obvious love of jubilee songs surprised Stoddard, who had not previously known this side of Mark Twain's character.

As soon as dinner was over Mark Twain dressed for the evening's performance. Always inclined to be careful about his appearance on the platform, he was especially meticulous in London, for he wished to appear especially well groomed before his fashionably dressed audience. Shortly after seven o'clock a carriage came and took them to the Queen's Concert Hall where they arrived at approximately seven-thirty. Just offstage, Stoddard reports, there was an anteroom with a few chairs where they waited while the audience assembled and where Stoddard could look out the window and count the carriages as they rolled up in the gloom of the fog to let out the occupants.

During the half-hour wait before curtain time, Mark Twain paced the room nervously, in sharp contrast with the careless, somewhat shambling manner which characterized his emergence from the wings. At precisely eight o'clock the audience signified its readiness for the progam to begin by applauding; and Mark Twain, waiting for the familiar signal, immediately prepared to make his appearance. Stoddard escorted him to the foot of the stairs that led to the stage and stood there long enough to see him move slowly toward the table, bow to the audience, and gaze intently about him for a minute or so before he began to speak. Stoddard then made his way by means of a hallway to the royal box where he took a seat, hidden from view by the drapery, and listened to the lecture. It was not long before he knew a good deal of it by heart and recognized any deviations which Mark Twain introduced from one lecture to the next.

Sometimes, as Stoddard looked from behind the drapes to get a view of the audience, the house was so filled with fog that he could scarcely see more than the area near him. It had come trailing in with the audience, filling the entire hall with a greyish gloom. One evening, when the fog had darkened the hall more than usual, Mark Twain called out to his audience, "Perhaps you can't see me, but I am here," and then proceeded with his lecture.

What interested Stoddard most about the lectures was the difference from one night to the next in the way in which Mark Twain's humor was received. Some evenings the audience seemed so cold that one could feel the depressing effect the moment one entered the hall. On other evenings a general cheerfulness pervaded the house, and Mark Twain felt it instantly and knew that it was the prelude to a good evening. What interested Stoddard, too, was the marked difference in the way certain humorous passages were received on different nights. Sometimes a particular joke produced laughter immediately all over the house. On another evening it caught hold feebly in one corner and then ran diagonally across the hall, exploding on the last bench. Other jokes which provoked loud and prolonged laughter one night scarcely brought a ripple the next.

When the lecture was over Stoddard met Mark Twain in the anteroom where Dolby presently joined them. Then, as soon as they were free, they proceeded to Mark Twain's room at the Langham, stoked up the fire in the fireplace, ordered cocktails, snacks, and cigars, and sat for hours going over the events of the evening, yarning about experiences of other days, and drifting into the sorts of stories which embarrassed Stoddard and sent him to the couch to sleep, or pretend to sleep, while the other two talked the night away.[39]

The London lectures came to an end on December 20. At Dolby's prodding, Mark Twain had agreed to a limited number of performances in the provinces, but with the London engagements over, and the Christmas season at hand, he grew impatient to return to the United States to be with his family. "I have *so much* to go home to and enjoy with a jubilant joy," he wrote Joseph Twichell,[40] as homecoming time neared, that he canceled tentative engagements at Glasgow, Edinburgh, Belfast, Dublin, and Cork, giving as an excuse that these provincial cities lacked halls large enough to suit him.[41] For some reason he filled an engagement at Leicester on January 8, 1874, before proceeding to Liverpool. There, on January 9, he gave the Roughing It lecture, and, on the following day, Our Fellow Savages of the Sandwich Islands.

On the evening January 9, in an affectionate gesture of

*Page of pictorial notes for Roughing It on the Silver Frontier
(England, 1873), presented to Charles Warren Stoddard as a
memento. Courtesy Henry W. and Albert A. Berg Collection of
the New York Public Library, Astor, Lenox, and Tildon Foundations. Copyright © 1967 by the Mark Twain Company.*

farewell after the lecture, he presented Stoddard with a page of notes on Roughing It which he had used on the platform. On the face of it, along a margin he inscribed, "We're done with this, Charles, forever! Yrs. Mark Twain, Liverpool, Jan. 9, 1874, 10:30 P.M."[42]

The next evening, at the close of the Sandwich Islands lecture, Mark Twain read, as an encore at the request of the audience, the Jumping Frog story.[43] The last performance over, Stoddard and Dolby, who had accompanied him to Leicester and Liverpool, joined Mark Twain at his hotel and spent the remainder of the evening with him. But in contrast with the gaiety of earlier after-lecture gatherings this one turned out to be quite solemn. Mark Twain had fallen into a state of vague forebodings about the trip home and his future. Presently something prompted him to quote the Biblical passage, "Remember the Creator in the days of thy youth," but he couldn't recall the rest of it. When they got a Bible and checked the passage, he found the story of Ruth and read it aloud to them so movingly that there were tears in his voice.[44] It was some time during this evening, probably, that Mark Twain tried to pay Stoddard for his services, and Stoddard refused to accept a penny. Eventually, Mark Twain reports, he had to smuggle the money to him through Dolby after leaving England.[45] It was five o'clock in the morning before the three men sought to get some rest. Later that morning, on January 13, Stoddard and Dolby returned to London, and Mark Twain boarded the "Parthia" for home.

It was about January 25 when he arrived in Hartford, and almost immediately Redpath besieged him with letters urging him to fill out the rest of the winter season on the American platform. With the prestige of the London lectures to support him, he could expect lucrative metropolitan engagements. But Mark Twain was adamant in his refusal. He informed Redpath that he had promised Livy there was not money enough in America to hire him to leave her for as much as a single day.[46] Nevertheless, after a few weeks, he relented enough to accept a few engagements here and there in large cities, concluding his lectures in Boston with a matinee and evening performance on Thursday, March 5. Two days earlier he had telegraphed Redpath, "Why don't you congratulate me? I never expect to stand on a lecture platform again after Thursday night."[47] And for a few months, perhaps, he kept that resolution.

CHAPTER TWELVE

ART OF READING

. . . telling the tale without the book you absorb the character. . . . —MARK TWAIN IN ERUPTION, P. 224.

AUTHORS' READINGS, which became, during Mark Twain's mature years, one of the most popular forms of public entertainment in the United States, derived their chief impetus from the much publicized and highly successful readings by Charles Dickens in New York and other eastern cities in 1867. Mark Twain had been fascinated by this form of entertainment ever since the memorable evening in December of that year, when he sat next to Olivia Langdon, his bride to be, and heard the celebrated Englishman read from his books to a large and distinguished audience in Steinway Hall.[1]

The performance was indeed impressive. Dressed in a black velvet coat with a brilliant red flower on the lapel, Dickens stood, as Mark Twain remembered it many years later, "under a red upholstered shed behind whose slant was a row of strong lights— just such an arrangement as artists use to concentrate a strong light upon a picture."[2] The audience sat in a half-darkened house while Dickens performed in the strong light cast upon him. He read dramatic passages with great force and vigor, for he acted as well as read, and stirred the audience profoundly.[3]

Though deeply moved by Dickens' masterful performance, Mark Twain gave no indication that he hoped, at some future time, to try his own hand at public readings. Perhaps he was too much overwhelmed by the impressive staging and lighting, and overawed by the celebrity of Dickens, who was then at the peak of his fame, even to think of it. At the moment he was far too busy earning his living with his pen and with occasional lectures to give much thought to this new form of entertainment. Besides, except for the *Celebrated Jumping Frog of Calaveras County,* which at that time he tended to regard as a "villainous backwoods sketch," he had no book to read from.

Precisely when and under what circumstances Mark Twain first undertook to read either to public or to private audiences is difficult to determine. He was constantly reading aloud, of course, to his wife and to the friends that came to the Clemens house to visit. By 1873, however, he had become sufficiently impressed with this new form of public entertainment to urge his friend Josh Billings to try readings, since "they are all the rage now."[4] He does not appear, however, to have followed his own advice at this time. The first record of a paid public reading by Mark Twain is contained in a letter to Thomas Nast, the famous cartoonist, proposing a joint tour. In the letter Mark Twain reveals that the preceding winter (that is, the winter of 1875–76) he had made a "little reading-trip" that had taken him to Philadelphia. He had received $300 for a fifteen minute reading given "in the midst of a concert."[5]

In November of 1876, he read, apparently for pay, twice in Boston, on November 21 in Music Hall and the next day in the Chelsea Academy of Music. How extensive his repertoire was for these performances is not known, but the Boston *Transcript,* November 22, mentions three selections, each of which became popular pieces on later programs—The Experience of the McWilliamses With the Membranous Group, My Late Senatorial Secretaryship, and An Encounter With an Interviewer.

Beginning with 1880 the record of readings increases somewhat, though most of the performances appear to have been given for charitable purposes. That year he read at a private house, for charity, A Telephonic Conversation, a highly amusing satire of women's conversation as heard by listening to one side of a dialogue over the telephone.[6] The following year, on February 26, he read in Twichell's chapel in Hartford, reporting later to William Dean Howells that he had had "a most rattling high time" of it, and that the piece that went best was Uncle Remus's "Tar Baby."[7] A few nights later, on February 28, he appeared before the literary society of the United States Military Academy at West Point and read for a full hour and a half to the assembled cadets.[8] Whether Mark Twain was paid for the performance beyond his expenses is not clear, but his program gave so much delight that on two later occasions he was again invited by the cadets to read.[9] About two weeks later he was reading again, this time in the African church for the colored residents of Hartford. No whites were allowed except those he brought with him. Again he read Uncle Remus's "Tar Baby" which he knew would please them because it was a tale they had heard from childhood. A colored choir sang Jubilee songs, which Mark Twain particularly loved, and the entire affair was very pleasing.[10]

If Mark Twain gave readings during the year 1882, they appear not to have been recorded. It was an extremely busy year with literary matters and with the Mississippi River trip which he had decided to take in preparation for writing *Life on the Mississippi*. Nevertheless, his interest in public readings was increasing, and presently he conceived what he regarded as a brilliant scheme. The plan was to gather about him a group of literary notables, William Dean Howells, Thomas Bailey Aldrich, and George W. Cable, and barnstorm the country on a reading tour. They were to travel comfortably in a Pullman car and have their own cook. Besides taking part in the program, Mark Twain was going to act as impresario. He guaranteed each of the others $75 a week and expenses.[11] It was an attractive scheme indeed, though actually too complicated to be practical. At any rate, the others couldn't see their way clear to commit themselves at the moment, and the plan was abandoned until a year later when Cable agreed to a joint tour for the season of 1884–85.

In the light of the record here presented it is clear that by the time Mark Twain undertook his tour with Cable he had given a good deal of thought to public reading, had observed with care other competent readers (Cable among them), and had acquired a good deal of practice and experience in it. The fact deserves some attention because in an autobiographic passage written many years later Mark Twain stated that before going on a tour with Cable he had never tried reading as a trade, presumably, that is, for money. He further stated that during the first week of that tour he made a botch of reading because he hadn't learned how to do it.[12] These statements are dramatic, but in the light of the evidence presented, scarcely accurate.

Before discussing the tour with Cable, however, it would be well to present briefly, at least, Mark Twain's theory of the art of reading. It was a matter that had long engaged his interest, and he found it difficult not to be critical of poor, ineffective reading wherever he encountered it. Clergymen as a class were very bad readers, he once charged, when one might reasonably expect good reading from them. They did not even learn to read the Lord's Prayer well. "A person who does not appreciate the exceeding value of pauses," he pointed out, "and doesn't know how to measure their duration judiciously, cannot render the grand simplicity and dignity of a composition like that effectively.[13] Fortunately, Mark Twain had a good deal to say about the art of reading, especially in his essay How To Tell a Story. This was partly because in later years he was obviously proud of his celebrity as a public reader, and partly because of his constant effort to perfect his own art in it.

It has often been observed that the distinction between lecturing and reading from one's own compositions can be a difficult one to make. The observation applies especially with reference to Mark Twain. The fact is that a considerable portion of all his early lectures could properly be termed readings. When in the Roughing It lecture, for example, he told such stories as The Mexican Plug, The Duel, or His Grandfather's Old Ram, they were no less readings because they happened to be parts of the lecture than they were when they later became parts of a reading program. The techniques which insured the platform success of these passages as parts of the one, also insured their success for the other. Indeed, a great many of the stories and anecdotes which in later years made up Mark Twain's repertoire of readings came from his three principal lectures, The Sandwich Islands, The American Vandal Abroad, and Roughing It.[14]

One of the first discoveries Mark Twain made about the art of reading, especially regarding humorous passages, was that the reader must dispense with the book. How early he had learned this imperative cannot be precisely determined. It is well known, however, that from the very beginning of his platform career he tried to commit his lectures to memory and do away with the manuscript as quickly as possible. That he had learned it by 1868 or 1869 is evident from his report of a reading in Music Hall, Boston, which P. V. Nasby, Josh Billings, and he attended one evening. The performance was by one De Cordova, a newcomer in the field of humor, and they had gone to see how formidable a competitor he might be. When Mark Twain observed that he brought his book with him to the platform and proceeded to read a humorous story from it, he was sure De Cordova would fail. He would fail anyway, Mark Twain believed, because he didn't know how to read even from a book. They had not long to wait. The laughter presently began to relax, the gaps of silence grew longer, and before long the whole house sat dead and emotionless.[15]

The reader, Mark Twain was convinced, must dispense with the book, for in reading from manuscript or printed page you are telling a story at second hand. "You are a mimic, and not the person involved; you are an artificiality, not a reality; whereas in telling the tale without the book you absorb the character, just as in the case of an actor."[16] Great actors, he maintained, would never be able to captivate an audience if they came on stage reading from a book. The "nicest shadings of delivery would be impossible."[17]

One of the most effective artifices lost by a person reading from a book, he believed, was the skilled use of the pause—that impressive, eloquent, and geometrically progressive silence which often accomplished more than the most felicitous combination of words. The reason one loses this powerful artifice is that in reading from a book he cannot measure the pause. It can only be measured in the faces of the audience. Their eyes alone reveal its proper length—the exact length; for nothing but the exact length will meet the needs of the highest skill.[18]

There was, however, a more fundamental objection to reading from a book. Written things, he held, were not for speech. Their form "is literary; they are stiff, inflexible, and will not lend themselves to happy and effective delivery with the tongue—where their purpose is merely to entertain, not instruct; they have to be limbered up, broken up, colloquialized and turned into common forms of unpremeditated talk."[19] This process of colloquializing written pieces and turning them into unpremeditated talk, in final analysis, amounted to a new act of artistic creation which transformed Mark Twain's book passages into different forms, forms far more natural and vital than the literary versions.

To illustrate the transformation of written selections which he gradually limbered up and turned into flexible talk, Mark Twain recorded in his autobiography the version which finally emerged of one of his favorite readings, His Granfather's Old Ram. He admits, on comparing the platform version with the original in Roughing It that he is unable to explain clearly why the one version is precisely suited to platform reading while the other is not. He can sense the difference, he asserts, but finds it impossible adequately to express it.[20] Actually, Mark Twain had previously expressed the difference sufficiently in general terms and did not believe a textual analysis would reveal it. Perhaps, if one may venture to express what seemed so elusive to Mark Twain, the success of the platform version was achieved at that moment when his language, inflection, tempo, and pauses exactly harmonized with the character and personality of the narrator of the story.

Mark Twain's final refinement in the art of reading came to him quite by accident one evening in 1899 during a reading performance in Vienna. He reported it to Howells with characteristic enthusiasm. Since he hadn't well memorized the selections he intended to read (he was apparently lecturing without charge), he did what he had always advised against doing—he appeared on the platform with book in hand. After reading a few lines, he remembered that the sketch needed "a few words of explanatory introduction; and so, lowering the book and now and then unconsciously using it to gesture with," he proceeded with the introduction and discovered that his remarks had carried him into the sketch itself. Fortunately, he had the substance of the sketch and its telling phrases sufficiently well in mind so that he could proceed without the book, "throwing the rest of it into informal talk," limbering it up as he went along, and giving it the snap and freshness of an impromptu.[21]

The peculiar effectiveness of the "new dodge, and the best one that was ever invented," derived, he believed, from two circumstances: first, he was through with the sketch before the audience was aware that he had begun it, supposing that his remarks were still preliminary; and second, "in the heat of telling a thing that is memorized in substance only," he flashed out "the happiest suddenly-begotten phrases every now and then." The second circumstance was actually nothing more than an application of his earlier theory of unpremeditated talk. The first circumstance, however, pretending that he was talking preliminary matter and leading the audience to believe that he would presently return to the book in hand—that was something new. It was "a dodge" he claimed he wished he had learned years ago, for it held an audience so firmly that their attention never wavered even for a moment.

After 1885, when he finished the tour with Cable, Mark

Twain read on a number of occasions and occasionally participated in authors' readings. The latter were sometimes elaborate
affairs with as many as eight or nine distinguished literary men
on the program. Since some of the authors did not time their
readings properly or chose passages that were too long, these
affairs often were stretched interminably;[22] consequently, Mark
Twain, who was meticulous in timing his readings well, usually
under fifteen minutes, went away bored and at times enraged by
these "witch's Sabbaths,"[23] as he once called authors' readings.
Nevertheless, whether he liked them or not, he continued to
participate in them, and to read at many public and private
affairs, always perfecting his art and never satisfied with anything
less than complete mastery.

The question occasionally arises why Mark Twain turned
from lecturing (that is, from such connected discourses as Our
Fellow Savages of the Sandwich Islands, The American Vandal
Abroad, and Roughing It) to readings. The answer that most
readily comes to mind is that he found a program of readings less
burdensome to prepare. It freed him of the necessity of assembling and organizing fresh materials for lyceum tours. In all
probability, however, there were two far more fundamental reasons for shifting from lectures to readings. A program of readings
relieved him of the charge, sometimes made by lyceum audiences,
that he had nothing to say, and that he employed his matter
chiefly as something to hang a joke on. With a program of readings he could unashamedly present a performance without a
moment's thought about instructing an audience. People who
came to hear him read did not expect to be instructed, or demand
a moral tidbit to carry home with them. As a consequence, he
was entirely free to do what he most of all wanted to do—entertain and amuse.

But along with this consideration, and equally important,
was Mark Twain's growing conviction that the art of reading required greater skill than the art of lecturing. People listening to
an informative lecture often felt rewarded by the substance even
though the presentation lacked skill. Not so with readings. To

Page from the Tauschnitz edition of The Adventures of Huckleberry Finn, *used by Mark Twain during world tour, showing how
he modified printed text for use on the platform. Copyright ©
1967 by the Mark Twain Company.*

O, it was a blessed thought!, I never can tell how good it made me feel — cuz I knowed I was doing right, now.

up on me—it ain't too late, yet—I'll paddle ashore
at the first light, and tell." I felt easy, and happy,
and light as a feather, right off. All my troubles
was gone. I went to looking out sharp for a light,
and sort of singing to myself. By-and-by one
showed. Jim sings out:

"We's safe, Huck, we's safe! Jump up and
crack yo' heels, dat's de good ole Cairo at las', I jis
knows it!" We's safe, H. we's safe, shore's you's
    I says: bacon, we safe!"

"I'll take the canoe and go see, Jim. It mightn't
be, you know."

He jumped and got the canoe ready, and put
his old coat in the bottom for me to set on, and
give me the paddle; and as I shoved off, he says:

"Pooty soon I'll be a-shout'n for joy, en I'll say,
it's all on accounts o' Huck; I's a free man, en I
couldn't ever ben free ef it hadn' been for Huck;
Huck done it. Jim won't ever forgit you, Huck;
you's de bes' fren' Jim's ever had; en you's de only
fren' ole Jim's got now." Bless de good ole heart o'
I was paddling off, all in a sweat to tell on him; you, Huck!
but when he says this, it seemed to kind of take
the tuck all out of me. I went along slow then, and
I warn't right down certain whether I was glad I
started or whether I warn't. When I was fifty yards
off, Jim says: Sings out across the water to me + says.
It kind of all unsettled me, + I couldn't
seem to tell whether I was doing right or
doing wrong.

capture and please his audience the reader had to depend almost entirely upon skill—upon manners and techniques and devices he found to be effective to his purpose. And in these skills Mark Twain sought perfection. Convinced by his own storytelling success on the lecture platform, and, as he claimed, by the experience he had gained from his long association with the most expert storytellers of the nation, he felt himself richly qualified to seek eminence in this difficult art.

That Mark Twain became one of the most distinguished readers of his day is universally acknowledged. Literary friends and acquaintances who knew him well and who heard him read were uniform in their praise. Robert Underwood Johnson declared him to be the most perfect reader he had ever known. William Dean Howells spoke of him as the most consummate public performer he had ever seen. "I would never want to read within a hundred miles of *you,* if I could help it," he once said.[24] George W. Cable's estimate was no less high. In 1922, at a meeting in Carnegie Hall, Cable said of his former platform companion, "It was the rigor of his art, an art which was able to carry the added burden beyond the burden of other men's art, the burden of absolutely concealing itself, of making him appear . . . as slipshod in his mind as he was in his gait."[25] Joseph H. Twichell, Richard Watson Gilder, Thomas Bailey Aldrich, and many other prominent contemporaries agreed that in the art of public reading Mark Twain had few if any peers.

CHAPTER THIRTEEN

READING TOUR WITH CABLE

I ought to have stayed home & written another book. It pays better than the platform. —MARK TWAIN, BUSINESS MAN, P. 207.

MARK TWAIN'S repeated and emphatic declarations in the early 1870's that he hated the platform and was giving it up forever, reflected momentary feelings rather than fixed resolves, at least so far as tour lecturing was concerned. During the years that followed there were times when James Redpath begged him to take to the platform again because of the pressure of requests from various parts of the country, and occasionally because he needed him as a replacement. In the fall of 1875, for example, when Henry Ward Beecher and Thomas Nast belatedly withdrew for the season, Redpath was in "the tightest sort of place," and begged Mark Twain to help him out. In response to the appeal, Mark Twain tentatively accepted engagements in Boston and New York during November, planning to repeat his Roughing It lecture,[1] but later withdrew.

Two years later, surprisingly, Mark Twain himself took the initiative in proposing a joint tour with his old friend Thomas Nast. He informed Nast that while he had never expected to take to the platform again until the time had come for him to say, "I die innocent," he was finding it hard to resist the offers that constantly kept arriving. He liked to talk to audiences, but traveling alone was dreary business. Besides, the responsibility of carrying a show alone was too burdensome. For Nast's consideration he proposed a plan for a joint tour through a long list of major cities, which he thought would net them somewhere between sixty and seventy-five thousand dollars.[2]

But the plan fell through and it was not until the summer of 1884 that the thought of another joint tour began to take shape in Mark Twain's mind. Two circumstances appear to have prompted the thought—the establishment of his own publishing house, the Charles L. Webster Company, a costly enterprise, and the forthcoming publication of *The Adventures of Huckleberry Finn*. Since the Webster Company was to publish the book, Mark Twain's investment as author and publisher was unusually heavy.[3] Consequently, as in the past, he again resolved to take to the platform as a rapid and promising way of acquiring funds. Furthermore, he hoped that by synchronizing the advertising of *Huckleberry Finn* with his public appearances on tour, the book sales might be greatly increased. He would thus earn money from lecturing, from increased royalties, and from publishing house profits. From every point of view the tour looked like a productive venture.

The plan this time, however, was not to lecture but to read from his books, and to include in his readings, all along the route, passages from the manuscript of *Huckleberry Finn*, which was scheduled to appear in February, immediately after the close of the lecture season. The decision made, he at once proceeded with the arrangements with characteristic enthusiasm and with a sharp eye to publicity. He proposed to gather about him what he called a menagerie of literary notables (such men as William Dean Howells, Thomas Bailey Aldrich, George W. Cable, "Uncle Remus" Harris, and others), charter a well-appointed Pullman car equipped with dining facilities, and move about the country in style and comfort.[4] It was a "gaudy" plan, as Tom Sawyer might have called it, but actually too complicated to be practical or profitable. In the end, as matters turned out, only Cable could go, or would go, the others declining for various reasons. To a reporter he confessed later that he might have gone on a reading expedition by himself, had no one joined him, but it would not have been pleasant. "I want somebody to keep me in countenance on the stage," he declared, "and to help me impose on the audience. But more than that I want good company on the road and at the hotels. A man can start out alone and rob the public, but it's dreary work. . . ."[5]

At Mark Twain's request, Charles L. Webster drew up a contract with J. B. Pond as agent. Pond was to furnish Cable $450 a week and expenses.[6] During the tour Cable was to be paid whether there were engagements or not, but was not to be paid when absent because of illness or for other reasons. In instances when there were more than two matinees a week he was to receive $60 additional. Pond's obligations were also carefully spelled out. He was personally to accompany them on tour, and in cases of absence, had to supply his brother Ozias. He was to furnish a treasurer and state his salary. It was specified that Pond attend to everything that pertained to business—the rental of halls, the determination of the route, the printing of announcements and programs, the price of admissions, and all other matters of a similar nature. It was Pond's menagerie, Mark Twain insisted, and he must put himself forward as boss and head ringmaster at all times and not ask advice from him. Remembering the hardships of earlier tours, Mark Twain specified that the journeys between engagements be made as short and convenient as possible. He especially insisted that the show must be exhibited from six to ten times in smaller communities before appearing in any big city. This procedure would give them time to prune their program and to "get our hands in."[7]

As was customary, Pond was to receive ten percent of the profits. At regular times, daily or weekly, he was to send Webster a detailed account of receipts and disbursements, and "to pay over to me daily what is coming to me."[8] There is every reason to believe that Mark Twain had complete faith in Pond's integrity as an agent. Indeed, he never waivered in that faith since he again employed him as agent ten years later for the American phase of his reading tour around the world. The record shows that the two men respected each other deeply and enjoyed each other's company. Yet now, because money was so urgent an objective, Pond's bills for expenses, which presently came in after the tour began, aroused his vigilance and prompted him at times to ask Webster to scrutinize them. "Do you watch Pond's accounts pretty carefully?" he wrote in January, 1885. "You know we paid him $300 just about the time I started out the second time; well, I had only reached Indianapolis when there came another expense bill for $1,600. I didn't doubt its correctness, still it was a rouser."[9] In the same letter he chided Webster for not giving him a regular weekly report of the sums of Pond's disbursements. Thereafter, since such reports appear to have reached him, concern about expense bills gave way to others.

In a special announcement concerning the joint reading program Pond listed the two men in such a way as to indicate that they were to have equal time on the program. Perceptively, he informed the public that the pathos of the one would alternate with the humor of the other, knowing from long experience that each, unrelieved, would fail to satisfy. Early in the tour he billed the pair as "Twins of Genius" and advertised the program as one of versatility and genius. Since Cable ordinarily opened the performance and usually sang as well as read, reporters fell into the habit of referring to Cable as supplying the versatility and Mark Twain the genius. And since Pond advertised Cable as a southern gentleman and Mark Twain as a resident of Connecticut, the newspapers soon heralded the joint program, with echoes of the Civil War, as a "literary bridging of the bloody chasm" and as a "rostrum of rapprochement of Louisiana and Connecticut."[10]

Cable began his readings alone about a month before Mark Twain joined him. The first joint program took place on November 5, 1884, in New Haven, Connecticut. Thereafter the tour proceeded through New England and New York. In December it continued west into Michigan, Ohio, and Pennsylvania. At Christmas time there was a recess of nine days. Beginning again on December 29 at Pittsburgh, the way led west through Indiana, Illinois, Missouri, Iowa, Minnesota, and Wisconsin. During the third week in February the two men turned northward into Canada and read before appreciative audiences in several Canadian cities—London, Toronto, Brockville, Ottawa, and Montreal. The final week took them back through New York to the eastern seaboard. The long tour finally came to a close on the last day of February in Washington, D.C., after they had been on the road four months and had covered thousands of miles in their travels. Counting matinees and two-night stands, they had performed over a hundred times in about eighty different cities. It was without question the most celebrated reading tour of the decade and came at a most propitious time for Mark Twain, for soon thereafter, author readings, as a form of platform entertainment in the United States, greatly declined.[11]

The repertoire of readings which Mark Twain had prepared for the tour with Cable was surprisingly extensive. An examination of his notebooks reveals that he selected, or at least marked for possible use, over fifty different passages. These were extracted from practically the entire range of his major and minor writings up to 1884, including the manuscript of *The Adventures of Huckleberry Finn*. From the latter alone he marked for reading (and during the season appears to have read at least once), as many as fifteen passages. The most frequently used were King Sollermun, and the Freeing of Jim by Tom and Huck. Others were The Waking of Nigger Jim, Jim's Bank, Huck's Struggle With His Conscience, Decorative Art (The Spider-armed Girl), Hamlet's Soliloqy, and This a Gov'ment. His notebook entries reveal that he also considered The Meeting of Huck and Aunt Sally, and the Mississippi Raftsmen's Fight.[12] There were times when he toyed with the idea of making up an entire program from *Huckleberry Finn*, though he apparently never did. There were times, too, as at Springfield, Massachusetts, on November 7, when the printed program contained no selections from his new book at all, though the program as actually given contained one.[13]

Of the entire repertoire of readings the most successful and the most frequently used selections, besides the two favorites from *Huckleberry Finn*, were the following: A Trying Situation (The Girl at Lucerne), The Tragic Tale of the Fishwife, The Ghost Story (The Golden Arm), The Jumping Frog, The Whistling (or Stammering) Story, and Telephone Talk. Others, apparently selected with a view to their suitablility to certain audiences and to certain areas of the country, were Reminiscences of Artemus Ward, Tom Bowline's Encounter With the Governor of Massachusetts, The Captain Explains a Difficult Point, The College Student Sailor, Why I Resigned the Editorship, and two stories from *Roughing It*—The Mexican Plug, and My Duel. He considered, but probably never used, something from Wakeman in Heaven.[14] A fact which deserves at least passing mention is that Mark Twain used none of his experiences as a Mississippi River pilot on the platform and appears never to have seriously considered using them. Yet it was a profession he always looked back upon with pride.

Occasionally he read numbers at special request, usually The Jumping Frog, and the well-known passages from *Innocents*

SPECIAL ANNOUNCEMENT!

"MARK TWAIN"—GEO. W. CABLE.

Season of 1884-5.

EVERETT HOUSE,

New York, July 25, 1884.

Major J. B. POND takes pleasure in announcing to the American public that he has succeeded in obtaining the consent of the two eminent and justly popular writers, MR. SAM'L L. CLEMENS (Mark Twain) and MR. GEORGE W. CABLE, the distinguished Southern novelist, to appear together in a unique series of literary Entertainments.

It is confidently believed that this will present for the first time a combination of genius in an entirely new form, and that the entertainment will appeal freshly to the intelligent public, with the double force of exquisite pathos and genuine humor.

MR. CLEMENS, who occupies a position as a humorist, entirely his own, will furnish to this combination a choice variety of matter in which his irresistible drollery and inimitable manner will be appreciated as they never have been before. As his name is already a household word wherever the English language is spoken, and American humor enjoyed, his appearance in propria persona as the reader of his own fun will afford for the first time the opportunity to see him at his very best.

The association of MR. GEO. W. CABLE with MR. CLEMENS will give, it is believed, a charm to the readings that could not otherwise have been secured. MR. CABLE, whose past season, when he appeared alone as the reader of his own peculiar narratives and the delineator of his own characters, made such an unexampled stir in the literary and artistic circles of New York and Boston, has equipped himself for this series with a fresh repertory in which all the quaint local color, the delicate portraitures, the novel dialect and the peculiar manners and methods of Creole life have been marvelously preserved and blended in a series of pictures, which for startling vividness and tender beauty have probably never been excelled.

These entertainments will be furnished by the two eminent gentlemen jointly. That is to say, each evening will be equally divided between them, so that the pathos of one will alternate with the humor of the other, and the genius of both will be presented in a rapidly changing programme.

In consenting to this co-operation, the Authors have done so with the laudable intention to make their series worthy not alone of the good taste of the literary public, but of the intelligent public at large, and the manager confidently believes that in presenting them jointly he is appealing to the popular heart, which now, as ever, responds promptly to what is original and has in it the broad elements of human sympathy and a humor that is at once irresistible and magnetic.

All the arrangements for the season are now completed by Major Pond, and he is prepared to receive applications from associations and committees having time to fill, and invites prompt correspondence from all parties desiring particulars as to dates, terms and other details.

Address,

JAMES B. POND,

Everett House, New York.

Special announcement of the Twain-Cable reading tour of 1884– 85.

Abroad about the European guides. Anything about foreign travel (he recorded in his notebook) was likely to please audiences a good deal.[15] Nevertheless, the record of programs given, so far as it is available, reveals that during the tour with Cable he made sparing use of such passages. As for The Jumping Frog, Mark Twain declared, nothing in the world could beat *"that yarn when one is feeling good & has the right audience in front of him."*[16]

Sometime during the period immediately preceding the opening of the tour, when Mark Twain was contemplating his repertoire of readings, he asked Cable to suggest Negro passages from the *Huckleberry Finn* manuscript suitable for use on the platform. The request was no doubt prompted by his respect for Cable's judgment, and by his desire to offer the passages which would evoke the greatest delight. Cable replied that he should like to hear him read runaway Jim's account of his investments, the passage which winds up with decision to give ten cents "To de po." More importantly, however, Cable ventured to advise Mark Twain against using, on a printed program, the title Can't Learn a Nigger to Argue. In the book text, he pointed out, the phrase was not objectionable, nor would it be objectionable when given, in context, from the platform. But to let it stand alone on a printed program seemed to him to invite erroneous conjectures of what the content of the reading might be. Furthermore, it carried a hint of grossness.[17] And Mark Twain, who was no less sensitive about the feelings of Negroes than Cable, appears to have followed the advice.

With the opening of the performances Mark Twain again resorted to the use of some of the devices for capturing audience interest as those he had previously used on the lecture circuit. Here, as with the lectures, he made use of the introductions as a source of humor and to set the tone of the evening's program. The presence of Cable made a number of practices possible. Rarely was there an introduction by a local chairman. Sometimes Cable came out alone and simply said, "I'm not Mark Twain." Often they came out together at the opening of the program, Mark Twain leading the way, with Cable, much shorter and slighter than his fellow performer, shyly following behind like a little boy. At other times each came out separately and introduced the other as he came on. "First he would introduce me," Cable once explained, "so the audience would know which of us was which; and then I would introduce him—so that they would know which of us was the other."[18]

Mark Twain's platform manner and his method of coming on stage invariably provoked comment by reporters. As in the early years, he either shuffled slowly from the wings as if unaware that an audience was present, and then showed perplexity and alarm at being discovered in so exposed a situation; or he came on in a funny little jog-trot, half-sideways, with a comical look of half inquiry and half appeal directed to the audience.[19] Years later Cable remembered him coming on stage, at the alternation of numbers, "the one side of him dragging, one foot limping after the other in the peculiar way, known to us all," and the house bursting into a storm of laughter at the sight of him.[20] Arriving at the reading desk, he lounged about it for a time as if not knowing just where to stand, thrust a hand deep into his trousers' pocket, and then stood there for a moment staring at the audience. Frequently after the reading started, he stood holding his right arm with his left hand, and fingered his chin or his mustache. On most occasions he used neither book nor manuscript, and gave the appearance of extemporizing.

As in earlier years, the reporters noted the slow drawling speech which, though natural to him, was always accentuated on the platform for the sake of effect. And there was the pause, a device which Mark Twain used with consummate skill. The mannerism most commonly noted, however, was his constantly serious, dead-pan expression. At the most humorous passages, when the whole house was convulsed with laughter, Mark Twain's face not only remained immobile, betraying not the slightest hint that anything funny had been said, but gave the impression that he was suffering from intense weariness. At the close of his numbers he often hippity-hopped off stage, in contrast to Cable who made his escape with a pigeonwing sort of movement.[21]

In personal appearance the two men offered a striking contrast which, with their differences in styles of reading, added novelty to the program. Both men wore evening dress. The reporters' descriptions of Mark Twain varied considerably. In general he gave the impression of being tall (he was actually about five feet, eight and a half inches), perhaps in contrast with Cable who was considerably shorter. The difference in height was noted especially on occasions when the two men came out from the wings together, the taller and heavier Mark Twain half pushing the smaller Cable onto the stage.[22] Mark Twain's unruly hair, always distinctive and now showing traces of gray, shone over his head like a halo. In contrast, Cable's jet black and glossy hair lay flat on his head, carefully parted and combed. His beard, though heavy, was neatly trimmed. Most often noted about Cable were his mustaches, twisted into surprisingly long strands that angled down past the corners of his mouth and nearly reached his collar. The total impression created by each of these men upon their audiences was powerful, and in general accurately reflected the differences in their characters, personalities, and literary styles. Cable, small in stature, neat, precise, and poised, give an air of intellectuality and culture. He read well and effectively, with a hint of preciseness and of training in elocution. Mark Twain, large and somewhat bumbling by contrast, with ruddy face and slowness of speech, gave an impression of carelessness, of impromptu act and unhurried thought—a simple, guileless, and unsuspecting man who was nevertheless natively shrewd.

These differences of impression, together with comments Mark Twain made about Cable after the tour ended, led some critics to assert that Cable was in every way a little man, moving in the shadow of his more illustrious companion, that he would have read to empty houses had it not been for his more famous co-worker, and that as a platform artist Mark Twain far outshone him.[23] Nothing is further from the truth. Some reporters liked Mark Twain's program better, while others preferred Cable's. The newspaper record reveals, indeed, that Cable was universally very well received. It was frequently noted that he was the more artistic of the two, and perhaps the better actor. If the audience at the end applauded one more than the other, the newspaper reporters rarely made a note of it. The following comment on the artistry of the two men, found in the London (Ontario, Canada) *Advertiser* of February 14, 1885, offers a penetrating analysis. It is typical in awarding Cable as high praise as it awards Mark Twain:

> Both are accomplished actors, always keeping themselves well in reserve, and not often striving for effect. Twain is the greatest sinner in the latter respect. Yet he is not obtrusively so. You feel that he knows he is grotesque and glories in it, but he is amusing, and it is plain to be seen that he keeps himself under control. His humour is undoubted and this is about the only quality that is observable on the stage. In his writings you admire the descriptive work—you feel that he has looked at every side of an object or an idea, and then turned it inside out for your inspection. But on the stage he seeks more for instantaneous effect, and it must be said he makes it. At the same time one can't help feeling that he is in the position of a man who is playing high comedy, but who knows there is more money in doing a song and dance. He is entertaining, but he is not doing his best work. Of the two Cable is the more artistic. He is a real actor, but one feels a doubt

as to whether he errs or not in attempting humour of the Twain kind. . . . The audience were highly pleased, as they should have been.

It may have been perceptive and frank appraisals of this kind that again opened up in Mark Twain the old wound, the disturbing thought that he was giving his audience mere drolleries. "Oh, Cable," he is reported to have said, "I am demeaning myself to be a mere buffoon. It is ghastly. I can't endure it any longer."[24]

But there were reasons other than platform artistry which accounted for Cable's popularity on the tour with Mark Twain. The fact was that his literary eminence during the season, 1884–85, was all but equal to that of his well-known companion. It must be remembered that Mark Twain's most famous book *The Adventures of Huckleberry Finn* had not yet been published. It is true that portions of it were appearing currently (December, January, and February) in *Century* magazine, but the great celebrity which subsequently came to him as a result of this masterpiece still lay in the future.

Cable on the other hand was never more in the public eye than precisely at this moment. *Old Creole Days, Madame Delphine,* and *The Grandissimes* had brought him national and international fame. Then in September of 1884, on the very threshold of his tour with Mark Twain, his book *Dr. Sevier* appeared. It caused a furor that surprised even Cable. The novel carried the statement that the northern cause in the Civil War was just and that "we of the South" could now admit it. Southerners were deeply incensed and voiced their angry objections in the public press. In November as the tour started, Cable defended his statement in an open letter to *Century* magazine. The controversy was still raging in January when an even greater storm arose as a result of another article by Cable, also appearing in *Century,* called "The Freedman's Case in Equity."[25] It was a well-reasoned, temperate plea for social justice for the Negro. In view of the publicity which Cable was receiving as the tour progressed, both because of his literary achievement and because of his powerful voice in the most urgent problem of social justice facing the nation, it is not surprising that when he stepped upon the platform to give his part of the evening's performance, he was at the moment more in the public spotlight than his associate. For that reason it probably never occurred to Cable that he was eclipsed by his famous co-worker. About a month after the joint tour had begun, he wrote his wife with becoming modesty, "I think it's a great thing to be able to hold my own with so great a platform figure."[26] William Dean Howells, who heard both men perform, confirmed Cable's self-appraisal when he declared that Cable was as fine a performer as Clemens, and that he could both read and sing the matter of his books.[27]

Financially the tour proved less successful than Mark Twain had hoped, and there were times when he felt he should have stayed home and written another book.[28] Nevertheless, it provided him quickly with a considerable sum of money and gave his new book *The Adventures of Huckleberry Finn* an immense amount of publicity which was presently translated into sales. But there was a sour note as the long journey came to an end, not on the surface to be sure, but present nonetheless so far as Mark Twain was concerned, though Cable may not then have been aware of it. The trouble that arose was of a nature bound to occur between traveling companions so closely associated over so long a period of time and so fundamentally different in their personal habits and beliefs. The things that chiefly stirred up Mark Twain's wrath were Cable's Presbyterian piety and his strict Sabbatarian practices. During the early days of the tour, for example, it is reported that Cable undertook to read the Bible aloud to Mark Twain during leisure moments. Mark Twain soon put a stop to that.[29] He was further irked by the fact that Cable adamantly refused to travel on public conveyances on Sundays. This fact frequently meant that the pair would be stranded in some small town over weekends. Cable, apparently, never felt stranded anywhere. On Sunday mornings he went to church and after church often accepted invitations to the homes of local parishioners.[30] Mark Twain rarely went to church. He loved to lie abed on Sunday mornings. But even after Cable's return to the hotel, the sociability between the two was somewhat restricted. Cable didn't smoke, he didn't drink intoxicating liquors, and he didn't play billiards, a game Mark Twain loved and found wonderfully relaxing. Nor would he attend theaters. All these things at times aroused Mark Twain's ire and provoked him to refer to Cable as a "Christ-besprinkled, psalm singing presbyterian."[31] To his wife he confided, "Livy, dear, you cannot imagine anything like this idiotic Sunday-superstition of Cable's. I would throttle a baby that had it. It is the most beggarly disease, the most pitiful, the most contemptible mange that ever a grown creature was afflicted withal."[32]

But there were other sources of irritation. Cable was objectionably economical. "He has not bought one single sheet of paper or an envelope in all these 3 ½ months—sponges all his stationery . . . from the hotels."[33] Pond confirmed Mark Twain's observation. Somewhere along the route he reported that when Cable paid his own expenses, he starved himself, and when someone else paid them his appetite was insatiable. He also reported that Cable was insulting and insolent to servants, and that all the servants at the Everett House in New York hated him.[34] "His body is small," Mark Twain wrote Livy as the long tour drew to a close, "but it is much too large for his soul. He is the pitifulest human louse I have ever known."[35]

Mark Twain's outbursts of irritation against his platform companion seem, however, to have had deeper roots than a mere conflict of religious beliefs, personality differences, and habits. As one examines the record, it is difficult to escape the conviction that a feeling of jealousy lay at the base of his criticisms. When he invited Cable as a companion on the tour, he had done so with the conviction that his southern friend was an able performer. "He's been training under an expert," he wrote Howells in November of 1883, "& he's just a rattling reader now—the best amateur I ever heard; & with 2 seasons of *public* practice, I guess he'll be the best professional reader alive."[36] That was high praise indeed from a man who had begun to train as a public reader himself and who took great pride in his own platform excellence. While it is true that later, in a moment of irritation, he confided to his notebook that Cable was not worth half the money he was paying him,[37] the fact remains that he never doubted his companion's skill.

What Mark Twain had not counted on was the widespread public attention which Cable's writings provoked during the tour, especially in January, 1885, after the appearance of "The Freedman's Case in Equity." Secretly no doubt, he felt that he was a better performer than Cable and a more popular author. And in such surmises he was probably correct. Nevertheless, moments of doubt assailed him as he observed the growing marks of respect and admiration which Cable's performances were receiving. During this period, Cable noted, though perhaps without divining the cause, that his companion was frequently "under a cloud," or "heavy as lead—all unstrung," and that at times he came off the platform into the wings vexed, disheartened, and full of lamentations.[38] Usually at such times, Mark Twain confessed that he could not account for the low spirits that engulfed him. At other times he attributed his difficulties to some physical circumstance like taking a warm bath just before the performance, resolving afterward that he would never do that again. Cable, on the other hand, was inclined to believe that it was the hard rail travel that was telling on them, and that it "has let out—slackened—our nerves."[39] Though Cable's conjecture may have had a good deal of truth in it, the fact remains that Mark Twain, contrary to his practice during earlier tours, complained very little about the hardships of traveling during the tour with Cable. There were, of course, causes for irritations and annoyances. At St. Louis, for example, Mark Twain flew into a rage because he had to catch a train at 9:40 in the morning and in a temper tantrum smashed a hotel window shutter with his fist.[40] On the whole, however, as recorded in his notebook, he was pleased to observe the many improvements that had taken place in rail travel and hotel accommodations since his days on the lyceum circuit, remarking that all of them added greatly to the traveler's comfort.[41]

It was chiefly in January, 1885, when his spirits seem to have been particularly low, that Mark Twain's feelings about Cable began to erupt in letters to Livy, revealing the deeper and truer sources of his irritations. "Cover the CHILD!" he raged, mimicking Cable's melodramatic line in his story Mary's Night Ride. "Do you know that infernal night ride of Mary's has grown from 6 minutes (in New Haven) to *fifteen!* And it is in *every* program. This pious ass allows an entirely new program to be announced . . . & then comes out without a wince or an apology & jerks that same old Night Ride on his audience again."[42]

What he failed to report to Livy was the universal popularity of that number, that audiences called for it as an encore when it had not been offered in the program, and that everywhere it was received with conspicuous favor. It was by far Cable's most effective selection, and he read it with dramatic power and skill. That Mark Twain eventually became surfeited with hearing the same melodramatic tale night after night can readily be understood. It can also be understood that he resented the extension of time in telling the story, especially since he himself was constantly attempting to reduce the time for some of his own selections without endangering their effectiveness. This endeavor was no doubt prompted by a number of considerations. First of all, he was concerned that the overall length of the program not exceed 115 to 120 minutes at the outside. The printed programs announced that carriages would be waiting at ten o'clock, thus allowing the audiences to expect the performance to be over at that time.[43]

To keep the programs within bounds required planning and constant vigilance. Mark Twain's notebook amply reveals how carefully he timed each selection, his own as well as Cable's, how he made allowances for delay at the opening of performances and tried to calculate the time to be allowed for encores. Nothing was left to chance. Only if an enthusiastic and insistent audience demanded, did he allow the program to run longer. It appears that he was prompted to reduce the time required for some of his own pieces because of his unusually slow rate of speech. Many of the program notes show that where Cable read six numbers, Mark Twain read only four, but that his four required longer time than Cable's six.[44] It pleased him greatly, therefore, when he succeeded in cutting the story of Tom and Huck freeing Jim (which he eventually divided into two numbers) from approximately thirty-five minutes to twenty-five, and The Jumping Frog to a record-breaking thirteen.[45]

Most of Mark Twain's objections to the shifts in Cable's program lose force, however, when one discovers that he was guilty of the very same charges. Early in the tour, for example, he informed his audience at Springfield, Massachusetts, that the printed programs they held in their hands, which had been distributed at great cost, were of no particular use, and explained why they were not, at some length. According to a reporter in the audience, he then proceeded to demonstrate the correctness of his statement by giving a number of readings "not one of which was mentioned on the program."[46] His objections lose force, further, when one discovers him reporting gleefully to Livy that during his performance in Central Music Hall in New York he extended a ten-minute yarn to thirty-five minutes and "no harm done."[47]

That the extension of time on the platform was a problem

THE
"Mark Twain" - Cable
READINGS.

MUSIC HALL, ORANGE, N. J.,

Thursday Ev'g, November 6, 1884.

1.
The Songs of Place Congo.
MR. GEO. W. CABLE.

2.
TELEPHONE TALK.
MARK TWAIN.

3.
FROM THE GRANDISSIMES.
a. Raoul Innerarity Exhibits his Pictures.
b. Aurora and Clotilde "Think it is doze Climate."
c. Raoul announces his marriage, and "don't care."

FROM DR. SEVIER.
Narcisse and the Richlings.
" Mistco 'Ichlin', in fact, I can baw that fifty dolla' myself."
MR. GEO. W. CABLE.

4.
FROM UNPUBLISHED SHEETS.
a. Colonel Sellers in a new role.
b. Colonel Sellers in a new role again.
c. A Dazzling Achievement.
MARK TWAIN.

J. B. POND, Manager.
Carriages at 10 o'clock.   EVERETT HOUSE, NEW YORK.

Program for Twain-Cable readings at Orange, New Jersey.

that needed to be watched is obvious; yet the fact remains that Mark Twain's plan for keeping it within bounds, as reported to Livy in mid-January, seems less than generous. "We've got a new plan, and it *works*. Cable goes on at the stroke of the hour, and talks 15 minutes to an *assembling* house, telling them not to be concerned about *him,* and he won't be bothered."[48] By following this plan, he indicated, they always managed to stay within the two-hour limit, including encores. But what pleased Mark Twain no less about the new arrangement was the fact that now only half the house heard Cable's first piece—"so there isn't too much of 'C' anymore—when as heretofore there has been a thundering sight too much of him."[49] The remark becomes more interesting as one observes from an examination of Mark Twain's notebooks that his time on the platform often ranged from ten to twenty minutes longer than that of Cable, despite the inference from Pond's "Special Announcement" that the two men were to have equal time. Later, when Cable's total reading time began to stretch out to a full hour, Mark Twain's irritation led him to consider cutting an entire number from Cable's program.[50]

How close Mark Twain's feelings approached malice in arranging to have Cable speak to an assembling house becomes apparent when one discovers how thoroughly he himself detested speaking under such circumstances. During his early tours on the lyceum circuit few things irritated him more than to have latecomers move down the aisles, rustle into their seats, and whisper greetings to their neighbors. There were times, as at Ottawa, Illinois, in 1869, when he became so exasperated that he interrupted his lecture to shout to the doorkeepers to shut the doors and keep them shut, and refused to continue the lecture until the house quieted down.[51]

It would be an error to suppose, however, that Mark Twain's exasperations about Cable erupted into quarrels or into outward manifestations of ill will. When he confided to William Dean Howells, at the close of the tour, that he liked Cable and found him pleasant company, he was no doubt sincere. "I rage and swear at him sometimes, but we do not quarrel."[52] It is nevertheless fair to surmise that the harmony was largely the result of Cable's equanimity and wise forebearance.[53] Indeed, newspaper interviews and Cable's notes made while the tour was in progress show that the three men—Mark Twain, Cable, and Pond—had many good times together. Evenings after the performance, when

they returned to the hotel and sat in the dining room taking refreshments before going to bed, they frequently fell to clowning,
especially if reporters were present to interview them. At Cincinnati, for example, in a mock altercation that arose when a reporter inquired what they thought of Bret Harte's work, Cable
and Mark Twain threatened each other with Mark Twain's empty
ale bottle (Cable had eaten ice cream), and Mark Twain threatened Pond for saying that the work Mark Twain liked best was a
sirloin steak. When a reporter asked Cable what he thought of
Mark Twain, he replied, "We fight all the time. I think that in
four three-minute rounds with soft gloves I could knock him out;
he's not much on science." Thereupon the twins of genius
wandered off to bed. Pond lingered long enough to affirm that
he was a very funny man himself, but that his two associates had
entered into a conspiracy "not to laugh at anything I do or say,
especially if I perpetrate a pun." He then warned the reporters
not to knock at Twain's or Cable's door before noon the next
day "no matter what happens. If they die before noon, let them
die; we can't help it."[54]

There were also a number of delightful personal experiences
which the two men shared and enjoyed. At St. Louis Mark
Twain gave Cable the rare opportunity of listening in on the conversation he had with his cousin James Lampton, the original of
Colonel Sellers of *The Gilded Age,* and hearing Lampton spin a
tale about a marvelous get-rich-quick scheme he was undertaking
with his son. Mark Twain had not told Cable who the visitor
was, but as Cable listened he recognized the character at once.[55]
At Rochester, New York, an important incident occurred when
Mark Twain, browsing in a book store, came upon Mallory's
Mort d'Arthur. It is likely that he had heard of the book, but
he had never seen it. Cable, standing at his elbow, immediately
recommended that he buy it, and predicted that once he had
started reading it, he would never lay it down till he had finished
it. The prediction proved correct, and Cable was gratified to
observe the lively interest which Mark Twain found in the book
which presently played so important a role in the planning of
A Connecticut Yankee in King Arthur's Court. Later, Mark
Twain acknowledged that Cable was its godfather.[56]

All along the route they were constantly besieged by people
who wanted to entertain them at dinner and have them in their
homes as overnight guests. Most of these invitations had to be

declined out of sheer protection against fatigue. Furthermore, Mark Twain had long ago discovered that a hotel offered more personal freedom than a private home, and therefore rarely accepted overnight hospitality. An exception was made, however, at Morristown, New Jersey, where they spent Thanksgiving day and night with Mark Twain's old friend Thomas Nast. Mark Twain occupied Miss Julia's room and was delighted to see how the young lady, about twenty years of age, had decorated its walls. Almost every inch of it was covered with the "most astounding variety of inexpensive & interesting trifles" of pictures, photographs, etchings, Christmas cards, menus, fans, and statuettes which one could imagine. As soon as he had an opportunity he wrote Livy that he wished Susy's room might be decorated in the same way.[57] But the visit at Nast's house was chiefly memorable for an incident that happened in the night. Unable to sleep because of the loud ticking of clocks, Mark Twain got up to remove them. Nast later pictorialized the incident in a cartoon showing a grim-faced Mark Twain in his nightshirt carrying out a big hall clock, with Cable, similarly dressed, standing by holding a candle.[58]

Cable's continued admiration and respect for his temperamental companion are also revealed in his notes. There was the occasion when the two men had supper one evening with David Ross Locke (Petroleum V. Nasby) at the latter's home in Toledo, and Cable silently recorded his observations—Nasby, disheveled hair, dowdy in dress, coarse, successful but unsatisfied; Mark Twain, neat, with facial lines that shone out. By implication, he also expressed his comfort in Mark Twain on another account. While he knew that his companion enjoyed an alcoholic drink, he also knew that his use of alcohol was well controlled, and that in no instance did its use in the least impair his artistry on the platform. Nasby, on the other hand, by his own confession during the dinner, declared that he was often so drunk he couldn't see his audience. Cable, who had an abhorrence for drunkenness, listened to Nasby's recital with disgust and later recorded in his notebook, "He's a bad dream."[59]

More significant, however, was Cable's praise of Mark Twain's artistry as a public reader. What a "fine instinctive art he has for the platform," he observed on the evening of January 30, during the performance at Rockford, Illinois.[60] A few days later at Chicago, where full houses greeted them, he noted with pleasure the splendid reception accorded one of Mark Twain's numbers. The "old surf-roar is booming," he noted with pleasure. "They will encore every number to the end. Ah! What a noble applause calls Mark back. . . ."[61]

That same evening he recorded an instance of Mark Twain's ingenuity and ready wit on the platform. Cable had finished a song and had retired to the wings. Mark Twain, always nervous at the change of numbers, had stepped out a bit too promptly and had unexpectedly met a pattering of applause intended for Cable. "He stood still a minute," Cable reported, and "then said in the drollest way imaginable—'I'll go back and get him,' and proceeded to the wings to call Cable back. The announcement was greeted with a roar of laughter and applause. In a moment he reappeared, and to the further delight of the audience said, 'He's sung all he knows.' "[62]

Another feature of Mark Twain's artistry that deeply impressed Cable was the extraordinary labor and care his companion exercised in planning and making up programs. "He has worked & worked incessantly," Cable reported, "until he has effected in all of them . . . a gradual growth of interest & humor so that the audience never has to find anything less, but always more, entertaining than what precedes it." He quoted Mark Twain as saying, "I don't want them to get tired out laughing before we get to the end." As a result of such planning and care, Cable reported, there was always "a steady crescendo, ending in a double climax. My insight into his careful, untiring, incessant labors are an education. . . ."[63]

Cable's observation of Mark Twain's diligence and care in making up programs is amply borne out by the notebook entries which Mark Twain made during the tour. There are several pages of programs, or proposed programs, with all selections listed and often timed, including the time to be allowed for encores, plus the total program time. Often the encores themselves are listed, sometimes with a question mark, indicating that a definite choice had not yet been made. There are reminders to prune and cut certain selections. There are lines with some of the words or syllables underscored, indicating exactly how they should be read, as for example one from *Huckleberry Finn,* "Hang it, Huck, ef I could ony c'lect de *in*trust I would let de *principal* go." There are suggestions for unexpected devices to arouse laughter and alert the audience. One of these was to have Cable come out and interrupt him once or twice while he was giving a number, as an introduction for his story about a man named Hayes, who, while trying to lecture was interrupted three times by someone paging a lady in the house and announcing that her husband had broken his leg. Whether Mark Twain ever attempted to carry out this complicated maneuver is not recorded. Interspersed throughout these entries are brief anecdotes (heard in the cars, perhaps), which he may have hoped to use on the platform, if opportunity offered. One was of a drunk man who had swallowed a small ball of thread, and tried to pull thread out of his mouth. Another was of a lady whose ninety-two-year-old husband had fallen down and broken his nose, and her remark afterward that it "came near disfiguring him for life." And there was the remark of the village no-account who was very sick. When the minister admonished him to call upon God, he replied he was "so kind of sick and lame I don't git out to call on anybody."[64]

Speaking of the tour with Cable many years later, Mark Twain remembered that his audiences were difficult and that he "had a hard time with them sometimes," because they were not trained in the reception of reading programs. However accurate that reflection may have been, one thing is amply clear—as a result of his careful and ceaseless labor toward the perfection of his art as a public reader he became one of the most effective performers of his time. He had few, if any, peers other than Cable.

In the days following the close of the tour, numerous invitations to read and lecture were extended to him. Only occasionally did he accept. His preoccupation with the affairs of the Webster Company, the Paige typesetter, kaolatype, and with a multitude of other enterprises, including plans for *A Connecticut Yankee in King Arthur's Court*, which presently began to engage his attention—all these things kept him enormously busy. The invitations he did accept from time to time were usually benefits for various enterprises. On April 28, 1885, he read in New York for the benefit of the American Copyright League. Howells, who was in the audience, wrote him later, "You . . . took that house up in the hollow of your hand and tickled it."[65] About five weeks later, on June 5, he read in Hartford for the benefit of local charities. The following year, on April 3, he read before the cadets and general garrison in the mess hall at West Point, probably free of charge except for expenses. On March 31, 1887, he participated in an authors' reading program for the benefit of the Longfellow Memorial Fund at the Boston Museum. About nine months later, on January 17, 1889, he read again in Baltimore, this time to relieve his friend Thomas Nelson Page who was unable to fill an engagement because of the sudden death of his wife. But even during these busy and in many ways troublesome years, as his notebooks reveal, he prepared his programs with care, experimenting with various selections, colloquializing and in other ways adapting them for public reading, timing them carefully, and arranging them in the order best calculated to produce a crescendo of interest and entertainment. During these years he importantly increased his repertoire by adding to it selections from the *Connecticut Yankee,* and from other writings of the period. By 1895, when he decided to undertake the reading tour around the world, he had at his command perhaps as many as seventy-five selections for use on the platform, and had arrived at a degree of mastery in the art of reading which few of his contemporaries could match.

CHAPTER FOURTEEN

THE WORLD TOUR

*Mrs. Clemens, Clara, and I started, on
the 15th of July, 1895, on our lecturing
raid around the world. We lectured and
robbed and raided for thirteen months.*
—MARK TWAIN IN ERUPTION, P. *194.*

AFTER THE TOUR with Cable in 1884–85, ten years passed
before the wolf at Mark Twain's door again compelled
him to return to the public platform as a tour lecturer.
They were harassing years, culminating in bankruptcy in 1894
when his publishing house, the Charles L. Webster Company,
finally collapsed.[1]

The story of Mark Twain's financial disasters in connection
with the Paige typesetter[2] and the Webster Company need not
be recited here. It need only be pointed out that by 1890 both
enterprises had put so heavy a strain upon his financial resources that he was forced to give up his house and expensive
way of living in Hartford and move to Europe where he could
live much more cheaply and privately.

The failure of Webster produced an indebtedness that ran
to approximately $94,000, not counting an additional $60,000
that Mrs. Clemens had invested in the company.[3] Sixty years old
and in uncertain health, he nevertheless immediately addressed
himself to the huge task of repaying his creditors. Inevitably
now, as in earlier years, his mind turned again to the public
platform. He needed money, and he needed it quickly and in

large amounts. He was working on *Joan of Arc* during these days, but he could not afford to wait for the royalty returns which that book might bring in. He felt he had to move without delay.

The decision to undertake another long and hateful lecture tour came, however, only after a bitter struggle. "Do you remember, Livy," Clara Clemens recalls her father saying to her mother after the tragic death of Susy, "the hellish struggle it was to settle on making that lecture trip around the world? How we fought the idea, the horrible idea, the heart-torturing idea. I, almost an old man, with ill health, carbuncles, bronchitis and rheumatism . . . with patience worn to rags, I was to pack my bag and be jolted around the devil's universe for what? To pay debts that were not even of my making. And you were worried at the thought of facing such hardships of travel, and SHE [Susy] was unhappy to be left alone. But once the idea of that infernal trip struck us we couldn't shake it."[4]

The "heart-torturing" decision made, Mark Twain wrote to his old friend Major J. B. Pond, who had managed his tour with Cable ten years earlier, tha the was considering "reading a few times in America," before sailing for Australia. The letter, dated May 1, was mailed from Paris.[5] Eighteen days later, he was back in the United States conferring personally with Pond and authorizing him to proceed with arrangements. Prior to this time, perhaps as early as February or March, he had already begun negotiations with R. S. Smythe, the famous Australian impresario, for a far eastern tour.[6] At any rate, by May 1, when he first wrote to Pond, Sydney newspapers were already announcing that Mark Twain would lecture in Australia.[7]

While wating for the tour to begin, the Clemenses had gone to Elmira to stay with their old friends and relatives, the Theodore Cranes. Mark Twain, as Clara reported, was not well. He was suffering from an undefined illness, complicated by a severe attack of carbuncles. Nor was he easy in mind; for one of his creditors, having learned that Mark Twain was back in the United States, brought suit against him, forcing him to make trips to New York to attend hearings. During these trips, and even while at Elmira, a nurse attended him constantly.[8] Though his health gradually improved, these were days when Mark Twain and his wife seriously wondered whether he would be well enough, when the time came, to undertake the long, hateful, and grueling journey to which he had committed himself.

In view of his precarious health, it was decided that Mrs. Clemens was to accompany her husband, in order to care for him and to protect him from needless and exhausting demands upon his energies. Clara, the middle daughter, now twenty-one, was also to go. Susy and Jean, for various reasons, were to remain behind and to join them in London on their return.

As manager of the American phase of the tour, Pond agreed to accompany the Clemenses in person all the way to Vancouver, British Columbia. He was to have complete charge of all arrangements and to relieve Mark Twain of all concerns except those relating to the lecture itself. In compensation he was to receive one-fourth of the profits. Partly for the trip and partly to be of service to the Clemenses, Mrs. Pond was also invited to join the group.[9]

The most important decision that now faced Mark Twain, in preparation for the tour, had to do with the kind of program he was to offer to the public. Should he lecture? Or should he read, as he had done on the tour with Cable? There was no reason why, outside the United States, he could not use his old favorite, the Sandwich Islands lecture, and also the lecture from *Roughing It*. They had always been very popular with the public. But they would hardly do for the American phase of the tour, since they were too well known. In the end, the decision in favor of readings was probably not very difficult. They too had met with enthusiastic audience approval. Furthermore, a program of readings had the additional virtue of allowing him more freedom on the platform, since he could include or omit stories and anecdotes according to the exigencies of the moment. In addition, with such a program he could easily prepare repeat lectures in large communities by simply selecting a new group of stories.

He was especially happy with his decision after he hit upon an ingenious plan for giving unity to a program of miscellaneous readings. The plan was to pretend that his lecture had a moral purpose—the regeneration of mankind. He intended to accomplish this regeneration by presenting a number of principles of moral improvement. The passages selected for reading were ostensibly chosen to illustrate these principles. Actually, of course, they were selected because Mark Twain knew from long experience that these passages had always been popular with his audiences and also because he loved to present them. The plan was unique and original. It allowed for the fullest exercise of his powers and provided him, in the transitions from one story to another, the widest opportunity to inject whatever thought came to him at the moment or a responsive audience might evoke.

The introductory remarks in which Mark Twain outlined his moral scheme were delightfully effective. People, he declared, wanted a lecturer to give them something solid, something educational, something that would improve them. And that was what he had come to do. He proposed to teach morals by the use of illustrations. He had a theory that a person should prize as priceless every crime, every transgression he commits—that is, the lesson he derives from it. By impressing the lesson of the crime upon his mind and heart, a person would never commit that crime again. There were, he said, 462 different crimes possible.[10] By committing each one of these and treasuring up the lesson derived from it, a person would become vaccinated against crime, so to speak, just as he becomes vaccinated against smallpox.[11]

Mark Twain then proceeded to illustrate some of the principles which he asserted he had learned in his own rise toward moral perfection (he was now, he said, more than two-thirds on his way up there and had not much further to go) by introducing various stories and anecdotes from his own writings. Since he lectured from two to five times in most towns, his repertoire of stories had, of necessity, to be quite extensive. An examination of news files reveals that he had at his command no less than twenty-five selections. (Some of these, however, do not seem to have been introduced for the purpose of illustrating moral lessons, but were casually introduced in connection with something previously said.)

The Jumping Frog and the story of the Mexican Plug, for example, were offered to teach a person never to put faith in a passing stranger; Jim Baker's Blue Jay, whatever you do, do with all your heart; The History of a Campaign That Failed, discretion is the better part of valor; Tom Sawyer's Crusade To Rescue the Holy Land, don't argue matters beyond your comprehension; The Corpse in His Father's Office, learn to gauge your courage early; The Awful German Language, the necessity of teaching patience; Huck Helps Jim Escape, a sound heart is better than a deformed conscience; The Christening of Mary Ann, don't jump to conclusions; The Small Pox story, a fellow has to start early in life if he wants to do right and learn how (sometimes adding to this precept the cynical reflection, "But what's the use of all the trouble in trying to do right when it's easier to do otherwise and the wages are the same").[12]

An item in his repertoire, added shortly after his arrival in Australia and deserving special mention, was his poem based upon the fauna of that country. About every thirty years, he told his audience, he experienced poetic inspiration. It had come upon him on his arrival in Australia. He had wanted to be original and write a poem about Sydney Harbor but people had discouraged him by stories of the violent deaths of others who had tried it before him. They had also offered him money to leave the city. But then he thought of the grand subject of the fauna of Australia, those wonderful beasts and birds, which existed nowhere else, and many of them not even there any longer. He had a lot of difficulty with his theme—perhaps he was too hasty—he was excited and anxious, he knew. The Poet Laureateship was still vacant then, and he wanted to get his sample in on time. He was willing to do the job cheaper than other men; but another man got it. He was sorry about that, because the present Poet Laureate was the same kind of a poet he was.

There were plenty of animals for the poetic theme—the emu, the auk, the kangaroo, the lyre, the laughing jackass, the ornithorhynchus, the dingo, the great moa, the boomerang, the dodo, the larrikin. His difficulty was that when the sense was right, there was nothing that would rhyme, and when the rhyme was right, there was no sense in it. His first attempt was

> Land of the ornithoryncus
> Land of the kangaroo
> Oh! ties of heredity link us.
> . . . .

He continued with fragments of the poem haltingly but with such delight to the audience, that in all his repertoire it proved one of the most widely applauded pieces.[13]

In advertising such a program as Mark Twain had devised, it is understandable that both Pond and Smythe were somewhat puzzled how to name it. In the ordinary sense of the term it was not a lecture at all; and it appears that Mark Twain at times objected when reporters referred to it as such, though he himself often used the term to describe it. Nor was it in the ordinary sense a mere program of readings; for it was noted that unlike Dickens, who read verbatim from his books, Mark Twain revised and amplified his stories, giving them a vitality and subtlety not present in the printed form. Pond's advertising usually avoided the word "lecture," instead presenting, "Mark Twain,

The World Famous Author In Talks and Readings From His own Rich Humor."[14] The American newspapers, on the other hand, were not so discriminating. They commonly referred to the program as a lecture. Throughout Australia, New Zealand, India, and South Africa, Smythe advertised the tour as a "Talking Tour," and referred to the specific programs as "At Homes," hoping, no doubt, to suggest in this manner their informal, personal quality.

The "greatest lecture tour of the century," as Pond sometimes called it,[15] began at Cleveland on July 15, 1895.[16] Cleveland was a propitious choice for the premier performance, for there he knew he could count on the enthusiastic support of the influential Cleveland *Herald*, and of the Solon Severances, old friends of "Quaker City" days. "Mother Fairbanks," as we have seen, had helped launch him at Cleveland a quarter of a century earlier.[17] He was sure that she would again do everything in her power to see him well started upon his new venture.

From Cleveland the tour proceeded through the Upper Michigan peninsula to Duluth, Minneapolis, and St. Paul, and then, after a two-day stopover in Winnepeg, across the northern tier of states to the principal cities of Montana and Washington, terminating in British Columbia with lectures at Vancouver and Victoria. At Cleveland Mark Twain had told his audience that he had barely recovered from an illness that had kept him in bed for forty-five days and that he had got out of bed only five days previously.[18] He was still noticeably weak and was suffering a good deal of pain from a carbuncle on his leg. All across the country the carbuncle troubled him so much that he was forced to spend considerable time in bed and forego a number of dinners and receptions that were planned in his honor.

By the time he reached Vancouver, however, he announced that his health was much improved, that he had gained nine pounds in twenty-eight days, and that he was twice as well as when he started out. Curiously enough, he attributed his improved health to lecturing, declaring it to be "gymnastics, chest expander, medicine, mind-healer, blues destroyer, all in one."[19] But Pond was not so optimistic about Mark Twain's health. Just before getting aboard the "Warrimoo" on August 23, Mark

Circular announcing itinerary of the American phase of the world tour.

MARK TWAIN'S TOUR

AROUND
THE WORLD,

BEGINNING IN CLEVELAND,

OHIO, JULY 15th, 1895,

CLOSING IN LONDON, MAY, 1896

ROUTE IN AMERICA.

JULY.

Mon 15.	Cleveland, Ohio	Stillman House
Tues 16.	" "	" "
Wed 17.	*Travel on Steamer.*	
Thur 18.	Sault Ste. Marie, Mich	Hotel Iroquois
Fri 19.	Mackinac.	Grand Hotel
Sat 20.	Petoskey, Mich	Arlington Hotel
SUN 21.	Mackinac..	Grand Hotel
Mon 22.	Duluth, Minn	Spalding Hotel
Tues 23.	Minneapolis, Minn	Hotel West
Wed 24.	St. Paul, Minn	Hotel Ryan
Thur 25.	*Travel.*	
Fri 26.	Winnipeg	The Manitoba
Sat 27.	"	" "
SUN 28.	"	" "
Mon 29.	Crookston, Minn	Crookston Hotel
Tues 30.	*Travel.*	
Wed 31.	"	

AUGUST.

Thur 1.	Butte, Montana	The Butte Hotel
Fri 2.	Anaconda, Mont	The Montana
Sat 3.	Helena, Mont	Hotel Helena
SUN 4.	" "	" "
Mon 5.	Great Falls, Mont	Park Hotel
Tues 6.	*Travel.*	
Wed 7.	Spokane, Wash	The Spokane
Thur 8.	*Travel.*	
Fri 9.	Olympia, Wash	The Olympia
Sat 10.	Tacoma, Wash	The Tacoma
SUN 11.	" "	" "
Mon 12.	Portland, Or	The Portland
Tues 13.	Seattle, Wash	The Rainier
Wed 14.	New Whatcom, Wash	
Thur 15.	Vancouver, B. C	Hotel Vancouver
Fri 16.	*Sails from Vancouver for Australia.*	

ADDRESS ALL COMMUNICATIONS TO

MAJOR J. B. POND,

EN ROUTE.

Twain had gone shopping and had laid in three thousand Manila Cheroots and four pounds of Durham smoking tobacco, wondering whether that would be enough to last him through to Australia.[20] A few days earlier Pond had written in his notebook, " 'Mark' has been in bed all day; he doesn't seem to get strength. He smokes constantly. . . . Physicians say it will eventually kill him."[21] Again he wrote, "If perpetual smoking ever kills a man, I don't see how 'Mark Twain' can expect to escape."[22]

Pond's concern for Mark Twain's health was genuine. The two men were old friends and had a warm regard for each other, despite occasional differences. Cheerful, hearty, and his "mill never idle," Pond was good company.[23] It was marvelous to hear him lie, Mark Twain reported, and the only fault one could find in him was that his lies lacked imagination, a sense of proportion.[24] A minor disagreement arose at the beginning of the tour, when Pond proposed to give his own lecture on Beecher, Sunday nights in churches. Mark Twain flatly rejected the plan, insisting that the tour was his private show and that "his manager wasn't to open his mouth in public while they were together." Pond apparently refrained until Mark Twain sailed from Vancouver, when, according to the humorist, he was immediately "at it in a Vancouver church."[25]

Before leaving Vancouver Mark Twain released a statement to the press, refuting a troublesome report that he had sacrificed for the benefit of his creditors the Webster Company property, and that he was now lecturing for his own benefit. This, he asserted, was completely erroneous. The money he earned lecturing, as well as the property, was intended for the creditors. The law, he claimed, recognized no mortgage on a man's brains. A merchant who had given up his possessions could start free again for himself. "But I am not a businessman, and honor is a harder master than the law. It cannot compromise for less than one hundred cents on a dollar, and its debts are never outlawed." He had, he declared, a two-thirds interest in the publishing house. Since Webster, his partner, had no resources, he expected to assume the total burden. He would ask his creditors to trust to his honor to discharge the full obligation as fast as he could earn it. "From my reception thus far on my lecturing tour," he continued, "I am confident that if I live I can pay off the last debt within four years."[26] Excerpts of Mark Twain's statement were widely reprinted in foreign newspapers all along the tour route.

Inevitably it had the effect of stimulating sympathy for the courageous, bankrupt American as well as curiosity to see him in the flesh.

The "Warrimoo" sailed for Australia by way of Hawaii, where Mark Twain was scheduled to lecture; but when they reached the Honolulu harbor no one was permitted to get off the ship because cholera had broken out in the city. It was a sore disappointment for Mark Twain, for he had looked forward with keen anticipation to revisiting the Islands after an absence of nearly thirty years. It was also a disappointment for another reason. $1,600 had to be returned to the purchasers of tickets for his lecture.[27]

Mark Twain landed in Sydney, Australia, on Monday, September 16. His "At Homes" there, four in number, began the following Thursday. From Sydney the itinerary led to Melbourne and Adelaide and to several smaller towns in Victoria Province. At Melbourne, where Mark Twain gave five performances, a new carbuncle formed on his leg. It gave him so much trouble that a doctor had to freeze and then lance it, after which he gave him a hypodermic. The consequence was that Mark Twain was in bed for a whole week, getting up only to keep his engagements on the platform.[28] There, fortunately, he was no longer conscious of the pain. "At such a time," he said, "one's mind is fully occupied, and one has no attention to waste on pain."[29]

On November 1, he boarded the "Mararoa" at Melbourne and proceeded, after a brief stopover at Hobart, Tasmania, to New Zealand. Five days later he arrived at Invercargill, South Island, and lectured there. The tour proceeded up the east coast of South Island, to Dunedin, Oamaru, Christchurch, and Nelson, and then to the North Island towns of Auckland, Gisborne, Napier, Hawera, New Plymouth, and Wellington. The lecture at Gisborne was canceled when Mark Twain refused to land. A stormy sea had made landing hazardous, and he did not want to put his wife and daughter in jeopardy by transferring them in that rough sea from their ship to a tugboat in a primitive basket-chair, manipulated by ropes and pulleys.[30]

At Napier he was again in bed with a carbuncle, the third since leaving Elmira. In a letter to Joe Twichell, dated November 29, he reported that the new one wasn't as bad as the second and that he lectured the evening before without inconvenience, but that the Napier doctors "thought best to forbid tonight's lecture."[31] The next day, November 30, his birthday, he was still in bed at Napier.

Two weeks later, on December 13, he reboarded the "Mararoa" for the return trip to Australia. Still troubled by the carbuncle and consequently irritable and easily annoyed, he found himself praying for a heavy storm that would keep the children in their cabins. "This is the damnedest menagerie of mannerless children," he complained, "I have ever gone to sea with."[32] He arrived at Sydney on December 17, and immediately resumed his Australian itinerary.

It was on December 19 on his way to Scone, a lecture stop not far from Sydney, that Mark Twain first heard of the strained relations that were developing between England and the United States, arising from a border dispute between Venezuela and British Guiana.[33] The Australian papers that night and the next day were so full of war-scare news that at the close of his Sydney lecture he felt moved to speak of the affair. Advancing to the edge of the platform and speaking with great earnestness, he said that in bidding the audience goodnight, it was his belief and earnest hope that the little war cloud would quickly be blown away. He trusted sincerely "that the fruitful peace which had reigned between the two nations for eighty years would not be broken, and that the two great peoples would resume their march shoulder to shoulder, as before, in the van of the world's civilization." The warm sincerity with which the words were spoken moved the audience deeply and they broke out in loud and prolonged cheering.[34]

On December 23 the Clemenses set sail for India by way of Melbourne, where they spent Christmas, and Adelaide, where they celebrated New Year's day.[35] During the long sea journey, which lasted about two weeks, Twain spent most of his time reading, finding particular fascination in Sir John Lubbock's books on ant life. As the ship neared Ceylon he contracted a cold which kept him in bed much of the time till they reached Colombo. Since no lecture had been scheduled during the two- or three-day stopover there, he went to bed at the Hotel Bristol and stayed till his boat left for Bombay, where his Indian tour was to begin. But when he arrived at Bombay on January 18 he was still suffering from the cold and was too hoarse to lecture. Here again the doctors ordered him to bed for an entire week.

Mr. and Mrs. Samuel L. Clemens in Melbourne, 1895.

As a consequence, the Bombay lectures didn't begin till January 25.[36]

From Bombay the itinerary included two side trips, one to Baroda and one to Poona. It then proceeded eastward across India to Allahabad and to Benares, where he watched the religious practices of the natives as they bathed themselves in the polluted waters of the sacred Ganges, and he reflected cynically upon the ignorance and superstition which oppressed mankind the world over. He interrupted his stay at Calcutta with a trip to Darjeeling, high in the mountainous country to the north, lecturing there twice before returning to Calcutta for a final performance.

The road now led westward and northwestward, carrying him eventually across northern India to Peshawar, near the border of Afghanistan. There were lectures at Mozufferpur, Lucknow, Agra, Delhi, Ambala, Rawalpindi, Ferozepore, Lahore, and other towns. If the long journeys by rail exhausted him, he kept silent about it. Perhaps the new and ever-changing scenery, the strange life in the villages, the people, the animals, the color of things, all engaged his attention and kept weariness away. At any rate, by the time he reached Lahore he was sufficiently recovered from his colds and carbuncles to look ahead with pleasure to the sea voyage from Calcutta to Ceylon.

At Colombo he lectured twice, on April 3 and 4. Unfortunately, April 3 was Good Friday, a circumstance that kept many people from attending a humorous performance, despite the celebrity of the lecturer. In addition, the weather was inclement. As a result, Mark Twain lectured that evening to a highly appreciative but disappointingly small audience. It was noted that though his health seemed good he was still troubled by a cough. The following afternoon at 5:30, at what was presumably a matinee performance, he lectured again, this time to a much larger audience despite another threatening downpour. Later that evening he and Mrs. Clemens and Clara, who had been sightseeing all day, boarded the "Wardha" bound for Mauritius.[37]

In that exotic little island, known to the western world chiefly through Saint Pierre's romantic story of *Paul and Virginia,* Mark Twain spent twelve delightful days which were marred only by the fact that his daughter Clara was still suffering from the ague which she had contracted in India. As for Mark Twain himself, he had completely recovered from his prolonged siege of carbuncles and was in the best of health. Much to the disappointment of both the English and French inhabitants of the island, however, he did not lecture, despite the fact that a public performance seemed promised and was anticipated by the news reporters. The French inhabitants were especially unhappy not to have an opportunity to hear the celebrated American, surmising that his failure to lecture indicated his scorn of them or that Mark Twain might have been offended by critical comments the French journalist Edmond About had made about him after one of About's visits to the United States.[38]

On April 28 Mark Twain sailed on the "Arundel Castle" for South Africa, the final stage of his long tour, arriving in Durban, Natal Province, on May 6.[39] Because his health was now quite restored, Smythe increased the number of engagements considerably, booking him at most stops for three or four performances, and leaving less time for sightseeing. From Durban he proceeded northwestward through Pietermaritzburg to Johannesburg, Pretoria, and Krugersdorp in the Transvaal; then far to the southward again to Bloemfontein in Orange Free State, and further southeastward to Queenstown, East London, and Port Elizabeth. From there the road led north again to Grahamstown and Cradock, up to the famous diamond mining town of Kimberley. Here he spent several days lecturing, visiting the great crater of the original diamond mine in that area, and later the office of the diamond mining company, where he saw a day's take of £10,000.[40] A week later he was in Capetown for his final series of lectures in South Africa. Precisely when he boarded the "Norman" bound for England is uncertain, but probably about July 15. He reached England the last day of July.[41] If he had any thoughts of accepting lecture engagements there, he soon abandoned them, for by August 15 word reached him of Susy's illness, and three days later the shattering news of her death. In a long lifetime Mark Twain suffered no greater shock than the death of Susy. He loved all his children, but Susy was the most imaginative of the three daughters and had the warmest personality.

An overall look at the entire itinerary of the world tour reveals that Mark Twain lectured in the neighborhood of one hundred ten times, with ninety-seven engagements positively identified. The American and New Zealand phases of the tour occupied about five weeks each, the Australian, Indian, and South African phases about seventy days each. He spent about

Announcement of program in Johannesburg. (Standard and Diggers News, May 18, 1896.)

Standard Theatre.

Lessees - - Messrs. B. & F. Wheeler

THIS EVENING, MAY 18.

A. BONAMICI has the honour to inform the public of Johannesburg and Suburbs that through the good offices of Mr. CARLYLE SMYTHE, the well-known Australian *Impressario*, he has been fortunate enough to induce

MR. S. CLEMENS,

THE GREATEST HUMOURIST

OF THE AGE,

The Celebrated American Author,

Under the Pseudonymnous of

MARK TWAIN,

to pay Johannesburg a visit previous to the other Colonial Towns, so as to change the heavy clouds which are hanging over these fields into a Rosy, Brilliant Atmosphere of

WIT,
HUMOUR,
HOPE, and
GOOD OMEN.

MARK TWAIN

— The STAR —

OF THE

Stars and Stripes

(Country of Freedom, Progress and Inventions), will give at the

STANDARD THEATRE,

4 "AT HOMES,"

On Different Subjects.

THIS MONDAY EVENING, MAY 18,
MARK TWAIN

WILL GIVE HIS

FIRST AT HOME.

Owing to the rush for seats a limited number of Chairs will be placed in the Orchestra.

Monday, the 18th,
Tuesday, the 19th,
Wednesday, the 20th,
Thursday, the 21st.

Gentlemen who have seats bespoken are kindly requested to call for them to avoid mistakes.

Prices : Boxes 4 and 3 guineas ; Stalls and Dress Circle 7s 6d, Family Circle 5s, Gallery 2s 6d.

Book early at Bonamici's.

eighty-five days on the water. The heaviest schedule of lecture engagements was in the United States and New Zealand; Africa was moderately heavy, Australia and India notably lighter. While Mark Twain's health may well have been a factor in determining the number of engagements in the various lands, it was probably not the only one, nor even the major one. The fact is that Mark Twain deliberately planned on doing a considerable amount of sightseeing, especially in Australia and India, and let it be known that he was making the tour as much to gather material for a proposed travel book as to lecture.[42] It is reasonable to surmise, therefore, that in arranging the itinerary, Smythe was instructed to keep this fact in mind, not only in choosing where to route him, but how often he was to lecture.

That Mark Twain took his sightseeing seriously is evident from the comments of the reporters as well as from his own accounts in the *Notebook* and in *Following the Equator*. The reporters frequently observed that he spent a great deal of time in collecting information about the localities he visited and in writing and assembling his notes. Nevertheless, despite all the time afforded by long sea voyages from one continent to another, Mark Twain complained that he had little opportunity to work at his notes and that he did not expect to begin serious work on his book till the Capetown lectures were over.[43] In explaining his slow progress with the book he confided to a reporter that "on a lecture tour one has to combine business with pleasure, and I can't say they mix very well."[44]

Mixing business with pleasure, or at least with social engagements, had long been one of Mark Twain's chief problems. By his own acknowledgement, as we shall see later, it seriously interfered with his writing and contributed to his failure, after the publication of *Huckleberry Finn,* to maintain a satisfactory rate of literary production. On the tour, the problem was no less great. His distinguished presence was everywhere noted. Invitations poured in constantly, and from all sides. American consular agents, prominent local and state officials, high ranking military personnel, clubs and organizations which had sponsored his lectures—all invited him to dinners, receptions, and other affairs, often late in the evening after the lecture. If he accepted, it usually meant exhausting hours that robbed him of rest and drained his energies. Frequently, of course, he could in good conscience, decline invitations because of ill health and a doctor's orders. His repeated colds and his carbuncles were, fortunately well known to the public through the press, permitting him to decline without giving offense.

There were many social affairs, however, which he felt he should not decline, nor did he wish to. At Baroda, India, for example, the Maharaja invited him to his capitol, and in the evening assembled three hundred distinguished guests in his honor.[45] There were many similar occasions when he considered it a matter of duty and international courtesy to represent his country, regarding himself as an ambassador of good will, which, indeed, he eminently was. It was in such a role that he asked for and received permission to visit the American prisoners in the Pretoria jail who were being held for their participation in the Transvaal Reform movement. In a long conversation he humored them by facetiously extolling the many advantages of confinement, asserting that Bunyan would never have written *Pilgrim's Progress* if he hadn't been in jail, nor would Cervantes have produced *Don Quixote* if he hadn't suffered "durance vile." He promised them that he would visit President Kruger and do his utmost to get their sentences extended. When he left, the prisoners, who enjoyed fully his ironic humor, cheered.[46] A few days later, Mark Twain, accompanied by the American consul, called upon President Kruger and interceded in behalf of the Americans. Though the President replied that it was his disposition to be lenient with the Americans,[47] the reporters present were less optimistic than Mark Twain that the reply was really encouraging.[48]

Thus, in view of his celebrity, the many social demands upon his time, the frequent interviews with reporters, the callers who came to pay their respects, and the thousand and one other interruptions, it is quite understandable that Mark Twain found that business and pleasure didn't mix very well.

In following Mark Twain's tour through newspaper reports in Australia, New Zealand, India, and South Africa, it quickly becomes evident that the American author and humorist was no stranger to his audiences in any of those lands. Throughout the whole English-speaking world, people were acquainted with *Innocents Abroad, Tom Sawyer,* and *Huckleberry Finn* and were eager to see the distinguished author and lecturer. His personal appearance had been made widely known by some excellent Sydney photographs which Smythe had especially ordered for the press.[49] There was much curiosity to see in person "the funniest man of the age" and "the greatest humorist of the century," as Smythe advertised him, and to hear the rich humor flow from his own lips. Thus, when Mark Twain stepped from the wings, a roar of applause invariably greeted him.

For a man sixty years of age and recently ill, his appearance was truly impressive. Bushy white hair circled his head like a halo. The brows were shaggy and thick, the mustache drooped. The complexion was ruddy. It was noted that his nose was strongly aquiline, the thin delicate nostrils suggesting nervous sensibility. The eyes, wonderfully keen and piercing, looked out gently from a furrowed, intellectual face. He appeared in full evening dress with a wide unornamented expanse of white shirt, and it occurred to some in the audience that he looked far too civilized to be the author of *Roughing It*.[50]

Emerging from the wings, his left hand thrust deep into his trouser pocket, he sauntered slowly toward the reading stand like a man out for a stroll who presently looks up and finds he has company. At times he walked out on the stage carrying a glass of water in such a casual and unstudied way as to appear that it was a perfectly natural thing for him to do. Then, stepping to the side of the stand, he stood with folded arms gazing at the audience with a quizzical look that betrayed no hint of a smile, and waited for the audience to quiet down.[51]

His method of opening the lecture varied from night to night. Sometimes when the greeting welled up loud and long and the warm welcome engulfed him, he was so deeply touched that his eyes veiled and he felt a break in his voice.[52] At such times he began by saying that such a greeting took away from him all sense of being a stranger in a far land and made him feel that he was among kind friends, a statement which usually evoked further applause. At other times he began by explaining how he happened to be out on a lecture tour and immediately introduced his scheme for the moral regeneration of mankind. Often he began simply by saying, "I once had an experience," and drifted immediately into one of his stories.[53]

His voice, it was observed, had none of the strident shrillness which, in their opinion, characterized the average American;[54] and while it had no particular strength, his speech was so distinct, clear, and penetrating that he could be heard everywhere in the hall, except occasionally when he lowered his voice. What impressed his audiences most, however, about his manner of speech was his slow, leisurely drawl (a Yankee drawl, as reporters characterized it) and his measured manner of speaking, never repeating or withdrawing a word once uttered. The extremely slow rate of speech, it was noted, made each story last a long time; too long, in fact, for the story of the discovery of the corpse in the father's office. This story, a reporter declared facetiously, lasted fifteen minutes, and in the hot Australian climate, where "the deceased doesn't keep for any considerable period, this prolonged exposure was unwise." Still, he acknowledged, it was a most interesting corpse.[55]

Foreign audiences, like those at home, were also greatly impressed by the distinguished humorist's subtle and masterful resources for capturing and holding audience interest. They noted, for example, the skillfully used pause, after which invariably followed a graphic word or a meaningful phrase purposely withheld; the serious, imperturbable demeanor; the dead-pan expression; the occasional groping for a word, though no one imagined that the word was not instantly at his command; and finally the complete naturalness and simplicity of manner by which he concealed the devices which made them laugh.

Try as they might, reporters confessed they found it almost impossible adequately to describe the effect which Mark Twain's performance exerted upon them. What was the magic, they asked themselves, which enabled him for nearly two hours to keep them under his sway?[56] As a lecture it was so utterly out of the ordinary, so unique in material, so delightfully rambling and inconsequential in treatment that no standard came to mind with which it could be critically compared.[57] Even if one were to reproduce his talk verbatim, the magic would be lost; for the reporters quickly sensed that the charm was not primarily in the stories themselves, but rather in the manner of telling, in the techniques, and in the whole speaking personality of the humorist. All of these blended themselves together so simply and naturally and effortlessly that no amount of specification could supply a true and adequate notion of the effect.

That Mark Twain was not merely a funny man, a mere laughter-maker, they also perceived. This man sensed the tears in human affairs. He perceived the acute suffering that afflicted the souls of men. Like Shelley he knew that our sincerest laughter is fraught with pain.[58] His humor was like the foam emerging from the deep streams of serious thought. It was liquid wisdom.[59]

And when he recited the pathetic passage from *Huck Finn,* where Huck starts off to turn "Nigger Jim" over to the authorities because his conscience bothers him, and Jim, unaware of Huck's intention, says, "Dah you goes, de ole true Huck; de on'y white gen'lman dat ever kep' his promise to ole Jim," the audience knew, unmistakably, that this humorist was capable of stirring their souls with purest pathos.

As an international celebrity, Mark Twain found reporters at almost every lecture stop, begging for interviews. In the early tour years, he had customarily avoided reporters. They took up his time, interfered with his rest, and distorted his statements. They were his natural enemies, especially those who reported extensive passages of his lectures verbatim. This practice, as we have seen, he resented from his earliest days as a public lecturer. But during the world tour his attitude toward reporters softened. He received them as often as his physical condition permitted, and received them graciously. At Hobart, Tasmania, for example, where he granted an interview, the reporter of the *Mail* was so impressed by his gracious reception that he commented about it at length. Here was a man who received you so simply and gently as to put away the slightest suspicion of arrogance. He made no attempt to be funny or to dazzle by a display of wit. Nor was he a cheap cynic. "He was content to meet you simply as Mr. Samuel L. Clemens, American gentleman, as distinct from Mark Twain, American humorist; and to talk to him was restful, for his ordinary conversation is subdued and companionable."[60]

The questions raised in interviews ranged all the way from his professional activity as a writer and lecturer to his opinions about wit and humor, his attitudes toward some of his contemporaries in the field of literature, and to matters of a more personal nature. With regard to lecturing he was asked whether he liked it as well as writing, whether he prepared his lectures carefully, and whether his memory sometimes failed him on the platform. "I like the platform," he said, "when I am there, but the thought of it makes me shudder . . . the prospect is dreadful."[61] As for preparing his lectures carefully, he wasn't going to pretend for a moment that he didn't. "I don't believe any public man," he asserted, "ever attained success as a lecturer to paid audiences (mark the qualification), who has not carefully prepared, and has not gone over every sentence, again and again, until the whole thing is fixed upon his memory. I write my lectures and try to memorize them, but I don't always succeed."[62] He confessed that his memory did occasionally fail him on the platform, but it was curious what could be done in such instances without the audience ever suspecting that anything was wrong.[63]

The question was sometimes asked why he hadn't written more. The answer was as frankly revealing as any Mark Twain ever made. "There was too much social life in my city for a literary man, and so for twenty years I gave up the attempt to do anything during the nine months of the twelve I am at home. It has only been during the three months that I have annually been on vacation . . . that I have written anything. It has been the same during the five years that I have been away from America . . . I wish now," he added regretfully, "that I had done differently and had persisted in writing when at home. I could easily have done it, although I thought I could not. . . . In my vacation I have steadily done four or five hours work every day at a stretch, and if only they would have let me alone, I would have done seven hours at a time without getting up from my chair."[64]

When asked about his method of work, he declared that when he worked at all he worked very regularly, every day and all day . . . till late at night. His family sometimes worried that he would overwork, but there was little reason to fear on that account, for he never considered any kind of writing he did as work. He always wrote in longhand. He had tried both a typewriter and a phonograph, but he couldn't get accustomed to the use of either one. As for dictation, he just couldn't learn the art. He could conceive its usefulness for commercial correspondence, but for his kind of writing it provided no inspiration. Nothing inspired a writer so much, he believed, as seeing one's own work go down on a page.[65]

He acknowledged that in general he wrote very slowly. When he wrote rapidly he found that he had to spend so much time the next day correcting his manuscript that he wasted rather than saved time.[66] The only book he ever wrote in a hurry was *Innocents Abroad*. In that case he had to meet a deadline. He finished it in sixty-two days, writing an average of three thousand words a day.[67] When asked what he found most helpful in his work, he replied tobacco. "I always smoke when I work. I couldn't do without it. I smoke by necessity."[68]

Though Mark Twain was almost always referred to in the advertising notices as a humorist, and rarely as a wit, reporters frequently sought his opinion on the differences between wit and humor. He admitted it was difficult to distinguish between them, and declared that he had never encountered a satisfactory definition that pointed up the difference.[69] There was, however, an imperceptible touch of something permanent about true humor that was not present in wit. Wit might be the mere conversational eruption of "smartness," a bright feather, an ornament.[70] It tends to be artificial. It need not be funny. It is something that flashes itself upon the hearer.[71] By general, if tacit, consent it is counted as a poor relation to humor. Pope, for example, was one of the world's wittiest writers, yet most agree he was artificial.[72]

Humor, on the other hand, is never artificial, declared Mark Twain. No man can be a humorist until he is capable of feeling the springs of pathos, and no man was ever properly funny who was incapable of being serious.[73] Life in general is a serious thing and man is the most serious part of it.[74] Humor and pathos are often simultaneous. But precisely what humor is and where it comes from are hard to say.[75] A scribbler like himself, who is serious if nothing else, may come upon a moment of enlightenment. A sudden thought may slip in, and then comes humor. It is a contribution the gods have sent his way. It is really not of man. "It comes from some place, the key of which he does not possess at will."[76]

Asked if some people didn't laugh as poets sing, simply because they must, Mark Twain demurred. True and proper laughter didn't come in that causeless way. Behind it is depth and purpose. "Look at the poor fool in 'Lear'; look at Lamb, getting the quaintest most spirit-moving effects, with the tears just trembling on the verge of every jest; look at Thackeray and Dickens. . . . Behind the broadest grins, the most exquisitely ludicrous situations, they know there is the grinning skull, and that all roads lead along the dusty road to death. . . . I say that the clown rolling in the sawdust at the circus to the shrieks of the children knows and feels the truth I have tried to explain." Garrick's assertion that one might fool the town in tragedy, but it wouldn't stand any nonsense in comedy was eminently true. Any pretender might cast up the whites of his eyes and deliver himself of mock heroics, but a true comedian must have a genuine ring in him; he must feel the deep seriousness of life.[77]

In one of the interviews Mark Twain was asked for his opinion about the duration of humorous books. He acknowledged that such books do not have the same chance of life as narratives, for humorous books depend upon style, in which the taste changes, while the other holds you with facts. He implied that *Innocents Abroad* would not endure, though he confessed it was still very popular. Books like *Roughing It* and *A Tramp Abroad*, on the other hand, offered entertainment in the shape of chaff and substance mixed up together; consequently they were of value and might endure longer. He believed that *A Connecticut Yankee in King Arthur's Court* was likely to have greater permanency than some of his other books because of the powerful political and social lessons which underlay its satire.[78]

Another question sometimes directed to Mark Twain concerned his opinions about various contemporary literary personalities. He was asked if he minded saying anything about Bret Harte. He replied he didn't mind, but if he spoke strongly he wished them to remember he was merely expressing a personal opinion. "I detest him," he declared, "because I think his work is 'shoddy.' His forte is pathos, but there should be no pathos which does not come out of a man's heart. He has no heart, except his name, and I consider he has produced nothing that is genuine. He is artificial."[79]

Mark Twain's harsh appraisal of Bret Harte and his work, while known to his friends and associates at this time, was not yet a matter of general public knowledge. His venturing to voice his true feelings about Harte to reporters, knowing that they would receive immediate and wide circulation through the press, supplies a basis for Twichell's remark that though Mark Twain was a tender and sensitive man, he was also a "hearty hater."[80] It also explains Robert Underwood Johnson's assertion that Mark Twain's "violence was almost unexampled among literary men," and that "no one who knew Mark Twain would have gone to him for a final estimate of a man."[81]

He confessed he had lost much of his admiration for Charles Dickens, one of his early favorites, but gave no reasons. Lewis Carroll was a true and subtle humorist. He was particularly impressed, however, with W. S. Gilbert, the famous librettist of comic operas. His gift for saying the wittiest things and saying them in verse never failed to astonish him.[82]

When Kipling's name was mentioned, Mark Twain reported that he had met the distinguished Englishman on several occasions and liked him very much. He admired his work prodigiously. There was no question that Kipling had genius, and if any one were disposed to find fault with him it would only be with regard to the accuracy of his presentation of Indian matters. There was bound to be criticism on that score. Since he didn't read Kipling for fact, he derived a good deal of pleasure from his books and was especially fond of his *Plain Tales*. As for his ballads, they were inimitable, unsurpassable.[83]

He confessed that he had come to the point where writers of fiction commanded little of his interest. He read little but the heaviest sort of literature and left modern writers severely alone, offering as a reason for his abstention a fear of falling into someone else's style if he dabbled too much among modern writers.[84]

During the American phase of the tour, reporters focused their attention upon Mark Twain's boys' books, *Tom Sawyer* and *Huckleberry Finn* and upon the Mississippi as a special field of interest. Concerning the characters of Tom and Huck, he claimed they were no creations of his own. "I simply sketched them from life. I knew both those boys so well that it was easy to write what they did and said. I've a sort of fondness for 'em anyway.

"I don't believe an author, good, bad, or indifferent, ever lived, who created a character. It was always drawn from his recollection of someone he had known. Sometimes, like a composite photograph, an author's presentation of a character may possibly be from the blending of two or more real characters in his recollection. But even when he is making no attempt to draw his character from life, when he is striving to create something different, even then, however ideal his drawing, he is yet unconsciously drawing from memory. It is like a star so far away that the eye cannot discover it through the most powerful telescope, yet if a camera is placed in proper position under that telescope and left for a few hours, a photograph of the star will be the result. So it's the same way with the mind; a character one has known some time in life may have become so deeply buried within the recollection that the lens of the first effort will not bring it to view. But by continued application the author will find, when he is done, that he has etched a likeness of someone he had known before.

"In attempting to represent some characters which he can-not recall, which he draws from what he thinks is his imagina-tion, an author may often fall into the error of copying in part a character already drawn by another, a character which im-pressed itself upon his memory from some book. So he has but made a picture of a picture with all his pains. We mortals can't create, we can only copy. Some copies are good and some are bad."[85]

He had seleceted the names of the two boys to suit his ear. Both boys were real characters, but "Tom Sawyer was not the real name of the former, nor the name of any person I ever knew, so far as I can remember, but the name was an ordinary one—just the sort that seemed to fit the boy, some way, by its sound, and so I used it. No, one doesn't name his characters haphazard. Finn was the real name of the other boy, but I tacked on the 'Huckleberry.' You see, there was something about the name 'Finn' that suited, and 'Huck Finn' was all that was needed to somehow describe another kind of a boy than 'Tom Sawyer,' a boy of lower extraction or degree. Now, 'Arthur Van de Vanter Montague' would have sounded ridiculous, applied to characters like either 'Tom Sawyer' or 'Huck Finn.' "[86]

As for the Mississippi being his special field of interest, he admitted it was, and for an obvious reason. "By a series of events —accidents—I was the only one who wrote about old times on the Mississippi. Wherever else I have been some better have been there before and will come after, but the Mississippi was a virgin field. No one could write that life but a pilot, because no one else but a pilot entered into the spirit of it. But the pilots were the last men in the world to write its history. As a class they did not naturally run to literature, and this was made more unlikely by another reason. Every pilot had to carry in his head thousands of details of that great river. Details, moreover, that were always changing, and in order to have nothing to confuse those details they entered into a compact never to read anything. Thus if they had thought of writing, they would have had no connected style, no power of describing anything; and moreover, they were so engrossed in the river that there was nothing in life unusual to them. Here then, was my chance, and I used it."[87]

When Mark Twain sailed from Capetown, South Africa, back to England in mid-July of 1896, the world tour at an end, the long ocean voyage afforded him an opportunity to take stock of the venture. Unquestionably he spent a good deal of time in his stateroom finishing his African notes, and in sorting and arranging those he had written in Australia, New Zealand, and India. He probably also spent some time in examining the many books, pamphlets, and magazines he had collected in all these countries with a view to their possible usefulness for his projected travel book. And since money was the primary reason for undertaking the world tour, one can well believe that he often sat in his room and tried to estimate his profits and plan how the money should be parceled out to his creditors.

On the long trip northward to England Mark Twain also had time to sit quietly on deck with his wife and daughter and review the panorama of incidents, some pleasant, some painful, that marked their travels through the four continents. He could not, of course, forget the carbuncles which had kept him in pain for nearly six months; nor the severe colds that had afflicted him at various places and had kept him in bed for days at a time, depriving him of valuable sightseeing opportunities and desirable social events; nor could he forget his deep disappointment in not being able to go ashore at Honolulu because of the cholera. There was the memory of the frightening prospect of transferring from ship to tug in a basket-chair in the turbulent harbor at Gisborne—on Livy's birthday—and his refusal to take the risk. And he recalled other moments of danger, or at least supposed danger. There was the day in Baroda when he first mounted an elephant. He didn't want to ride the elephant, for he was frankly afraid but he dared not reveal that fact.[88] There was also the day Mark Twain climbed into a canvas-canopied handcar, high in the mountains at Darjeeling, and made the thirty-five mile descent down the steep slopes to Calcutta at such a breakneck speed that it nearly took his breath away. The long glide downward produced a sensation of immense exaltation, mixed with deadly fright and unspeakable joy.[89]

And he recalled the excitement in Australia as the newspapers headlined the war scare and the warm friendliness of the people everywhere during the tense period, marred only in one instance when an English lady scornfully informed Mrs. Clemens that the British merely smile at the American threats of war.[90]

He recalled difficulties along the way with servants and waitresses at various inns and hotels. There was the big, frowsy blonde who waited upon them in the station restaurant at Invercargill, whose bad manners had made him homesick because she was so like certain American waitresses he had known.[91] And there was also the stunning Queen of Sheba-style barmaid at Palmerstone North who never failed to answer the bell, but always got up on her dignity and refused performing personal services as unbecoming to her position.[92] And there was the Indian servant whose custom it was to lie on the hard floor outside Mark Twain's door nights, there being no bell; and his other Indian servant, Brampy, whose beautiful black hair was combed back and knotted like a woman's, and who wore a white gown that reached from neck to heels also like a woman's, making Mark Twain feel uncomfortable about undressing unless the servant's back was turned.[93] He recalled with admiration the splendid, shining, dark bodies of Ceylonese children, dressed only in a rag or two of bright color, a perfect combination of body and dress, of grace, comfort, and beauty,[94] and concluded that nearly all black and brown skins were beautiful.[95]

And he recalled the incident at Bombay when a member of their party had sought to take a picture of the famous Parsee Towers of Silence and permission was refused because it was feared that Mark Twain wanted the pictures for the purpose of making fun of those grim receptacles of the Parsee dead.[96] More deeply impressed upon their memory were the things they had seen at Benares, the body burnings at the ghats, the people washing their mouths and drinking in the incredibly polluted waters of the Ganges, and the multitude of phallic symbols all through the city. He had seen ugliness in some of these countries, and poverty and disease and wretchedness one could not easily forget; yet there was beauty too, and strangeness which never failed to excite during the long train rides through pleasant and sometimes exotic rural countrysides and small native villages.

And there were memories of incidents relating to his lectures. He remembered the embarrassment during the performance at Port Elizabeth, South Africa, when a blind lady had to be taken out of the hall because she laughed so loud and so often during the lecture that her presence became a serious nuisance. She had assumed, because Mark Twain was a humorist, that everything he said was funny, and because of her sightlessness was not able to correct her false assumption.[97] And there was the night when the audience laughed at the wrong place, giving him no end of puzzlement, until he discovered later that a kitten had cavorted its way across the platform behind his back.[98] And there was the dogfight which loudly interrupted his lecture at Oamaru, and his surprise that dogs were allowed in New Zealand lecture halls until he read a sign in the hall at Napier, "Dogs positively forbidden in Dress Circle," implying that their presence elsewhere in the hall was not objectionable.[99] And there was the incident at Melbourne, as he stood on the platform just ready to begin his lecture, when a loud voice shouted from the gallery, "Is he dead, Mark? Is he dead?" and his standing there for a moment puzzling what to make of it till it dawned on him that the man was quoting the guide-destroying doctor in *Innocents Abroad*.[100] And there was the pleasant memory of the little girl who had sat close up front during his lecture at Lucknow, whose evident enjoyment of it had given him so much pleasure. That evening after the lecture and just before a banquet given in his honor, a guest had told him of a difference of opinion that had arisen between the girl and her parents concerning the precise number of sins he had mentioned in his lecture. The little girl happened to be right, whereupon he had insisted, before going in to the banquet, on writing his unknown little friend a note with a signed declaration that her recollection of the number was correct.[101] Less pleasant, on the other hand, was his memory of a recurrent and most disagreeable dream of appearing before lecture audiences in his shirt-tail.[102]

If there was in his train of memory any recollections of hardship other than of illness suffered during the long journey, the record fails to reveal them. The painful loneliness which had contributed so much to make the early tours under Redpath almost unendurable played no role on the world tour. With his wife and daughter at his side to share experiences with him and a whole strange new world to see, there was no question of loneliness. And on occasions when his wife and daughter stayed over at a particular place while he made certain segments of the tour without them, Smythe was always there for company and for billiards and to fend off trouble and annoyances.[103] And now the trip, which had loomed so horribly before them when they started out, holding only the prospect of being jolted about the devil's universe to pay off debts that he claimed were none of his making, was over at last. From every point of view, except the long separation from Susy and Jean, it had been eminently successful. As befitting the last tour he was ever to make, it gave him more satisfaction than any he had ever undertaken—except the very first one, the jubilant tour in California and Nevada thirty years previously. His one great hope now was to find a "house in some quiet English village away from the world and society," where he could sit down for a period of time and give himself the luxury of resting and writing.[104]

CHAPTER FIFTEEN

PLATFORM MANNERS AND TECHNIQUES

*I rely for my effects chiefly on a simu-
lated unconsciousness and intense absurdity.* . . . —LIFE OF JAMES REDPATH,
P. *173.*

IT TOOK JAMES R. REDPATH scarcely more than a season to
discover that he had in Mark Twain one of the most popular
lecturers and platform performers on his entire roster. Like
the late Artemus Ward's this young Westerner's art seemed remarkably natural and unstudied, a marvelous adaptation of
native skill and personality to the exigencies of the platform.
Actually, nothing was farther from the truth. While it is well
known that Mark Twain had little if any formal instruction in
public speaking or elocution, as it was called in that day, and
none at all in dramatic art, the fact remains that few of his distinguished contemporaries on the lecture platform, men like
Henry Ward Beecher, John B. Gough, and Wendell Phillips,
were more conscious artists than he.

The truth is that Mark Twain, like so many other so-called
self-made men, took pride in the fact that he had learned the
techniques of platform success through his own initiative and
effort. He made light of formal instruction in elocution, and
scoffed at George Washington Cable, his co-performer during the
tour of 1884–85, for having taken lessons in it. As a result, he
claimed, Cable had become artificial and theatrical, and less
pleasing and entertaining to his audiences than he had been in

the splendid early days of his ignorance.[1] It is now well known that this observation was quite unfair to Cable, who was indeed a highly skilled and effective platform reader and lecturer, and that Mark Twain's criticism of his companion stemmed not only from his distrust of the value of formal training in speaking, but from a somewhat thinly disguised jealously of Cable's obvious and unexpected popularity during the tour.[2]

But if Mark Twain had little exposure to formal instruction in public speaking, it is quite apparent that at the beginning of his career he made a conscious and determined effort to observe good speakers and to study the techniques and devices of his more successful contemporaries, especially those of Artemus Ward. But there were also others whose techniques he observed with absorbed interest. For example, during his stay in New York in the spring of 1867 before his departure on the Holy Land excursion, he visited Plymouth Church in Brooklyn to hear the famous Henry Ward Beecher preach. Carefully observing Beecher's techniques and manners as a speaker, he analyzed them at length in his next letter to the *Alta California,* praising the distinguished clergyman's rich and resonant voice, distinct enunciation, brilliant use of simile and metaphor, and his skillful blend of pathos, humor, and satire in the exposition of the great truths of his text.[3]

He appears to have been even more impressed with the eloquence and power of the Reverend Dr. Chapin, minister of the Universalist Church. There was a preacher! A man who could hold a congregation for as many hours as he wished! An invisible wire ran from every auditor's soul straight to a battery hidden somewhere in that preacher's head, and along those wires traveled in ceaseless flow the living spirit of words. Never before, he declared, had he looked on faces so eager, so rapt, and so fascinated. What was it, Mark Twain pondered, that chained the congregation so? It must have been Chapin's strong, deep, and unmistakable earnestness. There was nothing like that to convince people. But it was not *what* Chapin said that gave him power over his auditors, he concluded; it was his manner. "Manner is everything in these cases—matter is nothing."[4] For Mark Twain it was a truly momentous observation. It clarified for him a truth which he had previously perceived only dimly. It was a truth which, for the time being, he carefully stored away. It was not long, however, before it played a decisive and shaping role in his own performances.

His preoccupation with platform manners and techniques was also revealed in his detailed analyses of other famous speakers then in New York. There was Anna Dickinson, for instance, an extremely popular feminist lecturer whom he had heard speak in Cooper Institute to an audience of 2,500. He did not suspect then that within a year or two he might find himself in competition with her in various towns on the lecture circuit. Now, for his *Alta California* readers, he described her style in considerable detail, noting the qualities which in his opinion accounted for her unquestioned power and skill—her rapid and energetic talking, never using notes, never hesitating for the right word, keeping close to her subject, and reasoning well. There was only one defect. It was noticeable, he thought, in the speeches of most women—she dragged the climax when she should have exploded it.[5]

During the tours under Redpath, however, the people he observed with the greatest interest were his competitors in the field of humor—Josh Billings, Petroleum V. Nasby, Bill Nye, and others. All of these men were on Redpath's list of speakers, along with such "kings of the platform"[6] as have been mentioned earlier. In early October many of these people gathered in Boston as the lecture season opened and had as Mark Twain reports, a lazy and sociable time there, living at Young's hotel but meeting every day at Redpath's bureau and smoking, telling of their various experiences on the platform, discussing their successes and failures, and analyzing methods and techniques which struck them as most effective.[7] These frequent discussions and his attendance at the lectures of his friends whenever opportunity offered became for him fruitful sources of instruction.

But even more fruitful than these, perhaps, was his constant effort to analyze the successes and failures of his own performances, studying the reactions of his audiences, trying now one device, now another, worrying over his failures, and often working into the early morning hours at his hotel to correct mistakes, make revisions, and perfect his performance. While he was often pleased with his successes, the truth is that he never stopped tinkering with his lectures and trying new devices and effects. In everything that pertained to his hour and a half on the platform he was a perfectionist.

For Mark Twain the evening's performance began the instant he stepped from the wings. He had one immediate purpose in mind. That was to put the audience in a receptive frame of mind for a humorous lecture, and if possible, to get it laughing before he ever opened his mouth to speak. The devices by which he sought to achieve these happy effects Mark Twain called "starters," and he appears to have used them in one form or another from his earliest days on the platform. There is a report, for example, that in 1866 in Virginia City he arranged to have the rising curtain discover him at the piano, playing and singing an old favorite, "I Had an Old Horse Whose Name was Methusalem." Then, pretending surprise to be so discovered, he rose amid the shouts of laughter, ambled toward the front of the platform, and began to speak.[8]

One of his favorite starters, and one which he used throughout his early platform career, was his manner of progressing from the wings to the reading stand. As he moved forward he affected a careless shambling gait, and, with one hand in his pocket, proceeded as if he had no particular destination in mind and was completely unaware of the assembled house. Then, looking up suddenly and noticing the audience, he showed surprise and alarm as if he had not expected to be discovered in so exposed a position and did not know for a moment whether to advance or retreat.[9] Proceeding in the direction of the lectern, he walked slowly and hesitatingly around it, as if seeking the most comfortable place to stand. Now for the first time he deliberately faced the audience and stood for a full minute or more, gazing silently at it (with an idiotic stare, as some reporters noted), rubbing his hands together, adjusting his shoulders, turning his head from side to side, sometimes peering intently at the audience through bushy brows, or shading his eyes with his hands as if he were looking for someone.[10] At other times as he stood there, he fidgeted and looked perplexed, giving the impression of a schoolboy who had forgotten his piece. During all this time not a glimmer of a smile lighted his face. (It should be observed, however, that in later years, at the height of his reputation as a writer and speaker, his antics on the platform preceding the lecture became more restrained. During the World tour and later, for example, his celebrity as a humorist and his mere presence on the platform were in themselves sufficient provocations for laughter. The need for starters had all but disappeared.)

Perhaps the most effective and most frequently used starter which Mark Twain devised and used with much success was the self-introduction. Almost from the beginning of his lecturing career, formal introductions had bothered him. They were too long or too flattering or too full of errors. Besides, if there was an introducer (the chairman of the local committee, generally), he insisted upon sitting on the platform behind him, along with the rest of the committee, a circumstance which Mark Twain thoroughly detested. "The confounded chairman sat on the stage behind me," he complained to Livy in November of 1871. "He is the last one that can air his good clothes and his owlish mug on my platform."[11] Recalling his early experiences with local committees Mark Twain once wrote, "There was always a committee, and they wore a silk badge of office; they received us at the station and drove us to the hall; they sat in a row of chairs behind me on the stage, minstrel fashion, and in the earliest days their chief used to introduce me to the audience; but these introductions were so grossly flattering that they made me ashamed, and so I began to talk at a heavy disadvantage. It was a stupid custom. There was no occasion for the introduction; the introducer was almost always an ass, and his prepared speech a jumble of vulgar compliments and dreary efforts to be funny; therefore after the first season I always introduced myself—using, of course, a burlesque of the timeworn introduction."[12] By demanding the platform for himself, Mark Twain eliminated a troublesome source of distraction. He knew that his success depended on manner, on his ability as an actor, on slight but important gestures, on changes of voice, and on pauses rightly timed. Thus to have at his back a group of committeemen whose movements, though ever so slight, were sufficient to distract the audience at crucial moments always troubled and sometimes infuriated him.

The self-introductions, though often varied in minor ways, usually took the following form: "Ladies and Gentlemen, I have the pleasure of introducing to you Mr. Clemens, a gentleman whose numerous accomplishments, I may say, whose historical accuracy and high moral character are only surpassed by his natural modesty and sweetness of disposition." Then, as if speaking parenthetically, he said, "I refer in these general terms to myself, for I am the party. I have always been opposed to ceremonious forms of introduction to an audience as being entirely unnecessary after a lecture has been advertised. I had rather introduce myself, because then I can rely on getting in all the facts."[13] As an example of an introduction that had pleased him he then sometimes told the story of the big California miner who said, "I shall not waste time on this introduction. I do not know anything about this man except two things; one is, that he has never been in the penitentiary, and the other is, I cannot imagine why."[14] After a self-introduction at Wilmington, Delaware, he declared that an introduction by someone else was embarrassing to him because it put him in mind of that member of his family who was hanged, and of what was said of the affair afterward—that the hanging went off very comfortably but the sheriff's speech was annoying.[15]

During the early tours his self-introductions were most successful in those communities where he was not recognized and where momentarily the audience mistook him for a local introducer. When he then announced that he was the speaker, the surprise and laughter that followed served the purpose of a starter. After a few seasons, however, when he had become too well known to fool audiences in this manner, he made no further effort at deception, but relied only upon the laughter that ensued when he made routine local announcements for the chairman of the committee with unexpected touches of humor.

Whenever he allowed himself to be introduced, as occasionally happened, he used the introduction to lead into his lecture. At Peoria, Illinois, for example, where he spoke on The American Vandal Abroad, he declared that it did not *particularly* embarrass him to be introduced in so public a manner, for it reminded him of the European guides who introduced old relics and then described them with a trite story. Thereupon Mark Twain launched out on one of his most famous passages in *Innocents Abroad,* the story about the Roman guides exhibiting the handwriting and the statue of Christopher Columbus.[16]

When Mark Twain finally addressed himself to the reading stand, he usually placed a page of notes on it, or, on occasion, his manuscript. Since reporters often noted that his lectures gave the impression of spontaneity and his jokes were uttered as if he had just thought of them, a word about his attitude toward the use of notes and manuscript on the platform is in order. Almost from the beginning of his lecturing career Mark Twain was emphatic in his belief that a speaker should so impress his lecture upon his memory and understanding as to secure himself against a lame delivery.[17] An audience knows very well, he declared, that a speech is most worth listening to which has been so carefully prepared in private that it will seem impromptu;[18] consequently, any person preparing to make a speech at any time, anywhere, and upon any topic, "owes it to himself and to his audience to write the speech out and memorize it. . . ."[19] Mark Twain was amused that Nasby, after giving his lecture "Cussed Be Canaan," over a period of two or three seasons could not deliver a sentence of it without his manuscript except the opening one, "We are all descended from Grandfathers."[20] Years later, when William Dean Howells consented to give a series of lectures despite his fears of the public platform, Mark Twain earnestly admonished him to get his lecture by heart, or if he carried a manuscript with him to the platform, not to refer to it if at all possible.[21]

It is well known from various newspaper reports that during the first two or three nights of a new lecture, Mark Twain had his manuscript before him on the reading stand. Its mere presence gave him a sense of security. But even during those nights he seldom referred to it and regarded it as a misfortune when he had to refer to it at all. As soon as he had his lecture well in mind, he found the manuscript was more of a hindrance than a help. Free of it, he could introduce new anecdotes, shift their order, and venture upon variations in the telling of them without difficulty. It was a freedom that gave him tremendous advantage, for it allowed him a new measure of creativeness each night upon the platform. The eventual unimportance of the lecture manuscripts to Mark Twain probably explains why so few of them survived.

If Mark Twain dispensed with manuscripts at the earliest possible moment, it appears that he did rely more or less regularly upon a single page of notes which he placed upon the stand before him. There were exceptions, of course. A reporter at Fredonia, New York, noted that he lectured without notes and that this fact gave him an advantage over Nasby.[22] A year later, at Boston, on the other hand, it was observed that before beginning to speak, he placed a page of notes upon the stand.

The preparation and makeup of a page of lecture notes appears to have become a matter of considerable experimentation with Mark Twain. At first his notes consisted of the beginnings of sentences that introduced the major sections of his lecture. But they all looked about alike on the page, and though he committed the sentences to memory, he found he could not recall their order of succession. Consequently, he was in danger of getting mixed up or of skipping matter he wished to include. Compelled to devise a better system, he hit upon the scheme of marking the initial letter of each topic sentence on his finger nails. This also failed when he lost track of the finger he used last. "I couldn't lick off a letter after using it," he added humorously, "for while that would have made success certain, it would also have provoked too much curiosity. There was curiosity enough without that. To the audience I seemed more interested in my fingernails than I was in my subject; one or two persons asked me afterwards what was the matter with my hands."[23]

It was then that the idea of pictorial notes occurred to him. With his pen he rapidly sketched a set of pictures which suggested the various topics, "and did it perfectly. I threw them away as soon as they were made, for I was sure I could shut my eyes and see them any time."[24]

Since Mark Twain's manner of speech contributed so largely to his platform success, it is necessary to speak of his well-known drawl.

A reporter who claimed that he spoke at the rate of three words per minute by the watch was obviously exaggerating, but the rate was unquestionably very slow, a good deal slower than is commonly supposed today. In ordinary conversation, it is well known that Mark Twain was a "lazy" talker. On the platform he exaggerated his slowness, on the conviction that his slow manner of speech contributed importantly to his platform effects and because it appeared appropriate to the tone and character of his ancedotes. There were times when he even cautioned himself to remember to speak slowly, a fact which confirms the thought that slowness of speech on the platform was a deliberately cultivated device.[25]

As everyone knows, however, slowness of speech almost inevitably accompanies a drawl, and the drawl was by far Mark Twain's most pronounced speech characteristic, especially during the early years on the platform. There is evidence that Mark Twain sometimes looked upon his drawl in private conversation as an infirmity, something to be overcome; and it is noteworthy that he once remarked that his wife was as sensitive about her lack of physical strength as he was of his drawl.[26] One cannot escape believing that he came to regard it in ordinary social discourse in somewhat the same light as he had come to regard his slang and other indelicacies of speech, as a symbol of his un-regenerate days. That he made a conscious effort to control it is apparent from the fact as he grew older he often lost it entirely in private conversation, especially when strongly moved or not among close friends.[27] His daughter Clara reports that when the tragic and unexpected news of Susy's death reached her father, in his passionate outburst of grief and bitterness there was no drawl in his speech.[28] On the platform, however, Mark Twain made little or no effort to restrain it. On the contrary, he customarily exaggerated it, for he knew, as Clara Clemens confirmed, that it contributed greatly to the humorous effect of his performances.[29] The drawl was, without doubt, not only one of the most marked characteristics of his platform manner, completely harmonious with his total speaking personality, but also a most effective attention-holding device, especially among northern audiences.

A technique which played an extremely important role in Mark Twain's platform success was his dead-pan expression. It was one of the devices which he probably learned from Artemus Ward when he heard the showman lecture in Virginia City in 1863. "You know," Mark Twain once wrote Redpath, "that I rely for my effects chiefly on a simulated unconsciousness and intense absurdity."[30] He stressed the same point on another occasion when he declared that a humorous story must be told gravely, and that the teller must do his level best to conceal the fact that he even dimly suspects that his story is funny. In fact, to "string incongruities and absurdities together in a wandering and sometimes purposeless way and seem innocently unaware that they are absurdities," was in his opinion the very basis of American art in telling a humorous story.[31]

There were times, however, when the absurdities overcame him also, and he broke into laughter. There was the occasion, for instance, at Meriden, Connecticut, where he hit upon a new manner of telling the Jumping Frog story which so greatly increased its absurdity that he could not keep from laughing himself.[32] Another instance occurred at Paris, Kentucky, during the reading tour with Cable. It had been a splendid audience, which had applauded till their palms were sore and their feet tired. Then, Cable recalls, as Mark Twain came forward for the fourth alternation of their readings, "one side of him dragging, one foot limping after the other in that peculiar way known to us all," the house exploded into laughter and Mark Twain, "grim controller of his emotions at all times," also burst into laughter. And as he came off the platform, still laughing, he admitted to Cable that they had got him off his feet that time.[33]

No less effective than the simulated unconsciousness, the dead-pan, was the well-timed pause. It became one of Mark Twain's most studied devices and the one, perhaps, in which he took the most pride, because its effective use required great skill to avoid treacherous consequences. He once declared that he used to play with it (that is to say, experiment with it) as other children play with a toy.[34] Clara Clemens, who often heard her father lecture, reports that he not only knew the full value of the pause, but had the courage to make a long one when required for effect. As an example of the long pause effectively used, she offered the well-known passage from *Roughing It* which describes Mark Twain's effort to ride a vicious, bucking, Mexican plug. The platform version, slightly different from the book version, is reported as follows: "Well, that horse gave such a buck-jump at last that it sent me out of the saddle up and up— and up so high I came across birds I never saw before. I kept on going and just missed the top of a steeple. But when I got back, the horse . . . . . . was gone."[35]

Another story in which the pause was used with great skill was of the California miner who was hired by a company to blast rock for them. The story first appeared in Mark Twain's Sandwich Islands lecture but is not included in the fragment published by Albert Bigelow Paine in Mark Twain's *Speeches*. Since it is all but unknown to modern readers and yet always provoked uproarious laughter when Mark Twain told it, it is presented here in full:

> The miner drilled a hole four feet deep, put in powder, and began to tamp it down around the fuse. The crowbar struck a spark and caused a premature explosion, and that man and his crowbar shot up in the air, and he went higher and higher and higher until he didn't look bigger than a dog, and he kept on going higher and higher till he didn't look bigger than a bee, and then he went out of sight; and presently he came in sight again, looking no bigger than a bee; and he came further and further and further till he was as big as a boy, and he came further and further till he assumed the full size and shape of a man, and

he came down and fell right into the same old spot and
went to tamping again. (At this point there was loud
laughter and the audience thought the story was finished.
But after a pause, skillfully timed, Mark Twain continued),
And would you believe it, although that poor man was not
gone more than fifteen minutes, yet that company was
mean enough to dock him for the loss of time.[36]

But Mark Twain's most celebrated use of the pause was in
his famous Golden Arm story. In brief form the story ran as
follows: "Once 'pon a time there was a man, and he had a wife,
and she had a' arm of pure gold; and she died, and they buried
her in the graveyard; and one night her husband went and dug
her up and cut off her golden arm and tuck it home; and one
night a ghost all in white come to him and she was his wife; and
she says: 'W-h-a-r-r's my golden arm? . . . W-h-a-r-r's my golden
arm? . . . W-h-a-r-r's my golden arm?' "

Up to this point the story was told with deliberate slowness
and in a deep sepulchral tone, with a pause after the question
each time it was asked, producing a crescendo of suspense that
was heightened as the speaker bent toward the nearest of his
listeners and peered intently into their faces waiting for a reply.
Now came the pause which had to be timed with such delicate
care. Suddenly, with a blood-curdling shout, Mark Twain
sprang forward, thrust an accusing finger at one of the audience
and cried, "YOU'VE GOT IT!" The effect upon the person who
so suddenly and unexpectedly faced the accusing finger, was
electric, sometimes causing him to twitch with alarm, or rise in
his seat. Needless to say, part of the success of the climax depended upon Mark Twain's skill in selecting that person in front
of him who was following the story with the greatest emotional
intensity. Whenever he got the pause the right length, he declared, the closing remark had a startling effect. "But if the
length of the pause was wrong by the five-millionth of an inch
. . . it fell flat."[37]

It is interesting to note the variety of situations in which
Mark Twain used the pause with exceptional effectiveness. In
the Mexican plug story it separated a series of exaggerated statements, calmly spoken, from an equally calm statement of bare
but unexpected fact. In the miner's story the narrative, up to the
pause, has its own humorous climax based upon intense absurdity of situation and could stand alone as a unit. The state-

ment following the pause gives the narrative a sudden unexpected shift, placing all that preceded it into a framework of social criticism. In the Golden Arm story the pause is a prelude to intense shock on the part of the hearer as he finds himself suddenly and violently drawn into the action.

Brief mention has already been made of some of Mark Twain's gestures as he came on stage and during the moment or so he stood at the rostrum before he began to speak. It need only be added that ordinarily in the course of the lecture his manner was quiet and undemonstrative. But some gestures were noted. At times he snapped his fingers or rubbed his hands together softly. At other times he caressed the palm of his left hand with his index finger like the end man in a minstrel show propounding a conundrum. In a more demonstrative mood he put his arms akimbo or churned the air about his head with outspread hands as if fighting mosquitoes. On one occasion, according to a reporter who was himself a wit, he got his arms so twisted that three surgeons in the house edged toward the stage to offer their help.[38] As for other body movements which properly may be classed as gestures, it was frequently noted that his manner was peculiar; that he hung loosely around the desk or flirted around the corners of it, marching or counter-marching in the rear of it. He seldom stood still.

Though the manners and techniques which Mark Twain employed on the platform account for a large measure of his popularity, there were other factors which played important roles. He was by common acknowledgement a consummate actor. Furthermore, he had in a high degree what can best be described as "presence," both on and off the stage.

When he appeared on the platform even during the early years, the force of his personality was immediately felt—a subtle, indefinable attraction which few could escape or ignore, and which fewer could precisely analyze. In later years that force grew, enhanced, perhaps by his personal appearance—his bushy grey hair, his ruddy complexion, his somewhat aquiline nose, his moustache, and his quick-moving and piercing grey eyes under bushy brows. His entire bearing commanded attention. "Of all the men I have ever known," Robert Underwood Johnson, prominent American editor, author, and diplomat, once said, Mark Twain "had the intensest personality."[39] On meeting the American humorist for the first time, Matthew Arnold was no less powerfully attracted. At a reception given in his honor on the occasion of his visit to the United States, he saw a man enter the room. "Who—Who in the world is that?" he asked William Dean Howells with whom he was shaking hands. "Oh that is Mark Twain," Howells replied, and immediately arranged an introduction. And from that moment on, Howells reported, the two men spent most of the evening in each other's company.[40]

Manners, techniques, physical appearance, personality, bearing, voice, potent presence—all these and more made up the sum of Mark Twain's appeal, and made him, during his day, one of the most successful performers on the American platform.

CHAPTER SIXTEEN

AUDIENCE RECEPTION

*Ink actually refuses to photograph his
drolleries and peculiarities of manner.*
—PORTLAND « DAILY FREE PRESS » NOV. *15,
1871.*

MARK TWAIN'S RISE to platform popularity in the late
1860's was immediate and impressive. So rapid, indeed,
was his success that within two years after the memorable first lecture in San Francisco and after only one year on the
lyceum circuit, Redpath advertised him as the most popular
humorist then before the American public. The Cleveland
Herald praised him as the prince of humorists, and Warrington,
Boston correspondent for the well-known Springfield, Massachusetts, *Republican,* spoke of him as incomparably brilliant. It
was apparent that the young Westerner was bringing to the
lyceum audiences a new and very agreeable type of program,
chiefly entertaining but not devoid of instruction, which afforded
a pleasant relief from the heavily didactic programs which characterized the customary winter's course.

That James Redpath was elated about Mark Twain's success
can readily be understood. He had established his lecture bureau
in Boston at a time when many local lyceums were failing. While
he was aware that some of the failures were caused by poor management, he was convinced that a lack of variety in programs was
a more frequent cause. In addition to high class literary lectures,
he urged, the committees should include "a Reading, a Humor-

ous lecture, a Scientific lecture, and a Concert."[1] Lyceum lectures which succeeded only in imparting instruction, he contended, were bound to fail unless they afforded pleasure as well. Indeed, it was an impertinence to attempt to instruct an audience unless the instruction could be imparted pleasantly or eloquently.[2] It was not his intention, he assured the committees, to advise catering to the least educated taste in the local communities, but he felt it important not to neglect the average taste. Lyceum courses should contain something to engage the interest of every class.[3] As for a humorous lecturer, no one, in his opinion, was better suited to the needs of the lyceum than Mark Twain.

In presenting the public reception of Mark Twain's lectures during the early tour years, no attempt will be made to deal with each of the tours separately. For the most part, the audience response, as reflected by newspaper reporters and other observers, touched upon the same aspects of his performances regardless of what tour he happened to be on or of what he lectured on during a particular season. Furthermore, as Albert Bigelow Paine observed, Mark Twain's manner of delivery changed very little over the years, except to become more finished and more apparently artless.[4]

In the main, audience responses had to do with his platform manners and techniques, the nature and quality of his humor, and with his artistry on the platform. There were also, however, comments about the appropriateness of humorous lectures for lyceum courses, and, in connection therewith, serious questions about their worthwhileness—whether Mark Twain had something to say to his audiences or whether he was merely an entertainer.

Features of his performance which first caught the attention of audiences and which invariably provoked the comment of reporters were Mark Twain's platform manners and techniques. His awkward emergence from the wings and approach to the reading stand, the uncertain moving about it as if trying to find the right place to stand, his intent staring at the audience for several moments before making an attempt to speak, the self-introductions—all these were delightfully new to lyceum audiences who had never encountered anything quite like that before. Occasionally reporters expressed the opinion that the manners were clownish and that Mark Twain could well drop them without detriment to his fun,[5] but such instances were rare. Almost invariably, these platform devices were greeted with laughter and applause, and won for him that feeling of rapport with his audience which he deliberately sought to achieve during the opening moments of the evening's performance.

Though the self-introductions were occasionally singled out for criticism, the objection was never on the ground that they lacked humor, but that they deprived the chairman of the local committee of an opportunity to enjoy a moment of prominence before his fellow townsmen. The probability is strong that it was Mark Twain's obvious success with self-introductions that led Redpath to recommend to local committees everywhere that they abolish the practice of introducing lectures whenever possible as it was a nuisance and an excrescence.[6]

A never failing source of interest and pleasure for his audiences was Mark Twain's dead-pan expression—his simulated unconsciousness that he had said anything funny, even while reporting anecdotes of the intensest absurdity, though all the while the entire house was engulfed in laughter. Reporters commonly observed that during an entire evening's performance he did not smile once. Indeed, the more the audience laughed the more he looked as if he were about to cry, and, according to a reviewer for the Chicago *Tribune,* looking as solemn as an undertaker screwing down a coffin lid.[7]

No less pleasing to most audiences was Mark Twain's drawl. During the first lyceum tour some reporters professed to be annoyed with it on the assumption that it was a stage affectation, declaring that it spoiled the effect of many of his finest sentences.[8] Julia Newell, writing for the Janesville, Wisconsin, *Gazette,* in 1867, pronounced it abominable.[9] Others regarded it as a sort of platform trick of the same category as the tricks of spelling which characterized the writings of some of his humorous contemporaries. Actually, his drawling manner of speech was a characteristic from early childhood. When Horace Bixby, the Mississippi pilot who taught Mark Twain the river, once asked his cub, "What makes you pull your words that way?" Sam Clemens replied, "You'll have to ask my mother. She pulls hers too."[10] Henry Watterson, prominent American journalist and editor, who had met Mark Twain's mother, described her drawl as high-bred and patrician, not rustic and plebeian, and asserted that Mark Twain derived his drawl from her.[11]

The error of assuming that the drawl was a stage affectation did not long persist. Reporters soon discovered that it characterized his every-day manner of speech whether on the platform or in private interview. Nevertheless, his slow rate of speech, an inevitable concomitant of the drawl, occasionally provoked the charge of monotony. The reporter who asserted that Mark Twain spoke at the rate of three words per minute was obviously facetious, but the rate was, in fact, unusually slow even for a drawler. It was observed that he talked like a man extremely tired or extremely lazy, and that the words seemed to "drop rather than to be uttered."[12] More often, however, the "long drawn words" were declared an effective aid to the story and the joke,[13] and were regarded as sufficient of themselves to make an audience laugh.[14]

More disagreement arose about the volume and quality of his voice. From the earliest days of his platform career, Mark Twain seems to have encountered trouble in making himself heard. The difficulty resulted in part from a tendency to drop his voice at sentence ends. In the main, however, it arose from his failure to adjust to the accoustical properties of the lecture halls. In large city halls, designed especially for lectures, his voice carried fairly well. In smaller communities, where halls were built to serve a variety of purposes, and where the walls were bare, the floors uncarpeted, and the chairs movable, people had to strain to hear him. As a consequence, reporters frequently remarked that he should have spoken louder.[15]

The effort to raise his voice high enough to be easily heard in a hall with poor accoustical properties, however, created for Mark Twain a serious dilemma. To be sure, he wanted to be heard; but raising his voice made him feel that he was yelling, which, he feared, seriously minimized the feeling of naturalness which he wished to create—that "confidential conversational tone" which broke down all barriers between himself and his audience.[16] It was the unwelcome necessity of talking more loudly than he wished which precipitated some of Mark Twain's rages about squeaking floor boards, squeaking shoes, the rustling of programs, and the noise of latecomers moving down the aisles and into their seats. It is not without significance that he often referred to lecturing as "yelling." He soon recognized, of course, the importance of distinct articulation as an aid to his audiences and was pleased when reporters noted his effective use of it.[17]

Concerning the quality of Mark Twain's voice, reporters had relatively little to say. Though they seldom described it as pleasing, only rarely did they single it out for criticism. If newspaper accounts may be trusted, however, there appears to have been, especially during the early tour years, a slight nasal quality in his speech, which may have been exaggerated at times by a head cold. It may have been at such a moment of affliction that he lectured at Indianapolis and provoked a reporter to describe his speaking as a "singsong snuffling from the nose, never varying six notes"—the most miserable speaking he had ever heard.[18] Even as late as 1872, The Haverhill *Tri-Weekly Publisher* referred pointedly to the penetrating nasal quality of his voice.[19] Nevertheless, in spite of such comments, it is evident that any nasality which Mark Twain's voice may have possessed at times was ordinarily not sufficiently pronounced to be noticeable. Most reporters found the quality of his voice entirely acceptable and even agreeable.

Nor did the reporters have much to say about Mark Twain's language. If in any of his lectures he resorted to slang and crudities of diction, the record contains little evidence of it. Though some of his auditors found particular mental images presented in his lectures unpleasant and distasteful, the language employed to evoke such images escaped censure. His use of the vernacular and his familiar colloquial style of expression, especially when telling a story, invariably delighted audiences. They expected such language in a humorous lecture. At any rate, it was so simple and natural and so thoroughly in harmony with his casual platform manner that it probably never occurred to them to remark about it.

Though it was generally noted that Mark Twain possessed little eloquence, it was observed that his language flowed easily, gracefully, and eloquently[20] in the passages which described the Sphynx and the Parthenon in the Vandal lecture and the volcanic eruptions and the dreamy beauty of Hawaiian scenery in the Sandwich Islands lecture.

If Mark Twain succeeded in pleasing his audiences by the use of vernacular without resorting to slang and other crudities of speech, he also managed in large measure to escape the charge of bad taste. In this, fortunately, as in the use of proper language, the advice of Mrs. Fairbanks and of his wife unquestionably saved him; for the danger of giving offense by lapsing into bad taste was especially present in the early years and continued to bedevil him through the years, as his after-dinner speech on the occasion of Whittier's seventieth birthday dinner testifies.[21] During his California and Nevada lectures, as we have seen, he was charged in the Pilgrim Life lecture as having been too familiar with his audiences and that his humor verged on the improper and coarse. Precisely what evoked the charge, whether improper language or risque allusion, or both, was not indicated, but it was exactly the sort of criticism which Mrs. Fairbanks feared he might incur unless he disciplined his tongue.

Oddly enough the lecture which gave him the most difficulty on the score of propriety was his longtime favorite, Our Fellow Savages of the Sandwich Islands. To some the very title was an offense. Others were displeased by what they regarded as indelicate references to native dress, that is to say, native nudity of the Sandwich Islanders. Actually what appears to have displeased them was not the manner in which he spoke of these matters, but the fact that he mentioned the subject at all; for the text of the lecture as reported in the newspapers reveals nothing objectionable in the manner of language of telling. Still others professed to be revolted by Mark Twain's references to the Sandwich Islanders' fondness for certain kinds of food—"fricasseed cats" and "baked dogs," and by his statement that the latter was nothing more than our "cherished American sausage with the mystery removed," though both these remarks usually brought bursts of laughter.

The main causes of offense, however, were references to cannibalism in the Islands and particularly his account of the enterprising Kannaka in one of the back settlements who had become tired of eating his fellow tribesmen and wanted to see "how a white man would go with onions." He kidnapped an old whaler, Mark Twain reported, but "either the cuisine, or his conscience, or the weight of the whaler on his stomach killed him."[22] Perhaps conscious that the unpleasant image might arouse disgust, Mark Twain attempted to minimize the effects of the cannibal references by stating that he did not quite believe the stories himself. It was not till 1873 when he revised the Sandwich Islands lecture for the British public that he eliminated the Kannaka story and also the proposal which usually followed it, during the American tours, to illustrate cannibalism on the stage if any mother in the audience would bring up her child.

In the main, however, it can be said that Mark Twain avoided the pitfalls of bad taste. On the contrary, he was often pointedly praised because his lectures were free from obscenities, risqué allusions, and the smut popularly associated with humorous performances of his day. It was noted with approval that his humor did not degenerate into the coarse and stale jests of the endman in the burnt-cork fraternity, or into the buffoonery of a clown.[23]

The charge of irreverence which had frequently been leveled at his book *Innocents Abroad* was only occasionally directed against his lecture based upon that book. In preparing the Vandal lecture, thanks to the vigilant supervision of Mrs. Fairbanks and his wife, he deleted or toned down satiric attacks on the old masters of Europe, the priests, various Old World church practices, and the highly unflattering pictures of the Holy Land and its people. Such irreverence as appeared in the lecture he astutely attributed to the touring vandals rather than to himself.

As a consequence, the Vandal lecture largely escaped censure. The Sandwich Islands lecture, on the other hand, was not so fortunate. The passages which most frequently gave offense were those which appeared to put the labors of the Christian missionaries in the far-off islands of Hawaii in an unfavorable light. By stating that the white man and his civilization had brought all sorts of complicated diseases to the Islands and, as a consequence, had reduced the native population from 400,000 to 55,000 by 1865, he seemed to imply that part of the blame for the depopulation rested upon the missionaries. Thus at Jamestown, New York, one of the auditors aired his dissatisfaction by charging that the noble missionaries of the Sandwich Islands were abominably and jestingly misrepresented. Such ill-timed levity against the religious scruples of the community, he added, amounted to nothing less than a public offense.[24]

When Mark Twain realized that his comments about the missionaries might be unfavorably interpreted, he exercised care to prevent such instances from occurring; but here and there, as at Jamestown, he failed. That he was more concerned to avoid the charge of irreverence in his lectures on the lyceum circuit than he was in his books can readily be understood. There his performances were often sponsored by Y.M.C.A. and church organizations. Furthermore, many of his performances were given in churches. He was perceptive enough to know that under such circumstances, irreverence on the part of the lecturer would be altogether out of place. Nevertheless, restraint from indulging in godless utterances at times gave him a real pang. Being pious didn't particularly jibe with his principles he claimed. There was a fascination about meddling with forbidden things.[25] Indeed, a discriminating irreverence was, in his opinion, the creator and protector of human liberty.[26]

Of all the adverse criticism that appeared in the newspapers and other journals, none troubled Mark Twain more deeply than that concerning a lack of substance in his lectures and their questionable merit for lyceum courses. Was he, as some critics loudly asserted, merely a funny man on the stage, a jester, a joker, whose primary aim was to make comic capital of his materials? All these charges in one form or another were made against him during the lyceum tours. "Mark Twain has come and gone," one reporter declared, "and who is wiser and better for such trifling chatter? Small talk is getting altogether too common, and too popular, and too small."[27] Others declared flatly that his lectures were mostly nonsense, desultory trash, an occasion for laughter on a very small capital of wit, and that he sacrificed everything to make the audience roar.[28] While some admitted that his lecture imparted information, they were disappointed when a serious passage ended in a joke.

There were those who took their neighbors to task for demanding humorous lectures on the lyceum courses. Granted that they furnished variety, as Redpath claimed, did they not also tend to cheapen the course? Was a performance so obviously designed to evoke laughter compatible with the long established purposes of the lyceum? Wasn't it undignified to be seen laughing at it?[29] These same people, it was asserted, would not turn out to hear a sound and able exposition of ideas. Nonsense, not sense, was what they wanted.[30] Chiding his fellow townsmen for poor attendance at most of the season's programs, a reporter at Meriden, Connecticut, added despairingly, "but this is a minstrel-loving community, and there is no help in us."[31]

There were also those who, professing to enjoy Mark Twain's lectures, were willing to admit that he offered only deliberately designed nonsense—"only that and nothing more." In their opinion he was not a preacher, not a reformer, not a philosopher, not a teacher. He was and pretended to be "nothing but a joker."[32] It was a point of view, as we shall see, Mark Twain bitterly resented, but was not blameless in creating.

Joining the attack on humorous lecturers and lectures, and undoubtedly exercising considerable influence upon local lyceum committees and newspaper reporters, was J. G. Holland, influential editor of *Scribner's Monthly*, a writer of didactic and sentimental verse, novels, and miscellaneous prose, sometimes under the pseudonym "Timothy Titcomb." During the late 1860's and early 1870's while Mark Twain was touring the lyceum circuits, Holland was also a frequent performer on the lyceum platform. Nothing, it appears, distressed him more than the inclusion of humorous lectures on the lyceum courses. Such lectures, he declared, tended to degrade them to mere entertainment.

There was a time, he contended, when lectures were lectures, and the lecturer had something to say. Now, he charged, a lecture was any kind of nonsense that "any literary mountebank" could find an opportunity to utter. "Artemus Ward lectured," he declared, "and was right royally paid for acting the literary buffoon. He has many imitators." Nearly every lyceum course now contained the names of triflers on the platform, and in his judgment these members of the lecturing guild tended to exercise a degrading influence upon the public taste. Though these "drollerites" made money for the local associations, they should be banished from the lyceum platform.[33]

To what extent Holland's diatribes were aimed at Mark Twain personally can only be conjectured, but there was no doubt in Mark Twain's mind that he was a primary target, especially because in many quarters he was regarded as an imitator of Artemus Ward. In an article called "An Appeal From One That Is Persecuted" (which he fortunately had the good sense to withhold from publication), he reacted with characteristic heat and vigor. Holland's moralizing lectures, he charged had "hung crepe on more lyceum door knobs than those of any other man in America." What was ruining the lecture courses, he retorted, was not the inclusion of humorous lectures, but a whole season of dry old fashioned moralizing and strictly instructional lectures unrelieved by humor. In the end, Mark Twain asserted, the only thing that saved many of the local associations from going under was the inclusion of the very drollerites and triflers Holland complained about. And he supported his assertions by citing instances where it had been true.[34]

Fortunately, most of Mark Twain's auditors appeared untroubled in their enjoyment of his platform humor. What better way was there, they asked, to open the heart and enjoy every good impulse than to tingle the veins of humor. A lecturer who can administer to the mind the healthful relaxation provided by a hearty laugh was performing a valuable service.[35] This point of view was vigorously endorsed by others who were sure that many of Mark Twain's "touches" would be laughed over long after the more solid matter supplied during the winter's course would have been forgotten.[36] It was also, as we have seen, a point of view strongly endorsed by Redpath, whose judgment Mark Twain greatly respected.

It would be absurd, one writer asserted, "to attempt to describe a discourse which wandered from the gay to the grave continually, and kept the audience in alternate states of laughter and close attention. . . . It was a string of pearls from which the string had been lost."[37] Perhaps the best description of audience reaction was offered by a reporter who observed that the whole house just sat there and simmered.

Attempts to describe Mark Twain's humor inevitably led to comparisons with his fellow humorists, Artemus Ward, Josh Billings, and Petroleum V. Nasby. Comparisons with Ward were most frequent, many people believing that Mark Twain imitated the great showman, observing, however, that he lacked the valuable aid of Ward's panoramic views. One critic pointed out that the two were alike in passing abruptly from one topic to another, but that when Ward did this he changed his picture, whereas Mark Twain merely scratched his head.[38] More seriously it was observed that Mark Twain, unlike his celebrated fellow humorist, placed no dependence upon uncouth spelling and local vernacular. He had none of the swagger of the traditional Yankee joker, and his lectures were devoid of low phrases.[39]

The comparison with Nasby usually turned upon two points—that Mark Twain was humorous without indulging in Nasby's vulgarities, and that his platform style was much superior. Nasby, for example, read his lectures and hurried through them, whereas Mark Twain lectured without manuscript. To Mark Twain's credit, also, was the fact that his pseudonym did not suggest a different personality than his own, as did "Artemus Ward, Showman," "Petroleum V. Nasby, Cross-roads Politician," and "Josh Billings, Saturnine Philosopher." When Mark Twain faced his audience it was entirely in his own character.

One of the best and most extended comparisons of Mark Twain's humor with that of his humorous contemporaries appeared in the Albany, New York, newspaper in 1870, reporting

The Sandwich Islands lecture given in that city on the evening of January 10. Mark Twain, it flatly stated, was the best humorist then before the public. "His humor is in the idea, not in the mere use or misuse of words and phrases, which unfortunately seems to constitute the sole resort of most of the so-called humorists of the day. In genuine fun, both in the idea and in the setting, Mark Twain is immeasurably in advance of Nasby, Josh Billings and the whole miscellaneous tribe of bad spellers and verbal contortionists . . . the very 'Petroleum' of Nasby is affected, and his peculiarities give zest rather to partisan politics than to the multitude. Josh Billings has a deal of humor, but both he and Nasby shroud themselves in a mystery of infamous orthography, which becomes tiresome and even painful in a short time." As a consequence, it was asserted, the audience turns with unmingled satisfaction to the natural humor of Mark Twain. Artemus Ward in his lecture, Babes In the Wood, made a point of constantly evading his subject. Mark Twain did nothing of the kind. "His lecture with the fun out," it was perceptively observed, "would make a telling and accurate sketch of the Sandwich Islands and the natives thereof, but with the fun in it is a lecture that both amuses and instructs."

Of all the newspaper reports of his lyceum lectures none pleased Mark Twain more than that which appeared in a newspaper in the small Michigan town of Charlotte, following his lecture The American Vandal Abroad.[40] The report, which appeared over the signature "Brownie," opened with a compliment for Mark Twain's splendid mingling of humor and sense. This mingling made the lecture far more than a mere piece of drollery. In a few simple sentences, the lecturer had brought before the imagination clear and brilliant pictures more impressive than the real scene; for artists and poets, the writer asserted, see more in nature to love and admire than ordinary observers. Such lectures convinced an audience that far more satisfactory and enduring imagery can be impressed upon the mind by words, tone, and gesture than by painting or engraving.

"After holding the audience spellbound before the Sphinx, with its melancholy gaze over the past ages, or after contemplating Venice with its silent palaces, bridges, and gondolas, or Athens by moonlight from the Acropolis, Mark Twain then brought in his humorous vandalisms which served, by contrast, to heighten the enjoyment of what had preceded. "He mingled

in a little of the grotesque and just enough of the terrible . . . to
heighten the glow of his humorous descriptions, while these, in
turn served to enrich the splendor of his great pictures. It was
this artistic changing of the excitement for different faculties and
different sides of our nature, that so completely entertained, and
rested, and kept attention of the audience constantly fixed. This
[is] all art; the very highest kind; that consummate art which con-
ceals itself under perfect simplicity and naturalness."

Mark Twain, Brownie continued, was an artist who avoided
all effort at sublimity and pathos. He had learned what all artists
must learn—to know where he might fail and where he could
safely venture. He might have given his audience wit of a keen,
cold, and sparkling kind, but good taste and sympathy for his
fellow man, which Brownie asserted was the source of all genial
humor, had taught him to refrain. In the entire Vandal lecture
there was not a single unkind cut, nothing offensive. From every
point of view, he concluded, the lecture was a good one and
worthy of inclusion in the winter's lyceum course.

Brownie's critical appraisal delighted Mark Twain immensely. It was not only pleasingly detailed but presented him
to the public as something more than a mere platform comedian.
In every way, he believed, it was a perceptive appraisal. It was
especially welcome because it flattered him to believe that in
large measure he had succeeded in solving for some of his auditors
at least, the troublesome task of bringing into acceptable balance
his desire to amuse and the obligation to instruct. Certain that
the review would also please Mrs. Fairbanks and help allay her
fear that his humor in the Vandal lecture might appear ill-
natured or erupt into bad taste, he sent her a clipping from the
Charlotte paper, adding a word of praise for Brownie whom he
pronounced "a very good judge."[41]

Newspaper accounts concerning Mark Twain's grooming
and general appearance on the platform during the early tour
years vary a good deal. Some reporters found him pleasing in
dress and figure, and described him as a well-built, trim-looking
man, with intelligent features and a well-defined moustache. His
eyes, deep-set, twinkled like stars in the night. Bushy brows over-
hung them. His head, they declared, was an eminently good
one.[42]

Other reporters, however, asserted that he was not beautiful,
that his hair was carroty, and that he looked like a man who had

long worked in a brickyard without a hat. The observation attests the fact that Mark Twain's complexion during the early tour years was decidedly ruddy. Mark Twain's own description of himself some years later, humorously rendered in a delightful mixture of English and garbled German, is as follows:

"Fuss 8 ½ inches hoch; weight doch aber about 145 Pfund, sometimes ein wenig unter, sometimes ein wenig oben; dunkel braun Haar und rhotes moustache, full gesicht, mit sebr hobe Oren and leicht grau prachtvolles strahlenden Augen und ein Verdammtes gut moral character."[43]

Despite occasional comments to the contrary Mark Twain was usually meticulous about his personal appearance on the platform. On the lyceum circuit and later he always appeared in a frock coat, unless circumstances prevented, which occasionally happened when his baggage went astray. He recognized the importance of being well groomed on the platform, partly because he knew audiences expected it, but chiefly because he knew he could not be at his best unless all the circumstances regarding his appearance were right and he knew that they were right.

As many newspaper reporters confessed in attempting to describe Mark Twain's platform manner, pen and ink were simply inadequate to the task. As we have seen they commented on the slow speech, the drawl, the voice, the language, the simulated unconsciousness, the humor, the pause, and the personal appearance. They tried hard to indicate the naturalness, simplicity, and apparent artlessness of his performance. They noted that he uttered his jokes as if he had just thought of them, giving an effect of immediacy and spontaneity. They noted the impression he gave of being extremely lazy. Yet they well knew that the sum of the parts failed to provide either an adequate or an accurate description of his manner. It was as elusive to define as an aroma. Sitting before him in the lecture hall one could sense and enjoy the subtle influence of his remarkable personality and manner, but it was altogether beyond one's skill to encompass it in words. A personal magnetism seemed at once to capture the sympathy of his audience. Almost all agreed that to get a true comprehension of what Mark Twain was like on the platform one had to see him and hear him.

CHAPTER SEVENTEEN

ON AUDIENCES

*I know a great many secrets about audi-
ences—secrets not to be got out of books,
but acquired only by experience.* —MARK
TWAIN'S LETTERS, II, 542.

MARK TWAIN'S STATEMENT in 1891 to an unidentified
correspondent that he knew a great many secrets about
audiences was based upon long and abundant experience. By that year, however, whatever he had learned about
them could scarcely be called secrets, for on various occasions he
had expressed his thoughts about them, sometimes in vigorous
language.

It should be pointed out at once, however, that Mark Twain
was rarely harsh in his judgment of audiences. If, on a particular
evening he failed, or thought he had failed, it is to his credit that
he tended to place the blame upon himself, or upon circumstances and annoyances for which the audience as such was
scarcely to blame. Distractions caused by latecomers, people
sitting on the platform behind him, the presence of disturbing
children, or other irritating interruptions distressed him sometimes to the point of visible anger; but in such cases his fulmina-
tions were directed only against those who could and should have
prevented the annoyances. And only rarely did his comments
about particular audiences imply that they were dull-witted, or
that their lack of a sense of humor was a national trait.

One of Mark Twain's best known aversions was lecturing

to church audiences. "I never made a success of a lecture delivered in a church yet," he once complained to James Redpath.[1] People were afraid to laugh in a church. The moment they entered its doors, he felt, a mood, a state of mind, took possession of them which was alien to the reception of a humorous lecture. Consequently, the lecturer was immediately faced with a fundamental problem. He must somehow free them from the restraints of custom which made laughter seem inappropriate in a church and recreate a mood favorable to it, or fail. A humorous lecture that produced no laughter, or at best, only restrained and "respectable" laughter, could only be counted as a failure. An anecdote which delighted Mark Twain because it admirably illustrated the plight of the humorous lecturer who faced a church audience that was afraid to laugh found its way eventually into *A Connecticut Yankee in King Arthur's Court*. For a full hour the lecturer had flooded his audience with the killingest kind of jokes and they had remained silent. After the program was over and he had turned wearily to leave, a number of old graybeards came up to him, wrung his hand, and declared that his lecture was the funniest thing they had ever heard, and that it was all they could do to keep from laughing right out in meeting.[2]

The truth, of course, is that Mark Twain frequently did lecture in churches, despite his request that Redpath avoid such bookings where ever possible, and that he often came away well pleased with his church audiences. Indeed there were times when he noticed "divines" in his audience whose open enjoyment of his humor pleased him and made him feel grateful.[3] Once, when he thought he had failed, the failure came after he had lost his temper because of the constant and prolonged interruption of latecomers. The "idiot president" had insisted upon introducing him while people were still pouring in, and they had kept pouring in for several minutes after he had begun to speak. Finally, in exasperation, he interrupted his lecture and shouted to the doorkeepers to shut the doors and keep them shut. After this outburst of anger, his equanimity was completely ruined and the task of getting his audience back into a frame of mind to enjoy a humorous lecture was all but impossible. From that time on, he later reported to Livy, the "church was harder to speak in than an empty barrel would have been. . . ." At the close of the lecture he apologized so fervently for his outburst and for his poor performance that later in the evening the members of the local committee, out of sheer sympathy, had come to his room to comfort him.[4]

As between big city audiences and small town ones, it is quite evident that he preferred the former. Country audiences were difficult. They were less responsive and were slower, he believed, in their perception of humor. A passage that they would "approve with a ripple will bring a crash in the city."[5] City audiences were more sophisticated concerning humor and less restrained in their enjoyment of it. During the early tour years he had especially praised San Francisco, Carson City, San Jose, and St. Louis as places where "they snap up a joke before you can fairly get it out of your mouth."[6] Later he included New York, Chicago, Philadelphia, and Boston in the list. He had been a bit apprehensive about Boston when he first lectured there in November of 1869. It was regarded as a test town for lecturers, and he well knew that his success in New England would depend upon the way the Boston audience of four thousand critics received him.[7] He soon discovered, however, that he had nothing to fear and that the Bostonians were as warm and responsive as he could have wished.[8]

That Mark Twain preferred big audiences to small, whether in large cities or small towns, is easy to understand. Big audiences meant big box office receipts. When audiences were small, he fretted and complained, wondering whether the poor income was worth all the trouble and hardship. Money counted. He needed it. And since big cities were more likely to produce big audiences than small towns, the time came when, if he lectured at all for money, he lectured only in large cities. In later years, when he no longer lectured for pay and accepted speaking and reading engagements simply for his own gratification and that of his audience, small audiences no longer troubled him. Indeed, he found it in his heart to pay them a warm tribute. The lecturer or reader who had mastered all the arts of his trade could move a small audience most profoundly, he told his daughter Clara a few years before his death. Their faces, he declared, light up with pleasure, for they feel that though they are a small group they are very welcome to the speaker. And out of that feeling grew a warm sense of rapport.[9]

Mark Twain was sometimes especially wary of the Dutch audiences of Eastern Pennsylvania and parts of New York. Of

Kittaning, Pennsylvania, he wrote Livy in January, 1872, that it was a "filthy, stupid, hateful Dutch village," and that he had to lecture to "these leatherheads tonight."[10] At Allentown, he concluded, he would never be able to "handle these chuckle-headed Dutch" with his Reminiscences lecture.[11] As matters turned out, he soon discovered that he was unable to handle any audiences with it anywhere, and presently abandoned it. When he switched to the Artemus Ward lecture, he was more optimistic. He wrote Redpath hopefully that he expected to "fetch" the Pennsylvania Dutch with it,[12] and the record indicates that to some degree he did. Actually, he had considerable reason to be optimistic. Two years earlier, on January 10, 1870, he had given his Sandwich Islands lecture to an immense audience in Albany with much success. At that time he had written Livy proudly that though it was hard to make Albany Dutchmen laugh, "the subscriber did it."[13] But, of course, Albany was a sizable city and city audiences were more receptive of humor. Then, too, the gate receipts had pleased him.

Though Mark Twain rarely had occasion to lecture or read before all-Negro audiences, his liking and respect for their race led him happily to accept invitations to entertain them. It is not surprising, therefore, to find him, on one occasion, looking forward with much anticipation to a program he was invited to give to the colored members of the African Church in Hartford.[14] Had other colored groups expressed a wish to hear him, there is little doubt that Mark Twain would have made a sincere effort to grant it.

For a number of reasons Mark Twain preferred audiences where men largely outnumbered women. Where women were in the majority, he maintained, failure could invariably be counted on. Nothing could prevent it but a "carefully organized *claque*."[15] Men, he once declared, no matter how stupid, were more responsive than women, no matter how bright.[16] The reason? Simply this—"Ladies are cowards about expressing their feelings before folk; men *become* cowards in the presence of ladies."[17] The result was that the silence of the ladies gradually exercised a chilling effect upon the whole house. At this stage, Mark Twain declared, there was only one thing for the lecturer to do, and that was to introduce an uproariously comic anecdote, then announce that he had been smitten with a killing headache and retire from the platform.[18]

He also professed to dislike matinee audiences because of the predominance of women.[19] But this dislike appears to have troubled him much more during the early tour years than later. Even as early as 1872, however, it is apparent that the presence of women in the audience, especially attractive young women, posed no threat; for at Steubenville, Ohio, he was pleased to report, a "mighty handsome lot" of seventy young ladies from the Female Seminary had turned out to hear him.[20] Later, after the great tours were over, and even before, Mark Twain often lectured and read to groups made up entirely of women. Of such groups, none delighted him more than those of young women from Barnard and other colleges.[21]

His early liking for audiences made up mostly of men probably accounts in large measure for his enthusiasm for convict audiences. For example, he especially enjoyed lecturing at the Men's Reformatory at Elmira. It was the best audience in the world. Other lecturers and readers, he noted, were also favorably impressed with these audiences and came away wondering how to account for the splendid successes they had achieved before such groups. He was sure it was not because these audiences were the most intelligent and appreciative in the world, as some believed. The whole secret lay simply in one fact—the absence of ladies.[22]

There were, of course, certain towns where Mark Twain liked to lecture and others which he detested. As might be expected, the towns he liked best were those where his audiences were large, or where he encountered an especially warm and intelligent response. Cleveland, Newark, Utica, Indianapolis were some of the towns that he especially liked because they gave him splendid audiences. The town, however, which seems to have won his warmest affection was Fredonia, New York. His lecture there had given him immense satisfaction and he had felt so happy all through it that he introduced into his remarks a number of serious passages that were entirely impromptu. Jokingly he wrote to Livy that it was just about as good a lecture as he had ever listened to.[23] So delighted was he with the warmth and intelligence of the audience that, though he had come into Fredonia by night and had left in the night and had seen practically none of it, he presently settled his mother, sister, and niece there, partly because it was close to Buffalo where he then lived, but particularly because he was confident they would like the people.

The towns Mark Twain disliked to lecture in were usually those where on previous occasions he had failed to win his audience, or where for one reason or another he had felt mistreated. For, example, he found little pleasure in his audience at Worcester, New York, in November of 1871, because it was made up of "1,700 of the staidest, puritanical people" one ever saw, and one of the "hardest gangs to move that ever was."[24] At Buffalo it was not the audience but the lecture committee he had a grudge against. During his residence in that city he had once given them a packed house free of charge, and the committee had never even taken the trouble to thank him. Furthermore, they had allowed him to shift for himself in getting to the lecture hall. "I mortally hate that society," he wrote Redpath, and requested not to be looked there.[25]

His dislike for Jamestown, New York, was even more violent. Here, again, his objection was not so much because of the audience, which appears to have received his Sandwich Islands lecture (January 21, 1870) well enough, but because of the violent attacks upon it which appeared in the newspapers following the lecture. A feud had broken out between local editors concerning the merit of the various speakers which the lyceum committee had engaged for the season. Mark Twain's lecture, humorous, satirical, and here and there apparently disrespectful of the Sandwich Islands missionaries, brought the feud unpleasantly into the open.[26] On the one hand his lecture was attacked as worthless and insulting; on the other defended as good humorous entertainment. Caught in the middle, Mark Twain was furious. "Don't lecture me in Jamestown," he warned Redpath two seasons later. He had no intention of lecturing there. All lecturers, he supposed, hated that place.[27]

On the basis of the evidence presented, it is clear that no matter where or when or under what circumstances Mark Twain lectured, there was for him one indispensible criterion of a good audience—its laughter. An audience which was deterred from laughter by conventional restraints or by fear of laughter was a poor audience. So, too, were audiences which were slow in their perception of humor. It would be unfair to Mark Twain, however, to imply that laughter was his sole criterion of success. There were in his lectures and reading performances passages of pathos and descriptive passages of beauty and power not intended to evoke laughter, where laughter would patently have been inappropriate. He took great pride in doing such passages well. Furthermore, as he matured he was no longer content with *any* laughter, but was concerned that his audiences laugh at really good things—that his humor was worthy of the laughter. And if in any performance the audience failed to laugh where humor was intended, it is to Mark Twain's credit, as pointed out earlier, that he tended to blame not his audience but only himself, and his own ineptness.

CHAPTER EIGHTEEN

PROFITS FROM THE ALTERNATE CAREER

Every night the question is, well, who
does this day's earnings belong to? —THE
LOVE LETTERS OF MARK TWAIN, P. *172.*

IT IS REPORTED that Oliver Wendell Holmes once remarked, while contemplating whether or not he should take to the platform, that a public lecturer was a literary strumpet who prostituted himself for an abnormally high fee.[1] While Mark Twain might greatly have admired Holmes' vigorous and descriptive language, it is doubtful that at any time during his career he would have agreed with the sentiment. Though it is evident that he was deeply troubled at the thought that his humorous performances did not sufficiently satisfy the expectation of many of his auditors to be instructed and that his public image might be too much that of a man wearing cap and bells, the idea that he was prostituting himself for money by lecturing never entered his head. On the contrary, from the very beginning of his platform career money was always and frankly a primary objective. He needed money, often desperately, to pay off debts, to buy time for his pen, or merely to live, and the platform offered a quick and relatively easy way of providing it.

In 1866 in San Francisco, at the very beginning of his platform career, when someone asked him what he needed most at the moment, money or literary reputation, he declared emphatically, "Money, by _____!"[2] And when a reporter told him after the lecture that some people had characterized his performance as a "bilk and a sell," he shrugged off the charge saying that everyone had a right to his own opinion, but that he had the consolation of slapping his pockets and hearing the money jingle.[3] Indeed, during most of his touring career, far from being concerned about whether or not he deserved the fees he received from lecturing, he was more often unhappy because they were not higher.

In order to present a background for a discussion of Mark Twain's profits from tour lecturing, a glance at the fee structure which prevailed during the late 1860's and the early 1870's, the period in which Mark Twain rose to platform celebrity, may be helpful. Among the best known names in the field at this time were Henry Ward Beecher, John B. Gough, Anna Dickinson, Olive Logan, Horace Greeley, Wendell Phillips, Artemus Ward, Petroleum V. Nasby, and Josh Billings. All these people commanded large fees. Of these, according to Mark Twain, Beecher, Gough, and Dickinson were the only ones who knew their own value and exacted it. Their price, he declared, was $400 a night.[4] Actually, their fees ran that high only in large cities. In smaller communities they ranged between $200 and $250.

J. B. Pond, who acquired the Boston Lyceum Bureau in 1884, reports that after James Redpath became Gough's manager, his lecture fees ran from $200 to $500 for each performance, and that during his last year of touring, his income exceeded $30,000.[5] Nasby's fees appear to have been equally high. He is said to have boasted that his first lecture tour was the most lucrative ever recorded in the annals of the lyceum.[6] An estimate of Artemus Ward's income for a full season's tour with his popular lecture Babes in the Wood, as reported in the Portland, Oregon, *Daily Press*, November 17, 1871, also ran to over $30,000.

For the group just below these extremely popular and highly paid lecturers the fee was usually $100 "with modifications," which meant, as pointed out elsewhere, that well-established lyceums in large cities paid more, whereas those in smaller towns ordinarily paid less. It was to this second group that Mark Twain belonged during his tours under Redpath. That he eventually became acutely unhappy about his status as a $100 performer, however, became unpleasantly clear one evening at Norristown, Pennsylvania, in 1871, when he twice gratuitously reminded his audience, in his lecture on Artemus Ward, that in comparison with the fees paid Ward, his own fee for the evening's performance was painfully inadequate.[7] It was not till after he had achieved considerable literary reputation that Mark Twain was able to command larger fees. By that time, however, he was no longer willing to subject himself to the loneliness and rigors of the lyceum circuit. In the summer of 1874, for example, when Redpath offered him $30,000 for a season of fifty lectures, Mark Twain "just smiled in derision" though the offer meant an average of $600 a lecture.[8]

At the bottom of the fee structure came a host of minor lecturers whom Redpath listed at $50, "with modifications." In cities, he explained, their fees would run from $60 to $70; but in villages, where lyceums were struggling under difficulties and were willing to take "off nights," they could be supplied at $30 to $40.[9] These, according to Mark Twain, were the "house-emptiers" on the lecture circuit who hastened the decline of lyceum popularity. On Redpath's list for the season of 1869–70, for example, was William R. Emerson, elder brother of Ralph Waldo Emerson, who offered the public a choice of three lectures: "American Traits," "The Coming Age of the Coming Man," and "Popular Arts."[10] But even at the low fee of $50, William R. Emerson does not appear to have been much in demand.

In discussing Mark Twain's profits from tour lecturing, no attempt will be made to present in any precise way his net or even his gross earnings for each of the various tours. The data upon which such a determination could be made are simply not available. Mark Twain apparently kept no detailed record of earnings for an entire tour, or if he did it is no longer extant. Nor have Redpath's records been preserved. For the later tours, those under Pond's management (the tour with Cable and the World Tour), some helpful records are available, but even these do not reveal a final figure of net earnings after expenses.

Nevertheless, an examination of Mark Twain's comments about his platform earnings found in his correspondence and other writings and in the writings of Redpath, Pond, and others, throws a good deal of light on the matter. It reveals, at least, his approximate earnings from what has been called his parallel career, and indicates his attitude toward platform profit and the importance of the income derived from tour lecturing.

Concerning the earnings of the first California-Nevada tour of 1866, a good deal of uncertainty exists. The opening lecture in

San Francisco had brought in, as we have seen, about $1,200, a truly handsome amount, of which Mark Twain was able to retain about $400. Sacramento and Virginia City also seem to have been profitable; but in small towns like Maryville, Red Dog, Nevada City, Grass Valley, and San Jose he claimed to have lost money. Speaking of the first California-Nevada tour many years later, Mark Twain declared that it had brought in somewhere between twelve and fifteen hundred dollars.[11] This amount, he claimed, was only about half of what he should have had and that the doorkeeper, who "was an old circus man and knew how to keep door," had got the rest.[12] Even if we accept Mark Twain's more modest figure of $1,200 as net income for the first tour (involving fifteen or sixteen lectures and about ten weeks of his time), it made a splendid return for an impecunious young man making his debut upon the lecture circuit. It not only catapulted him suddenly from poverty to comparative affluence, but, even more importantly, opened for him a new vista of activity and destroyed his fears about how he might earn a living. The leisure to write and the opportunity to acquire funds for his contemplated trip around the world now seemed assured. The lecture platform promised to be a bonanza.

Of his income during the brief tour in the Middle West, which immediately followed, the record is all but silent. There were five engagements: two in St. Louis and one each in Hannibal, Keokuk, and Quincy. A severe storm during the second St. Louis lecture so greatly reduced his audience that fewer than a hundred were in attendance. Though he was on home ground in Hannibal and Keokuk and may have had good houses there, as reported in the local papers,[13] it is doubtful that his earnings for all five engagements netted him more than $175 to $200. But even this amount, added to his savings from the California-Nevada tour, was extremely important, for by this time he had committed himself to the "Quaker City" Holy Land Excursion and was desperately saving money to supplement the amount the *Alta California* was paying him for correspondence.

Back in New York again by mid-April, Mark Twain resumed his correspondence for the *Alta California,* but he was now no longer content to depend solely on remuneration from writing while waiting for the "Quaker City" to sail. He saw no reason why he should not attempt to increase his earnings and his reputation by lecturing in the New York area. To this end

he immediately directed his energies. As we have seen, he lectured three times, twice in New York and once in Brooklyn.
Unfortunately the first lecture, at Cooper Institute, though an
immensely pleasing platform success, failed financially. According to Frank Fuller, who had taken charge of the business arrangements for the performance, the advertising expenses and
hall rent amounted to approximately $600, which Fuller paid
out of his own pocket, while the sale of tickets brought in under
$300.[14] The good press notices of the Cooper Institute lecture
appear, however, to have provided good houses for the remaining
two lectures; and since there is no evidence that these houses
were "papered" with complimentary tickets as was true at Cooper
Institute, one may conjecture that his net income from each of
the two lectures ranged from $50 to $100. Whether he now re-
paid Fuller part of the loss incurred from the Institute lecture,
or begged off for the time being in order to preserve a maximum
amount of cash for the Holy Land trip cannot be determined.
That he still owed Fuller a considerable sum after his return
from the "Quaker City" excursion is evident, from the correspondence of the two men, which reveals that Fuller, hoping
to recover in full or in part the money he had so generously advanced for the Institute venture, had urged Mark Twain to undertake a new lecture tour in the far West.[15] Whether in the
end Mark Twain ever reimbursed Fuller is unknown. Many
years later, recalling Fuller's help, he declared that though the
affair had cost his friend four or five hundred dollars, Fuller
had never mentioned it.[16] The remark seems to imply that
the debt remained unpaid. The episode with Fuller along with
other evidence indicates that during the early years, at least,
when the pressure for money was a heavy and constant burden,
Mark Twain was a slow payer. If at times he did not actually
seek to evade payment of some of his debts, he was at least willing
to let them ride until repayment was convenient.[17]

Concerning his income from the second California-Nevada
tour during the spring and early summer of 1868, little is known.
He appears to have lectured about twelve times. Since three of
these engagements were in San Francisco, and the itinerary included Sacramento, Virginia City, and Carson City, it is likely
that the financial reward for the entire tour equaled or slightly
exceeded that of two years earlier. Certainly the first San Francisco lecture paid off handsomely, since the gross receipts ran to

$1,600.[18] But the smaller towns were disappointing. In consequence of his increased reputation because of the Holy Land letters in the *Alta California,* he had hoped for substantial rewards even in the smaller communities. But this hope proved false. The *Alta,* he discovered, had copyrighted the entire series of Holy Land letters and had threatened suit against newspapers that reprinted them without permission. As a result, since few small town newspapers had printed his correspondence, his reputation had not filtered inland as widely as he had expected. Nevertheless, the income from the tour was large enough to serve Mark Twain well. It enabled him to live with some comfort in a San Francisco hotel while he worked hard on the manuscript for *Innocents Abroad.*

In the summer of 1868, Mark Twain placed himself under Redpath's management for a season's tour on the lyceum circuit, apparently entirely prompted by the need for money. Though the manuscript for *Innocents Abroad* was already in the hands of the publisher, it would be many months before any hoped-for royalties might come from that source. In the meantime he had met Olivia Langdon, and his thoughts had turned toward courtship and marriage. Needing money and needing it quickly, his mind again turned naturally and promptly to lecturing. His successes on the platform in New York, Brooklyn, and San Francisco were sufficiently well known to Redpath to warrant a place for the young humorist among the $100 people on his lyceum list.[19]

To arrive at a dependable estimate of Mark Twain's earnings for the tours under Redpath, it would be necessary to know in each case the fees he received and the number of engagements he filled. Such figures are extremely difficult to compute, since complete itineraries for these years are not available except for the season of 1871–72. Furthermore, while he kept jottings of his earnings from time to time, he kept no consistent, detailed record then or later, either with regard to his lectures or his books. This fact was clearly revealed in July of 1895, when he was summoned to a hearing held in the office of Stern and Rushmore, attorneys, at 40 Wall Street, New York, in connection with the failure of the Charles L. Webster Company. When asked what the exact proceeds from his books had been he declared he had never tried to keep track of it. He had received checks and cashed them and spent the money. That was all he knew and all he could tell them.[20] Nevertheless, a careful examination of his comments about earnings, found in his correspondence and other writings, throws some light on the matter. Thus on June 4, 1869, some months after the close of the first season, he wrote his family in St. Louis that he had made eight or nine thousand dollars (gross income before expenses) and that of this amount he then had less than $3,600 in the bank.[21] He had expected to be able to save half the gross,[22] but his expenses had been unusually heavy. He was not only planning for marriage but supplying himself with clothes and other appurtenances which a rising young man so much before the public eye should have.

In the seasons immediately following the tour of 1868–69 Mark Twain occasionally demanded and got fees up to $150. In 1871, for example, he received $150 at Norristown, Pennsylvania. He notified Redpath that he wanted $150 at Rondout (now Kingston), New York, because it was hard to get to and the lyceum there now had a larger hall.[23] Perhaps he was determined to make up in these towns what he had lost at others, as for example, at Wilkes-Barre, where his fee was only $75; or it may be that he was convinced that he now deserved a higher fee rating than during previous seasons on the circuit and was in a mood to try out the local committees to see how they would react. Whatever his motive for demanding higher fees, it is apparent that during the season of 1871–72 he was as usual in urgent need of money and that he depended chiefly upon his proceeds from lecturing to meet his debts. In a letter to Livy, written on January 7, 1872, about a month before the season ended, he confided that of the $10,000 the tour would bring in, he would hardly have enough left to get home on. Everything had gone or was going for debts. "Every night the question is, "Well, who does *this* day's earnings belong to?"[24] The chief debts, of course, were those incurred through the sale of his interest in the Buffalo *Express*, which he had sold at a loss. Nevertheless, he managed to get home with a little more money than he had indicated to Livy, for on February 13, after the tour had ended, he informed Mrs. Fairbanks that he had come out of the campaign "with less than $1,500 to show for all that work and misery."[25] The fact, however, that a season of lecturing provided sufficient money to meet his debts, pay a good share of his current living expenses, and allow a remainder of $1,500, helps explain why Mark Twain, though professing to hate the platform and becoming increasingly reluctant to subject himself to its hardships, repeatedly succumbed to the pressures that harassed him and allowed Redpath to book him.

Concerning Mark Twain's fees for the London lectures during the closing months of 1873, little is known, but they appear to have been more substantial than those of the tours recently concluded under Redpath's management. He had refused engagements for the season of 1872–73 partly because the financial pressure had eased, and partly because he was no longer willing to be counted among Redpath's $100 lectures. His growing literary reputation through the publication of *Innocents Abroad* and *Roughing It* (recently off the press) had given him an increased sense of his own value. "When I yell again for less than $500," he informed Redpath, "I'll be pretty hungry."[26] In the same letter he nevertheless indicated that he was going to yell again in London shortly and that he was polishing up his Roughing It lecture for his audiences there, thus allowing Redpath to infer that his London fees would range up to $500 a lecture. As a consequence, Redpath, not wishing to lose a good moneymaker like Mark Twain, presently offered more lucrative terms. But Mark Twain turned them down until the rewards approximated the fees he had determined upon. By February of 1873, apparently, the conditions had been met and Mark Twain lectured twice in New York and once in Brooklyn. The two New York lectures, February 5 and 10, under the auspices of the Mercantile Library Association, brought him, on a profit-splitting basis, $1,300, or about $650 a lecture. It was thus clear that his judgment concerning his own value had been confirmed. He was no longer a $100 man, but like Gough, Dickinson, and others he knew his own value and exacted it. He could now go to London as a top-paid lecturer from his own country.

Despite the fact that a complete schedule of Mark Twain's famous reading tour with George W. Cable, during the season of 1884–85, is available, as is also a cash book which James Pond kept of the engagements, Mark Twain's net profit for the season's performances can only be estimated. It must be remembered that he owned the show; that is, he assumed all the financial risks, paid Cable $450 each week ($60 in addition for matinees), and paid all Cable's expenses. There was also, of course, Pond's share for management, which on this occasion included travel expense since he accompanied the two performers. As

Mark Twain scrutinized the expense bills for all three men, as they reached him from time to time through Charlie Webster's office, he was shocked at what he considered their exorbitance. They were "rowsers," and Webster should check them carefully.[27] What especially troubled Mark Twain was that, despite the popularity of their performances, their audiences were often disappointingly small. Too many of their engagements were in small communities where no amount of advertising was likely to produce profitable houses. In many instances the gross receipts for an evening amounted to less than $400, and occasionally to less than a hundred. The matinees also proved financially disappointing. Boston, for example, brought in only $168. It was in the metropolitan areas where he depended upon earnings large enough to compensate for the inadequate income from smaller towns. Yet even here the gross receipts fell below his expectations. Baltimore brought in only $754. Washington did a little better with $789. Even Brooklyn, where he hoped for one of his largest paying audiences, yielded only $983. So disappointed was Mark Twain about the small audiences his performances were attracting during the opening weeks of the tour that he pressed Pond to step up the advertising. Otherwise he might as well close the show. Along with larger and more colorful placards and signs, he suggested a parade of men draped with billboards walking about the streets announcing the programs.[28] Pond hastened to comply and appears to have achieved some improvement, but rarely, it seems, sufficient to please Mark Twain. The best paying house of the entire tour appears to have been Chicago, which brought in $1,216, a satisfactory amount, but not one to be particularly jubilant about.

Pond's cash book reveals that the total gross receipts for the tour came to $46,201. Cable received $6,750 beyond expenses. Precisely how much the total expense bill amounted to and precisely what Mark Twain's net return was are not specifically indicated. Assuming that as owner of the show his earnings were calculated to be well above Cable's, which is a permissible assumption, it appears that the long tour, which lasted from four to five months, and comprised about 93 performances brought him in the neighborhood of $12,000 to $14,000. It should be observed, however, that this amount reflects only partially what the tour earned for Mark Twain in terms of dollars. It had been undertaken, in part, at least, to promote the sale of *Huckleberry*

Finn, and in order to get his newly erected publishing house, the Charles L. Webster Company, off to a profitable start. A determination of the ultimate net profit resulting from the tour should properly include an undetermined amount arising from the increased sale of the book through the advertising it received on the platform. Such a calculation, however, would patently be impossible.

Information about Mark Twain's income from the world tour of 1895–96 is sketchy at best, but enough is at hand to warrant estimates. Since his wife and daughter Clara accompanied him, his travel expenses were unusually high. So, too, were his medical expenses because of the carbuncles and colds which afflicted him during much of the first half of his long journey. During the American phase of the tour, as we have seen, Pond was his agent, and he and his wife accompanied the Clemenses all the way across the continent to Vancouver. Presumably Pond paid his wife's expenses out of his own pocket. The agent during the foreign phase of the tour was R. S. Smythe of Australia. Concerning the amount of his fee nothing is known, nor are any of his records available. Nevertheless, items of information are at hand which supply something of a basis for determining Mark Twain's earnings. At various stages of the tour, we find, he forwarded money to Henry Rogers, who had recently taken charge of his financial affairs. From Vancouver, for example, after 22 engagements, Paine reports that he sent Rogers $5,000.[29] To the extent to which this figure represents earnings after expenses, it may be assumed that his average net profit for each lecture during the American phase amounted to approximately $227.

In order to arrive at a dependable estimate of profits from the foreign phase of the tour, it would first of all be necessary to know the number of engagements. While no completely recorded itinerary appears to exist, a fairly accurate schedule of engagements may be worked out by examining *Following The Equator, Mark Twain's Notebook,* his correspondence, and the reports of his activities found in foreign newspapers. From these sources one may conclude that his lectures abroad numbered about 110. With few exceptions, all these performances were given in large metropolitan areas or at least in areas with large concentrations of English speaking people. During the foreign phase, too, he forwarded money to Rogers for the retirement of

Mark Twain's

TALKING TOUR

ROUND THE WORLD.

——)o(——

Nights of Wit and Wisdom.

——)o(——

THE SUBJECTS FOR EACH EVENING BEING ENTIRELY DIFFERENT.

———

"What a blest relief Mark Twain will be! And what a royal reception he will meet with everywhere! There is probably no other man living, except perhaps Mr. Gladstone, so universally known or whom so many persons in every civilised country have to thank for having brought new interests into their lives, and given them something to think and talk about."—Sydney DAILY TELEGRAPH, May 1, 1895.

———

Sydney—THURSDAY, SEPTEMBER 19.

Melbourne—(Bijou Theatre) SEPTEMBER 25.

Adelaide—(Theatre Royal) OCTOBER 12.

Wellington, N.Z.—(Opera House) DECEMBER 7.

———

For Particulars see Daily Papers.

R. S. SMYTHE.

his debt. On October 3, 1895, for example, he recorded in his *Notebook* that on that day he sent £437.[30] At the current rate of exchange, that amounted to about $2,100. The entry was made after Mark Twain had given nine lectures (four in Sydney and five in Melbourne), indicating that in Australia, also, his net profit for each lecture averaged in the neighborhood of $230. If we use this average for the entire tour, which appears justifiable in view of the excellent press notices which presently began to circulate in the areas where he was scheduled to lecture, and Carlyle Smythe's fulsome praise of Mark Twain's splendid audiences, we arrive at a total of approximately $25,000. If to this we add the $5,000 from the American phase of the tour, it appears that the world tour brought Mark Twain a net profit of about $30,000.

In his book *Eccentricities of Genius,* Pond asserts that Mark Twain earned from the world tour enough money with his voice and pen to pay all his publishing house debts in full, with interest, and that he did it almost a year sooner than he had originally expected.[31] Not counting a claim of $70,000 which his wife had against the company, Mark Twain's debts from the Webster failure amounted to approximately $80,000.[32] Thus it is clear that the income from lecturing alone contributed between a third and a half to the final retirement of that burdensome debt.

At various times after the world tour Pond again tried to persuade his old friend to return to the platform. In July of 1897 he wrote Clemens, who was still in London after completing *Following the Equator,* offering $50,000 and all expenses for 125 engagements in the United States.[33] It was a splendid offer of $400 clear for each lecture, but Mark Twain turned it down. His wife was no longer willing that he should subject himself again to so grueling a task. Nor was he himself willing. In 1899, while he was in Sweden to seek medical aid for his daughter Jean's epilepsy, Pond made a final serious effort to induce the celebrated humorist to return to the platform. This time he offered a thousand dollars a night for ten nights,[34] hoping no doubt that the large fee and the limited number of engagements would prove irresistibly attractive. But by this time no amount of money or inducements could lure Mark Twain back to tour

Announcement of performance in Sydney. (Sydney Bulletin, *September 21, 1896.)*

lecturing. He was now financially comfortable and the very thought of resuming the burdens and miseries of a tour made him shudder.

If anyone had asked Mark Twain after the world tour had closed what his total income had been over the years from his parallel career as a public lecturer, it is doubtful that he would have ventured a reply. Though it is obvious the income from his pen greatly exceeded that from tour lecturing, without it, at very crucial periods of his career, the wolf would have sat longer and more often at his door, his pen would have lain unused more often at his desk, and his whole scale of living would have been considerably reduced. To Mark Twain tour lecturing meant many things—reputation, freedom for his pen, pleasure on the platform, artistry, and money—always and especially money.

CHAPTER NINETEEN

RETIREMENT FROM TOUR LECTURING

I do not believe you could offer me terms
that would dissolve my prejudice against
the platform. —ECCENTRICITIES OF GENIUS,
P. 226.

SINCE MARK TWAIN became one of the most popular and best
paid lecturers on the American platform, the question may
well be asked why he so often declared his hatred for it and
his intention never to return to it again. Before attempting an
answer, however, it should be pointed out that at various times
in his career his declarations about quitting the platform meant
different things. During the years when he was lecturing on the
lyceum circuit, under James Redpath's management, what he
hated and obviously never intended to return to was *tour* lecturing. After 1874, for a period of about ten years, it appears he
meant to include all public lecturing. These were the years of
his greatest literary productivity, when "scribbling," as he sometimes called authorship, had become his major preoccupation. In
later years, especially after the world tour of 1895, what he clearly
meant to retire from was lecturing for pay. It has often been
observed by those who knew Mark Twain well, that, far from
hating the platform, he loved the time spent there. As his daughter Clara perceptively observed, he detested the thought of lecturing all his life, "yet when on the stage, he almost always succeeded
in electrifying himself to the point of pleasure."[1] Furthermore,
it is inconceivable that a person who really hated the platform

would have continued to lecture, as Mark Twain did on both public and private occasions, up to the very closing year of his life.

His reasons for wanting to give up tour lecturing were both simple and complex, but all were compelling. There were many simple reasons: the toil, fatigue, and irritations of travel (most of it during the severities of northern winters), the loneliness of long separations from his family, his preference for writing rather than for tour lecturing, his fear that lecturing on the lyceum circuit would become a habit from which he might never escape, and finally his wife's emphatic insistence during their early married years that he give it up.

The record of Mark Twain's disenchantment about tour lecturing began with the season of 1868–69. Lasting nearly four months, the schedule that season took him in a series of criss-crosses all the way from New York to Iowa. For a number of reasons it was an exhausting experience. As the season began, his courtship of Olivia Langdon was not prospering. Though she consented to be his "sister" and to write to him, the arrangement was altogether frustrating. And when, toward the end of November, she capitulated and there was a tentative engagement, the thought of his unstable and insecure way of life became a matter of immediate and deep concern. Furthermore, the fatigue of travel as the tour ground on made him so irritable at times that it got him into senseless quarrels with all sorts of people—doormen at the lecture halls, members of local committees, and hotel managers. That season, the record amply shows, life on tour was a constant series of harassments.

The following June in a letter to his folks in St. Louis, Mark Twain confided his hopes for escape. If he could get a suitable position with a good newspaper, he would give up lecturing. He would rather do with less money than to submit again to wearing travel of another long tour. "I most cordially hate the lecture field," he declared, and shuddered to think that he might never get out of it. His talks with Gough, Nasby, and other lyceum lecturers of the day had convinced him that old troupers never expected to get out of it; and he was sure he did not want to become wedded to it as they had.[2]

In the end, however, his decision whether or not to lecture always hinged upon one consideration—the immediate and urgent need for money. In the spring of 1870, for example, when he was temporarily affluent, he happily informed Redpath that he was never "going to lecture any more forever," and saw no reason why he should crucify himself nightly on the platform.³ But scarcely a year later, after he had sold his interest in the Buffalo *Express* at a loss and was again in immediate need of money, he allowed Redpath to book him. By this time it had become a matter of pride with Mark Twain not to accept further financial help from the affluent Langdons. He was determined to make his own way, and if that meant going on tour again, so it would have to be. The fact is, he was still smarting from the sting of certain remarks Charlie Langdon, Olivia's brother, had made during Mark Twain's courtship visits at the Langdon home. At that time, in his resentment, he had told Mrs. Langdon that if he and Livy ever got into financial trouble they would sell their "point lace and eat shucks in a foreign land, and fight it out, but we won't come back and billet ourselves in the old home, and have Charlie charging us for board 'on the European plan' as he is always threatening to do with me when I linger there a few days."⁴ So, Mark Twain let Redpath know that he would be available for the season ahead.

By mid-October he was on the road again and hating it. Lonesome as he was, however, Livy was even more lonesome. In need of her husband's loving and reassuring presence, her letters voiced her deep discontent. She hoped it was the last season it would be necessary for him to lecture, she wrote. "It is not the way for a husband and wife to live if they can possibly avoid it, is it? Separation," she gloomily reminded him, "comes soon enough."⁵ A few weeks later she wrote again, this time more firmly, "I *cannot* and I *will not think* about your being away from me this way every year, it is not half-living. . . ." And if it was going to be necessary, she added, for him to be away so much in order to maintain their present mode of living, there was only one answer—they would then change their mode of living.⁶ That season, while he was spending a lonesome Christmas in Chicago, where the tour had taken him, Livy was at home more wretchedly lonesome and unhappy than ever.

Pondering his wife's deep discontent and the circumstances which made lecturing necessary, Mark Twain sat down in his hotel room one evening and took stock of his debts. Though his lectures for the season would bring him about $10,000, after paying all his bills he would scarcely have enough money to get home on. "I *do* hate lecturing," he again assured her, and he would try to do as little of it thereafter as possible,[7] but, she must realize, necessities had to be met even if it meant temporary separations. While there is little doubt that Livy Clemens possessed the courage and the spirit to face the facts of their financial difficulties, it is quite apparent that during the early period of marriage she perceived the facts only dimly and probably never quite comprehended her husband's pride in his ability to support his family entirely through his own efforts and his firm refusal to accept help from her family even when the need appeared urgent. When the tour closed in mid-February, he reaffirmed his resolutions to retire. "I ain't going to *ever* lecture any more," he wrote Mrs. Fairbanks, "unless I get in debt again."[8] But he did not expect to get into debt again soon, for that month his new book *Roughing It* appeared on the book stalls and he was confident it would sell well and bring him a golden harvest.

During the season of 1873–74 he lectured in London and thereafter in a few large cities in the United States, but there was no tour, and, except for about a month during the final series of the London lectures, there was no lonesomeness, for his wife had gone to England with him. For this reason, probably, and because of the increased reputation her husband would derive by remaining in London and continuing the lectures there, Livy voiced no complaints.

When the question of lecturing arose again the next season, Mark Twain publicly announced that he would never again appear on the platform unless driven by a lack of bread. Nevertheless, some months later, he lectured free of charge in Hartford, in behalf of the poor in Father Hawley's congregation. In view of his recent public announcement that he had given up lecturing entirely, he felt it necessary to offer an explanation. And the one he offered was ingenious—that though he *had* quit the lecture platform never to return to it unless driven by a lack of bread, he had consented to lecture on the present occasion for "this last and final time" since he was, in fact, being driven by a lack of bread in Father Hawley's flock.[9]

If Mark Twain gave any public lectures for pay in the ten-year period between 1874 and 1884, they were extremely infrequent. On New Year's Day, at the end of that decade, he strengthened a resolution, frequently made, never to make another speech, by imposing a money penalty upon himself for any violation.[10] And during that decade there were at least no tours.

But in 1884, to no one's real surprise, he again took to the platform, this time on an extensive reading tour with George W. Cable that lasted over four months. With Cable as a companion there was, of course, no trouble about lonesomeness. Nevertheless, for a man who had so often declared his hatred for tour lecturing and for the hardships and fatigue of traveling, the motives for undertaking it must have been exceptional.

That Mark Twain felt an explanation was called for is indicated by a statement made to a reporter of the New York *Sun* not long after the tour had gotten underway. They say, he declared, that "lecturers and burglars never reform. I don't know how it is with burglars . . . but it is quite true of lecturers. They . . . say they are going to leave the lecture platform, never to return. They mean it. . . . But there comes, in time, an overpowering temptation to come out on the platform and give truth and morality one more lift. You can't resist."[11]

Albert Bigelow Paine suggested that after all his resolves to quit the platform forever, Mark Twain was willing in the fall of 1884 to engage in another long season's tour because reading from his books seemed less objectionable than lecturing.[12] Mr. Paine's suggestion is plausible, for during the past ten years Mark Twain had become much interested in the art of reading and had acquired some skill in it. Understandably, he wished to see what he could do with it on the public platform.

But there were other and obviously more compelling reasons *why* Mark Twain, at this time, could not resist going on tour again. He was urgently in need of money. At great expense he had recently established his own publishing house, the Charles L. Webster Company, and was planning to bring out through that enterprise his new book *The Adventures of Huckleberry Finn*. The success of both the publishing house and the book was now at stake. In what better way could it be assured than by means of a reading tour, with a repertoire that included some judiciously selected passages from the new book? Whatever truth there may be in the charges that Mark Twain was a gullible and muddleheaded businessman, there is no question that in the matter of bringing both his books and his lectures into public notice, he was unusually resourceful and enterprising. At any rate, Mark Twain went on tour. Pushed aside or forgotten were the old complaints about the fatigues and hardships of travel and separation from home and family. Of his hatred for the platform nothing was now said. This was business—very important busi-

ness—and by this time even his wife understood and raised no objections.

The period between 1885 and 1895 marked a sharp downward spiral in the financial affairs of Mark Twain. The failure
of the Paige typesetting machine, the collapse of his publishing
house, together with other misadventures brought him, at the age
of sixty, to the verge of bankruptcy and saddled him with a debt
that might well have disheartened a man of less courage. It was
inevitable that the thought of lecturing as a rapid and profitable
means of income again came to the forefront. It was a hateful
decision to make, but what else was there to do? The tour that
was presently agreed upon was to be worldwide. It was planned
to provide a double income—one from lecturing and one from a
travel book *(Following the Equator)* based upon the trip.
Though the tour lasted a full year, there was no lonesomeness
this time, for Mrs. Clemens and his daughter Clara accompanied
him. Besides, there was a whole new world to see—Australia, New
Zealand, exotic Ceylon, India, and South Africa. Instead of the
usual complaints about the fatigue, there were now expressions
of delight about the ever-changing scenery, and regret that his
wife and daughter sometimes missed seeing things that had excited his own interest.[13] And though the carbuncles which gave
him so much trouble during the first half of the trip sometimes
turned the evening's performance into an ordeal, there were no
outbursts, as in the old days, about his hatred for the platform.
Nevertheless, when the long tour finally came to an end he was
glad. Never again, he hoped, would circumstances drive him
across "the devil's universe," to pay off debts.

As a result of the splendid success of his global tour and
the worldwide celebrity that followed it, Pond tried hard to engage the famous humorist for one more big American tour with
a lecture based upon his book *Following the Equator;* but the
effort proved futile. Mark Twain could no longer be tempted.[14]

In addition to the simple answers that explain why Mark
Twain soon grew to hate tour lecturing, there are two others, of
varying complexity, that deserve consideration. The first of
these was based on a belief which the Langdons had, while they
were considering his suitability as a husband for their daughter,
that he was at heart and by habit a wanderer, unrooted, and
basically unstable; and that their daughter's life with such a man
would be an endless and restless roaming.[15] And they had reasons

Mark Twain (left) and George Washington Cable (sitting) with Mark Twain's relatives at Quincy, Illinois, Jan. 13, 1885

for their belief. Had he not wandered West after quitting the river? Had he not drifted through the mining camps of Nevada before taking up newspaper work in Virginia City? And after only two years there had he not moved again, to California? Had he not then wandered off to Hawaii; and almost immediately after his return from those remote islands had he not started off on the "Quaker City" excursion to the Holy Land? And since his return from that trip, what had his life been like? A trip again to California, and now long lecture tours that kept him on the move for months at a time. Where was Mark Twain at home? What was his address? And if their daughter married this wanderer, what would her address be?

In a letter to Mark Twain Olivia confided her parents' fears about his apparent instability. No other accusation against his suitability as a husband stirred him so deeply. In his heart he felt that the charge was fundamentally untrue; yet how could he prove it? The record certainly seemed to confirm it. Against so disturbing a charge some defense seemed imperative. Carefully, and at length, he undertook to explain to her that he was not a wanderer by choice but by necessity. His profession as a journalist had made wandering a necessity. *All* men knew that things done from necessity had little fascination about them. Wandering was neither a *habit* with him nor a proclivity. "Does a man, five years a galley-slave, get in the habit of it & yearn to be a galley-slave always? Does a horse in a tread-mill get infatuated with his profession & long to continue in it? Does the sewing girl, building shirts at sixpence apiece grow fascinated with the habit of it at last & find it impossible to break herself of it without signing the pledge? And being pushed from pillar to post & compelled so long to roam, against my will, is it reasonable to think that I am really fond of it & wedded to it? I think not."[16]

Nevertheless, despite his defense and self-justification, the charge that he was a wanderer struck deeply home. And though he could honestly say that lecturing trips were a necessity, he realized that for the well-rooted and splendidly established Langdons and their daughter, they served, during the early tour years, as a symbol of instability, and constituted a stigma—a reflection upon his character. In retrospect, it is safe to say that Mark Twain would have abandoned tour lecturing for writing, had the need for money been less compelling, even without the damning implications suggested by the Langdons; but with the implications once made, he at least *seemed* guilty.

While the charge that he was by heart a wanderer unquestionably played an important role in his decision to give up
tour lecturing as soon as he could free himself from debt, there
was still another reason for his growing hatred of it—a more
subtle and fundamentally far more disturbing one than any so
far considered. It was bedded in a deep-lying uncertainty as to
his proper role as a lecturer before American lyceum audiences.
Was that role, Mark Twain asked himself, primarily to amuse?
Or was it primarily to instruct? To Archibald Henderson he
once confessed that when he first began to lecture, his sole idea
was to make comic capital out of everything he saw or heard.
"My object was not to tell the truth, but to make people laugh."[17]

Indeed, so intent was he at times to make them laugh, that
he even risked spoiling the effect of an eloquent descriptive passage by resorting to a trick of anticlimax. Years later he recalled
how Tom Fitch, a friend during his early Virginia City days, had
cautioned him against it after attending one of his lectures.
"Clemens," he said, "your lecture was magnificent. . . . Never in
my life have I listened to such a magnificent piece of descriptive
narrative. But you committed an unpardonable sin—*the* unpardonable sin. . . . you closed a most eloquent description, by
which you had keyed your audience to a pitch of interest, with
a piece of atrocious anticlimax which nullified all the really fine
effect you produced. My dear Clemens, whatever you do, never
sell your audience."[18] Precisely what anticlimax Tom Fitch had
in mind cannot now, with certainty, be established. Most probably, it was the parenthetical remark which Mark Twain sometimes made in a low voice, in the nature of an aside, immediately
following his eloquent description of Hawaiian scenery and the
grandeur of a volcanic eruption—"There, I'm glad I've got that
volcano off my mind." Despite Fitch's warning, however, and
Mark Twain's statement to Archibald Henderson that it was his
"first really profitable lesson," it appears that he learned the
lesson with difficulty; for during the tour of 1869–70, when he
lectured on the Sandwich Islands, he still occasionally made use
of the anticlimactic trick because he knew from experience that
it did evoke laughter, and laughter was always his main criterion
of success.[19]

Mark Twain's ability to make his audiences laugh made him
for many years America's leading humorist on the public platform, and he was not unaware of this distinction. Nevertheless,
he well knew that there were always people who left the lecture

hall disappointed. They had enjoyed the humor but had expected more substance, more instruction, a message, a moral. The old troublesome question persisted. Was a humorous lecture appropriate to the objectives of the lyceum course? Was it worth the fee they had paid for admission? Wasn't he giving them mostly froth? When one summed it all up, wasn't Mark Twain *merely* a humorist, a joker, a funny man on the platform, a jester, a man with cap and bells?

And it is highly significant that his concern about his role on the platform was deep-lying enough to get into his dreams. In his autobiographical sketch "My Platonic Sweet-Heart" he supplies a vivid account of one of those dreams which he experienced in January, 1867, not long after his first public lecture in San Francisco, at a time when he was contemplating a series of lecturers before eastern audiences.

The dream took him back to the first public lecture. He was again standing on the stage in Maguires Opera House. He began to speak and then suddenly stopped in fright. ". . . I discovered I had no subject, no text, nothing to talk about." He made a few lame attempts at humor, but the audience remained silent and unsmiling, and presently "broke into insulting cries, whistlings and hootings, and catcalls. . . ." Then the audience arose and struggled in mass toward the doors.

Even if one admits that the dream had its origin in the natural fear of failure which anyone might experience on the occasion of a first public performance, or that it was rooted in a vague uneasiness at the thought that the eastern audiences he expected soon to face might be more cultured and therefore more exacting than those of California and Nevada, one cannot escape noting that at the base of that fear was the thought that he had no subject—nothing to talk about. It strongly suggests that Mark Twain thought of his lectures primarily in terms of the amusement they would afford his audiences, and if they failed in that, they failed in everything. Thirty years later, in his *Notebook,* he again recorded it, apparently for the last time. "I come on the platform with no subject to talk about, and not a note."[20]

"I hate that dream worse than any other," he confessed to Albert Bigelow Paine. "In it I am always getting up before an audience with nothing to say, trying to be funny; trying to make my audiences laugh, realizing that I am only making silly jokes. Then the audience realizes it, and pretty soon . . . get up and leave. That dream always ends by my standing there in the semidarkness talking to an empty house."[21]

To add to his uneasiness during the lyceum tours was his wife's expressed concern about her husband's public image as a humorist and her earnest hope that people might yet learn to know something of his deeper and larger nature.[22] "She thinks a humorist is something perfectly awful," he confided to Mrs. Fairbanks, and added that anybody who could convince her that he was not a humorist would earn her eternal gratitude.[23] Nor did he derive any comfort from Livy's anger when she heard a lady ask one day if there were anything of Mr. Clemens except his humor.[24]

That Mark Twain made a deliberate effort during the years on the lyceum circuit to give his audiences enough substance to minimize the charges of his critics is quite apparent. He made the effort also in deference to the prodding of his motherly critic, Mrs. Fairbanks, whose judgment he generally respected and whose help he sought in creating for him a favorable image as a lyceum performer. Indeed, he even bowed to the demand that he supply his lectures with a moral even where, in his opinion, none was needed, frankly informing his audiences that he offered it only because it seemed to be expected. And when, despite all his efforts to satisfy his critics, the charges still persisted that he was a mere humorist, he was understandably irked, for he honestly believed that his lectures *had* substance.

What Mark Twain apparently failed to realize, or failed to find a solution for, was the fact that his humor obscured the instruction to such a degree that his lectures did not *seem* to inform. As people left the lecture hall they did not *feel* instructed. They remembered the humor and the outbursts of laughter, but it took an effort to remember, if they tried to remember at all, what he had come to tell them.

At the heart of his problem, it is now evident, lay the simple fact that his overriding aim in a lecture was to amuse, not to instruct. The inescapable proof for this assertion lies in the one fact: whenever he believed a lecture had failed, he always attributed the failure to his inability to make the audience laugh. If the audience simmered with amusement, as it did on good nights, he regarded the lecture a success. It was for this reason, as we have seen, that he dreaded lecturing in the churches. There, people were afraid to laugh. It was for that reason, too, that he dreaded lecturing to "chuckle headed" Dutch audiences in Pennsylvania and New York. It was difficult to evoke from them free and hearty laughter. Always, always for Mark Twain laughter was the primary thing.

To amuse or instruct? And in the answer to that question lay his dilemma. He wanted to amuse, but many of his auditors had paid their lyceum fees expecting instruction, the primary purpose for which the lyceum "courses," as they were commonly called, had been established. And Mark Twain felt an inescapable obligation to satisfy that expectation if he were going to accept lyceum engagements.

The effect of this dichotomy between desire and obligation was far more disturbing to Mark Twain than he liked to admit. True, he could take comfort in the fact that his lectures commonly attracted large audiences and made money for the local lyceums. In some instances, as Redpath well knew, they served to keep some of them alive by offsetting the losses incurred by other less popular programs, a fact which supplied Mark Twain with powerful ammunition against such detractors as Josiah Holland. Nevertheless, he could not absolutely rid himself of nagging doubts about the real value of humorous lectures to paying audiences. Weren't his lectures, in very fact, a form of highway robbery, as he himself sometimes spoke of them—taking money from people without giving them real substance in return?

And it was one of Mark Twain's greatest misfortunes that the dichotomy in his own attitude toward the value of a humorous lecture was but a reflection of the same dichotomy prevalent in the public attitude of his time. Humor in and for itself had not yet, during most of his lecturing career, achieved full respectability.

In the light of these considerations, it is easy to see why Mark Twain eventually gave up lecturing for pay, but never gave up the "gratis" platform. Lecturing without charge he was no longer in the uncomfortable position of taking people's money for an evening of amusement under the guise of offering instruction. His only obligation was to send them home happy. And with this change in practice there came to him a growing confidence in the value of humorous performances. By 1889 he could say to Andrew Lang, the distinguished British critic, that simply to have amused the masses would have satisfied his dearest ambition, for they could get instruction elsewhere, adding that amusement was a good preparation for study and a good healer of fatigue after it.[25]

By the time he made the world tour he was even more confident—confident enough so that he could jokingly speak of his lecture as a "morals" lecture and make comic capital out of the pretense that it offered a scheme for the moral regeneration of man. Yet even then, at times the old doubts assailed him, as on the occasion in South Africa when he was asked to eliminate serious items from his evening's program and offer only humorous ones. Did they expect him, he raged, to stand before them and merely crack jokes for an hour or two? Didn't they have any respect for the senatorial dignity of his years? But even as he raged he was forced to acknowledge that they had a prescriptive right to expect only mirth from him. He had long encouraged them in that mistake.[26] In any event he was now through. When the tour was over he would lecture no more.

He did, as the record shows, continue to lecture occasionally (there was one in Budapest and one in Vienna in 1899), but now strictly for fun. All his debts were paid and he was quietly living in Europe, solvent at last. He happily informed Pond that he could now live comfortably without any further help from the platform. "I like to talk for nothing about twice a year," he confessed, "but talking for money is *work*, and that takes the pleasure out of it. I do not believe you could offer me terms that would dissolve my prejudice against the platform. I do not expect to see the platform again until the wolf commands. Honest people do not go robbing the public on the platform, except when they are in debt."[27]

Thereafter, the question of tour lecturing never again arose to trouble Mark Twain's mind, for under the astute management of his financial affairs by Henry H. Rogers, Manager and Director of Standard Oil Company, the wolf never again commanded. On Roger's part it was an act of friendship for which Mark Twain was profoundly grateful. "Who achieved this miracle for us? Who saved us from separations, unendurable toil on the platform, and public bankruptcy? *Henry Rogers. . . .* His name is music to my ears."[28]

In 1906, when invited to lecture to a large and distinguished gathering in Carnegie Hall for the benefit of the Robert Fulton Monument Association, he refused a fee of a thousand dollars, and reiterated the reasons for his refusal. He had, he declared, retired from the pay-platform a number of years ago; but he loved to hear himself talk and therefore wouldn't retire from the gratis platform until after he was dead and courtesy required him "to keep still and not disturb the others."[29] So, he agreed to speak without charge, announcing on the handbill made up for the occasion that it was to be his "farewell" lecture.[30]

Actually it was not. He continued now and then to accept invitations to speak at various occasions till the closing year of his life. But now the old doubts, the dilemmas, the fears about paid public performance no longer rose to haunt him. He knew that the people who came to hear him loved him for his humor. And for their frank and wholehearted enjoyment of it he, in turn, loved them with a free and grateful heart.

His last public appearance was on June 10, 1909, ten months before his death, when he gave the commencement address at a girls' school at Cantonsville, Maryland.

CHAPTER TWENTY

TEXTS OF TOUR LECTURES

*They will feast you on raw fish, with the
scales on, cocoanuts, plantains, baked
dogs and fricasseed cats, all the luxuries
of the season.* —OUR FELLOW SAVAGES OF
THE SANDWICH ISLANDS.

OUR FELLOW SAVAGES OF THE SANDWICH ISLANDS

DURING THE TOUR OF 1866–67 this lecture was advertised as
Sandwich Islands! A Serio-Humorous Lecture Concerning Kanakadom, or simply as The Sandwich Islands.
During the tour of 1869–70 and later it was sometimes called
Our Fellow Citizens of the Sandwich Islands, but usually as
Our Fellow Savages of the Sandwich Islands.

When one speaks of the text of this lecture one must bear
in mind that in addition to the text of the original lecture there
were two revisions—one for the tour of 1869–70 which took Mark
Twain through the eastern states, and one made in the late fall
of 1873 for British audiences. In a letter dated January 1, 1894,
Mark Twain wrote Frank Fuller, who apparently had asked for
information concerning the manuscript of "that old lecture"
(that is, of the San Francisco lecture of October 2, 1866), that it
was no longer in existence. "I tore it up," he said.[1] But Albert
Bigelow Paine reports in his Introduction to *Mark Twain's
Speeches* that "some considerable portions of this first lecture
have been preserved," and offers extensive extracts, purportedly
from the original manuscript. Whether he actually derived them
from original manuscript or from a newspaper report of the

lecture he does not specifically say. It is apparent from internal evidence that the extracts of the "First Lecture Delivered October 2, 1866" which he supplied in *Mark Twain: A Biography*, III, Appendix D are from a newspaper.

Today, at any rate, it appears that only two pages of the original "old manuscript" are still in existence. One, numbered page 15, is reproduced in Frear's *Mark Twain and Hawaii*, facing page 176. Frear reported that the original page was then in possession of Arthur F. Brown of Woodbridge, Connecticut. The other, page 58 (reproduced on the page opposite), is in the Berg Collection of the New York Public Library. Along the edge of this page, which he was evidently presenting to someone as a gift, Mark Twain wrote, "Will this do? Though it is not a 'sentiment' strictly speaking. It is original MS of first lecture. Delivered October 1867 in San Francisco." (The date should be 1866.) Following the note he entered the date April, 1873.[2] If Mark Twain had destroyed the manuscript of the "old lecture" except for the two pages still extant prior to 1894 when he claimed it was no longer in existence, it is highly dubious that Albert Bigelow Paine ever saw "considerable portions" of it, unless, of course, Mark Twain was in error about having torn it up.

No manuscript of the revised version of the lecture for the tour of 1869–70 has been uncovered. Fortunately, reporters in various cities reproduced it extensively in their newspapers. These versions differ from Paine's alleged extracts from the original manuscript offered in *Mark Twain's Speeches* chiefly by a change in introductory material and by the addition of anecdotes. Nor does a manuscript for the 1873 version appear to exist. Before going to England to lecture that year, Mark Twain tried out a newly revised form of the lecture on a few metropolitan audiences at home. Of this revision Mrs. Clemens wrote to Mrs. Fairbanks ". . . that lecture is so good and so well rec'd, you know you have not heard it since he rewrote it—and it is much better than before."[3] Again, fortunately, a reporter reproduced a good deal of it—this time for the Brooklyn *Eagle*, February 8, 1873. It was this version that Mr. Frear reprinted in *Mark Twain and Hawaii*, Appendix D2. It also appears to be the version which Thomas B. Reed selected for inclusion in Volume IV of *Modern Eloquence*. Reed's statement in a prefatory note to his version of the lecture, that Mark Twain delivered it in the Academy of Music in New York in 1877, is obviously an

dome of bloody lava 85
as large as a small cottage,
this bursts & sends a million
sparkling gems aloft that
shed a blinding radiance
... & from the midst
of the exploding dome a filmy
jet of light green flame flashes
out & floats away like a dis-
embodied soul — & then the
monstrous mass crushes back
into the lake & attests its ponderous weight by the deep,
funnel-like depression it
makes in the surface. In a
few moments a black crust
of cooling lava forms upon
the lake like a cream, & over
it dance a myriad of beauti-

error. The correct date was 1873 and the place the Brooklyn Academy of Music.

Selected for reprinting here is the version Mark Twain prepared for the tour of 1869–70. It has more of the flavor of Mark Twain than the 1873 version, since it preserves some of the inelegancies which distinguished his early manner, and which he pruned out of the later lecture in deference to a supposed greater delicacy of taste among British audiences.[4] But it is also offered for another reason. It was this version of the lecture which contributed most to his popularity on the lyceum circuit.

The text which follows is that found in the Meriden, Connecticut, *Daily Republican*, December 13, 1869; supplemented by a passage from the Troy, New York, *Daily Times*, January 12, 1870; one from *Mark Twain's Speeches*, pp. 18 and 19; and one from Frear's *Mark Twain and Hawaii*, pp. 61 and 62. While the composite here presented is incomplete, it clearly exhibits Mark Twain's early humor on the platform, his felicitous manner of combining instruction and entertainment, and his power of description.

I HAVE the pleasure of introducing to you Mr. Samuel Clemens, otherwise Mark Twain, a gentleman whose high character and unimpeachable veracity are only surpassed by his personal comeliness and native modesty. I am the gentleman referred to. I suppose I ought to ask pardon for breaking the usual custom on such occasions and introducing myself, but it could not be avoided, as the gentleman who was to introduce me did not know my real name, hence I relieved him of his duties.

UNPLEASANT OBJECTS

The first object I saw in the Sandwich Islands was an unpleasant one, and hence it suggested the beginning of my lecture. We cannot forget unpleasant things. In an old cathedral in Milan they showed me relics and other unpleasant objects, but one above all I remember simply because it was a very unpleasant thing. It was a curious, ancient statue, ascribed to Phidias, because it was imagined that no other artist could have ever copied nature so delicately and accurately. It was a figure carved in stone of a man without skin. It was a thoroughly skinned man, and every vein, artery, fiber, tendon, and even the tissue of the human frame, were marvelously and faithfully portrayed even to the minutest detail. It was not a pleasant thing to look at, but, somehow, there was a fascination about it because it looked so natural. It did. It looked as if it was in pain, and you felt that a thoroughly skinned man could only look like that. I have tried to get rid of such an unpleasant association, and dreamed and dreamed—that he had come to stay a week with me. I remember once when a mere girl—a child, so to speak—I ran away from school. I was afraid to go home at night—not that I cared anything about it myself, but my parents were prejudiced against that sort of thing, and although my judgment was quite as good as theirs, still as they had the majority they generally settled everything their own way, and so I was afraid to go home. I went to my father's office and laid myself on the lounge. It was late at night. The moon was beginning to creep up and to cast a few beams of light upon the floor. Looking upon the floor I discovered a long and mysterious looking shape. I turned my back upon it. It annoyed me; not that I was frightened, oh no, but just when I knew the moon's rays must have lighted up the spot I turned and looked, and lo! it was a dead man, his white face turned up to the moonlight, and he was cold and stiff and stark. I never before felt so sick in my life. I never before wanted to take a walk so badly as I did then. I did not go away in a hurry. I simply went through the window and took the sash with me. I did not need the sash, but it was handier to take than it was to leave it. I was not scared but a good deal agitated. I have never got rid of that man yet. He had—it appeared—fallen lifeless in the street, and they had brought him in to hold an inquest upon him, or to try him, and of course they found him guilty. It is not advisable to go to one's subject in a direct line and that accounts for the foregoing remarks. If a man is going to pop the question he begins a long way from his subject and talks of the weather. So it is with me; great subjects should be approached cautiously. I shall tell the truth as nearly as I can and quite as nearly as *any* newspaperman can. The nonsense with which I shall embellish it will not detract from its truthfulness; that will be but as the barnacle to the oyster. I don't know—*sotto voce*—whether the barnacle does stick to the oyster or the oyster to the barnacle—that figure is of my own invention. I was born and reared a long way from tidewater and I don't know whether the barnacle does stick to the oyster, but if it don't I do.

THE SANDWICH ISLANDS

These islands are situated some twenty-one hundred miles southwest from San Francisco. The prevailing opinion—that they are in South America—is a mistake. They are situated in the Pacific Ocean, and their entire area is not greater, I suppose, than that of Rhode Island and Connecticut combined. They are of volcanic origin; of volcanic construction I should say. They are composed of lava harder than any statement I have made for three months. There is not a spoonful of legitimate dirt in the whole group, unless it has been lately imported. These islands were discovered some eighty or ninety years ago by Captain Cook, though another man came very near discovering them before, and he was diverted from his course by a manuscript found in a bottle. He wasn't the first man who has been diverted by suggestions got out of a bottle. Eight of these islands are inhabited, four of the eight are entirely girdled with a belt of mountains comprising the most productive sugar lands in the world. The sugar lands in Louisiana are considered rich, and yield from 500 to 1,700 pounds per acre, but those of the Sandwich Islands yield from 2,500 to 13,000 pounds per acre. A 200-acre crop of wheat in the states is worth $20,000 or $30,000; a 200-acre crop of sugar in these islands is worth $200,000.

You could not do that in this country, unless you planted it with stamps and reaped it in bonds. When these islands were discovered the population was about 400,000, but the white man came and brought various complicated diseases, and education, and civilization, and all sorts of calamities, and consequently the population began to drop off with commendable activity. Forty years ago they were reduced to 60,000, and the educational and civilizing facilities being increased they dwindled down to 55,000, and it is proposed to send a few more missionaries and finish them. It isn't the education or civilization that has settled them; it is the imported diseases, and they have all got the consumption and other reliable distempers, and to speak figuratively, they are retiring from business pretty fast.

MANNERS OF THE PEOPLE

There are about three thousand white people in the islands; they are mostly Americans. In fact they are the kings of the Sandwich Islands; the monarchy is not much more than a mere name. These people stand as high in the scale of character as any people in the world, and some of them who were born and educated in those islands don't even know what vice is. The natives of the Sandwich Islands of color are a rich, dark brown, a kind of black and tan. The tropical sun and the easygoing ways inherited from their ancestors have made them rather idle, but they are not vicious at all; they are good people. The native women in the rural districts wear a loose, magnificent, curtain calico garment, but the men don't. Upon great occasions the men wear an umbrella, or some little fancy article like that—further than this they have no inclination towards gorgeousness of costume. In ancient times the king was the ruler of all the land, and supreme head of the church and state; his voice was superior to all law; he was absolute; his power was sacred. After the king in authority came the high priests of the ancient superstition, and after them the great chiefs, little better than slaves to the king. Next came the common plebians, and they were slaves to the whole party, *were* abused and killed at the slightest pretext. And below them, away down at the bottom of this pile of tyranny and superstition, came the women, and they were the abject slaves of all; they were degraded to the level of the beasts, and thought to be no better. They were cruelly maltreated. By the law of the land it was death for a woman to eat at the same table with her husband, or to eat out of the same dish with him. Even those darkened people seemed to have a glimmering idea of the danger of the women eating forbidden fruit, and they didn't want to take the risk. Now the Sandwich Islanders are the best educated of any people on the earth, and I don't suppose there is a single *Kannacker* of 18 years and upward, but what can read and write. And all this wonderful work was accomplished by our American missionaries. And what is curious further, this great work was paid for in great part by the American Sunday school children with their pennies. Though it is beyond all comprehension that many a bad little boy has reaped a lucrative income, by confiscating the pennies given him for missionary contributions, dropping into the box such brass buttons as he could spare from his garments. It is the proudest reflection of my life that I never did that—never did it but once or twice, anyhow. These natives are an exceeding hospitable people. If you want to stay two or three days and nights in a native cabin you will be welcome. They will feast you on raw fish, with the scales on, cocoanuts, plantains, baked dogs and fricasseed cats, all the luxuries of the season. But if you want to trade with one of them, that's business. He will tell one falsehood after another right straight along, and not ordinary lies either, but monstrous incredible ones, and when a native is caught in a lie it doesn't incommode him at all. All these natives have a dozen mothers at least, not natural mothers, but adopted ones. A California man went down there and opened a sugar plantation. One of his hands came and said he wanted to bury his mother. He gave him permission. In a few days the man wanted to go and bury another mother. He gave him permission. In a few days the man wanted to go and bury another mother. The Californian thought it strange, but said "Well, go and plant her." Within a month the man wanted to bury some more mothers. "Look ye here," said the planter, "I don't want to be hard upon you in your affliction, but it appears to me your stock of mothers holds out pretty well. It interferes with business, so clear out and never come back till you have buried every mother you have in the world."

DOGS

They are very fond of dogs, these people; not the great Newfoundland or the stately mastiff, but a species of little mean, contemptible cur, that a white man would condemn to death on general principles. There is nothing attractive about these dogs—there is not a handsome feature about them, unless it is their bushy tails. A friend of mine said if he had one of these dogs he would cut off his tail and throw the rest of the dog away. They feed this dog, pet him, take ever so much care of him, and then cook and eat him. I couldn't do that. I would rather go hungry for two days than devour an old personal friend in that way; but many a white citizen of those islands throws aside his prejudices and takes his dinner off one of those puppies—and after all it is only our cherished American sausage with the mystery removed.

CANNIBALISM

It used to be popular to call these Sandwichers cannibals. They are not cannibals. There was one, however, who opened an office in a back settlement and did a good business, eating up a good many *Kannackers* in his time. In other cities I usually illustrate cannibalism on the stage, but being a stranger here

I don't feel at liberty to ask favors, but still, if anyone in the audience would lend me an infant, I will
go on with the show. However, it is of no consequence. I know that children have grown scarce lately
on account of the neglect with which they are treated
since the woman's movement began. That cannibal I
was speaking about reduced the Democratic vote a
good deal, but getting tired of *Kannackers*—they are
not good for a steady diet—he thought he would
see how a white man would go with onions. So he
kidnapped an old whaler who had been in the service
sixty-five years, but either the crime or his conscience,
or the weight of the whaler on his stomach, or both
together, killed him. I was told this. I don't believe
it quite myself, and only told it on account of the
moral it conveys. There must be a moral in it somewhere, because I have told the story thirty or forty
times, and never got it out yet. They have some curious customs there; among others, if a man makes a
bad joke they kill him. I can't speak from experience
on that point, because I never lectured there. I suppose if I had I should not be lecturing here.

CLIMATE AND CUSTOMS

The climate of these islands is delightful, it is
beautiful. In Honolulu the thermometer stands at
about 80 or 82 degrees pretty much all the year
round—don't change more than 12 degrees in twelve
months. In the sugar districts the thermometer stands
at 70 and does not change at all. Any kind of a thermometer will do—one without any quicksilver is just
as good. That climate is very healthy—as healthy as
ours; indeed, a man told me it was so hot in Wall
Street the other day that gold went up to 160 in the
shade.

If you would see magnificent scenery—scenery on
a mighty scale—and get scenery which charms with its
softness and delights you with its unspeakable beauty,
at the same moment that it deeply impresses you with

its grandeur and its sublimity, you should go to the islands.

Each island is a mountain or two or three mountains. They begin at the seashore—in a torrid climate where the cocoa palm grows and the coffee tree, the mango, orange, banana, and the delicious cherimoya; they begin down there in a sweltering atmosphere, rise with a grand and gradual sweep till they hide their beautiful regalia of living green in the folds of the drooping clouds, and higher and higher yet they rise among the mists till their emerald forests change to dull and stunted shrubbery, then to scattering constellations of the brilliant silver sword, then higher yet to dreary, barren desolation—no tree, no shrubs, nothing but torn and scorched and blackened piles of lava; higher yet, and then, towering toward heaven, above the dim and distant land, above the waveless sea, and high above the rolling plains of clouds themselves, stands the awful summit, wrapped in a mantle of everlasting ice and snow and burnished with a tropical sunshine that fires it with a dazzling splendor! Here one may stand and shiver in the midst of eternal winter and look down upon a land reposing in the loveliest hue of summer that hath no end.

The volcano of Kee-law-ay-oh is 17,000 feet in diameter and from 700 to 800 feet deep. Vesuvius is nowhere. It is the largest live volcano in the world; shoots up flames tremendously high. You witness a scene of unrivaled sublimity; and witness the most astonishing sights. When the volcano of Kee-law-ay-oh broke through a few years ago, lava flowed out of it for twenty days and twenty nights, and made a stream forty miles in length, till it reached the sea, tearing up forests in its awful fiery path, swallowing up huts, destroying all vegetation, rioting through shady dells and sinuous canyons. Amidst this carnival of destruction, majestic columns of smoke ascended, and formed a cloudy, murky pall overhead. Sheets of green, blue, lambent flame were shot upwards and pierced this vast gloom, making all sublimely grand.

With all their kindly ways these people practice some cruelties. They will put a live chicken into the hot ashes simply to see it hop about. They would burn the flesh before the missionaries came, and would put out an eye, or a tooth, when a chief died. And if their grief was deep, and they could get relief in no other way, they would go out and scalp a neighbor. In the season of mourning for a great person they permit any crime that will best express sorrow.

They do everything differently from other people. They mount a horse from the off side. They turn to the left instead of the right. They say the same words for "good bye" and "how do you do." They always, in beckoning for you to come, motion in the opposite direction. Even the birds partake of this peculiarity. The native duck lives four thousand feet above the level of the sea, and never sees water except when it rains. They (the islanders) groan in a heartbroken way when they are particularly happy. They have some customs we might import with advantage. I don't call any to mind just now.

In Honolulu they are the most easygoing people in the world. Some of our people are not acquainted with their customs. They started a gas company once, and put the gas at $13 a thousand feet. They only took in $16 the first month. They all went to bed at dark. They are an excellent people. I speak earnestly. They do not know even the name of some of the vices in this country. A lady called on a doctor. She wanted something for general debility. He ordered her to drink porter. She called him again. The porter had done her no good. He asked her how much porter she had taken. She said a tablespoonful in a tumbler of water. I wish we could import such a blessed ignorance into this country. They don't do much drinking there; it is too expensive. When they have paid the tax for importing the liquor they have got nothing left to purchase the liquor with. They are very innocent and drink anything that is limpid— kerosene, turpentine, hair oil. In our town on a

Fourth of July an entire community got drunk on a barrel of Mrs. Winslow's soothing syrup.

LIARS

These Sandwichers believe in a superstition that the biggest liars in the world have got to visit the Islands some time before they die. They believe that because it is a fact—you misunderstand—I mean that when liars get there they stay there. They have had several specimens they boast of. They treasure up their little perfections, and they allude to them as if the man was inspired—from below. They had a man among them named Morgan. He never allowed anyone to tell a bigger lie than himself, and he always told the last one too. When someone was telling about the natural bridge in Virginia, he said he knew all about it, as his father helped to build it. Someone was bragging of a wonderful horse he had. Morgan told them of one he had once. While out riding one day a thunder shower came on and chased him for eighteen miles, and never caught him. Not a single drop of rain dropped onto his nose, but his dog was swimming behind the wagon the whole of the way. Once, when the subject of mean men was being discussed, Morgan told them of an incorporated company of mean men. They hired a poor fellow to blast rock for them. He drilled a hole four feet deep, put in the powder, and began to tamp it down around the fuse. I know all about tamping, as I have worked in a mine myself. The crowbar struck a spark and caused a premature explosion, and that man and his crowbar shot up into the air, and he went higher and higher and higher till he didn't look bigger than a bee, and then he went out of sight; and presently he came in sight again, looking no bigger than a bee; and he came further and further and further till he was as big as a dog, and further and further and further till he was as big as a boy, and he came further and further till he assumed the full size and shape of a man, and he came down and fell right into the same old spot and went to tamping again. And would you believe it—concluded Morgan—although that poor fellow was not gone more than fifteen minutes, yet that mean company docked him for the loss of time.

THE AMERICAN VANDAL ABROAD

A T THE BEGINNING of the tour of 1868–69 this lecture was advertised as Brother Jonathan Abroad[5] or as American Vandals in the Old World.[6] After the tour got under way, it was invariably announced as The American Vandal Abroad.

Fifty-seven pages of the lecture manuscript are preserved among the Mark Twain Papers (DV No. 52). It was from this source, probably, that Albert Bigelow Paine extracted portions for inclusion in his book *Mark Twain's Speeches.*[7] The text which follows, slightly edited here and there for the sake of continuity, has been composited from several sources: Paine's extracts, various newspaper reports, and a manuscript fragment of the concluding portion of the lecture, found in the Webster Collection. It is reprinted here with Mark Twain's deletions and emendations. Concerning this lecture, as with his others, it must be remembered that when Mark Twain had once committed it to memory, he departed freely from the manuscript text and introduced new matter on the spur of the moment. Thereafter, none of his manuscripts represented his lecture on any particular occasion. The composite provides a fairly accurate overview of the various components of the lecture. The sources of the various parts of the composite are indicated in brackets. It should be noted that Mark Twain was careful to define "Vandal," fearing the term might otherwise give offense.

[After being introduced by a local citizen Mark Twain said]

I T DOES NOT exactly embarrass me to be introduced in so public a manner, but it does remind me of those European guides who brought out every old relic and described it with a trite story and who if interrupted were obliged to begin again at the beginning.[8]

I like anything that reminds me of them because I hate them. They expect you to go into ecstasies over what they show you. After we learned their distinguishing characteristics we determined to affect as much imbecility as possible. The surgeon of the ship was capable of asking the stupidest questions without moving a muscle. He was elected spokesman of the party. We worried our guide. He showed us the bust of Columbus. The Doctor examined. He asked, "Is he dead? What did he die of?" He also asked, "Are his parents dead? Which is the bust and which is the pedestal? Has he been on a bust before?"[9]

I am to speak of the American Vandal this evening, but I wish to say in advance that I do not use this term in derision or apply it as a reproach, but I use it because it is convenient; and duly and properly modified, it best describes the roving, independent, free and easy character of that class of traveling Americans who are *not* elaborately educated, cultivated and refined, and gilded and filigreed with the ineffable graces of the first society.[10]

The American Vandal goes everywhere and is always at home everywhere. He attempts to investigate the secrets of the harems; he views the rock where Paul was let down in a basket, and seriously asks where the basket is. He will choke himself to death trying to smoke a Turkish pipe and swears it is good. He goes into ecstasies over the insufferable horrors of the Turkish bath, though he is thinking the while that he may never come out alive. He learns to ride a camel. He packs his trunk with figs and other little vegetables. He looks picturesque when beholding Rome from the dome of St. Peter's. His soul is full of admiration. He rises above earthly cares. It is grand to be an American, he feels. He is proud and looks proud. His countenance is beaming. He does not fail to let the public know that he is an American. This is not a fault. It is commendable. I have seen him in the company of kings and queens, lords and popes. He is always self possessed, always untouched, unabashed—even in the presence of the Sphinx.[11] The

Sphinx, whose great face was so sad, so earnest, so longing, so patient. There was a dignity not of earth in its mien, and in its countenance a benignity such as never anything human wore. It was stone, but it seemed sentient! If ever image of stone *thought*, it was thinking. It was looking toward the verge of the landscape, but looking *at* nothing—nothing but distance and vacancy. It was looking over and beyond everything of the Present, and far into the Past. It was gazing over the ocean of Time—over lines of century—waves, which, further and further receding, closed nearer and nearer together, and blended at the last into one unbroken tide, away toward the horizon of a remote antiquity.

It was thinking of the wars of departed ages—of the empires it had seen created and destroyed—of the nations whose birth it had witnessed, whose progress it had watched, whose annihilation it had noted—of the joy and sorrow, the life and death, the grandeur and decay, of five thousand slow-revolving years.

It was the type of an attribute of man—of a faculty of his heart and brain. It was MEMORY—RETROSPECTION—wrought into visible tangible form. All who know the pathos there is in memories of days that are accomplished and faces that have vanished—albeit only a trifling score of years gone by, will have some appreciation of the pathos that swells in these grave eyes that look so steadfastly back upon the things they knew before History was born—before Tradition had being—things that were, and forms that moved, in a vague era that even Poetry and Romance scarce know of—and passed one by one away and left the stone dreamer solitary in the midst of a strange, new age and uncomprehended scenes!

The Sphinx is grand in its loneliness; it is imposing in its magnitude; it is impressive in the mystery which hangs over its story. There is that in the overshadowing majesty of the eternal figure of stone, with its accusing memory of the deeds of all ages, that reveals to one something of what he shall feel when he stands at last in the awful presence of God![12]

The true home of the Vandal is Paris, where he is most officious and conceited. He drinks oceans of champagne, and is *non-chalant,* what ever that means. It is a good word though. He attends all the plays, weeps when the crowd weeps, and claps and stamps when other people do. He learns to talk French so well in six weeks that he is constantly abusing the Parisians for not knowing their own language. I knew one Vandal who, on his return home, failed to answer the salutations of his friends, having become so familiar with the French pronunciation of his name that he found it difficult to recognize his original one.[13]

When the Vandal gets through with France, he generally takes in Italy. He thinks it is proper to visit Genoa, that stately old City of Palaces, whose vast marble edifices almost meet together over streets so narrow that three men can hardly walk abreast in them, and so crooked that a man generally comes out of them about the same place he went in. He only stays in Genoa long enough to see a few celebrated things and get some fragments of stone from the house Columbus was born in—for your genuine Vandal is an intolerable and incorrigible relic gatherer. It is estimated that if all the fragments of stone brought from Columbus' house by travelers were collected together, they would suffice to build a house fourteen thousand feet long and sixteen thousand feet high— and I suppose they would.[14]

He generally takes mementos from everywhere he goes. One of them was very successful till he got into the Crimea. He found nothing there but the hipbone of a horse. The Vandal took it and labeled it "The jawbone of a Russian General." Travelers' labels are not always reliable.[15]

Next he hurries to Milan and takes notes of the Grand Cathedral (for he is always taking notes). Oh, I remember Milan and the noble Cathedral well enough—that marble miracle of enchanting architecture. I remember how we entered and walked about its vast spaces and among its huge columns, gazing

aloft at the monster windows all aglow with bril-
liantly colored scenes in the life of the Savior and his
followers. And I remember the sideshows and the
curiosities there, too. The guide showed us a coffee-
colored piece of sculpture which he said was considered to have come from the hand of Phidias, since it
was not possible that any other man, of any epoch,
could have copied nature with such faultless accuracy.
The figure was that of a man without skin; with every
vein, artery, muscle, every fiber and tendon and tissue
of the human frame, represented in minute detail. It
looked natural, because it looked somehow *as if it
were in pain.* A skinned man *would be likely to look
that way*—unless his attention were occupied by some
other matter.[16]

[The recollection of the statue of the skinned
man reminded him of a painful incident that had
happened when he was a boy. Having played truant
from school and fearing to go home, he went to his
father's office to spend the night, unaware that a
corpse had been laid on the floor of the office waiting
for a coroner to pass sentence upon him, that is, hold
an inquest. He lay down and went to sleep. After a
while he awoke, and in the moonlight he felt almost
sure there was something on the floor. As the moonlight crept along the floor the outlines of the mysterious object were gradually revealed. He felt inclined
to get up and examine it and yet he didn't want to.
He began to feel uncomfortable. He wanted to go
somewhere. He desired to take a walk. He made up
his mind to leave. It was inconvenient to go out by
the door, so he went through the window. He was in
no hurry but he took the sash with him. Not that he
needed the sash, but it was more convenient to take
it than to leave it.][17]

In Milan the Vandal goes to see the ancient and
most celebrated painting in the world, "The Last
Supper." We all know it in engravings: the disciples
all sitting on one side of a long, plain table and Christ
with bowed head in the center—all the Last Suppers
in the world are copied from this painting. It is so

damaged now, by the wear and tear of three hundred years, that the figures can hardly be distinguished. The Vandal goes to see this picture—which all the world praises—looks at it with a critical eye, and says it's a perfect old nightmare of a picture and he wouldn't give forty dollars for a million like it (and I endorse his opinion), and then he is done with Milan.

He paddles around the Lake of Como for a few days, and then takes the cars. He is bound for Venice, the oldest and proudest and the princeliest republic that ever graced the earth. We put on a great many airs with our little infant of a republic of a century's growth, but we grow modest when we stand before this gray old imperial city that used to laugh the armies and navies of half the world to scorn, and was a haughty, invincible, magnificent republic for fourteen hundred years! The Vandal is bound for Venice! He has a long, long, weary ride of it; but just as the day is closing he hears someone shout, "Venice!" and puts his head out of the window, and sure enough, afloat on the placid sea, a league away, lies the great city with its towers and domes and steeples drowsing in a golden mist of sunset!

Have you been to Venice, and seen the winding canals, and the stately edifices that border them all along, ornamented with the quaint devices and sculptures of a former age? And have you seen the great Cathedral of St. Mark's—and the giant's Staircase—and the famous Bridge of Sighs—and the great Square of St. Mark's—and the ancient pillar with the winged Lion of St. Mark that stands in it, whose story and whose origin are a mystery—and the Rialto, where Shylock used to loan money on human flesh and other collateral?[18]

Here, perchance, the Vandal may hear the song of the romantic gondolier. However, despite Byron, his private opinion is that as a singer the gondolier is a humbug. He feels it is grand to glide down the street in a gondola instead of a street car. He sees businessmen step out, put on their gloves, and glide

down to their counting rooms. The ladies kiss good-
bye, play all the secret deceptions of the sex in our
own land, but keep the gondolier waiting instead of
the private carriage. They go shopping just the same
and compel the poor clerks to lay down tons of silks,
bombazines, corduroys and the like, and then buy a
paper of pins and have it sent home by the errand
boy. Ladies there are the same angels as at home,
have dresses cut "bias" and have their back hair held
up by a crupper just the same way.[19]

I had begun to feel that the old Venice of song
and story had departed forever. But I was too hasty.
When we swept gracefully out into the Grand Canal
and under the mellow moonlight the Venice of poetry
and romance stood revealed. Right from the waters
edge rose palaces of marble; gondolas were riding
swiftly hither and thither and disappearing suddenly
through unsuspected gates and alleys; ponderous
stone bridges threw their shadows athwart the glitter-
ing waves. There were life and motion everywhere,
and yet everywhere there was a hush, a stealthy sort
of stillness, that was suggestive of secret enterprises of
bravos and lovers; and clad half in moonbeams and
half in mysterious shadows, the grim old mansions of
the republic seemed to have an expression about them
of having an eye out for just such enterprises as these.
At that same moment music came stealing over the
waters—Venice was complete.

Our Vandals hurried away from Venice and scattered abroad everywhere. You could find them breaking specimens from the dilapidated tomb of Romeo
and Juliet at Padua—and infesting the picture galleries of Florence—and risking their necks on the
Leaning Tower of Pisa—and snuffing sulphur fumes
on the summit of Vesuvius—and burrowing among
the exhumed wonders of Herculaneum and Pompeii—
and you might see them with spectacles on, and blue
cotton umbrellas under their arms, benignantly contemplating Rome from the venerable arches of the
Coliseum.

And finally we sailed from Naples, and in due

time anchored before the Piraeus, the seaport of Athens in Greece. But the quarantine was in force, and so they set a guard of soldiers to watch us and would not let us go ashore. However, I and three other Vandals took a boat, and muffled the oars, and slipped ashore at 11:30 at night, and dodged the guard successfully. Then we made a wide circuit around the slumbering town, avoiding all roads and houses—for they'd about as soon hang a body as not for violating the quarantine laws in those countries. We got around the town without any accident, and then struck out across the Attic Plain, steering straight for Athens—over rocks and hills and brambles and everything—with Mt. Helicon for a landmark. And so we tramped for five or six miles. The Attic Plain is a mighty uncomfortable plain to travel in, even if it *is* so historical. The armed guards got after us three times and flourished their gleaming gun barrels in the moonlight, because they thought we were stealing grapes occasionally—and the fact is we *were*—for we found by and by that the brambles that tripped us up so often were grapevines—but these people in the country didn't know that we were quarantine-blockade runners, and so they only scared us and jawed Greek at us and let us go, instead of arresting us.

We didn't care about Athens particularly, but we wanted to see the famous Acropolis and its ruined temples, and we did. We climbed the steep hill of the Acropolis about one in the morning and tried to storm that grand old fortress that had scorned the battles and sieges of three thousand years. We had the garrison out mighty quick—four Greeks—and we bribed them to betray the citadel and unlock the gates. In a moment we stood in the presence of the noblest ruins we had ever seen—the most elegant, the most graceful, the most imposing. The renowned Parthenon towered above us, and about us were the wrecks of what were once the snowy marble Temples of Hercules and Minerva, and another whose name I have forgotten. Most of the Parthenon's grand columns are still standing, but the roof is gone.

As we wandered down the marble-paved length of this mighty temple, the scene was strangely impressive. Here and there in lavish profusion were gleaming white statues of men and women, propped against blocks of marble, some of them armless, some without legs, others headless, but all looking mournful and sentient and startlingly human! They rose up and confronted the midnight intruder on every side; they stared at him with stony eyes from unlooked-for nooks and recesses; they peered at him over fragmentary heaps far down the desolate corridors; they barred his way in the midst of the broad forum, and solemnly pointed with handless arms the way from the sacred fane; and through the roofless temple the moon looked down and banded the floor and darkened the scattered fragments and broken statues with the slanting shadows of the columns!

What a world of ruined sculpture was about us! Stood up in rows, stacked up in piles, scattered broadcast over the wide area of the Acropolis, were hundreds of crippled statues of all sizes and of the most exquisite workmanship; and vast fragments of marble that once belonged to the entablatures, covered with bas-reliefs representing battles and sieges, ships of war with three and four tiers of oars, pageants and processions—everything one could think of.

We walked out into the grass-grown, fragment-strewn court beyond the Parthenon. It startled us every now and then, to see a stony white face stare suddenly up at us out of the grass, with its dead eyes. The place seemed alive with ghosts. We half expected to see the Athenian heroes of twenty centuries ago glide out of the shadows and steal into the old temple they knew so well and regarded with such boundless pride.

The full moon was riding high in the cloudless heavens now. We sauntered carelessly and unthinkingly to the edge of the lofty battlements of the citadel, and looked down, and, lo! a vision! And such a vision! Athens by moonlight! All the beauty in all the world combined could not rival it! The prophet that thought the splendors of the New Jerusalem were revealed to him surely saw this instead. It lay in the level plain right under our feet—all spread abroad like a picture—and we looked down upon it as we might have looked from a balloon. We saw no semblance of a street, but every house, every window, every clinging vine, every projection, was as distinct and sharply marked as if the time were noonday; and yet there was no glare, no glitter, nothing harsh or repulsive—the silent city was flooded with the mellowest light that ever streamed from the moon, and seemed like some living creature wrapped in peaceful slumber. On its farther side was a little temple whose delicate pillars and ornate front glowed with a rich luster that chained the eye like a spell; and nearer by, the palace of the King reared its creamy walls out of the midst of a great garden of shrubbery that was flecked all over with a random shower of amber lights—a spray of golden sparks that lost their brightness in the glory of the moon and glinted softly upon the sea of dark foliage like the palled stars of the Milky Way! Overhead, the stately columns, majestic still in their ruin; underfoot, the dreaming city; in the distance the silver sea—not on the broad earth is there another picture half so beautiful!

We go back to the ship safely, just as the day was dawning. We had walked upon pavements that had been pressed by Plato, Aristotle, Demosthenes, Socrates, Phocion, Euclid, Xenophon, Herodotus, Diogenes, and a hundred others of deathless fame, and were satisfied. We got to stealing grapes again on the way back, and half a dozen rascally guards with muskets and pistols captured us and marched us in the center of a hollow square nearly to the sea—till we were beyond all the graperies. Military escort—ah, I never traveled in so much state in all my life.

I leave the Vandal here. I have not time to follow him farther—nor *our* Vandals to Constantinople and Smyrna and the Holy Land, Egypt, the islands of the sea, and to Russia and his visit to the emperor. But I wish I *could* tell of that visit of our gang of "Quaker

City" Vandals to the grandest monarch of the age. America's staunch old steadfast friend, Alexander II, Autocrat of Russia.[20]

In conclusion I will observe that even galloping as we did about the world, we learned something. The lesson of the Excursion was a good one. It taught us that foreign countries are excellent to travel in, but that the best country to live in is America, after all. We found no soap in the hotels of Europe, & they charged us for candles we never burned. We saw no ladies anywhere that were as beautiful as our own ladies here at home & especially in this audience. We saw none anywhere that dressed with such excellent taste as do our ladies at home here. I am not a married man, but—but—I would like to be. I only mention it in the most casual way, though, &—do not mean anything—anything personal by it. We saw no government on the other side *like our own*—not *just* like our own. The Sultan's was a little like it. One of his great officers came into office without a cent, & went out in a few years & built himself a palace worth 3 million. It brought tears to my eyes in that far foreign land—it was so like home. The Sultan confiscated it. He said he liked to see a man prosper, but he didn't like to see him get wealthy on $2,000 a year & no perquisites. ~~That officer would make a name for himself over here. He would shine in whiskey and cotton frauds.~~

We saw no energy in the capitals of Europe like the tremendous energy of New York, & we saw no place where intelligence & enterprise were so widely diffused as they are here in our country. We saw nowhere any architectural achievement that was so beautiful to the eye as the national capitol of America, at Washington, & we saw nowhere any building that was—that was—just like our Washington Monument. We saw no people anywhere so self-denying, & patriotic & prompt in collecting their salaries as our own members of Congress. ~~We saw many bad pictures, but we saw none so execrable as those in the Capitol Rotunda.~~ . . . We saw nothing in Europe, Asia or

Africa to make us wish to live there, & when the voyage was done (& it was a very, very pleasant one, take it all together), we were glad to get back to our own country where moral & religious freedom prevail,— where politicians are incorruptible,—where accident policies are cheap & where the chances to get your money back are good on all railroads. . . .

Ah I had rather live here than in Turkey—in Constantinople, with its beggars, its dogs, its ugly overpraised Mosques, its hen-pecked Sultan, who has 800 wives and yet isn't happy, ~~& ought to be happy, if there is such a thing as happiness in the Married State, & yet isn't~~. It is a perfect *unanswerable* argument against matrimony. If a man can't be happy with 800 wives, what chance is there for him with only *one?* None in the world. People tell me that it makes a man happy to have a woman love him—& I used to be innocent enough to believe it before I went to Constantinople. Theorizing is all very well, but facts and figures are better. If the love of just one woman could make a man so happy, what ought to be the natural result, how would it be with him if he had the love of 800 of them? Why he just simply couldn't *stand* so much bliss, that is all. He couldn't live through it. Such a deluge of sweetness as that would be bound to swamp him. He couldn't contain all that sweetness any more than a 1-gallon jug could contain 800 gallons of clarified sugar house molasses honey. Sentiment is all very well, but sentiment can't stand the test of mathematics. Travel has made me wise—& I warn the youth of Brooklyn to beware of matrimony. It is a delusion & a snare. I have seen it under the most favorable aspect, & I ought to know where of I speak. It is my deliberate judgment that a man—that a man—wouldn't be happy with 40,000 wives! The Sultan of Turkey talked to me like a father. He saw that I sympathized with him, & he opened his heart & told me all his troubles. He said, why Governor, you can't imagine the expense and bother that all those women cost me. Why it isn't 15 minutes ago, since my ugliest wife, no. 642 (and she is a spectacle to look

at)—I have forgotten her name, was in here trying to
get me to buy her $100,000 worth of jewelry; oh an
ugly woman hasn't got any effrontery, you know, &
another one, no. 422, came right after her with a black
eye—she'd had a brief fight with no. 764 & got the
worst of it. . . .[21]

If there is a moral to this lecture it is an injunc-
tion to all Vandals to *travel.* I am glad the American
Vandal *goes* abroad. It does him good. It makes a
better man of him. It rubs out a multitude of his old
unworthy biases and prejudices. It aids his religion,
for it enlarges his charity and his benevolence, it
broadens his views of men and things; it deepens his
generosity and his compassion for the failings and
shortcomings of his fellow creatures. Contact with
men of various nations and many creeds teaches him
that there are *other* people in the world besides his
own little clique, and other opinions as worthy of attention and respect as his own. He finds that he and
his are not the most momentous matters in the universe. Cast into trouble and misfortune in strange
lands and being mercifully cared for by those he never
saw before, he begins to learn that best lesson of all—
that one which culminates in the conviction that God
puts *something* good and something lovable in every
man his hands create—that the world is *not* a cold,
harsh, cruel, prisonhouse, stocked with all manner of
selfishness and hate and wickedness. It *liberalizes* the
Vandal to travel. You never saw a bigoted, opinion-
ated, stubborn, narrow-minded, self-conceited, *almighty mean man* in your life but he had stuck in one
place ever since he was born and thought God made
the world and dyspepsia and bile for *his* especial comfort and satisfaction. So I say, *by all means* let the
American Vandal go on traveling, and let no man
discourage him.[22]

I thank you for listening so patiently to this out-
pouring of Truth.

Will repeat in this house on Saturday evening, &
will be glad if you will mention it to your friends, &

if you like the lecture tell them to come, & if you don't
like it tell them you do & get them to come, so that we
can fool as many people as we can.[23]

ARTEMUS WARD

THE TITLE of this lecture was variously reported in the
newspapers as Artemus Ward, Humorist; The Life and
Sayings of Artemus Ward; or simply Artemus Ward. The
original manuscript has not been discovered, nor did any newspaper report the lecture fully, probably because Mark Twain's
audiences and people generally were quite familiar with the life
and sayings of Artemus Ward. The text which follows has been
composed from the reports of the lecture found in a number of
newspapers, but mainly from the Hartford *Daily Times* of November 9, 1871, and the Toledo *Blade,* December 12, 1871. Obviously, much of the lecture is missing, especially those parts, unfortunately, which contributed most to the humor—the stories
and anecdotes. Fortunately, however, the substance of some of
these portions could be identified from comments in the newspapers. They have been indicated by brackets and inserted at
the proper places.

LADIES AND GENTLEMEN, I ask leave to introduce
to you the lecturer of the evening, Mr. Samuel
B. [sic] Clemens, otherwise known as "Mark
Twain," a gentleman, I may say, whose devotion to
science, aptness in philosophy, historical accuracy,
and love of—truth are in perfect harmony with his
majestic and imposing presence. I—ah—refer—ah—in-
directly to—to myself! It is not, I know, customary
to introduce a lecturer after having the amount of
advertising that I have had; but as the management
desired that the introduction should be made, I preferred making it myself, being sure by this means of
getting in all the—facts!

It is my purpose to show that Artemus Ward was
America's greatest humorist, and I will give you a
skeleton outline—I have not time for more—of his

life. In this outline I shall not load you down with historic fact to such an extent that you will be unable to get home, nor will I even make for you any of my philosophical deductions. This last promise is, on my part, a sacrifice, for I admire my philosophical deductions as I admire few other things on earth. Strange as it may seem, I have always found that the effect produced by them upon an audience was that of intense and utter exasperation.[24] [Artemus Ward was] one of the greatest humorists of his age. He . . . [was] thrown so early and suddenly into reputation and fortune that he did not develop into the polished wit he might have become. He was, however, no manufactured humorist. Humor was born in him. He was a humorous baby, he was a humorous boy, he was a funny man. [I cannot] go back and show just how he was a funnier baby than any other baby. But it [is] evident that he early displayed the genius that was in him.[25]

Once when a schoolboy, a friend and he got hold of a pack of cards and indulged heavily in euchre. A Baptist minister was stopping at the house, and to secrete the cards they placed them in his black gown, which hung in a closet. But what was his horror to see the minister one day, in the river baptising his converts, and presently the cards commenced to float upon the water, the first cards being a couple of bowers and three aces. Well, he got walloped for this, and his aunt pictured to him the humiliation of the minister. Said she: "I don't see how he got out of it." Artemus replied: "I don't see how he could help going out on a hand like that."[26]

[At this point, Mark Twain explained that he had not begun exactly at the beginning and that he would go back to that point.][27]

Artemus Ward's real name, as most of you are probably aware, was Charles F. Browne. He was born in Waterford, Maine, in 1834.[28] As a boy he was long, lank, and lean, and a victim of disease always.[29] His personal appearance was not like that of most Maine men. He looked like a glove-stretcher. His hair, red, and brushed well forward at the sides, reminded one of divided flame. His nose rambled on aggressively before him, with all the strength and determination of a cow catcher, while his red mustache—to follow out the simile—seemed not unlike the fortunate cow. He was of good old Puritan descent, and he was proud of it. He says himself: "The Wards are descended from that noble race who fled from despotism to a land where they could enjoy their own religion, and prevent everybody else from enjoying *his'n*."

I don't know whether it is treasonable to speak in this way about those reverend old chaps, the Pilgrim Fathers. I am a Puritan Father, myself, at least I am descended from one. One of my ancestors cut a conspicuous figure in the "Boston massacre," fighting first on one side and then on the other. He wasn't a man to stand foolin' round while a massacre was goin' on. Why, to hear our family talk you'd think that not a man named anything but Twain was in that massacre—and when you come to hear all about it you'd wish that such was the case. Then I had another ancestor in the battle of Bunker Hill. He was everything, that ancestor of mine—killed, wounded and missing. He was a prompt, business-like fellow, and to make sure of being the last of the three, he did it first of all—did it well too, before a shot was fired.[30]

Why, I could stand here for a week and tell you of my distinguished ancestors, and I think I'll do it. On second thought, I think I won't, but go back to my subject.[31]

Ward never had any regular schooling; he was too poor to afford it for one thing, and too lazy to care for it for another. He had an intense ingrained dislike of work of any kind; he even objected to see other people work, and on one occasion went so far as to submit to the authorities of a certain town an invention to run a treadmill by steam. Such a notion could not have originated with a hardhearted man![32] The father of Artemus had a farm, and tried to make the son scare the crows away by firing a shotgun at them; but the boy was too indolent for this; he loaded the gun and the father fired it. The report was like a young earthquake.

Old Mr. Ward was laid up for a week. The senile gentleman, upon recovering asked his son to come forward. He questioned him about the loading of the fowling piece—why he didn't make a report. The precocious youth replied he supposed the gun would report for itself, and so it did. That was enough.[33] He was fond of his early village home, and often referred to it in his writings, and later in life went back and secured the old homestead to his aged mother.

While still young, he apprenticed himself to a printer in Skowhegan. [I] don't know where Skowhegan is, but anyhow it is around here somewhere. Artemus was pleased with the place and used often to pronounce the name; it reminded him so much of the names of old Spain and Portugal, because it was so different.[34]

His first literary venture was as typesetter in the office of the old Boston *Carpet Bagger* [sic], and for that paper he wrote his first squib. He tried every branch of writing, even going so far as to send to the Smithsonian Institute—at least so he himself said— an essay on some deep scientific subject which has never been revealed to the public. He soon tired of settled life and poor pay in Boston, and came to the West to better his fortune. He was for a time in Tiffin, afterward in Toledo, and finally obtained a position in Cleveland as a reporter at $12.00 per week. This was a good salary for a reporter in those days.[35]

It was while acting as a reporter in Cleveland that, in an idle hour, Browne penned an ill-spelled letter, chiefly for his own entertainment, and signed it "Artemus Ward." There was something in Artemus that took the country by storm, and the American showman, who was ready to turn an honest penny by exhibiting an eclipse from a tent with a hole in the top, immediately had the whole world running to his show. [Here Mark Twain digressed on showmen as coarse, illiterate Americans, always endeavoring to suit their conversation to their company, always keeping their eye on the almighty dollar, always mingling the ridiculous with the sublime, and never losing an opportunity to perpetrate a joke.]

The flood tide of his popularity soon bore Artemus to New York, where for a time he infused new life into the columns of *Vanity Fair*, a comic journal published in that city. The quickening was but for a time, and the paper had already entered upon that rapid decline which every American comic journal seems destined to even in its early youth. Artemus watched *Vanity Fair* in its death agonies, saw it expire, and said above its grave that he had always been of the opinion that an occasional joke improved a comic paper.

The idea of lecturing then occurred to Artemus. Encouraged in this proposal by his friends, he strung together a series of jokes and stories, under the title of My Seven Grandmothers, which title he subsequently changed at the suggestion of a friend, to that of The Babes in the Wood, and appeared with this production before an audience first in Norwich. At Christmas time, in 1861, he opened his Babes in New York, and subsequently in California and elsewhere. His profits during that season amounted to something like $30,000 or $40,000—a very considerable sum for that day, but a gas-fitter in the New York Court House does better than that now.

[At this point Mark Twain, speaking of some of Artemus Ward's characteristics, illustrated his patience and good humor with the story of his (Mark Twain's) friend Oliver of Nevada, originally told in *Innocents Abroad*.[36] This story, frequently referred to by reporters as especially delightful to the audience, was not reproduced in any of the newspapers examined. He also cited the reply given by Artemus to the California manager, who inquired of him, "What'll you take for one hundred nights?" to which Artemus replied, "Brandy and water." He also quoted the story of the stranger hunting a victim:

While riding on the railroad train Artemus was accosted by a stranger, a fellow traveller, who inquired of him if he had heard the last thing about Horace Greeley. "Horace Greeley? Who's he? I never heard of him." Again the stranger put a question, in reference to George Francis Train. Artemus replied, "I don't remember hearing that name before." The stranger, intent on getting information from him about someone, said: "What do you think of General Grant?" Artemus replied: "Hang it all, man, you know more strangers than any one I ever knew of." The stranger was still undaunted, and asked, "Did you ever hear of Adam?" Artemus looked at him and inquired, "What was his other name?"]

Having lectured for three months in California,[37] Artemus went over to England, and opened with his panorama in Egyptian Hall, London, and lectured to the nobility as well as common people. His success was so great that he threatened at one time to compel the Royal Family to remain away from his exhibition. Some of the pictures in his exhibitions were most wretchedly painted. Concerning one of these pictures, that of some impossible animal, he assured his audience that some of the greatest artists in the city came to the hall every morning before daybreak, with lanterns, to inspect it. "They say they never saw anything like it before, and hope they never will again." He was always tender-footed in matters of criticism. He said that some people found fault and slurred at him for not saying things like Edward Everett. "Why are they so one-sided?" he asked; "Edward Everett ought to be slurred some, I think, because he can't make a speech like me." No man had ever such respect paid to him in England, as Artemus, except Joaquin Miller.

[Here Mark Twain quoted a number of stories from Artemus Ward's lecture The Babes in the Wood.]

Artemus Ward was a man of good impulses. He was not deep, nor great brained; but he did not live in vain.[38] His speeches in print were flat, but his talk was interesting. It was unkind to report him. There was more in his pauses than in his words. And so no reporter's pen could do him justice.

Artemus had one favorite device in his speeches and that was a sudden transition in the statement of sublime facts to a rehearsal of something decidedly ridiculous. The climax was spoiled, but the laugh came in, and that was just what was needed.

The wit of Mr. Ward was very lively. He was a great humorist, nevertheless. True, he must not be compared with Holmes or Lowell. These men have a refinement that he did not possess; but this does not detract from the great showman's ability to create fun for the million.[39]

[In England] he lectured until his health was in such condition that he was nightly attended by his physician at the theatre.[40] The English climate of cold and fog seemed to have the effect of eating away his life and, although he struggled hard, he had to relinquish his vocation. When he knew that he must die, his only desire was to get home . . . he longed for some familiar face to be with him in his last hours and take his last messages, but it was not to be so. . . . [41] One night in January, four years ago, the people found the doors of Egyptian Hall closed against them. In the thirty-fourth year of his age, at Southampton, he died. Death at any time is sad, but under such circumstances as these it wrings the sigh of pity from every heart.[42]

[In concluding his lecture Mark Twain most frequently asked leave to recite a touching poem on the death of Artemus Ward which had originally appeared in the *Spectator*.[43] But sometimes, if the occasion seemed right, he risked closing with a humorous story. The poem from the *Spectator* is offered here.]

> Is he gone to the land of no laughter
>   This man that made mirth for us all!
> Proves death but a silence hereafter
>   From the sounds that delight or appall?

Once closed, have the lips no more duty,
    No more pleasure the exquisite ears;
Had the heart done o'er flowing the beauty,
    As the eyes have with tears?

Nay, if ought be sure, what can be surer
    Than that Earth's good decays not with Earth?
And of all the heart's springs none are purer,
    Than the springs of the fountains of mirth,
He that sounds them has pierced the heart's hollows,
    The place where tears are, and sleep;
For the foam-flakes that dance in life's shadows
    Are wrung from life's deep.

He came with a heart full of gladness,
    From the glad-hearted world of the West,
Won our laughter, but not with mere madness,
    Spake and joked with us not in mere jest;
For the pain in our heart lingered after,
    When the merriment died in our ears,
And those that were loudest in laughter
    Are silent in tears.

ROUGHING IT

DURING THE TOUR of 1871–72, this lecture was advertised as Roughing It. In England, in 1873–74, the title was Roughing It on the Silver Frontier.

No original manuscript of the lecture is known to exist. In 1871, however, a reporter for the Lansing, Michigan, *State Republican* reproduced it for his newspaper "entire" on the facetious assumption that "Mark Twain's feelings might be hurt unless we give him a pretty extended notice. . . ." It constitutes perhaps the fullest report in existence of any of Mark Twain's tour lectures.

How extensively he revised the lecture for British audiences cannot with certainty be known, though it is probable that in the opening remarks he took into account the fact that the American Silver frontier in Nevada was largely unknown to his foreign auditors. That he was particularly concerned to describe its main features and contrast it with the English countryside is evident from a page of pictorial sketches and notes which Mark

Twain used on the platform to remind him of the particulars he wished to stress.[44] One of the notes read "Physically Nev. does not resemble England." The text which follows is that found in the Lansing *State Republican,* December 21, 1871.

LADIES AND GENTLEMEN: By request, I will ask leave to introduce the lecturer of the evening, Mr. Clemens, otherwise Mark Twain—a gentleman whose great learning, whose historical accuracy, whose devotion to science, and whose veneration for the truth, are only equaled by his high moral character and his majestic presence. I refer in these vague and general terms to myself. I am a little opposed to the custom of ceremoniously introducing a lecturer to an audience, partly because it seems to me that it is not entirely necessary, I would much rather make it myself. Then I can get in all the facts.

But it is not really the introduction that I care for—I don't care about that—that don't discommode me—but it's the compliments that sometimes go with it. That's what *hurts.* It would hurt anybody. The idea of a young lady being introduced into society as the sweetest singer or the finest conversationalist! You might as well knock her in the head at once. I never had but one public introduction that seemed to me just exactly the thing—an introduction brimful of grace. Why, it was a sort of inspiration. And yet the man who made it wasn't acquainted with me; but he was sensible to the backbone, and he said to me: "Now you don't want any compliments?" Of course I did not want any compliments at all. He said: Ladies and gentlemen—I shan't fool away any unnecessary time in this introduction. I don't know anything about this man; at least I only know two things: One is, that he has never been in the penitentiary; and the other is, I don't know why." Such an introduction as that puts a man at his ease right off.

I must not forget to make the announcement of the next lecture, the second of course, to be delivered by President Angell of the State University on Tuesday evening, the 26th of December. I don't know what his subject is going to be, but it will be good and well handled no doubt. In fact I forgot to ask what the subject is going to be.

Now when I first started out on this missionary expedition, I had a lecture which I liked very well, but by-and-by I got tired of telling that same old stuff over and over again, and then I got up another lec-ture, and after that another one, and I am tired of that: so I just thought tonight I would try something fresh, if you are willing. I don't suppose you care what a lecturer talks about if he only tells the truth—at intervals. Now I have got a book in press (it will be out pretty soon), over 600 octavo pages, and illus-trated after the fashion of the *Innocents Abroad*. Terms—however I am not around canvassing for the work. I should like to talk a little of that book to you tonight. It is very fresh in my mind, as it is not more than three months since I wrote it. Say 30 or 40 pages—or if you prefer it the whole 600.

Ten or twelve years ago, I crossed the continent from Missouri to California, in the old overland stage-coach, a good while before the Pacific Railway was built. Over 1,900 miles. It was a long ride, day and night, through sagebrush, over sand and alkali plains, wolves and Indians, starvation and smallpox—every-thing to make the journey interesting. Had a splen-did time, a most enjoyable pleasure trip, in that old stagecoach. We were bound for Nevada, which was then a bran' new Territory nearly or about as large as the state of Ohio. It was a desolate, barren, sterile, mountainous, unpeopled country, sagebrush and des-erts of alkali. You could scarcely cast your eye in any direction but your gaze would be met by one signifi-cant object, and that was the projecting horns of a dried, shrunken carcass of an ox, preaching eloquent sermons of the hardships suffered by those emigrants, where a soil refused to clothe its nakedness, except now and then a little rill (or, as you might call it, a river) goes winding through the plain. Such is the Carson River, which clothes the valley with refresh-ing and fragrant hayfields. However, hay is a scant crop, and with all the importations from California the price of that article has never come under $300 per ton. In the winter the price reaches $800, and once went up to $1,200 per ton, and then the cattle were turned out to die, and it is hardly putting the figure too strong to say that the valleys were paved with the remains of these cattle.

It is a land where the winters are long and rigorous, where the summers are hot and scorching, and where not a single drop of rain ever falls during eleven tedious months; where it never thunders, and never lightens; where no river finds its way to the sea or empties its waters into the great lakes that have no perceptible outlet, and whose surplus waters are spirited away through mysterious channels down into the ground. A territory broad and ample, but which has not yet had a population numbering 30,000, yet a country that produced $20,000,000 of silver bullion in the year 1863, and produces $12,000,000 to $16,-000,000 every year, yet the population has fallen away until now it does not number more than 15,000 or 18,000. Yet that little handful of people vote just as strongly as they do anywhere, are just as well represented in the Senate of the United States as Michigan, or the great state of New York with her 3,000,000 or 4,000,000 of people. That is equality in representation.

I spoke of the sagebrush. That is a particular feature of the country out there. It's an interesting sort of shrub. You see no other sort of vegetable, and clear from Pike's Peak to California's edge the sage-bushes stand from three to six feet apart, one vast greenish-gray sea of sage brush. It was the emigrant's fast friend, his only resource for fuel. In its appearance it resembles a venerable live oak with its rough bark and knotty trunk, everything twisted and dwarfed, covered with its thick foliage. I think the sagebrush are [sic] beautiful—one at a time is, anyway. Of course, when you see them as far as the eye can reach, seven days and a half in the week, it is different. I am not trying to get up an excitement over sagebrush, but there are many reasons why it should have some mention from an appreciative friend. I grant you that as a vegetable for table use sagebrush is a failure. Its leaves taste like our ordinary sage; you can make sage tea of it; but anybody in this audience who has ever been a boy or a girl, or both, in a country where doctors were scarce and measles and grandmothers plenty, don't hanker after sage tea. And yet after all there was a manifest providence in the creation of the sagebrush, for it is food for the mules and donkeys, and therefore many emigrant trains are enabled to pull through with their loads where ox teams would lie down and die of starvation. That a mule will eat sagebrush don't prove much, because I know a mule will eat anything. He don't give the toss up of a copper between oysters, lead pipe, brick dust, or even patent office reports. He takes whatever he can get most of.

In our journey we kept climbing and climbing for I don't know how many days and nights. At last we reached the highest eminence—the extreme summit of the great range of the Rocky Mountains, and entered the celebrated South Pass. Now the South Pass is more suggestive of a straight road than a suspension bridge hung in the clouds though in one place it suggests the latter. One could look below him on the diminishing crags and canyons lying down, down, down, away to the vague plain below, with a crooked thread in it which was the road, and tufts of feathers in it which were trees—the whole country spread out like a picture, sleeping in the sunlight, and darkness stealing over it, blotting out feature after feature under the frown of a gathering storm—not a film or shadow to mar the spectator's gaze. I could watch that storm break forth down there; could see the lightnings flash, the sheeted rain drifting along the canyon's side, and hear the thunder crash upon crash reverberating among a thousand rocky cliffs. This is a familiar experience to traveling people. It was a miracle of sublimity to a boy like me, who could hardly say that he had ever been away from home a single day in his life before.

We visited Salt Lake City in our journey. Carson City, the capital of Nevada, had a wild harem-scarem population of editors, thieves, lawyers, in fact all kinds of blacklegs. Its desperadoes, gamblers, and silver miners went armed to the teeth, every one of them dressed in the roughest kind of costumes, which looked strange and romantic to me and I was fascinated.

Now, instead of making a tedious description, I will say that they had a curious and peculiar breed of horses out there. I will give you the main points in regard to a little personal adventure which I had with one of these horses, leaving your imaginations to do the rest. Everybody rode horseback there. They were most magnificent riders. I thought so at least. I soon learned to tell a horse from a cow, and I was just burning with impatience to learn more. I was determined to have a horse to ride, and just as the thought was rankling in my mind an auctioneer came along on a beast crying him for sale, going at 22, 22, horse, saddle, and bridle. I could hardly resist. There was a man standing there. I was not acquainted with him (he turned out to be the auctioneer's brother). He observed to me, "That is a remarkable horse to be going at that price." I said I had half a notion to buy it. He said: "I know that horse—know him perfectly well. You are a stranger, and you may think that he is an American horse. He's nothing of the kind; he's a genuine Mexican plug; that's what he is." Well, I didn't know what a "genuine Mexican plug" was, but there was something about that man's way of saying it that I made up my mind to have that horse if it took every cent I had, and I said: "Has he any other advantages?" Well, he just hooked his forefinger into the breast pocket of my army shirt, led me off one side, and said in a low tone that no one else could hear, said: "He can outbuck any horse in this part of the country. Yes," he repeated, "he can outbuck any horse in America." The auctioneer was crying him at

24, 24, going at 24. I said, 27—"and sold." I took the
"genuine Mexican plug," paid for him, put him in
the livery stable, had him fed, then I let him rest
until after dinner, when I brought him out into the
plaza, where some of the citizens held him by the
head while others held him down by the tail, and I
got on him. As soon as they had let go, he put all his
feet together in a bunch. He let his back sag down
and then he arched it suddenly and shot me 180
yards into the air. I wasn't used to such things, and
I came down and lit in the saddle, then he sent me up
again and this time I came down astride his neck, but
I managed to slide backward until I got into the saddle
again. He then raised himself almost straight up on
his hind legs and walked around awhile, like a member of Congress, then he came down and went up the
other way, and just walked about on his hands as a
schoolboy would, and all the time kept kicking at the
sky. While he was in this position I heard a man say
to another, "But don't he buck!" So that was "bucking." I was very glad to know it. Not that I was particularly enjoying it, but I was somewhat interested in
it and naturally wanted to know what the name of it
was. While this performance was going on, a sympa-
thizing crowd had gathered around, and one of them
remarked to me: "Stranger, you have been taken in.
That's a genuine Mexican plug," and another one
says: "Think of it! You might have bought an American horse, used to all kinds of work, for a very little
more money." Well I didn't want to talk. I didn't
have anything to say. I sat down. I was so jolted up,
so internally, externally, and eternally mixed up, gone
all to pieces. I put one hand on my forehead, the
other on my stomach; and if I had been the owner of
16 hands I could have found a place for every one of
them. If there is a Californian in this audience he
knows what a Mexican plug is, and he knows that I
have hardly exaggerated that exasperating creature.

Now if you would see the noblest, loveliest inland
lake in the world, you should go to Lake Tahoe. It is
just on the boundary line between California and

'Nevada. I have seen some of the world's celebrated lakes and they bear no comparison with Tahoe. There it is, a sheet of perfectly pure, limpid water, lifted up 6,300 feet above the sea—a vast oval mirror framed in a wall of snowclad mountain peaks above the common world. Solitude is king, and in that realm calm silence is brooding always. It is the home of rest and tranquility and gives emancipation and relief from the griefs and plodding cares of life. Could you but see the morning breaking there, gilding those snowy summits and then creeping gradually along the slopes until it sets, the lake and woodlands, free from mist, all agleam, you would see old Nature, the master artist, painting these dissolving views on the still water and finally grouping all these features into a complete picture. Every little dell, the mountains with their dome-turned pinnacles, the cataracts and drifting clouds, are all exquisitely photographed on the burnished surface of the lake, suffused with the softest and richest color. This lake is ten miles from Carson City, and in company with a friend we used to foot it out there, taking along provisions and blankets—camp out on the lake shore two or three weeks at a time; not another human being within miles of us. We used to loaf about in the boat, smoke and read, sometimes play seven-up to strengthen the mind. It's a sinful game, but it's mighty nice. We'd just let the boat drift and drift wherever it wanted to. I can stand a deal of such hardship and suffering when I'm healthy. And the water was so wonderfully clear. Where it was 80 feet deep the pebbles on the bottom were just as distinct as if you held them in your hand; and in that clear white atmosphere it seemed as if the boat was drifting through the air. Out in the middle it was a deep dark indigo blue, and the official measurement made by the State Geologist of California shows it to be 1,525 feet deep in the center. You can imagine that it would take a great many churches and steeples piled one upon another before they would be perceptible above its surface. You might use up a great deal of ecclesiastical architecture in that way. Now, notwithstanding that lake is lifted so high up among the clouds, surrounded by the everlasting snowcapped mountain-peaks, with its surface higher than Mt. Washington in the East, and notwithstanding the water is pretty shallow around the edges, yet the coldest winter day in the recollection of humanity was never known to form ice upon its surface. It has no feeders but the little mountain rills, yet it never rises nor falls. Donar [sic] Lake, close by, freezes hard every winter. Why Lake Tahoe does not is a question which no scientist has ever been able to explain.

If there are any consumptives here I urge them to go out there, renew their age, make their bodies hale and hearty, in the pure, magnificent air of Lake Tahoe. If it don't cure you I'll bury you at my own expense. It *will* cure you. I met a man there—he had been a man once, but now he was only a shadow, and a very poor sort of shadow at that. That man took the thing very deliberately. He had fixed up things comfortable while he did stay, but he was in dead earnest. Thought he was going to die sure, but he made a sickly failure of it. He had brought along a plan of his private graveyard, some drawings of different kinds of coffins, and he never did anything but sit around all day and cipher over these plans, to get things to suit him, and try to find out which coffin would be the most becoming. Well, I met that man three months afterward. He was chasing mountain sheep over mountains seven miles high with a Sharp's rifle. He didn't get them, but he was chasing them just the same. He had used up his graveyard plans for wadding and had sent home for some more. Such a cure as that was! Why, when I first saw that man his clothes fitted him about as a circus tent fits the tentpole; now they were snug to him; they stuck to him like postage stamps, and he weighed a ton. Yes, he weighed more than a ton, but I will throw in the odd ounces, I'm not particular about that, eleven I think it was. I know what I am talking about, for I took him to the hay scales and weighed him myself. A lot of us stood on there with him. But I hope you won't mind my nonsense about it. It was really a wonderful cure, and if I can persuade any consumptive to go out there I shall feel at any rate that I have done one thing worth having lived to accomplish. And if there is a consumptive in this house I want to say to him. Shoulder your gun, go out there and hunt. It's the noblest hunting ground on earth. You can hunt there a year and never find anything—except mountain sheep; but you can't get near enough to them to shoot one. You can see plenty of them with a spyglass. Of course you can't shoot mountain sheep with a spyglass. It is our American Shamwah (I believe that is the way that word is pronounced—I don't know), with enormous horns, inhabiting the roughest mountain fastnesses, so exceedingly wild that it is impossible to get within rifleshot of it. There was no other game in that country when I was there—except seven-up; though one can see a California quail now and then— a proud, stately, beautiful bird, with a curved and graceful plume on top of its head. But you can't shoot one. You might as well try to kill a cast-iron dog. They don't mind a mortal wound any more than a man would mind a scratch.

I had supposed in my innocence that silver mining was nice, easy business, and that of course all you had to do was to pick it up, and that you could tell it from any other substance on account of its brightness and its white metallic look. Then came my disenchantment; for I found that silver was merely scattered through quartz rock. Gold is found in cement veins, in quartz veins, loosely mingled with the earth, in the sand in beds of rivers, but I never heard of any other house or home for silver to live in than quartz rock. This rock is of a dull whitish color faintly marbled with blue veins. A fine powder of silver ore makes these blue veins and this yields $30 in bullion. A little dab of silver that I could crowd in my mouth came out of this 2,000 pounds of solid rock. I found afterward that $30 rock was mighty profitable. Then they showed me some more rock which was a little more clouded, that was worth $50 a ton. The bluer and darker the rock the richer it was. Sometimes you could find it worth $400, $500, and $600 a ton. At rare intervals rock can be found that is worth $1,500 and $2,000 per ton, and at rarer intervals you would see a piece of quartz that had a mass of pure silver in its grip, large as a child's head—more than pure, because it always had a good deal of gold mixed up in its composition. The wire silver is Nature's aristocratic jewelry. The quartz crystallizes and becomes perfectly clear, just as clear and faultless as the diamond, and almost as radiant in beauty. Nature, down there in the depths of the earth, takes one of these quartz rocks, shapes a cavity, and right in its heart imprisons a delicate little coil of serpentine, pure white, aristocratic silver.

It was uphill work, this silver mining. There were plenty of mines but it required a fortune to work one; for tons of worthless rock must be ground to powder to get at the silver. I was the owner of a hundred silver mines, yet I realized that I was the poorest man on earth. Couldn't sell to anybody; couldn't pay my board; so I had to go to work in a quartz mill at ten dollars per week. I was glad to get that berth, but I couldn't keep it. I don't know why; I was the most careful workman they ever had. They said so. I took more pains with my work than anybody else. I was shoveling sand—tailings as they call it. It is silver-bearing rock that has been ground up and worked over once. It is then saved and worked over again. I was so particular about it that I have sat still for one hour and a half and studied about the best way to shovel that sand; and if I couldn't cipher it out in my mind I wouldn't go shoveling around recklessly—I would leave it alone until the next day. Many a time when I have been carrying sand from one pile to another 30 or 40 feet apart I would get started with a pailful when a splendid idea would strike me and I would carry that sand right back and sit down and think about it. Like as not I would get so absorbed in it as to go to sleep. I most always go to sleep when I am excited.

I knew there was a tiptop splendid way to move that sand from one pile to another and I told the boss so. "Well," he replied, "I am all-fired glad to hear it," and you never saw a man so kind of uplifted as he was. He seemed as if a load had been lifted from his breast—a load of sand.

I said to him: "What you want now is to get a cast-iron pipe about 14 feet in diameter—boiler iron will do—and about 42 feet long. Have one end raised up 35 or 40 feet, and then you want to have a revolving belt. Work it with the waste steam from the engine. Have a chair fastened to that belt and let me sit in that chair. Have a Chinaman to load up that big box, pass it to me as I come around, and I will up it into that pipe." You never saw a man so overcome with admiration. He discharged me on the spot. He said I had too much talent to be fooling away my time in a quartz mill.

If you will permit me, I would like to illustrate the ups and downs of fortune in the mining country with just a little personal experience of my own. I had a cabinmate by the name of Higby—a splendid good fellow. One morning the camp was thrown into a fearful state of excitement, for the "Wide West" had struck a lead black with native silver and yellow with gold. The butcher had been dunning us a week or two. Higby went up and brought a handful away and he sat studying and examining it, now and then soliloquizing in this manner: "That stuff never came out of the Wide West in the world." I told him it did, because I saw them hoist it out of the shaft. Higby went away by himself, and came back in a couple of hours perfectly overcome with excitement. He came in, closed the door, went and looked out of the window to make sure there was nobody in the neighborhood, and said to me, "We are worth a million of dollars. The Wide West be hanged—that's a blind lead." Said I: "Higby, are you *really* in earnest? Say it again: say it strong, Higby." He replied: "Just as sure as I am standing here, it's a blind lead. We're rich." Poverty had vanished and we could buy that town and pay for it, and six more just like it. A blind lead is one that doesn't crop out above the ground like an ordinary quartz lead. The Wide West had simply tapped it in their shaft and we had discovered it. It belonged to us. It was our property and there wouldn't anybody in the camp dispute that fact. We took into partnership the foreman of the Wide West, and the Wide West had to stop digging. We were the lions of Esmeralda. People wanted to lend us money; other people wanted to sell us village lots on time; and the butcher brought us meat enough for a barbecue and went away without his pay.

Now there is a rule that a certain amount of work must be done on a new claim within the first ten days, or the claim is forfeited to any one who may first take it up. Now I was called away to nurse an old friend who was dangerously ill up at the Nine-Mile Ranch, and I just wrote a note and threw it into the window telling Higby where I was gone. The fellow I went to nurse was an irascible sort of fellow. and while carrying him from the vapor bath because I let my end of him fall we had a quarrel and I started for home. When I reached there, I saw a vast concourse of people over at the claim and the thought struck me that we were richer than ever, probably worth two million certain. Presently I met Higby looking like a ghost, and says I: "What on earth is the matter." "Well," he says, "you didn't do the work on the mine. I depended on you. The foreman's mother dying in California, he didn't do the work, our claim is forfeited and we are ruined. We haven't a cent." We went home to the cabin. I looked down at the floor. There was my note, and beside it was a note from Higby, telling me that he was going away to look for another mine which wouldn't have amounted to anything even if he had found it, in comparison with our claim.

It don't seem possible that there could be three as big fools in one small town, but we were there, and I was one of them. For once in my life I was absolutely a millionaire for just ten days by the watch. I was just ready to go into all kinds of dissipation and I am really thankful that this was a chapter in the history of my life, although at the time of course I did a great deal of weeping and gnashing my teeth. When I lost that million my heart was broken and I wanted to pine away and die, but I couldn't borrow money enough to live on while I did so, and I had to give that up. Everything appeared to go against me. Of course, I might have suicided, but that was kind of disagreeable.

I had written a few letters for the press, and just in the nick of time I received a letter from the Virginia City *Daily Enterprise* offering me $25 a week to go and be a reporter on that paper. I could hardly believe it, but this was no time for foolishness and I was in for anything. I never had edited anything, but if I had been offered the job of translating Josephus from the original Hebrew I should have taken it. If I had translated Josephus I would have thrown in as many jokes as I could for the money and made him readable. I would have had a variety, if I had to write him all up new.

Well, I walked that 130 miles in pretty quick time and took the berth. Have you ever considered what straits reporters are sometimes pushed to in furnishing the public with news? Why, the first day items were so scarce, I couldn't find an item anywhere and just as I was on the verge of despair, as luck would have it, there came in a lot of emigrants with their wagon trains. They had been fighting with the Indians and got the worst of it. I got the names of their killed and wounded, and then by-and-by there was another train came in. They hadn't had any trouble and of course I was disappointed, but I did the best I could under the circumstances. I cross-questioned that boss emigrant and found that they were going right on through and wouldn't come back to make trouble, so I got his list of names and added to my killed and wounded, and I got ahead of all the other papers. I put that wagon train through the bloodiest Indian fight ever seen on the plains. They came out of the conflict covered with glory. The chief editor said he didn't want any better reporter than I was. I said: "You just bring on your Indians and fetch out your emigrants, leave me alone, and I will make the fur fly. I will hang a scalp on every sage-bush between here and the Missouri border." That was all first rate, but by-and-by items got low again and I was downhearted. I was miserable, because I couldn't strike an item. At last fortune favored me again. A couple of dear delightful desperadoes got into a row right before me and one of them shot the other. I stepped right up there and got the victim to give me his last words exclusively for the *Enterprise,* and I added some more to them so as to be sure and get ahead of the other papers, and then I turned to the desperado. Said I, "You are a stranger to me, sir, but you have done me a favor which I can never sufficiently thank you for. I shall ever regard you as a benefactor." And I asked him if he could lend me half a dollar. We always borrowed a piece whenever we could—it was a public custom. The thought then struck me that I could raise a mob and hang the other desperado, but the officers got ahead of me and took him into custody. They were down on us and would always do any little mean thing like that, to spite us. And so I was fairly launched in literature, in the business of doing good. I love to do good. It is our duty. I think when a man does good all the time his conscience is so clear. I like to do right and be good, though there is a deal more fun in the other thing.

Now you see by my sort of experience a man may go to bed at night not worth a cent and wake up in the morning to find himself immensely wealthy, and very often he is a man who has a vast cargo of ignorance. To illustrate my point I will give you a story about a couple of these fresh nabobs whose names were colonels Jim and Jack. Colonel Jim had seen considerable of the world, but Colonel Jack was raised down in the backwoods of Arkansas. These gentlemen after their good luck suddenly determined on a pleasure trip to New York; so they went to San Francisco, took a steamer, and in due time arrived in the great metropolis. While passing along the street, Colonel Jack's attention was attracted by the hacks and splendid equipages he saw, and he says: "Well I've heard about these carriages all my life and I mean to have a ride in one. I don't care what it costs." So Colonel Jim stepped to the edge of the sidewalk and ordered a handsome carriage. Colonel Jack says: "No, you don't. None of your cheap turnouts for me. I'm here to have a good time, and money's no object. I'm going to have the best rig this country affords. You stop that yellow one there with the pictures on it." So they got into the empty omnibus and sat down. Colonel Jack says: "Well! ain't it gay? Ain't it nice? Windows and pictures and cushions, till you can't rest. What would the boys think of this if they could see us cut such a swell in New York? I wish they could see us. What is the name of this." Colonel Jim told him it was a barouche. After a while he poked his head out in front and said to the driver, "I say, Johnny, this suits *me*. We want this shebang all day. Let the horses go." The driver loosened the strap and passed his hand in for the fare. Colonel Jack, thinking that he wanted to shake hands, shook him heartily and said: "You understand me. You take care of me and I'll take care of you." He put a $20 gold piece into the driver's hand. The driver says: "I can't change that." Colonel Jack replied: "Put it into your pocket, I don't want any change. We're going to ride it out." In a few minutes the bus stopped and a young lady got in. Colonel Jack stared at her. Pretty soon she got out her money to pay the driver. Colonel Jack says: "Put up your money, Miss; you are perfectly welcome to ride here just as long as you want to, but this barouche is chartered and we can't let you pay." Soon an old lady got in. Colonel Jack told her to "sit down. Don't be at all uneasy, everything is paid for and as free as if you were in your own turnout, but you can't pay a cent." Pretty soon two or three gentlemen got in, and ladies with children.

Colonel Jack says, "Come right along. Don't mind us. Free blowout." By and by the crowd filled all the seats and were standing up, while others climbed up on top. He nudged Colonel Jim and says: "Colonel, what kind of cattle do they have here? If this don't bang anything I ever saw. Ain't they friendly, and so awful cool about it, but they ain't sociable." But I have related enough of that circumstance to illustrate the enormous simplicity of these unfledged biddies of fortune.

When I told the chairman of the society this evening that I wanted to change my subject he said it was a little risky; he didn't know about it, but I pleaded so hard and said the only reason was I didn't want to talk that Artemus Ward lecture because it had been printed in the papers. I told him that I would put in a little scrap from that Artemus Ward lecture, just enough to cover the advertisement, and then I wouldn't be telling any lies. Besides this anecdote had a moral to it. Well, the moral got him.

As nearly as I can cipher it out, the newspaper reporter has got us lecturers at a disadvantage. He can either make a synopsis or do most anything he wants to. He ought to be generous, and praise us or abuse us, but not print our speeches. Artemus Ward was bothered by a shorthand reporter and he begged him not to do him the injustice to garble his speech. He says, "You can't take it all down as I utter it." The reporter said, "If you utter anything I can't take down I will agree not to print the speech." Along in the lecture he tipped the reporter the wink and then he told the following anecdote:

(Whistle wherever the stars occur. If you can't, get somebody that can.)

He said that several gentlemen were conversing in a hotel parlor and one man sat there who didn't have anything to say. By and by, the gentlemen all went out except one of the number and the silent man. Presently the silent man reached out and touched the gentleman and says: "** I think, sir, I have seen you somewhere before. I am not ** sure

where it was or ** when it was ** but I know I have
** seen you." The gentleman says: "Very likely: but
what do you whistle for?" "** I'll tell you all about
it ** I used to stammer ** fearfully and I courted a
** girl ** and she wouldn't ** have me because I
was afflicted with such an **infirmity. I went to a
doctor and ** he ** told me that every time I ** went
to stammer ** that I must whistle, which I ** did,
and it completely cured me. But don't you know that
** girl ** wouldn't have me at last, for she ** said
that **she wouldn't talk to a man that whistled as I
did. ** She'd as soon hold a conversation with a
wheelbarrow that wanted ** greasing."

Ladies and gentlemen, For three or four days I
have had it in my mind to throw away that other
lecture, but I never had the pluck to do it until tonight. The audience seemed to look friendly, and as
I had been here before I felt a little acquainted. I
thought I would make the venture. I sincerely thank
you for the help you have given me, and I bid you
goodnight.

THE MORALS LECTURE

NO MANUSCRIPT TEXT of this lecture, or "talk," as J. B.
Pond called it, has been discovered, if, indeed, there
ever was one. The text which follows is almost entirely
that of the opening performance at Cleveland, July 15, 1895, as
reported in the *Plain Dealer*, July 19. Two passages from other
reports have been added, partly for their interest, and partly
to show how the lecture grew in repetition. These passages appear in brackets. The first, which develops the idea of moral
vaccination, was reported in the Johannesburg, South Africa,
Standard and Diggers News, May 29, 1896; the second, on the
subject of forbidden fruit, appeared in the Calcutta, India, *Englishman*, February 11, 1896. Part of the second passage is also
to be found in Mark Twain's *Notebook*, p. 275. The text in the
Plain Dealer is by far the most extensive one found in any newspaper in America or abroad.

THE MORALS LECTURE

I WAS SOLICITED to go round the world on a lecture tour by a man in Australia. I asked him what they wanted to be lectured on. He wrote back that those people were very coarse and serious and that they would like something solid, something in the way of education, something gigantic, and he proposed that I prepare about three or four lectures at any rate on just morals, any kind of morals, but just morals, and I like that idea. I liked it very much and was perfectly willing to engage in that kind of work, and I should like to teach morals. I have a great enthusiasm in doing that and I shall like to teach morals to those people. I do not like to have them taught to me and I do not know any duller entertainment than that, but I know I can produce a quality of goods that will satisfy those people.

If you teach principles, why, you had better let your illustrations come first, illustrations which shall carry home to every person. I planned my first lecture on morals. I must not stand here and talk all night; get out a watch. I am talking the first time now and I do not know anything about the length of it.

I would start with two or three rules of moral principles which I want to impress upon those people. I will just make the lecture gradual, by and by. The illustrations are the most important so that when that lecture is by and by written and completed it will just be a waveless ocean with this archipelago of smiling green islands of illustrations in the midst of it.

I thought I would state a principle which I was going to teach. I have this theory for doing a great deal of good out there, everywhere in fact, that you should prize as a priceless thing every transgression, every crime that you commit—the lesson of it, I mean.

Make it permanent; impress it so that you may never commit that same crime again as long as you live, then you will see yourself what the logical result of that will be—that you get interested in committing crimes. You will lay up in that way, course by course, the edifice of a personally perfect moral character. You cannot afford to waste any crime, they are not given to you to be thrown away, but for a great purpose. There are 462 crimes possible and you cannot add anything to this, you cannot originate anything. These have been all thought out, all experimented on and have been thought out by the most capable men in the penitentiary.

[Mark Twain then declared that he planned to carry out his scheme of moral regeneration along purely scientific lines, amounting to nothing less than moral vaccination. Medical men vaccinated against physical disease. Sin was a moral disease, and he proposed to vaccinate against it as such. (Here Mark Twain described briefly the vast importance of the healing art and its wonderful future prospects. Then came the anticlimax.) Why it was quite possible in another fifty years that medical men would have succeeded in driving away all deadly disease entirely. He was ruining his own trade, true, but that was his business, not ours. In the future the medical man would not wait for his patient to grow up and contract diseases—no, he would vaccinate him in his cradle against all the diseases there were—vaccinate him all over. It would make him a spectacle to look at; but that child would come to stay—to live for ever. He could not be got rid of by any of the ordinary methods—it would be necessary to get him struck by lightning if he was to be removed.]

Now, when you commit a transgression, lay it up in your memory, and without stopping, it will all lead toward moral perfection. When you have committed your 462 you are released of every possibility and have ascended the staircase of faultless creation and you finally stand with your 462 complete with absolute moral perfection, and I am more than two-thirds up there. It is immense inspiration to find yourself climbing that way and have not much further to go. I shall have then that moral perfection and shall then see my edifice of moral character standing far before the world all complete. I know that this should pro-

duce it. Why, the first time that I ever stole a watermelon—I think it was the first time, but this is no matter, it was right along there somewhere—I carried that
watermelon to a secluded bower. You may call it a
bower and I suppose you may not. I carried that
watermelon to a secluded bower in the lumberyard,
and broke it open, and it was green.

Now, then, I began to reflect; there is the vir-
tual—that is the beginning—of reformation when you
reflect. When you do not reflect that transgression is
wasted on you. I began to reflect and I said to myself,
I have done wrong; it was wrong in me to steal that
watermelon—that kind of a watermelon. And I said
to myself: now what would a right-minded and right-
intentioned boy do, who found that he had done
wrong—stolen a watermelon like this. What would he
do, what must he do; do right; restitution; make restitution. He must restore that property to its owner,
and I resolved to do that and the moment I made that
good resolution I felt that electrical moral uplift
which becomes a victory over wrong doing. I was
spiritually strengthened and refreshed and carried
that watermelon back to that wagon and gave it to
that farmer—restored it to him, and I told him he
ought to be ashamed of himself going around working
off green watermelons that way on people who had
confidence in him; and I told him in my perfectly
frank manner it was wrong. I said that if he did not
stop he could not have my custom, and he was
ashamed. He was ashamed; he said he would never
do it again and I believe that I did that man a good
thing, as well as one for myself. He did reform; I was
severe with him a little, but that was all. I restored
the watermelon and made him give me a ripe one. I
morally helped him, and I have no doubt that I
helped myself the same time, for that was a lesson
which remained with me for my perfection. Ever
since that day to this I never stole another one—like
that.

Then I have another theory, and that is to teach
that when you do a thing do it with all your might;

do it with all your heart. I remember a man in California Jim What-is-his-name, Baker. He was a hearty man of most gentlemanly spirit and had many fine qualities. He lived a good many years in California among the woods and mountains; he had no companionship but that of the wild creatures of the forest. To me he was an observant man. He watched the ways of the different creatures so that he got so that he could understand what the creatures said to each other and translate it accurately. He was the only man I ever knew who could do this. I know he could, because he told me so himself, and he says that some of the animals have very slight education and small vocabulary and that they are not capable of using figures and allegory, but there are other animals that have a large vocabulary. These creatures are very fond of talking. They like to show off, and he placed the bluejay at the head of that list. He said: "Now there is more to the bluejay than any other animal. He has got more different kinds of feeling. Whatever a bluejay feels he can put into language, and not mere commonplace language, but straight out and out book talk, and there is such a command of language. You never saw a bluejay get stuck for a word. He is a vocabularized geyser. Now, you must call a jay a bird, and so he is in a measure, because he wears feathers and don't belong to any church, but otherwise he is just as human nature made him. A bluejay hasn't any more principle than an ex-congressman, and he will steal, deceive and betray four times out of five; and as for the sacredness of an obligation, you cannot scare him in the detail of principle. He talks the best grammar of all the animals. You may say a cat talks good grammar. Well, a cat does; but you let a cat get excited, you let a cat get at pulling fur with another cat on a shed nights and you will hear grammar. A bluejay is human; he has got all a man's faculties and a man's weakness. He likes especially scandal; he knows when he is an ass as well as you do."

[At this point Mark Twain went on to tell that

story about the bluejay that bit off more than he could chew.]

Now that brings me by a natural and easy transition to Simon Wheeler of California; a pioneer he was, and in a small way a philosopher. Simon Wheeler's creed was that pretty nearly everything that happens to a man can be turned to moral account; every incident in his life, almost, can be made to assist him, to project him forward morally, if he knows how to make use of the lesson which that episode teaches, and he used—well, he was a good deal of a talker. He was an inordinate talker; in fact, he wore out three sets of false teeth, and I told about a friend of his one day—a man that he had known there formerly, and who he had a great admiration for, of one Jim Smiley, and he said it was worth a man's while to know Jim Smiley. Jim Smiley was a man of gift; he was a man of parts; he was a man of learning; he was—well, he was the curiousest man about always betting on anything that turned up that you ever see, if he could get anybody to bet on the other side, and if he couldn't he would change sides. As soon as he got a bet he was satisfied. He prepared himself with all sorts of things—tomcats, rat terriers and all such things, and one day he ketched a frog; said he calculated to educate him. And he took him home and never done nothing but set in his back yard and learn that frog how to jump. Yes, sir, and he did learn him to—he did learn him to. When it came to jumping on a dead level there wasn't no frog that could touch him at all. Come to jump on the dead level, why, he could lay over any frog in the profession, and Smiley broke all the camps around there betting on that frog. Bye and bye he got a misfortune. He used to keep his frog in a little lattice box. The frog's name was Daniel Webster, and he would bring that box down town and lay for a bet. And one day a fellow came along, a stranger in the camp he was, he says, "What might it be that you have got in the box?" "Well," Smiley says, "It ain't anything particular, it's only just a frog," "Well," he says, "What is he good for?" "Well,"

Smiley says, "I don't know, but I think he is good enough for one thing; he can outjump any frog in Calaveras County." The stranger took that box, turned it around this way and that way, and he examined Daniel Webster all over very critically, and handed it back, and he said, "I don't see any points about that frog that is any better than any other frog." "Oh," Smiley said, "It may be that you understand frogs and may be that you are only an amateur, so to speak; anyway I will risk $40 that he can outjump any frog in Calaveras County." Well, that stranger looked mighty sad, mighty sorrowful-grieved, and he said, "I am only a stranger in camp and I ain't got no frog, but if I had a frog I would bet you." Smiley says, "That's all right, just you hold my frog a minute; I will go and get you a frog." So Smiley lit out to the swamp and that stranger took that box and he stood there—well, he stood, and stood, and stood the longest time. At last he got Daniel Webster out of the box and pried his mouth open like that (indicating), took a teaspoonful and filled him full of quail shot, filled him full up to the chin and set him down on the floor. Daniel set there.

Smiley he flopped around in the swamp about half an hour. Finally he cotched a frog and fetched him to this fellow. They put up the money, and Smiley says: "Now, let the new frog down on the floor with his front paws just even with Daniel's, and I will give the word." He says, "One, two, three, scoot," and they touched up the frogs from behind to indicate that time was called, and that new frog, he rose like a rocket and came down kerchunk a yard and a half from where he started, a perfectly elegant jump for a nonprofessional that way. But Smiley's frog gave a heave or two with his shoulders—his ambition was up, but it was no use, he couldn't budge, he was anchored there as solid as an anvil. The fellow took the money, and finally, as he went over, he looked over his shoulder at Daniel, and he said: "Well, I don't see any points about that frog that is any better than any other frog." And Smiley looked down at Daniel Webster, I never see a man so puzzled. And he says: "I do wonder what that frog throwed off for? There must be something the matter with him, looks mighty baggy somehow." He hefted him, and says, "Blame my cats, if he don't weigh five pounds." Turned him upside down and showered out a hatfull of shot. And Simon Wheeler said, "That has been a lesson to me." And I say to you, let that be a lesson to you. Don't you put too much faith in the passing stranger. This life is full of uncertainties, and every episode in life, figuratively speaking, is just a frog. You want to watch every exigency as you would a frog, and don't you ever bet a cent on it until you know whether it is loaded or not.

[The transitional sentences which lead into the following story refer, apparently, to an unreported section of the lecture.]

Now you think from that man's language, which is not very refined, that he was the bravest man that ever was. That man was not afraid of anything. I never was afraid of anything. I have always had nerve, abundance of nerve. I never lost my nerve but once. Once I lost part of my nerve. I will not say all of it. That time it humiliated me so that I always remember it. [When a schoolboy it often fell to my lot to come across a rainy day—one of those days which schoolboys all the world over regard as too rainy to go to school, and just rainy enough to go fishing. Forbidden fruit had the same attraction for me as it had for Adam. Some unthinking people criticize Adam—find fault with him because he was weak, and yielded. Oh, that is not fair, that is not right. He hadn't any experience. We have had ages and ages of experience and tuition—we who criticize him and yet see what we are—just see what we are when there is any forbidden fruit around. I have been around a good deal, but I have never been in any place where that apple would have been safe—except Allahabad. Why, it is the *prohibition* that *makes* anything precious. There is a charm about the forbidden that makes it unspeakably desirable. It was not that Adam ate the apple for the apple's sake, but because it was forbidden. It would have been better for us—oh infinitely better for us—if the serpent had been forbidden.]

My father was a magistrate and being a magistrate he was also coroner, sheriff and lord mayor and he had a little bit of an office in what was the sole room in a small house that stood by itself. And that little office had a sofa in it and that used to come handy to me now and then, because often I noticed on my way to school that the weather was not suitable for school and I better go fishing, so I went. But when I came back, when I returned from those excursions, it was not prudent to go home. I always met so many companions and preferences that it was better for me to lodge in that little office, and once while I was off on one of those excursions there was a fight late in the afternoon in that little street and a man was killed and they carried him to that little office and straightened him out there on the floor on his back and got him ready for the inquest in the morning, went away and left him there. I arrived about midnight and I did not know about this circumstance and I slipped in the back way and groped my way through the dark to that sofa and lay there. But just as I was drowsing off to sleep it seemed to me that I could make out a dim outline of a large black mass of some kind stretched on the floor and it made me a little uncomfortable. My first thought was to go and feel of it, but I concluded I would not do that. I sat and watched that thing as it lay in parallelograms and squares of moonlight and I thought I would just wait till that moonlight crept to that thing. It was so slow, that waiting, that finally I got another idea and thought I would turn my face to the wall and I turned over and counted, and counted. I did not get as far as I intended, but at last I forced myself to count the full hundred and then I turned over and there was a man's hand lying in the square of that moonlight. Why, I never felt so embarrassed in my life. I could not take my eyes away from that object; I watched that moonlight line by line, first revealing an arm, then the white shoulder. By that time it seemed to me that I could stand it no longer; I must pull myself away and I did. Putting my hand on my heart and holding it there a moment, I took one glimpse, only the one glimpse, thank God, and there lay that white, white face, snow white face, and the glassy eyes. But something made me think what is the matter with me, as I sat there with my heart beating. I was not scared. I got just that one glimpse and then I went away from there. I did not go in what you might call a hurry, not a great hurry; I went out the window. I took the sash with me; I did not need the sash, but it was handier to take it than to leave it, so I took it.

I shan't have time; the time is too late altogether. I will have to skip that next and come to a matter which illustrates another moral point which I will tell you about presently and that is an episode in the lives of three persons who lived in Missouri a great many years ago. Two boys, Tom Sawyer and Huck Finn, and a very particular old friend of theirs, a middle-aged slave named Jim, and these three were generally disputing about some subject which was rather too large for them. I (Huck Finn) asked him (Tom Sawyer) what was the trouble and he said it was heartbreaking to see the days and the years slip away and him a getting older and older and no wars breaking out, no way for him to make a name for himself, and he started in to plan out some way to make him celebrated. Pretty soon he struck it and offered to take me and Jim in. We went up in the woods and he told me what, and he said it was a crusade. I asked him what a crusade is, and he said, "Is it possible you don't know what a crusade is?" I told him I didn't and what is more I didn't care. I have lived through to this time without it and I had my health and if you will tell me what it is all right. I'd as soon I didn't know, for I don't care for stacking my head full of information. What is a crusade? I can tell you. Is it a sort of patent right? No, a crusade is war; it is war to rescue the holy land from the heathen cannibals.

Which holy land is it? Why there is only one holy land. Do you think there is a million? Well, I said, Tom Sawyer, how did we come to let them get it? We did not come to let them get hold of it. They always had it. If they always had it, it belongs to them. "Why, certainly," he said. "I understand that now. It seems to me that if I had a farm and it was my farm and it belonged to me and another fellow wanted it, would it be right for him to take it? If they own anything at all there it is just the mere land: just the land and nothing else. As for the holiness they can take that if they want it." You don't understand it at all. You don't get the hang of it at all. It has nothing to do with farming. It is on a higher plane. It is religious. "What, religious to go and take the land from the people who own it?" Why, of course it is, it has always been considered so.

I shan't attempt to go on with the rest of that program, but I will just close with that which is at the bottom. I have been in bed stretched on my back forty-five days and I am only five days out of that bed and I am, perhaps, not strong enough to stand here and talk. I will just close. It is unbusinesslike to jump at conclusions on too slight evidence and I will close with the case of christening a baby in a Scotch-Irish family. A little clergyman came and when he found that there was a great host of people assembled there he would attempt to exploit his peculiar vanity. He could not resist that temptation. When he took the baby from the father's hands and hefted it, he said: "My friends, he is very little; very little; well, he is a very little fellow, but what of that? I see in your faces disparagement of him because he is little; disparagement for no cause but that he is little. You should reflect that it is from the little things that the great things spring. What is smaller than a grain of granite or sand, and yet it is from grains of granite and sand that this earth is formed. Very little is he. Take the little drop of water and out of little drops of water the great ocean is made. And very little is he and yet he may become like Napoleon, or like Caesar, or like both of them in one. He may conquer empires, he may turn all the world to looking at him. He may be like Hannibal, or like Alexander, or both in one, and become master of the universe. But what is his name? Mary Ann, is it?"

I thank you very cordially for the indulgence with which you have listened to my scheme for revolutionizing the morals of the globe as I go round and I wish to say that I hope to succeed in the work which I have undertaken.

NOTES

APPRENTICESHIP

1. Henry Nash Smith and William M. Gibson (eds.), *Mark Twain—Howells Letters*, I, 252–57.

2. Albert Bigelow Paine (ed.), *Mark Twain's Letters*, I, 322–24.

3. For Orion's brief entry in the field of lecturing, see Fred W. Lorch, "Orion Clemens," p. 379.

4. Henry Nash Smith and Frederick Anderson (eds.), *Mark Twain of the Enterprise*, p. 135.

5. Pages 204–5.

6. Bernard DeVoto (ed.), *Mark Twain in Eruption*, p. 115.

7. *Ibid.*, pp. 110–18. For Mark Twain's report of his participation in a mesmerizing performance in Hannibal in 1850, see *Ibid.*, pp. 118 ff.

8. Albert Bigelow Paine, *Mark Twain: A Biography*, I, 84. The autobiographical papers of Orion Clemens, from which Paine was able to extract much information about Mark Twain's early life, are no longer accessible. In a letter to me (April 24, 1927) Paine wrote: "There is no hope of your seeing those odds and ends of Orion's *Autobiography*. It was Mark Twain's wish that all should be destroyed, and most of them *were* burned. Some fragments may remain, but I am not sure. . . ." Up to the present time, however, no fragments have been discovered. The destruction of these papers constituted, it must be confessed, an unfortunate act of literary mayhem.

9. *Ibid.*

10. *The Twainian*, IV, No. 8 (May, 1945), 1.

11. Paine, *Biography*, I, 84.

12. Fred W. Lorch, "Mark Twain in Iowa," p. 421.

13. *Ibid.*, p. 420.

14. Paine, *Biography*, I, 107.

15. Paine, *Letters,* I, 49.
16. For information about Mrs. Holliday see Dixon Wecter, *Sam Clemens of Hannibal,* pp. 157–58.
17. Lorch, "Mark Twain in Iowa," p. 456.
18. Paine, *Biography,* I, 39.
19. Wecter, *Sam Clemens of Hannibal,* p. 127.
20. *Ibid.,* p. 46.
21. For a detailed discussion of the influence of the Florida, Missouri, experiences upon Mark Twain as a writer, see Harold Roberts, "Sam Clemens; Florida Days," pp. 4–7.
22. Paine, *Biography* I, 77; Albert Bigelow Paine (ed.), *Mark Twain's Speeches,* pp. 140–41.
23. Paine, *Biography* I, pp. 226–67.
24. *Ibid.,* p. 271.
25. William M. Clemens, *Mark Twain, The Story of His Life and Work,* pp. 54–55. San Francisco, 1892.
26. For a description of the "Third House" and its origin and purposes, see Richard C. Lillard, "Studies in Washoe Journalism and Humor."
27. Effie Mona Mack, *Mark Twain in Nevada,* pp. 273–74. Also see Smith and Anderson, *Mark Twain of the Enterprise,* p. 102.
28. Paine, *Letters,* I, 94.
29. "Doings in Nevada" appeared Feb. 7, 1864; "Those Blasted Children," Feb. 21, 1864.
30. Mark Twain, *How To Tell a Story,* p. 8.
31. See Chapter 20.
32. Mark Twain's early soubriquet, "Wild Humorist of the Pacific Slope," was probably suggested by a similar nickname applied to Artemus Ward ("Wild Humorist of the Sage Brush Hills") which he acquired during his lecture trip to the Far West. Charles Henry Webb, publisher of the Jumping Frog book, had known both Mark Twain and Artemus Ward in San Francisco and had obviously associated them in his mind as kindred humorists. His other soubriquet for Mark Twain in the advertisement of the Frog book, "Moralist of the Main," may also have been suggested by references to Artemus Ward in San Francisco advertising as a "moral lecturer." (See Franklin Walker, *San Francisco's Literary Frontier,* p. 159.)
33. January 29, 1864.
34. January 30, 1864. In the Nevada mining districts a "dusty" miner was one who possessed gold dust. The expression "dusty Christian" described a devout, practicing Christian.
35. Smith and Anderson, *Mark Twain of the Enterprise,* p. 145.
36. *Ibid.*
37. *Ibid.*
38. Years later, in a reply to a letter from a lady whose sister wished to go upon the lecture platform, Mark Twain wrote: "There is an unwritten law about human successes. . . . In brief this law is: 1. No occupation without an apprenticeship; 2. No pay to the apprentice." (See J. B. Pond, *Eccentricities of Genius,* p. 229.)

FIRST PUBLIC LECTURE

1. Years later, in "The Turning-Point of My Life," Mark Twain said of the Sandwich Islands assignment, "By and by, Circumstance and the Sacramento *Union* sent me to the Sandwich Islands for five or six months, to write up sugar. I did it; and threw in a good deal of extraneous matter. . . ." (*What is Man? And Other Essays*, p. 136.)

2. Albert Bigelow Paine (ed.), *Mark Twain's Notebook*, p. 29.

3. Albert Bigelow Paine, *Mark Twain: A Biography*, I, 291.

4. Albert Bigelow Paine (ed.), *Mark Twain's Letters*, I, 119. Years later Mark Twain reported that the proprietors of the *Union* were so enthusiastic about the Sandwich Islands letters that when he asked for an additional $300 for his full three-column story of the "Hornet" disaster, they cheerfully paid it. (See *The Man That Corrupted Hadleyburg* [New York: Harper and Brothers, 1898] p. 73.)

5. Paine, *Biography*, I, 291. Also see *Alta California*, Nov. 17, 1866. Mark Twain apparently worked seriously to make a book of his Sandwich Islands letters as he later succeeded in doing with his Holy Land letters. By the following June (1867) he appears to have had it nearly completed. On June 7 he wrote his family in St. Louis, "I have withdrawn the Sandwich Islands book—it would be useless to publish it in these dull publishing times" (Paine, *Letters*, I, 127). Of the precise nature of the book, nothing is known.

6. G. Ezra Dane (ed.), *Letters From the Sandwich Islands*, p. 216. See also *Alta California*, April 9 and July 7, 1867. Years later, in the winter and spring of 1883–84, Mark Twain again took up the project of writing a book on Hawaii, this time an historical narrative. This, too, he abandoned, in favor of *A Connecticut Yankee in King Arthur's Court*. (See Fred W. Lorch's "Hawaiian Feudalism and Mark Twain's *A Connecticut Yankee in King Arthur's Court*," *American Literature*, 30 [March, 1958], 50–66. Also A. Grove Day, *Mark Twain's Letters From Hawaii*, pp. xiv and xv.)

7. Paine, *Biography*, I, 287.

8. *Evening Bulletin*, Oct. 3, 1866.

9. *Mark Twain's Autobiography*, II, 351.

10. Mark Twain, *Roughing It*, II, 292. Also see G. E. B., "Mark Twain as He Was Known During His Stay on the Pacific Slope."

11. *Roughing It*, II, 292.

12. Sept. 29, 1866.

13. Oct. 2, 1866.

14. *Ibid.*

15. *Roughing It*, II, 293. About seven months after the first San Francisco lecture, Mark Twain was jailed in New York one night for interfering in a street brawl (though probably for drunkenness). The next morning, while idly examining the scribbling on the jail walls, he was startled to read, "The Trouble Will Begin at Eight O'Clock." He

well remembered inventing that sentence in the office of the *Morning Call* "when I was writing the advertisement for my first lecture in San Francisco. . . . I smiled at the conceit when I first wrote it, but when I thought how sad-hearted and full of dreams of a happier time the poor fellow might have been who scribbled it here, there was a touching pathos about it. . . ." (Franklin Walker and G. Ezra Dane (eds.), *Mark Twain's Travels With Mr. Brown,* pp. 187–90 and 292.

16. Melville D. Landon, *Kings of the Platform and Pulpit,* p. 74.

17. Paine, *Biography,* I, pp. 291–94; Ivan Benson, *Mark Twain's Western Years,* pp. 149–50; Walter Frear, *Mark Twain and Hawaii,* pp. 164–69; *Roughing It,* II, 292–96.

18. *Roughing It,* II, 293.

19. *Ibid.,* pp. 293–94.

20. *Ibid.,* pp. 294–95.

21. *Evening Bulletin,* Oct. 3, 1866.

22. *The Golden Era,* Oct. 7, 1866.

23. *News Letter,* Oct. 6, 1866.

24. *Autobiography,* I, 242–43. Also see Albert Bigelow Paine (ed.), *Mark Twain's Speeches,* p. 303.

25. *Evening Bulletin,* Oct. 3, 1866.

26. Will Clemens, "Mark Twain on the Lecture Platform," p. 25. According to one account of the first San Francisco lecture, Mark Twain began as follows: "Julius Caesar is dead, Shakespeare is dead, Abraham Lincoln is dead, and I am far from well myself." (Frear, *Mark Twain and Hawaii,* p. 198.)

27. *Evening Bulletin,* Oct. 3, 1866.

28. Paine, *Biography,* III, 1601.

29. *Evening Bulletin,* Oct. 3, 1866.

30. *Roughing It,* II, 296.

31. *Evening Bulletin,* Oct. 3, 1866.

32. *Ibid.*

33. *The Golden Era,* Oct. 7, 1866.

34. Oct. 3, 1866.

35. *The Golden Era,* Oct 7, 1866.

36. Frear, *Mark Twain and Hawaii,* pp. 181–82.

37. Howells, *Speeches,* XIV.

38. Springfield, Massachusetts, *Republican,* Nov. 10, 1866.

39. Paine, *Biography,* I, 294.

40. T. E. Pemberton, *The Life of Bret Harte,* p. 73.

41. Bernard DeVoto (ed.), *Mark Twain in Eruption,* pp. 304–5.

42. In his *Mark Twain's Speeches* and in Appendix D of *Mark Twain: A Biography,* Albert Bigelow Paine offers extracts from Mark Twain's first lecture in San Francisco, but fails to supply the source. In view of the fact that the San Francisco newspapers refrained from printing extended portions of the lecture verbatim, and the original manuscript of the lecture was not available to Paine, one must assume that he derived the extracts from newspaper reports of the lecture given elsewhere. Furthermore, since relatively few reporters were capable of making a verbatim stenographic transcription of a lecture (though Mark Twain's notably slow drawl would have made an effort to do so less

difficult), one cannot accept the extracts which Paine offers as a true and accurate copy of Mark Twain's text. Paine's judgment, therefore, based upon these extracts, that the literary qualities of the opening San Francisco lecture were superior to those of the Sandwich Islands letters, must be accepted with reservation. A sufficiently accurate text of the first San Francisco lecture simply does not exist as a basis for making such a judgment.

NOTES TO CHAPTER THREE

THE JUBILANT TOUR

1. Albert Bigelow Paine, *Mark Twain: A Biography*, I, 291–94; *Roughing It*, II, 297.
2. Albert Bigelow Paine (ed.), *Mark Twain's Letters*, I, 121.
3. Paine, *Biography*, I, 205.
4. The Sacramento *Union*, Oct. 10, 1866.
5. *Ibid.*, Oct. 12, 1866.
6. The Sacramento *Bee*, Oct. 12, 1866.
7. The Grass Valley *Daily Union*, Oct. 20, 1866.
8. Paine, *Biography*, I, 295.
9. *Ibid.*
10. *Ibid.* It was during this tour also, after a lecture in one of the California mining camps, that an old miner delighted him by asking, "Be them your natural tones of eloquence?" *(Ibid.)*
11. May 30, 1864.
12. Gold Hill *Evening News*, Oct. 30, 1866.
13. Virginia City *Enterprise*, Oct. 30, 1866.
14. *Ibid.*, Oct. 31, 1866.
15. *Ibid.*, Nov. 1, 1866.
16. Paine, *Letters*, I, 121.
17. *Ibid.*
18. *Ibid.*
19. For a full account of Mark Twain's mounting troubles in Virginia City and Carson City, which precipitated his departure in May, 1864, see Henry Nash Smith and Frederick Anderson (eds.), *Mark Twain of the Enterprise*, Part III, "The Affair Was a Silly Joke."
20. Walter Frear, *Mark Twain and Hawaii*, Appendix D5, p. 449.
21. Paine, *Biography*, I, chap. IV; *Roughing It*, II, chap. XXXVIII.
22. William M. Stewart, whose testimony about Mark Twain in other particulars is of dubious reliability, reports that during the hold-up Mark Twain "was the scaredest man west of the Mississippi." *(Reminiscences*, p. 27.)
23. *Alta California*, Dec. 14, 1866. When asked after his return to San Francisco what the lecture trip had been like, he is reported to have replied that everything had gone well except that Denis McCarthy had mistaken it for a spree *(Morning Call*, April 17, 1887).
24. Nov. 18, 1866.

25. About three years later Mark Twain told James Redpath that all 1,400 seats in Platt's Hall had been reserved at a dollar a ticket and had sold out in five hours (Will Clemens, "Mark Twain on the Lecture Platform," p. 27).

26. Frear, *Mark Twain and Hawaii*, p. 209.

27. Nov. 18, 1866.

28. Nov. 17, 1866.

29. *Morning Call*, Nov. 17, 1866.

30. For Mark Twain's extended account of the experiment to compel humor by repetition see Charles Neider (ed.), *The Autobiography of Mark Twain*, (New York, 1959), pp. 143–46.

31. Nov. 21, 1866.

32. Nov. 23, 1866.

33. Nov. 29, 1866. Frear *(Mark Twain and Hawaii*, p. 447) conjectures that the editor's unfavorable criticism of Mark Twain as a lecturer, while acknowledging that he was a "racy and humorous writer," was provoked by "the non-receipt of advertisements and complimentary tickets." The conjecture was obviously based upon assertions to the same effect made in the Santa Rosa *Sonora Democrat*, Dec. 1, 1866, which ridiculed the editor of the Petaluma *Journal and Argus* for his criticisms.

34. Notebook No. 32, June 2–July 24, 1897, MTP. On his return to San Francisco, perhaps to make up for the unsatisfactory receipts at Oakland, Mark Twain began writing a series of letters for the *Evening Bulletin* concerning business conditions in the principal towns he had visited during the tour. These letters appeared under the heading "Interior Notes," Nov. 30, Dec. 6, and Dec. 7, 1866. Unfortunately, they reveal nothing about his experiences as a lecturer.

35. *Evening Bulletin*, Dec. 10, 1866.

36. *Alta California*, Dec. 6, 1866.

37. *Ibid.*, Dec. 10, 1866.

38. *Ibid.*, Dec. 11, 1866.

39. Dec. 11, 1866.

40. Dec. 11, 1866.

41. *Alta California*, Dec. 15, 1866.

NOTES TO CHAPTER FOUR

ON HOME GROUND

1. Franklin Walker and G. Ezra Dane (eds.), *Mark Twain's Travels With Mr. Brown*, p. 122.

2. Albert Bigelow Paine, *Mark Twain: A Biography*, I, 308. The book appeared in May, 1867, under the title, *The Celebrated Jumping Frog of Calaveras County, and Other Sketches*.

3. Walker and Dane, *MTTWB*, pp. 111–12.

4. *Ibid.*, p. 116.

5. Samuel C. Webster (ed.), *Mark Twain, Business Man,* p. 91.

6. Walker and Dane, *MTTWB,* p. 135.

7. *Ibid.,* p. 136.

8. Mark Twain's humorous reference to auger holes may have been suggested by the flowery oratory of Tom Fitch, his old California friend, who, in one of his lectures, had referred to the planets as the "auger holes of heaven." The phrase had evoked satire among Fitch's associates in San Francisco. (Franklin Walker, *San Francisco's Literary Frontier,* p. 99.)

9. The reference to female suffrage in the advertising blurb had special interest for the people of St. Louis because some days earlier (Mar. 13, 14, and 15) Mark Twain's satiric views on the subject had appeared in the *Daily Missouri Democrat.*

10. Walter Frear, *Mark Twain and Hawaii,* p. 177; Paine, *Biography,* I, 460.

11. Members of William A. Moffett's family lived in Quincy. Moffett was Pamela Clemens' husband. What connection Mark Twain had with General Singleton, at whose house he spent a night in Quincy, is not clear. (See Walker and Dane, *MTTWB,* pp. 148 and 289.)

12. Keokuk *Gate City,* April 6, 1867.

13. Keokuk *Constitution,* April 9, 1867.

14. *The Twainian,* I, No. 5.

NOTES TO CHAPTER FIVE

NEW YORK AND BROOKLYN

1. Dixon Wecter (ed.), *The Love Letters of Mark Twain,* pp. 26–27.

2. Walter Frear, *Mark Twain and Hawaii,* pp. 454–55.

3. Albert Bigelow Paine, *Mark Twain: A Biography,* I, 312.

4. *Alta California,* Mar. 28, 1867.

5. Frank Fuller, "Utah's War Governor Talks of Many Famous Men," *New York Times,* Oct. 1, 1911.

6. *Ibid.*

7. Frear, *Mark Twain and Hawaii,* p. 455.

8. Newspaper clipping in the MTP, not dated or identified.

9. Frear, *Mark Twain and Hawaii,* p. 455.

10. Albert Bigelow Paine (ed.), *Mark Twain's Letters,* I, 124.

11. Fuller, "Utah's War Governor."

12. Paine, *Biography,* I, 315.

13. *Ibid.*

14. *Mark Twain's Autobiography,* II, 355.

15. Paine, *Biography,* I, 316.

16. *Autobiography,* II, 355.

17. June 16, 1867.

18. Fuller, "Utah's War Governor."

19. It is possible, of course, that Nye failed to keep his promise because Mark Twain had dealt with him rather severely in his "Governor's Message to the Third House" in Carson City in 1864. (See Clemens' letter to sister Pamela, Mar. 18, 1864, MTP.)

20. *The Twainian,* Fifteenth Year, No. 4 (July-August, 1956), 1.

21. It was Edward (Ned) House of the *Tribune* who had gone down to the "Quaker City" office with Mark Twain to make inquiries about the Holy Land trip.

22. Fuller, "Utah's War Governor."

23. Brooklyn *Union,* May 10, 1867.

24. *Alta California,* June 30, 1867.

25. Paine, *Letters,* I, 125.

NOTES TO CHAPTER SIX

RETURN TO THE FAR WEST

1. *What Is Man? And Other Essays,* p. 136.

2. Albert Bigelow Paine, *Mark Twain: A Biography,* I, chap. LXIII.

3. Concerning Mark Twain's relations with Senator William Morris Stewart, see Paine, *Biography,* I, 346–47, and Stewart's *Reminiscences.*

4. Paine, *Biography,* I, 352.

5. *Ibid.,* p. 353.

6. Edward Wagenknecht *(Mark Twain: The Man and His Work,* p. 33) reports that Mark Twain, as a boy, may have shied away from Dickens because his brother Orion had prodded him to read his books. The evidence of the time, however, suggests that he read Dickens with pleasure. Mark Twain's description of Dickens as a public reader, supplied to the *Alta California* (Feb. 5, 1868), was less reverential: "a thin-legged old gentleman, gotten up regardless of expense, especially as to shirt-front and diamonds, with a bright red flower in his button-hole, grey beard and moustache, bald head, and with side hair brushed fiercely and tempestuously forward. . . ."

7. Bernard DeVoto (ed.), *Mark Twain in Eruption,* pp. 213–14.

8. Will Clemens, "Mark Twain on the Lecture Platform," p. 26.

9. Albert Bigelow Paine (ed.), *Mark Twain's Letters,* I, 143.

10. *Ibid.,* p. 144.

11. Washington, D.C., *Daily Morning Chronicle,* Jan. 11, 1868.

12. According to Mark Twain's version, "Little George, with his face all smeared with mashed cherries (strong circumstantial evidence), went to his father and confessed the act, saying that he could not tell a lie, whereupon his father clasped him to his arms, and told him that he wished he had gone into all the cherry orchards in the vicinity, and chopped all the trees, for this confession would then have been a greater evidence of his love for the truth." *(Daily Morning Chronicle,* Feb. 24,

1868. Also see Albert Bigelow Paine (ed.), *Mark Twain's Speeches,* p. 349.)
    13. *Daily Morning Chronicle,* Feb. 24, 1868.
    14. Paine, *Biography,* I, 359.
    15. Apr. 12, 1868.
    16. Apr. 15, 1868.
    17. Apr. 18, 1868.
    18. Apr. 19, 1868.
    19. Sacramento *Union,* Apr. 18, 1868.
    20. Dixon Wecter (ed.), *Mark Twain to Mrs. Fairbanks,* p. 26. Also see Paine, *Letters,* I, 153.
    21. Apr. 15, 1868.
    22. Apr. 16, 1868.
    23. Apr. 18, 1868.
    24. The Nevada City *Daily Transcript,* Apr. 15, 1868.
    25. Wecter, *Fairbanks,* pp. 25–26.
    26. Apr. 24, 1868.
    27. Virginia City *Enterprise,* Apr. 28, 1868.
    28. Will Clemens, "Mark Twain on the Lecture Platform," p. 26.
    29. The Carson City *Silver Age,* Apr., 1868.
    30. Wecter, *Fairbanks,* p. 28, n. 1.
    31. A complete copy of the handbill may be found in Paine, *Biography,* III, Appendix H, pp. 1614–17. In *Innocents Abroad* Mark Twain claimed to have discovered in the ruins of the Coliseum at Rome the only playbill of that "establishment now extant." While the general tone and substance of the mock Roman playbill are different from that of the San Francisco handbill, the one probably suggested the other, for Mark Twain was busily engaged at the time on the manuscript of *Innocents Abroad.*
    32. *Alta California,* July 3, 1868.
    33. *Ibid.*
    34. July 3, 1868.
    35. Wecter, *Fairbanks,* p. 33.
    36. *Mark Twain's Autobiography,* I, 243–44.
    37. The letter appeared in the Herald Nov. 21, 1867.

NOTES TO CHAPTER SEVEN

ON THE LYCEUM CIRCUIT

    1. "The Treaty With China" appeared Aug. 4, 1868.
    2. "Letter From Mark Twain," dated Aug. 17, appeared Aug. 23, 1868.
    3. Actually, *Innocents Abroad* was not published until July, 1869.
    4. See Mark Twain's letter to Abel Fairbanks, dated Oct. 5. For an account of the Association whose services Mark Twain secured and of which G. T. Torbet of Dubuque was secretary in the summer of 1868,

see Luella M. Wright's "Culture Through Lectures," *Iowa Journal of History and Politics*, XXXVIII, No. 2 (April, 1940), 115–62; and H. H. Hoeltje's "The Associated Western Literary Societies," *Ibid.*, XXV, 120–31. The Association, started in 1865, was interested in booking lectures by easterners in the Middle West.

5. Dixon Wecter (ed.), *Mark Twain to Mrs. Fairbanks*, p. 33.

6. Her articles appeared in the *Herald* under the pen name "Myra." For a brief biographical sketch of Mary Mason Fairbanks see Wecter, *Fairbanks*, pp. xx-xxi.

7. B. A. Booth, "Mark Twain's Friendship With Emeline Beach," p. 220.

8. Albert Bigelow Paine omitted the offending phrase, "ours as a general thing," in *Mark Twain: A Biography*, III, Appendix G, but retained it in *Mark Twain's Speeches*, p. 31.

9. Wecter, *Fairbanks*, p. 13.

10. *Ibid.*, p. 16.

11. *Ibid.*, pp. 24–32.

12. The New York *Herald* article, Nov. 21, 1867, was titled "The Quaker City Pilgrimage, A Malcontent Passenger's Story of the Excursion—The Serio-Comic Features of the Enterprise."

13. Wecter, *Fairbanks*, p. 38.

14. *Ibid.*, p. 46.

15. *Ibid.*

16. *Ibid.*

17. *Ibid.*, pp. 44–45.

18. *Ibid.*, p. 46.

19. Samuel C. Webster (ed.), *Mark Twain, Business Man*, pp. 102–3.

20. The passage reported in the *Herald* is identical with the one in *Innocents Abroad*. Mark Twain himself probably supplied the text for it from his lecture manuscript. The passage is reprinted in Chapter 20.

21. Dixon Wecter (ed.), *The Love Letters of Mark Twain*, pp. 23–24.

22. Albert Bigelow Paine (ed.), Mark Twain's *Letters*, I, 155–56.

23. Webster, *Mark Twain, Business Man*, p. 103.

24. *The Twainian*, Tenth Year, No. 3 (May-June, 1951), p. 4.

25. Wecter, *LL*, p. 58.

26. Cleveland *Plain Dealer*, Jan. 23, 1869.

27. This verbatim transcription from the Cleveland *Daily Leader*, Jan. 23, 1869. The lecture netted the Orphan Asylum over $800. (See Wecter, *LL*, p. 58.)

28. Feb. 3 to 11 he had no engagements and spent the time in Elmira (Wecter, *LL*, p. 68, n. 3).

29. Paine, *Biography*, I, 379.

30. Wecter, *Fairbanks*, p. 68.

31. A careful search has brought to light only nine lectures during February and two during March.

32. Paine, *Letters*, I, 156.

UNDER REDPATH'S MANAGEMENT

1. Albert Bigelow Paine, *Mark Twain: A Biography,* I, 373.
2. Albert Bigelow Paine (ed.), *Mark Twain's Letters,* I, 155.
3. Redpath's letter of April 24, 1869, recently discovered, is offered here by permission of C. E. Backman, manager of the Western Department of the Redpath Bureau, Chicago. Its fortunate discovery helps to clear up false assumptions initiated by Albert Bigelow Paine, concerning Mark Twain's first association with Redpath's Boston Lyceum Bureau. It also corrects an erroneous statement by James B. Pond that Redpath invited Mark Twain to come East for the season of 1872–73 and that he made his first appearance in Boston *(Eccentricities of Genius,* p. 199).
4. Paine, *Letters,* p. 158.
5. Dixon Wecter (ed.), *Mark Twain to Mrs. Fairbanks,* pp. 101, 104.
6. Paine, *Letters,* I, 158.
7. Wecter, *Fairbanks,* p. 99.
8. *Ibid.,* p. 104.
9. Charles F. Horner, *Life of James Redpath,* p. 177.
10. Dixon Wecter (ed.), *The Love Letters of Mark Twain,* p. 108.
11. Wecter, *Fairbanks,* p. 107.
12. Paine, *Letters,* I, 168.
13. Wecter, *Fairbanks,* p. 107. Mark Twain probably abandoned the California lecture not because its curiosities lacked interest but because he found it difficult to evoke humor from material that of necessity consisted largely of descriptive detail concerning the physical features of the state.
14. Pittsburgh *Post,* Nov. 1, 1869. The Redpath Bureau *Special News Letter* (Fall, 1966), reports that Mark Twain's fee at Pittsburgh was $120, a handsome figure for a relative newcomer to the lecture field.
15. Wecter, *LL,* p. 112.
16. *Ibid.,* p. 116.
17. *Ibid.,* pp. 116–17.
18. *Ibid.,* p. 117.
19. Nov. 2, 1869. The Pittsburgh *Dispatch* printed an angry review of Mark Twain's lecture, but whether it presented a synopsis is not known, since the file is no longer extant. Associated with the *Dispatch* was J. H. Foster, a fellow passenger on the "Quaker City." (See Paine, *Biography,* III, 1609.) He may have been one of the many excursionists who were offended by Mark Twain's satirical letter about his "Quaker City" associates which appeared in the New York *Herald,* Nov. 21, 1867.
20. See, for example, Mark Twain's letter to William Dean Howells, Jan. 28, 1882, about the suspected hostility of the New York *Times* (Henry Nash Smith and William Gibson (eds.), *Mark Twain–Howells Letters,* I, 386–69). For additional comment about Mark Twain

and the reporters see Arthur L. Vogelback's "The Literary Reputation of Mark Twain."

21. Albert Bigelow Paine (ed.), *Mark Twain's Speeches*, p. 51.

22. Years later Mark Twain told Mrs. Fairbanks that it was his inflexible rule to be content with anything a newspaper might say about him because anything they said was not "so low down as my private opinion of myself." (Wecter, *Fairbanks*, p. 265.)

23. William Dean Howells (ed.), *Mark Twain's Speeches*, p. 387.

24. "Glimpses of the Past."

25. Wecter, *LL*, p. 171.

26. Pittsburgh *Post*, Nov. 2, 1869.

27. Paine, *Letters*, I, 168.

28. Springfield, Mass., *Republican*, Nov. 13, 1869. "Warrington" was the pen name of William S. Robinson, one of the most distinguished reporters ever to serve with the *Republican*. He is said to have derived his pen name from the friend of Pendennis in Thackeray's novel, *Pendennis*.

29. Wecter, *LL*, p. 120.

30. Springfield *Republican*, Nov. 13, 1869.

31. *Mark Twain's Autobiography*, I, 150–51.

32. Paine, *Letters*, I, 168.

33. Wecter, *LL*, p. 137. As late as 1880 he was still adamant in his objection to the practice of synopsizing. Before lecturing in Hartford in April of that year, he made all newspapermen swear that they would not say a single word about his lecture either before or after the performance. (Samuel C. Webster, *Mark Twain, Business Man*, p. 145.)

34. Jan. 28, 1870.

35. Clara Clemens, *My Father, Mark Twain*, pp. 69–70. For a more extended account of Mark Twain's experience in Jamestown see Fred W. Lorch, "Mark Twain's Sandwich Islands Lecture and the Failure at Jamestown."

36. Paine, *Biography*, I, 394.

NOTES TO CHAPTER NINE

THE MOST DETESTABLE CAMPAIGN

1. Will Clemens, "Mark Twain on the Lecture Platform," p. 27.

2. Albert Bigelow Paine (ed.), *Mark Twain's Letters*, I, 172.

3. *Ibid.*, pp. 172–73. But also see a fragment of the May 10 letter in Will Clemens, "Mark Twain on the Lecture Platform." In this instance, as in many others, Paine apparently failed to indicate that he had omitted part of the letter.

4. *The Lyceum*, July 1870, p. 4.

5. *Ibid.*, p. 16. The book was *Innocents Abroad;* the relative was, of course, his father-in-law, Jervis Langdon, who had made his daughter and new son-in-law a gift of a furnished house in Buffalo without Mark

Twain's prior knowledge. He had also advanced money for the purchase of part interest in the Buffalo *Express*. The *F* in the signature refers to George L. Fall, Redpath's business partner.

6. Dixon Wecter (ed.), *Mark Twain to Mrs. Fairbanks,* p. 128.

7. *Ibid.,* p. 131.

8. *Ibid.,* p. 149. The only person he seems to have been fond of in Buffalo was David Gray, the poet-editor of the Buffalo *Courier.*

9. In the *American Publisher,* I, No. 4 (July, 1871), Orion Clemens reported that Mark Twain had two new lectures, one an appeal in behalf of boys' rights, and one entitled simply D.L.H. As Bernard DeVoto points out in *Mark Twain at Work,* p. 6, Mark Twain made a marginal notation in his manuscript of *The Adventures of Tom Sawyer* as follows: "Put in thing from Boy-lecture." The "boy-lecture" manuscript, unfortunately, does not appear to have been preserved. That it had a shaping influence on the Tom Sawyer story seems probable.

10. Paine, *Letters,* I, 189. In a letter to Mrs. Fairbanks he reported that the lecture included Artemus Ward; an eccentric, big-hearted newspaperman (Riley); the king of the Sandwich Islands (Kamehameha); Dick Baker (Dick Stoker in *Roughing It*); Reeves A. Jackson (the guide-destroying doctor in *Innocents Abroad*); and Emperor Norton (a pathetic San Francisco lunatic). (See Wecter, *Fairbanks,* p. 155).

11. William M. Clemens, "Mark Twain on the Lecture Platform," p. 28.

12. SLC to James Redpath, June 10, 1871, MTP.

13. Paine, *Letters,* I, 189.

14. *Ibid.,* pp. 190–91.

15. Charles F. Horner, *Life of James Redpath,* p. 167.

16. Paine, *Letters,* I, 190.

17. Horner, *Life of James Redpath,* pp. 172–73.

18. Franklin Walker and G. Ezra Dane (eds.), *Mark Twain's Travels With Mr. Brown,* p. 104.

19. *Mark Twain's Autobiography,* I, 157–60.

20. Walker and Dane, *MTTWB,* p. 105.

21. Horner, *Life of James Redpath,* pp. 173–74.

22. Dixon Wecter (ed.), *The Love Letters of Mark Twain,* p. 161.

23. Oct. 16, 1871.

24. Scranton *Morning Republican,* Oct. 19, 1871.

25. Wecter, *LL,* p. 161.

26. Oct. 24, 1871.

27. Philadelphia *Inquirer,* Nov. 21, 1871; and Lowell *Weekly Journal,* Nov. 24, 1871.

28. Wecter, *LL,* pp. 163–64.

29. Norristown *Herald and Free Press,* Nov. 2, 1871.

30. Erie *Weekly Observer,* Dec. 14, 1871.

31. Paine, *Letters,* I, 193.

32. The *Tribune* printed large portions of his lecture in Chicago Dec. 20 and 24, 1871. The complete stenographic report of his lecture in the Lansing, Michigan, *State Republican,* Dec. 21, 1871, had apparently escaped his notice.

33. Wecter, *LL*, p. 171; Wecter, *Fairbanks*, p. 159.
34. Letter to Redpath, Jan. 17, 1872, in Will Clemens, "Mark Twain on the Lecture Platform," p. 29.
35. Paine, *Letters*, I, 194.
36. Wecter, *Fairbanks*, pp. 159–60; Wecter, *LL*, p. 172.
37. Wecter, *Fairbanks*, p. 158.
38. *Daily Morning Democrat*, Dec. 16, 1871; See also the Lansing *State Republican*, Dec. 21, 1871. *Roughing It* was copyrighted Dec. 6, 1871. It did not appear on the bookstalls until near the end of February, a few days before the tour ended.

NOTES TO CHAPTER TEN

LIFE ON THE LECTURE CIRCUIT

1. *Alta California*, July 25, 1869. Also see *The Twainian*, VIII, No. 3 (May-June, 1949), 3–6.
2. Dixon Wecter (ed.), *The Love Letters of Mark Twain*, p. 50.
3. *Ibid.*, p. 68.
4. *Ibid.*, p. 172.
5. *Ibid.*, pp. 169–70. The great Chicago fire began on the night of Oct. 9, 1871. Mark Twain drove through the ruins nine weeks later.
6. Dixon Wecter (ed.), *Mark Twain to Mrs. Fairbanks*, p. 54.
7. Clara Clemens, *My Father, Mark Twain*, p. 52.
8. Wecter, *LL*, p. 129.
9. *Ibid.*, p. 130.
10. For an instance of Mark Twain's annoyance with "soiled & nasty imps" he sometimes encountered in private homes, see Wecter, *LL*, pp. 115–16.
11. Albert Bigelow Paine, *Mark Twain: A Biography*, I, 446.
12. Clara Clemens, *MF, MT*, p. 52; Wecter, *LL*, p. 122.
13. Wecter, *LL*, p. 122.
14. Clara Clemens, *MF, MT*, pp. 48–49. Sometimes, as at Bethlehem, Pennsylvania, Oct. 15, 1871, he registered under a pseudonym (*Ibid.*, p. 50).
15. Paine, *Letters*, I, 290–91.
16. Wecter, *LL*, p. 170.
17. Iowa City *Republican*, Jan. 20, 1869.
18. Wecter, *LL*, pp. 52–53.
19. Iowa City *Republican*, Jan. 20, 1869.
20. Clara Clemens, *MF, MT*, p. 50.
21. Danville, Illinois, *Commercial*, Jan. 4, 1872.
22. Wecter, *LL*, pp. 73–74.
23. *Ibid.*, p. 121.
24. Clara Clemens, *MF, MT*, p. 50.
25. Wecter, *LL*, p. 55.
26. *Ibid.*, p. 53.

27. *Ibid.*, p. 70.
28. *Ibid.*, p. 34.
29. *Ibid.*, p. 132.
30. *Ibid.*, p. 76.
31. *Ibid.*, p. 126.
32. *Ibid.*, p. 164.
33. *Ibid.*, pp. 172–73.
34. *Ibid.*, pp. 129–30.
35. *Ibid.*, pp. 135–36. It appears that Mark Twain gave up smoking for a brief period in 1869, but when he began writing *Roughing It* in 1871 he resumed his monthly quota of three hundred cigars *(Ibid.*, p. 139).

NOTES TO CHAPTER ELEVEN

LECTURES IN ENGLAND

1. Letter dated Boston, July 12, 1872, MTP. © 1967 by The Mark Twain Co.
2. Albert Bigelow Paine, *Mark Twain: A Biography*, I, 458.
3. Charles W. Stoddard, *Exits and Entrances*, p. 61.
4. Paine, *Biography*, I, 469.
5. Nov. 7, 1872.
6. Will Clemens, "Mark Twain on the Lecture Platform," p. 29.
7. Paine, *Biography*, I, 474.
8. Franklin Walker, *San Francisco's Literary Frontier*, p. 340.
9. Paine, *Biography*, I, 489.
10. Moncure D. Conway, *Autobiography*, II, 129.
11. Paine, *Biography*, I, 490.
12. *Ibid.*, p. 491.
13. Fred W. Lorch, "Mark Twain's Public Lectures in England in 1873," pp. 297–304.
14. *Punch*, Dec. 20, 1873.
15. *Standard*, Oct. 14, 1873. The *Standard* reported that P. T. Barnum, the great American showman, was in the audience opening night.
16. *Daily Telegraph*, Oct. 14, 1873.
17. *Morning Post*, Oct. 14, 1873.
18. *Ibid.*
19. Undated clipping from London *Cosmopolitan*, MTP.
20. *The Twainian*, Thirteenth Year, No. 1, p. 4.
21. Will Clemens, "Mark Twain on the Lecture Platform," p. 29.
22. *The Twainian*, Thirteenth Year, No. 1, p. 4.
23. *Ibid.*
24. Liverpool *Journal*, Oct. 25, 1873.
25. *Times*, Oct. 19, 1873.
26. Stoddard, *Exits and Entrances*, p. 62.

27. Liverpool *Evening Express,* Oct. 21, 1873; and Liverpool *Mercury,* Oct. 21, 1873.

28. Dixon Wecter (ed.), *Mark Twain to Mrs. Fairbanks,* p. 181. "I rather dread to have him change," she told Mrs. Fairbanks, "as that lecture is so good and so well rec'd, you know you have not heard it since he rewrote it—and it is so much better than before."

29. London *Morning Post,* Dec. 10, 1873.

30. Conway, *Autobiography,* II, 129–30.

31. Summary based upon Mark Twain's page of lecture notes for Roughing It on the Silver Frontier lecture, the London *Daily News* and the *Daily Telegraph,* Dec. 9, 1873.

32. Conway, *Autobiography* II, 129–30.

33. *Morning Post,* Dec. 9, 1873.

34. *Daily Telegraph,* Dec. 9, 1873.

35. SLC to OLC, Dec. 13, 1873, MTP.

36. Walker, *San Francisco's Literary Frontier,* pp. 340–41.

37. Henry Nash Smith and William Gibson (eds.), *Mark Twain-Howells Letters,* I, 154.

38. *The Twainian,* Thirteenth Year, No. 1, p. 4. Tichborne was an illiterate impostor who tried to establish his claim as rightful heir to a great estate. Mark Twain's interest in the case led to the creation of a similar claimant in his book *The American Claimant.*

39. Stoddard, *Exits and Entrances,* pp. 61–70.

40. Paine, *Biography,* I, 499.

41. *Ibid.*

42. Later that evening he still had enough energy to write Frank Fuller and report that he had full houses in England and "a jolly good time with them." See *The Twainian,* IV, No. 1, p. 1.

43. Stoddard, *Exits and Entrances,* p. 73.

44. *Ibid.,* pp. 73–74.

45. Smith and Gibson, *Mark Twain–Howells Letters,* I, 154. A few years after the London episode Mark Twain tried to help Stoddard get a consulship. In this connection he wrote Howells that he had known "poor, sweet, pure-hearted, good-intentioned, impotent Stoddard" for twelve years and in all that time "he had never been fit for anything but a consul."

46. Paine, *Biography,* I, 502.

47. *Ibid.*

NOTES TO CHAPTER TWELVE

ART OF READING

1. Albert Bigelow Paine, *Mark Twain: A Biography,* I, 353.

2. Bernard DeVoto (ed.), *Mark Twain in Eruption,* pp. 213–14.

3. Mark Twain, *A Tramp Abroad,* II (Hartford, 1880), 81.

4. New York *Weekly,* July 14, 1873.

5. Albert Bigelow Paine (ed.), *Mark Twain's Letters,* I, 302.
6. Henry Nash Smith and William Gibson (eds.), *Mark Twain—Howells Letters,* I, 302.
7. *Ibid.,* p. 356.
8. *Ibid.*
9. Mark Twain read again at West Point in Apr., 1886, and Jan., 1890 (Smith and Gibson, *Mark Twain—Howells Letters,* II, 551–53 and 625).
10. *Ibid.,* I, 356.
11. Paine, *Biography,* II, 783; also William Dean Howells, *My Mark Twain,* p. 53.
12. DeVoto, *Mark Twain in Eruption,* p. 216.
13. *A Tramp Abroad,* II, 81.
14. In view of Mark Twain's often expressed love for his career as a Mississippi River pilot, the question arises why he never included passages from *Life on the Mississippi* or from "Old Times on the Mississippi" in his repertoire of readings. Mark Twain himself offers no answer. One may conjecture, however, that the materials in these accounts which he might have considered were in his judgment too instructional in nature (piloting, he explains in Chapter XIII of *Life on the Mississippi* is eminently one of the "exact" sciences) to fit into a program aimed primarily at entertainment.
15. *Mark Twain's Autobiography,* I, 152–53.
16. DeVoto, *Mark Twain in Eruption,* p. 224.
17. *Ibid.*
18. *Ibid.,* p. 225.
19. *Ibid.,* p. 116.
20. *Ibid.,* pp. 217–24.
21. Smith and Gibson, *Mark Twain—Howells Letters,* II, 705–6.
22. See, for example, his comment about the Authors' Reading Program for the benefit of the Longfellow Memorial Fund held on the afternoon of Mar. 31, 1887, in Boston *(Ibid.,* pp. 589–90).
23. *Autobiography,* II, 147.
24. Smith and Gibson, *Mark Twain—Howells Letters,* I, 530.
25. American Academy and the National Institute of Arts and Letters, *Academy Notes and Monographs,* p. 77.

NOTES TO CHAPTER THIRTEEN

READING TOUR WITH CABLE

1. Albert Bigelow Paine (ed.), *Mark Twain's Letters,* I, 262.
2. *Ibid.,* pp. 311–12.
3. Charles L. Webster was the husband of Annie Moffatt, Mark Twain's niece. For an extended account of Mark Twain's venture into the publishing business and his relations with Webster see Samuel C. Webster (ed.), *Mark Twain, Business Man.*

4. Albert Bigelow Paine, *Mark Twain: A Biography*, II, 783.

5. Minneapolis *Tribune*, Jan. 25, 1885.

6. In 1907 Mark Twain mistakenly reported that he "hired Cable as a helper at six hundred dollars a week and expenses," (Bernard DeVoto (ed.), *Mark Twain in Eruption*, p. 216). Actually, the $600 included expenses.

7. Webster, *Mark Twain, Business Man*, pp. 268–69.

8. *Ibid.*, p. 269.

9. *Ibid.*, p. 294.

10. Boston *Daily Advertiser*, Nov. 15, 1884.

11. Mark Twain claimed many years later that when he and Cable began their tour in 1884 there had been "a holy silence" in the field of lecturing and reading for a period of ten years, and that a generation had grown up who were ignorant of such programs and "didn't know how to take them. . . ." These untrained audiences, he declared, sometimes gave him and Cable a hard time. (DeVoto, *Mark Twain in Eruption*, p. 215.) The claim was, of course, considerably exaggerated.

12. See Notebook No. 18 (Oct. 24, 1884–April 4, 1885), pp. 4–5, MTP. Not all the entries are dated, nor do the program notes indicate where the programs were given, except for the one at Madison, Wisconsin, and the first performance at Chicago. The selection called the Raftsmen's Fight probably refers to the raft passage which originally formed a part of the manuscript of *The Adventures of Huckleberry Finn* before it became a part of *Life on the Mississippi*.

13. *Daily Republican*, Nov. 8, 1884. The passage he read from *Huckleberry Finn* appears to have been the King Sollermun episode.

14. Notebook No. 18, p. 6.

15. *Ibid.*, p. 4.

16. Dixon Wecter (ed.), *The Love Letters of Mark Twain*, p. 231. Cable confirmed the splendid audience reception of The Jumping Frog story, declaring it was "superbly received." See Arlin Turner, *George W. Cable*, (Durham, North Carolina, 1956), p. 181.

17. Folder dated 1884-C-E, MTP. The question is sometimes asked why Mark Twain never lectured in the Deep South. A number of explanations offer probable answers. First, while Mark Twain was lecturing under Redpath's management, Redpath's bureau was new and developed its clientele through the lyceums in the northern states, where they chiefly flourished. Then, too, in the decade following the Civil War Northern lecturers were not popular in the South. Even had opportunities been offered to lecture there, Mark Twain might have refused, fearing that he might be abused as a renegade. Certainly, when he chose Cable as a reading companion for the tour of 1884–85 any thought of performing in the South was out of the question in view of Cable's pro-Negro stand. Finally, it is doubtful that Mark Twain could have expected a sympathetic audience in the South for his readings from *The Adventures of Huckleberry Finn* with its sympathetic treatment of Jim and its satire of certain aspects of Southern white society and culture.

18. *Critic*, V (Dec. 27, 1884), 308.

19. Minneapolis *Tribune*, Jan. 25, 1885.

20. American Academy and the National Institute of Arts and Letters, *Academy Notes and Monographs,* p. 76.

21. St. Paul *Dispatch,* Jan. 24, 1885. Hamlin Garland, who attended the Twain–Cable readings in Music Hall, Boston, on the evening of November 13, recorded in his Notebook that Mark Twain's calm face and "easy homelike style," put the entire audience at ease. He noted the flexibility and fine compass of the humorist's voice which ran easily to very fine deep notes and observed that he hit off his best things with a raspy, dry, "rozen" voice. A dry cough added a quizzical note to his wit, and deep sighs produced an irresistibly comic effect. At no time was there even the ghost of a smile. Mark Twain, he concluded, was "altogether a man whom you would take for anything but the funny man he is." See James B. Stronk, "Mark Twain's Boston Stage Debut as seen by Hamlin Garland," *New England Quarterly,* XXXVI, No. 1 (March, 1963), 86.

22. Grand Rapids *Daily Eagle,* Dec. 15, 1884.

23. See, for example, Edward L. Tinker's "Cable and the Creoles," pp. 321, 322; and William E. Broadfield's "Mark Twain as Keokuk Printer."

24. Paine, *Biography,* II, 786.

25. XXIX, 268–78.

26. Lucy L. C. Bickle, *George W. Cable. His Life and Letters,* p. 134.

27. William Dean Howells, *My Mark Twain,* pp. 53–54.

28. Webster, *Mark Twain, Business Man,* p. 297. Henry Nash Smith and William Gibson, the editors of the *Mark Twain–Howells Letters,* II, 519, report that the tour brought Mark Twain a great deal of money. For a discussion of earnings on the tour see Chapter 18.

29. Paine, *Biography,* II, 784.

30. *Ibid.*

31. Tinker, "Cable and the Creoles," p. 322.

32. Wecter, *LL,* p. 234.

33. *Ibid.,* p. 237.

34. *Ibid.,* p. 235.

35. *Ibid.,* p. 237. For a detailed and sound report of the relationship between Mark Twain and Cable, before, during, and after the tour, see Arlin Turner's *George W. Cable,* especially Chapter XIII, "The Highway Robbery Business."

36. Smith and Gibson, *Mark Twain–Howells Letters,* I, 451. About a quarter of a century later Mark Twain reversed his opinion on the value of Cable's training under teachers of elocution, claiming it had made him theatrical and artificial. (See DeVoto, *Mark Twain in Eruption,* p. 216.)

37. Notebook No. 18, p. 19, MTP.

38. Turner, *George W. Cable,* p. 182.

39. *Ibid.,* p. 180.

40. *Ibid.,* p. 175.

41. Albert Bigelow Paine (ed.), *Mark Twain's Notebook,* pp. 172–73.

42. Wecter, *LL,* p. 236.

43. See Illustration on p. 176.

44. Paine suggested that the program he offered in *Biography,* II, 785, was the one the two men "were likely to use after they had proved its worth." This program lists four numbers for each reader. The record shows, however, that the programs were constantly altered and that such a neat balance in the number of selections read was seldom maintained. It must be remembered also that the number of selections read by either man fails to indicate the time required for the reading, a matter Mark Twain tried hard to control, often, it appears, in his favor.

45. Wecter, *LL,* p. 230.

46. Springfield *Daily Republican,* Nov. 8, 1884.

47. Wecter, *LL,* p. 231.

48. *Ibid.* Cable soon discovered that it would not be wise to sing to an assembling house. Though his voice was described as clear, it was not strong enough to rise above the rustling in the seats and the movement of latecomers.

49. *Ibid.*

50. *Ibid.,* p. 236.

51. *Ibid.,* p. 49. Mark Twain's testiness concerning annoyances while he was on the platform was further illustrated at Hamilton, Ohio, during the tour with Cable. When a man walked out of the hall with creaking shoes, he called out "Take your shoes off, please; take your shoes off." Indeed, as the tour progressed, according to Pond, Mark Twain's nerves became so taut that the mere rustling of the printed program upset him. To avoid the distraction he devised small programs printed on stiff card paper, that did not rustle and that could not be used as fans. ("Memories of the Lyceum," p. 896.)

52. Paine, *Letters,* II, 450.

53. As Arlin Turner points out *(George W. Cable,* p. 175), "In the hundred or more letters he wrote home while on the road with Mark Twain he never indicated the slightest irritation with Mark or his traveling manager . . . though there was irritation, or room for irritation, all the way round."

54. Cincinnati *Inquirer,* Jan. 3, 1885. The register of the St. Nicholas Hotel, where the men stayed, showed the entry, "J. B. Pond and Servants." Pond explained that this registry was "for the purpose of eluding autograph hunters and other nuisances."

55. See Arlin Turner's "James Lampton, Mark Twain's Original for Colonel Sellers," *Modern Language Notes,* LXX (Dec., 1955), 592–94.

56. *Academy Notes and Monographs,* p. 81.

57. Wecter, *LL,* pp. 220–21.

58. Paine, *Biography,* II, 788.

59. Turner, *George W. Cable,* pp. 174–75.

60. *Ibid.,* p. 180.

61. *Ibid.,* p. 181.

62. *Ibid.*

63. *Ibid.,* pp. 180–81. Mark Twain's care in perfecting a program and in carefully planning how best to achieve success in the telling of

particular stories was not new to the reading tour with Cable. As early as 1869, during his second lyceum tour, he wrote Livy an enthusiastic account of how he had improved the telling of the Jumping Frog story by a change in the manner of its telling, without altering a single word of the text. The change in manner made the story so absurd that he couldn't control his own laughter, and arrived at a particular point three different times "before he could get by it & go on." (Wecter, *LL*, p. 41.)

64. All these entries are to be found in Notebook No. 18, MTP. © 1967, The Mark Twain Co.

65. Smith and Gibson, *Mark Twain–Howells Letters*, II, 530.

NOTES TO CHAPTER FOURTEEN

THE WORLD TOUR

1. The Charles L. Webster Company was organized in 1884, failed in 1890, was reorganized, and failed again in April, 1894. (For detailed reports concerning Mark Twain's venture in owning and operating his own publishing house see Albert Bigelow Paine, *Mark Twain: A Biography*, II, Chaps. CXLIX and CLXXXVIII; Samuel C. Webster (ed.), *Mark Twain, Business Man*, Chap. 24 ff.; and the Elmira, New York, *Telegram*, July 14, 1895.

2. How much Mark Twain lost on the Paige typesetter is uncertain, but on Jan. 15, 1894, when news of the final collapse of the enterprise reached him, he claimed he and his wife were $160,000 in debt. (Albert Bigelow Paine (ed.), *Mark Twain's Notebook*, p. 235.)

3. For the figure $94,000 see Paine, *Notebook*, p. 381. For the $70,000 figure see the Elmira *Telegram*, July 14, 1895. Henry Rogers, who later took charge of Mark Twain's financial affairs, put Mark Twain's losses, on account of the failure of Webster, at $100,000, and his wife's at $60,000. (Paine, *Biography*, II, 984–85.)

4. Clara Clemens, *My Father, Mark Twain*, p. 179.

5. J. B. Pond, *Eccentricities of Genius*, p. 200.

6. As matters turned out, however, R. S. Smythe was unable, personally, to accompany Mark Twain after the lecture at Adelaide. Smythe had proceeded from Adelaide to Melbourne on the "Cuzco," which was declared, on arrival, to be a cholera infested ship. He was ordered into quarantine just as they were about to sail for New Zealand. (Otago *Daily Times*, Nov. 6, 1895.) Precisely when his son Carlyle took over as manager is uncertain. The Hawkes Bay *Herald* (Napier) reported that Hugo Fisher was in the city representing R. S. Smythe, in behalf of Mark Twain. Carlyle Smythe seems to have joined Mark Twain shortly thereafter for the remainder of the tour. (See *Taranaki Herald*, New Plymouth, Dec. 6, 1895.) In an interview in India, Carlyle Smythe reported that Mark Twain's world tour was the result of twelve years of negotiation. As early as 1884 R. S. Smythe had visited Mark

Twain in Hartford to suggest such a tour, but Mark Twain was then too busy with literary matters to consider it. In 1888 another attempt was made, but he again refused. His eventual decision to attempt so ambitious a tour, Smythe reported, was probably due to the counsels of his friend Henry M. Stanley, who had frequently been asked while on his own Far Eastern tour if Mark Twain would ever visit the antipodes. During the winter of 1894–95 negotiations were again renewed, this time successfully. (The Natal *Mercury*, undated but probably May, 1896.)

7. The Sydney *Bulletin*, Sept. 21, 1895.

8. The Elmira *Telegram*, July 14, 1895.

9. For Pond's account of the American phase of the tour, see *Eccentricities of Genius*, pp. 197–230. Also see Fred W. Lorch's "Mark Twain's 'Morals' Lecture During the American Phase of the World Tour in 1895–1896;" and Paine, *Biography*, II, 999–1019. Despite Mark Twain's agreement that Pond was to have complete charge of all arrangements, he did not hesitate to suggest ways in which his tour was to be advertised. He especially wanted Pond to emphasize that Mark Twain was "on his way to Australia and thence around the globe on a reading and talking tour to last twelve months; that traveling *around the world* is nothing, as everybody does it. But what he was traveling *for* was unusual; everybody didn't do that." (Pond, *Eccentricities of Genius*, p. 200.)

10. The number changed with almost every lecture, Mark Twain merely picking a number at random each night.

11. Johannesburg *Standard and Diggers News*, May 29, 1896. Also the Pretoria *Press*, May 26, 1896.

12. Other selections included in the repertoire were The Golden Arm; Cure for Stammering; Punch, Brother, Punch; Stealing the Watermelon; Decay of the Art of Lying; Encounter With an Interviewer; The McWilliamses and the Lightning; The Man Caught Up in the Carpet Making Machinery; The Death of Buck Fanshaw; The Duel With the Rival Editor; The Mean Company that Docked Worker; and The Australian Poem.

13. Johannesburg *Standard and Diggers News*, May 29, 1896; also see Calcutta *Englishman*, Feb. 13, 1896.

14. Missoula, Montana, *Missoulian*, Aug. 3, 1895.

15. Pestosky, Michigan, *Daily Reporter*, July 20, 1895.

16. Actually, Mark Twain gave a trial run of his Morals lecture two days earlier, Sunday evening, July 13, to the prisoners at the Elmira Reformatory. The prison newspaper, *Summary*, July 21, reported that the audience enjoyed the talk immensely, many being "on the verge of apoplexy."

17. See Fred W. Lorch's "Mark Twain's Lecture Tour of 1868–1869: The American Vandal Abroad," pp. 518–19.

18. Cleveland *Plain Dealer*, July 19, 1895.

19. Pond, *Eccentricities of Genius*, p. 225.

20. *Ibid.*, p. 224.

21. *Ibid.*, p. 223.

22. *Ibid.*, p. 224. In his lecture "Memories of the Lyceum" Pond stated that Mark Twain ate only when hungry, that he knew him to go days without a particle of food, but smoked constantly while awake.

23. Henry Nash Smith and William Gibson (eds.), *Mark Twain–Howells Letters*, II, 715.

24. *Ibid.*, p. 704.

25. William W. Ellsworth, *The Golden Age of Authors*, p. 226. Ellsworth regarded Pond as the greatest of the lecture managers. As a lecturer, however, he found him boring *(Ibid.*, pp. 251–53).

26. William Dean Howells (ed.), *Mark Twain's Speeches*, pp. 351–52.

27. Pond, *Eccentricities of Genius*, p. 200.

28. Paine, *Notebook*, p. 251. "The dictionary," Mark Twain added, "says the carbuncle is a kind of jewel. I never cared for jewelry."

29. Tasmanian *Weekly Mail*, Nov. 9, 1895.

30. For accounts of the Gisborne episode see Paine, *Notebook*, p. 257; *Following the Equator*, I, 298–99; and Clara Clemens, *MF, MT*, p. 149. In the latter source Clara Clemens mistakenly places the incident at Napier. She also implies, erroneously, that a landing in the basket-chair was made.

31. Paine, *Letters*, II, 629.

32. Paine, *Notebook*, p. 262.

33. *Ibid.*, p. 263.

34. Sydney *Morning Herald*, Dec. 21, 1895.

35. *Following the Equator*, II, 3.

36. Calcutta, *Indian Daily News*, Jan. 26, 1896; Paine, *Notebook*, p. 270. For an account of Mark Twain's visits to Colombo, see "Mark Twain In Ceylon," by Coleman O. Parsons, *The Twainian*, January-February, 1963, p. 4, and March-April, 1963, pp. 3–4; also the *Ceylon Observer*, Apr. 4, 1896.

37. Port Louis, Mauritius, *Merchants and Planters Gazette*, Apr. 18, 1896.

38. Port Louis, Mauritius, *Le Journal de Maurice*, Apr. 27, 1896.

39. *Following the Equator*, II, 317.

40. Paine, *Notebook*, p. 302.

41. Paine, *Letters*, II, 634.

42. Calcutta *Indian Daily News*, Jan. 25, 1896; Calcutta, *The Englishman*, Feb. 6, 1896.

43. Durban, Natal, *Natal Mercury*, May 7, 1896.

44. Tasmanian *Mail* (Weekly), Nov. 9, 1895. Also see *the Natal Mercury*, May 7, 1896.

45. Calcutta *Englishman*, Feb. 6, 1896.

46. Pretoria *Press*, May 25, 1896.

47. Transvaal *Advertiser*, May 25, 1896.

48. *Ibid.*, May 28, 1896. Carlyle Smythe reports that American journals were so eager to secure correspondence from Mark Twain concerning the Reform prisoners at Pretoria, that they cabled him blank checks, practically speaking, for anything he might send them. But Mark Twain declined, despite his need for money, probably because he in-

tended to use the material in *Following The Equator.*

49. The photograph had been made by Falk, a well-known Sydney photographer. See Melbourne *Age,* Sept. 27, 1895.

50. Melbourne *Age,* Sept. 29, 1895.

51. Capetown *Cape Argus,* July 8, 1896.

52. *Following the Equator,* I, 148.

53. Calcutta *Englishman,* Feb. 19, 1896.

54. Calcutta *Indian Daily News,* Jan. 24, 1896, copied from the Ceylon *Observer.*

55. Sydney *Bulletin,* Sept. 28, 1895.

56. Johannesburg *Standard and Diggers News,* May 19, 1896.

57. Invercargill, New Zealand, *Southland Times,* Nov. 6, 1895.

58. Melbourne *Age,* Sept. 29, 1895.

59. Timaru *Herald,* Nov. 11, 1895.

60. Tasmanian *Mail* (Weekly), Nov. 19, 1895.

61. Bombay *Gazette,* Jan. 23, 1896.

62. *Ibid.*

63. *Ibid.* Also see Clara Clemens, *MF, MT,* p. 46.

64. *Ibid.* Also see *Natal Mercury,* May, 1896.

65. *Current Indian News,* Jan. 27, 1896. About ten years later, of course, Mark Twain dictated large sections of his autobiography to Albert Bigelow Paine.

66. Bombay *Gazette,* Jan. 23, 1896.

67. *Current Indian News,* Jan. 27, 1896.

68. *Ibid.*

69. Tasmanian *News,* Nov. 2, 1895; Sydney *Morning Herald,* Sept. 17, 1895.

70. Sydney *Morning Herald,* Sept. 17, 1895.

71. *Daily Telegram,* Sept. 17, 1895.

72. Sydney *Morning Herald,* Sept. 17, 1895.

73. Tasmanian *News,* Nov. 2, 1895.

74. Sydney *Argus,* Sept. 17, 1895.

75. Sydney *Morning Herald,* Sept. 17, 1895.

76. Sydney *Argus,* Sept. 17, 1895.

77. Sydney *Morning Herald,* Sept. 17, 1895.

78. Melbourne *Age,* Sept. 27, 1895. In the interview Mark Twain reported that he had got *A Connecticut Yankee* out "in a hurry, at a high price, and it went through a comparatively limited edition of 35,000 or 40,000 copies."

79. Sydney *Argus,* Sept. 17, 1895.

80. Joseph H. Twichell, "Mark Twain," p. 825.

81. Robert Johnson, *Remembered Yesterdays,* p. 319.

82. Tasmanian *News,* Nov. 2, 1895.

83. *Current Indian News,* Jan. 27, 1896.

84. Tasmanian *News,* Sept. 2, 1895.

85. Portland *Oregonian,* Aug. 11, 1895.

86. *Ibid.* Mark Twain's memory failed him here. "Finn" was not the real name of the other boy. His name was Blankenship.

87. Winnepeg *Tribune,* July 27, 1895.

88. *Following the Equator,* II, 84.
89. *Ibid.,* chap. XX.
90. Paine, *Notebook,* p. 274.
91. *Ibid.,* p. 256.
92. *Ibid.,* p. 259.
93. *Ibid.,* p. 270.
94. *Ibid.,* p. 269.
95. *Following the Equator,* II, 51.
96. Carlyle Smythe, "The Real Mark Twain," p. 29.
97. *Ibid.,* p. 33.
98. Paine, *Notebook,* p. 249.
99. *Ibid.,* p. 261.
100. Pietermaritzburg, *Natal Witness,* May 18, 1896.
101. Smythe, "The Real Mark Twain," p. 35.
102. Paine, *Notebook,* p. 249.
103. *Ibid.,* p. 298.
104. Smith and Gibson, *Mark Twain–Howells Letters,* II, 661. Mark Twain expressed this hope to Howells in a letter dated Aug. 5, 1896. Two weeks later the hope was shattered when word reached him of his daughter Susy's death on August 18.

NOTES TO CHAPTER FIFTEEN

PLATFORM MANNERS AND TECHNIQUES

1. Bernard DeVoto (ed.), *Mark Twain in Eruption,* p. 216.
2. Fred W. Lorch, "Cable and His Reading Tour With Mark Twain in 1884–85," p. 479. In his essay "Taming the Bicycle," however, Mark Twain takes a contrary view, declaring that a self-taught man seldom knows anything accurately. ". . . he does not know a tenth as much as he could have known if he had worked under teachers. . . ." (*What is Man? And Other Essays,* p. 290.) He seems never to have changed his mind, however, that platform arts are best learned by observation and practice. "Who taught you to read?" he asked Howells in 1885. "Observation & thought, I guess." "And practice at the Tavern Club?"—"Yes; that was best teaching of all." (Henry Nash Smith and William Gibson (eds.), *Mark Twain–Howells Letters,* II, 527.)
3. *Alta California,* Mar. 30, 1867.
4. *Ibid.,* June 16, 1867.
5. *Ibid.,* Apr. 5, 1867.
6. The phrase is taken from the title of Melville D. Landon's *Kings of the Platform and Pulpit.*
7. *Mark Twain's Autobiography,* I, 151.
8. Albert Bigelow Paine, *Mark Twain: A Biography,* I, 295–96.
9. Mark Twain's shambling gait, though obviously used as a platform device and probably exaggerated for effect, appears to have been a natural characteristic of his manner of walking when offstage. (See

Twichell's comment, American Academy and the National Institute of Arts and Letters, *Academy Notes and Monographs*, p. 34. For a description of its peculiar effectiveness, see Cable's comment, *Ibid.*, p. 76.)

    10. Worcester *Evening Gazette,* Nov. 10, 1871.

    11. Clara Clemens, *My Father, Mark Twain,* p. 45. The lecture was at Worcester, Nov. 10, 1871.

    12. *Autobiography,* I, 160.

    13. Portland, Maine, *Daily Eastern Argus,* Nov. 16, 1871.

    14. Paine, *Biography,* I, 295.

    15. *Daily Commercial,* Oct. 25, 1871.

    16. Peoria *Daily Transcript,* Jan. 12, 1869.

    17. Dixon Wecter (ed.), *The Love Letters of Mark Twain,* pp. 23–24.

    18. Albert Bigelow Paine (ed.), *Mark Twain's Speeches,* p. 2.

    19. DeVoto, *Mark Twain in Eruption,* p. 301. Even his so-called impromptu speeches, Mark Twain admits, were written out days ahead of time, with all pauses and hesitations properly indicated and carefully memorized. (See Mark Twain's speech "To the Whitefriars," London, June 20, 1899, in William Dean Howells, *Mark Twain's Speeches,* p. 380.)

    20. *Autobiography,* I, 148–49.

    21. Albert Bigelow Paine (ed.), *Mark Twain's Letters,* II, 684. Howells replied that if he had Mark Twain's great histrionic ability he would gladly follow his advice, but lacking it, he had better rely on manuscript. (Smith and Gibson, *Mark Twain–Howells Letters,* II, 707.)

    22. Fredonia *Censor,* Jan. 19, 1870.

    23. *What is Man?* pp. 141–42.

    24. *Ibid.,* p. 142.

    25. Notebook No. 28a (I) May 15–Aug. 23, 1895; No. 30 (I) May 1–30, 1896, MTP.

    26. Dixon Wecter (ed), *Mark Twain to Mrs. Fairbanks,* p. 97.

    27. Clara Clemens, *MF, MT,* p. 139.

    28. *Ibid.,* p. 179.

    29. *Ibid.,* p. 139.

    30. Charles F. Horner, *Life of James Redpath,* p. 173.

    31. *How To Tell a Story and Other Essays,* p. 8.

    32. Wecter, *LL,* p. 41.

    33. *Academy Notes and Monographs,* 75–76.

    34. *Mark Twain in Eruption,* p. 226.

    35. Clara Clemens, *MF, MT,* p. 139.

    36. See the Sandwich Islands lecture reprinted in Chap. 20.

    37. DeVoto, *Mark Twain in Eruption,* p. 226.

    38. Harrisburg *Daily Patriot,* Jan. 17, 1872.

    39. Robert Johnson, *Remembered Yesterdays,* p. 324.

    40. William Dean Howells, *My Mark Twain,* p. 28.

NOTES TO CHAPTER SIXTEEN

AUDIENCE RECEPTION

1. *The Lyceum,* No. 1, August, 1869.
2. Charles F. Horner, *Life of James Redpath,* pp. 193–94.
3. *The Lyceum,* No. 1, August, 1869.
4. Albert Bigelow Paine (ed.), *Mark Twain's Speeches,* p. xiv.
5. Norwich, Connecticut, *Daily Advertiser,* Nov. 15, 1869.
6. Horner, *Life of James Redpath,* p. 195.
7. Dec. 20, 1871.
8. Detroit *Free Press,* Dec. 23, 1868.
9. June 3, 1867.
10. Albert Bigelow Paine, *Mark Twain: A Biography,* I, 118.
11. Report of a public meeting held at Carnegie Hall, New York, Nov. 30, 1910, in memory of Samuel Langhorne Clemens, American Academy and the National Institute of Arts and Letters, *Academy Notes and Monographs,* p. 83.
12. Portland, Maine, *Advertiser,* Nov. 17, 1871.
13. Jamestown, New York, *Journal,* Dec. 10, 1869.
14. Toledo *Blade,* Jan. 21, 1869.
15. Cleveland *Plain Dealer,* Nov. 18, 1869.
16. *Alta California,* Apr. 16, 1868.
17. Decatur, Illinois, *Republican,* Jan. 14, 1869.
18. Indianapolis *Daily Sentinel,* Jan. 5, 1869.
19. Nov. 24, 1872.
20. Decatur *Herald,* Jan. 14, 1869.
21. Paine, *Biography* II, 603–4.
22. See Chapter 20.
23. Decatur *Herald,* Jan. 14, 1869. While he professed to wish with all his heart that there were no irreverent passages in the book, he was privately convinced that the success of *Innocents Abroad* was in no small measure attributable to their presence. (Dixon Wecter (ed.), *Mark Twain to Mrs. Fairbanks,* p. 110.)
24. Jamestown *Journal,* Jan. 28, 1870. See also the Utica *Morning Herald,* Jan. 18, 1870.
25. Wecter, *Fairbanks,* p. 107.
26. *The American Claimant,* p. 80.
27. Haverhill *Weekly Gazette,* Nov. 24, 1871.
28. Chicago *Tribune,* Jan. 8, 1869.
29. Portland, Maine, *Daily Eastern Argus,* Nov. 16, 1871.
30. From an undated and unidentified Geneseo, New York, newspaper [Feb., 1869].
31. *Daily Republican,* Dec. 13, 1869.
32. Jamestown *Journal,* Jan. 28, 1870.
33. Josiah G. Holland, "Triflers on the Platform," p. 489. See also his "Lecture Brokers and Lecture Breakers," 560–61; and "The Literary Bureaus Again," pp. 362–63.

34. The manuscript is the Berg Collection of the New York City Public Library. Though undated, the internal evidence points to 1872.
35. Philadelphia *Press*, Dec. 8, 1869.
36. Lockport, New York, *Daily Union*, Mar. 4, 1869.
37. Fort Wayne *Daily Gazette*, Jan. 4, 1869.
38. Mount Vernon, New York, *Daily Chronicle*, Dec. 18, 1869.
39. Peoria, Illinois, *Daily Transcript*, Jan. 12, 1869.
40. *Republican*, Dec. 30, 1868.
41. Wecter, *Fairbanks*, p. 66.
42. Decatur *Republican*, Jan. 12, 1869.
43. John Ritchie Schultz, "New Letters of Mark Twain," p. 48.

NOTES TO CHAPTER SEVENTEEN

ON AUDIENCES

1. Albert Bigelow Paine (ed.), *Mark Twain's Letters*, I, 189.
2. Chap. IX.
3. The Newton, Massachusetts, *Journal*, Dec. 4, 1869.
4. Dixon Wecter (ed.), *The Love Letters of Mark Twain*, p. 49.
5. *Mark Twain's Autobiography*, I, 151.
6. *Alta California*, May 19, 1867.
7. Paine, *Letters*, I, 168.
8. It is apparent that Mark Twain perceived the trouble that might arise when a wide cultural gap existed between the lecturer and his audience. Audiences, he believed, prefer speakers with the same weaknesses and virtues which they themselves possess. If the lecturer is too highbrow for his audience, or the audience too highbrow for the lecturer, there is bound to be trouble. (Opie Read, *Mark Twain and I*, p. 53.)
9. See Caroline Thomas Harnsberger's *Mark Twain at Your Finger Tips*, p. 15. He was probably thinking of speaking before small groups, however, when he warned against speaking across a long narrow room. The lecturer should always be at the end of the room facing his audience. In this position he would avoid the necessity of turning first one way and then another to look at his auditors and having some of them always behind him. No part of the audience should ever be behind him, for "you can never tell what they are going to do." (William Dean Howells (ed.), *Mark Twain's Speeches*, p. 151.)
10. Wecter, *LL*, p. 173.
11. *Ibid.*, 161.
12. Paine, *Letters*, I, 193.
13. Clara Clemens, *My Father, Mark Twain*, p. 209.
14. Henry Nash Smith and William Gibson (eds.), *Mark Twain–Howells Letters*, I, 356.
15. Albert Bigelow Paine (ed.), *Mark Twain's Notebook*, pp. 200–201.

16. Notebook, No. 23 (I), July 1–Nov. 1, 1888, MTP.
17. Paine, *Notebook,* p. 201.
18. *Ibid.*
19. *Ibid.,* p. 200.
20. Wecter, *LL,* p. 172.
21. Paine, *Notebook,* p. 202.
22. *Ibid.,* p. 201.
23. Wecter, *LL,* p. 140–41.
24. Clara Clemens, *MF, MT,* p. 45.
25. Paine, *Letters,* I, 190–91.
26. Fred W. Lorch "Mark Twain's 'Sandwich Islands' Lecture and the Failure at Jamestown, New York," pp. 314–25.
27. Charles F. Horner, *Life of James Redpath,* p. 167.

PROFITS FROM THE ALTERNATE CAREER

1. Leon Howard, *Herman Melville: A Biography,* Berkeley, 1951, p. 256.
2. G. E. B., "Mark Twain as He Was Known During His Stay on the Pacific Slope," Mark Twain's ever urgent need of money and his ceaseless attempts to get it probably accounts for Robert Barr's uncomplimentary remark in 1898 that "If ever the eyes and beak of the American eagle were placed in a man's face, Samuel L. Clemens was that man." *(McClure's Magazine,* Jan., 1898. Also see *The Twainian,* IV, No. 6 (March, 1945) , 4.)
3. Oakland *Daily News,* Oct. 10, 1866.
4. *Mark Twain's Autobiography,* I, 157.
5. J. B. Pond, *Eccentricities of Genius,* p. 4.
6. *Ibid.,* p. 193.
7. Norristown *Herald* and *Free Press,* Nov. 2, 1871.
8. Redpaths *The Lyceum,* 1874.
9. *Ibid.,* August, 1869.
10. *Ibid.*
11. Will M. Clemens, "Mark Twain on the Lecture Platform," p. 29.
12. *Autobiography,* II, 351.
13. Fred W. Lorch, "Lecture Trips and Visits of Mark Twain in Iowa," pp. 507–7.
14. Frank Fuller, "Utah's War Governor Talks of Many Famous Men," New York *Times,* Oct. 1, 1911.
15. Typescript copies of letters from S.L.C. to Frank Fuller dated Aug. 7, Nov. 24, and Dec. 2 and 5, 1867, MTP.
16. *Autobiography,* II, 356.
17. Washoe *Evening Slope,* Nov. 21, 1866, declared that the proceeds of Mark Twain's lecture in San Francisco had been attached for

the benefit of one of his creditors. A few days later, on Nov. 23, an article in the Gold Hill *Daily News* implied that Mark Twain's departure for the East had been delayed on account of difficulties arising from non-payment of debt.

18. Albert Bigelow Paine (ed.), *Mark Twain's Letters,* I, 153.

19. Pond claims Redpath invited Mark Twain to come East to lecture on the advice of Petroleum V. Nasby *(Eccentricities of Genius,* p. 199).

20. The Elmira *Telegram,* July 14, 1895.

21. Paine, *Letters,* I, 158.

22. Samuel C. Webster (ed.), *Mark Twain, Business Man,* p. 103.

23. Paine, *Letters,* I, 189–90.

24. Dixon Wecter (ed.), *The Love Letters of Mark Twain,* pp. 171–72.

25. Dixon Wecter (ed.), *Mark Twain to Mrs. Fairbanks,* p. 160.

26. Will Clemens, "Mark Twain on the Lecture Platform," p. 29.

27. Webster, *Mark Twain, Business Man,* p. 294.

28. Letter to Pond dated Nov. 15, 1884, Berg Collection.

29. Paine, *Letters,* II, 628.

30. Albert Bigelow Paine (ed.), *Mark Twain's Notebook,* p. 251.

31. Pond, *Eccentricities of Genius,* p. 199.

32. See Elmira *Telegram,* July 14, 1895.

33. Paine, *Notebook,* p. 328.

34. Pond, *Eccentricities of Genius,* p. 226.

NOTES TO CHAPTER NINETEEN

RETIREMENT FROM TOUR LECTURING

1. Clara Clemens, *My Father, Mark Twain,* p. 139.

2. Albert Bigelow Paine (ed.), *Mark Twain's Letters,* I, 158–59.

3. *Ibid.,* pp. 172–73.

4. Dixon Wecter (ed.), *The Love Letters of Mark Twain,* pp. 66–67.

5. *Ibid.,* p. 164.

6. *Ibid.,* pp. 168–69.

7. *Ibid.,* p. 172.

8. Dixon Wecter (ed.), *Mark Twain to Mrs. Fairbanks,* p. 160.

9. Albert Bigelow Paine (ed.), *Mark Twain: A Biography,* I, 540–41. Also see the Hartford *Courant,* Mar. 6, 1875, and the Hartford *Daily Times* of the same date. *The Daily Times* stated that it withheld a full report of the lecture at Mark Twain's request. William Dean Howells conjectured that Mark Twain's desire to give up public lecturing, during middle life was that he came more and more to hate "the swarming of interest upon him, and all the inevitable clatter of the thing." (See *My Mark Twain,* p. 55.)

10. Albert Bigelow Paine (ed.), *Mark Twain's Speeches,* p. 1.

11. Nov. 19, 1884.
12. Paine, *Biography,* II, 783.
13. Paine, *Letters,* II, 633.
14. J. B. Pond, *Eccentricities of Genius,* p. 226.
15. Wecter, *LL,* p. 60.
16. *Ibid.,* pp. 60–61.
17. Archibald Henderson, *Mark Twain,* p. 99.
18. *Ibid.* Tom Fitch, associated with the Virginia City *Union,* had considerable reputation locally as an orator.
19. Springfield, Massachusetts, *Republican,* Nov. 13, 1869.
20. Albert Bigelow Paine (ed.), *Mark Twain's Notebook,* p. 351.
21. Paine, *Biography,* III, 1368.
22. Wecter, *Fairbanks,* p. 67.
23. *Ibid.,* p. 63.
24. *Ibid.,* p. 67.
25. Paine, *Letters,* II, 527–28.
26. Carlyle Smythe, "The Real Mark Twain," *Pall Mall Magazine,* XVI, No. 65 (Sept. 1898), 34.
27. Pond, *Eccentricities of Genius,* p. 226.
28. Clara Clemens, *MF, MT,* p. 83.
29. Paine, *Letters,* II, 791.
30. Paine, *Biography,* III, 1288.

NOTES TO CHAPTER TWENTY

TEXTS OF TOUR LECTURES

1. Walter F. Frear, *Mark Twain and Hawaii,* p. 177.
2. For an account of the discovery of this page see Frank Fuller's letter dated 1910 to Albert Bigelow Paine *(The Twainian,* The Fifteenth Year, No. 5, Sept.-Oct., 1956, p. 4).
3. Dixon Wecter (ed.), *Mark Twain to Mrs. Fairbanks,* p. 181.
4. Fred W. Lorch, "Mark Twain's Public Lectures in England in 1873," pp. 297–304.
5. Newark *Daily Advertiser,* Dec. 8, 1868.
6. Norwich, New York, *Chenango Union,* Dec. 9, 1868.
7. See his pp. 21–30.
8. Peoria, Illinois, *Daily Transcript,* Jan. 12, 1869.
9. Chicago *Republican,* Jan. 8, 1869.
10. Albert Bigelow Paine, *Mark Twain's Speeches,* p. 21.
11. Chicago *Republican,* Jan. 8, 1869.
12. Cleveland *Herald,* Nov. 18, 1868.
13. Peoria *Daily Transcript,* Jan. 12, 1869.
14. Paine, *Speeches,* pp. 21–22.
15. Peoria *Daily Transcript,* Jan. 12, 1869.
16. Paine, *Speeches,* p. 22.
17. Mohawk Valley *Register* and Fort Plain *Journal,* Dec. 25, 1868.

18. Paine, *Speeches,* pp. 22–24.
19. Peoria *Daily Transcript,* Jan. 12, 1869.
20. Paine, *Speeches,* pp. 24–29.
21. From the Webster Collection.
22. Paine, *Speeches,* pp. 29–30.
23. From the Webster Collection.
24. To this point from Toledo *Blade,* Dec. 12, 1871.
25. Hartford *Daily Times,* Nov. 9, 1871.
26. Toledo *Blade,* Dec. 12, 1871.
27. Hartford *Daily Times,* Nov. 9, 1871.
28. Toledo *Blade,* Dec. 12, 1871.
29. Hartford *Daily Times,* Nov. 9, 1871.
30. Toledo *Blade,* Dec. 12, 1871. Word "his'n" from Hartford *Daily Times,* Nov. 9, 1871.
31. Homer, New York, *Courtland County Republican,* Dec. 8, 1871.
32. Toledo *Blade,* Dec. 12, 1871.
33. Philadelphia *Inquirer,* Nov. 21, 1871.
34. Hartford *Daily Times,* Nov. 9, 1871.
35. Toledo *Blade,* Dec. 12, 1871.
36. Published in Hartford, 1869, pp. 284–87.
37. Artemus Ward's lecture tour in the Far West included Virginia City, where Mark Twain worked as a reporter on the *Territorial Enterprise.* It was at this time, during a period of about twelve days, that the two met and became friends. Somewhere in the course of the lecture Mark Twain alluded to his personal acquaintance with Ward, but no portion of those comments has been discovered.
38. From n. 35 to this point from Hartford *Daily Times,* Nov. 9, 1871.
39. Toledo *Blade,* Dec. 12, 1871.
40. Hartford *Daily Times,* Nov. 9, 1871.
41. Toledo *Blade,* Dec. 12, 1871.
42. Hartford *Daily Times* and Toledo *Blade,* dates cited.
43. Mar. 16, 1867.
44. Albert Bigelow Paine (ed.), *Mark Twain's Letters,* I, 213.

BIBLIOGRAPHY

American Academy and the National Institute of Arts and Letters. *Academy Notes and Monographs.* New York, 1922.

Aldrich, Mrs. Thomas Bailey. *Crowding Memories.* New York, 1920.

Armstrong, C. J. "Sam Clemens Considered Becoming a Preacher," *The Twainian,* IV, No. 8 (May, 1945), 1.

Ashbaugh, Kraid. "Mark Twain as a Public Speaker," *Western Speech,* XIV (January, 1950), 10–14.

"As I Like It," *Scribner's Magazine,* 95 (June, 1934), 433–34.

G. E. B. "Mark Twain as He Was Known During His Stay on the Pacific Slope," San Francisco *Call,* April 17, 1887.

Barr, Robert. "Samuel L. Clemens; Mark Twain; A Character Sketch," *McClure's Magazine,* X (January, 1898), 246–51.

Bellamy, Gladys Carmen. *Mark Twain as a Literary Artist.* Norman, Oklahoma, 1950.

Benson, Ivan. *Mark Twain's Western Years.* Stanford, 1938.

Benton, Joel. "Reminiscences of Eminent Lecturers," *Harper's,* XCVI, No. DLXXIV (March, 1898), 603–14.

Bickle, Lucy L. C. *George W. Cable: His Life and Letters.* New York, 1928.

Bode, Carl. *The American Lyceum.* New York, 1956.

Booth, B. A. "Mark Twain's Friendship With Emeline Beach," *American Literature,* XIX (November, 1947), 221–30.

Brashear, Minnie. *Mark Twain, Son of Missouri.* Chapel Hill, North Carolina, 1934.

Broadfield, William E. "Mark Twain as Keokuk Printer," Keokuk *Gate City,* October 24, 1911.

Brooks, Noah. "Mark Twain in California," *Century,* N.S. XXXV (November, 1898), 97–99.

Burnett, Ruth A. "Mark Twain in the Northwest," *Pacific Northwest Quarterly,* XLII (July, 1951), 187–202.

Buxbawm, K. "Mark Twain and American Dialect," *American Speech*, II (February, 1927), 23–26.

M. B. C. "Mark Twain as a Reader," *Harper's Weekly*, LV, No. 2820 (January 7, 1911), 6.

Camp, James E. *Mark Twain's Frontier*. New York, 1963.

Cardwell, Guy A. "Mark Twain's 'Row' With George Cable," *Modern Language Quarterly*, 13, No. 4 (December, 1952), 363–71.

———. *Twins of Genius*. East Lansing, Michigan, 1953.

Clemens, Clara. *My Father, Mark Twain*. New York, 1931. Passages reprinted by permission of Harper and Row, Publishers.

Clemens, Cyril. *Josh Billings, Yankee Humorist*. Webster Groves, Missouri, 1932.

———. *Petroleum V. Nasby*. Webster Groves, Missouri, 1936.

——— (ed.). *Republican Letters*. Webster Groves, Missouri, 1941.

Clemens, William M. *Mark Twain, His Life and Work*. San Francisco, 1892.

———. "Mark Twain on the Lecture Platform," *Ainslee's Magazine*, VI, No. 1 (August, 1900), 25–32.

Coleman, Rufus A. "Mark Twain in Montana, 1895," *Montana Magazine of History*, III (Spring, 1953), 9–17.

Conway, Moncure D. *Autobiography*. 2 vols. London, 1904.

Critic, The, V (December 27, 1884).

Dane, G. Ezra (ed.). *Letters From the Sandwich Islands*. Stanford, 1938.

Day, A. Grove (ed.). *Mark Twain's Letters From Hawaii*. New York, 1966.

DeVoto, Bernard. *Mark Twain at Work*. Cambridge, Massachusetts, 1942.

——— (ed.). *Mark Twain in Eruption*. New York, 1940.

——— (ed.). *The Portable Mark Twain*. New York, 1946.

Donner, Stanley T. "Mark Twain as a Reader," *Quarterly Journal of Speech*, XXXIII (October, 1947), 308–11.

———. "Mark Twain's First Lectures," *Western Speech*, XIV (March, 1950), 40–42.

Duckett, Margaret. *Mark Twain and Bret Harte*. Norman, Oklahoma, 1964.

Ellsworth, William W. *The Golden Age of Authors*. New York, 1919.

Fatout, Paul. "Mark Twain Lectures in Indiana," *Indiana Magazine of History*, XLVI, No. 4 (December, 1950), 363–73.

———. *Mark Twain on the Lecture Circuit*. Bloomington, Indiana, 1960.

———. *Mark Twain in Virginia City*. Bloomington, Indiana, 1964.

———. "Mark Twain's First Lecture: A Parallel," *Pacific Historical Review*, 25, No. 4 (November, 1956), 347–54.

———. "The Twain–Cable Readings in Indiana," *Indiana Magazine of History*, LIII, No. 1 (March, 1957), 19–28.

Flanagan, John T. "Mark Twain on the Upper Mississippi," *Minnesota History*, XVII, No. 4 (December, 1936), 377–84.

Frear, Walter Francis. *Mark Twain and Hawaii.* Chicago, 1947.

Gilder, Richard Watson. "A Glance at Mark Twain's Spoken and Written Art," *Outlook*, 78 (December 3, 1904), 842–44.

"Glimpses of the Past," *Missouri Historical Society Publication.* St. Louis (October, 1935).

Harnsberger, Caroline Thomas. *Mark Twain at Your Finger Tips.* New York, 1948.

Hayes, Cecil B. *The American Lyceum.* Washington, D. C., 1932.

Henderson, Archibald. *Mark Twain.* New York, 1912.

Hingston, Edward P. *Genial Showman.* London, 1871.

Hoeltje, Hubert H. "Notes on the History of Lecturing in Iowa," *Iowa Journal of History and Politics*, XXV (January, 1927), 62–131.

———. "When Mark Twain Spoke in Portland," *The Oregon Historical Quarterly*, LV (March, 1954), 73–81.

Holland, Josiah G. "Lecture Brokers and Lecture-Breakers," *Scribner's Monthly*, I, No. 5 March, 1871), 560–61.

———. "The Literary Bureaus Again," *Scribner's Monthly*, IX. (July, 1872).

———. "The Popular Lecture," *Atlantic Monthly*, XV (March, 1865), 364.

———. "Triflers on the Platform," *Scribner's Monthly*, III, No. 4 (February, 1872), 489.

Horner, Charles F. *Life of James Redpath.* New York, 1926.

Howells, William Dean. *My Mark Twain.* New York, 1910.

——— (ed.). *Mark Twain's Speeches.* New York, 1910. Copyright © 1923, 1951 by the Mark Twain Company.

Johnson, Robert Underwood. *Remembered Yesterdays.* Boston, 1923.

Kaplan, Justin. *Mr. Clemens and Mark Twain.* New York, 1966.

King, Frederick A. "The Story of Mark Twain's Debts," *Bookman*, 31 (June, 1910), 394–96.

Krause, Sydney J. "Mark Twain's Method and Theory of Compositions," *Modern Philosophy*, LVI, No. 3 (February, 1959), 167–77.

Landon, Melville DeLancy (Eli Perkins). *Kings of the Platform and Pulpit.* New York, 1900.

La Vegne, Gary W. "The Day Mark Twain Came to Geneseo, New York," *The Twainian*, Twentieth Year, No. 6 (November-December, 1961), 1–4.

Leacock, Stephen. "Mark Twain and Canada," *Queen's Quarterly*, XLII (Spring, 1935), 68–81.

———. "More of Mark Twain in Canada," *Queen's Quarterly*, XLII (Summer, 1935), 272–74.

Leary, Lewis. *Mark Twain's Letters to Mary.* New York, 1961.

"Lecturing Experience," *Book Buyer*, 22 (April, 1901), 179.

Lederer, Max. "Mark Twain in Vienna," *The Mark Twain Quarterly,* III (Summer-Fall, 1945), 1–12.

Lennon, E. James. "Mark Twain Abroad," *The Quarterly Journal of Speech,* 39, No. 2 (April, 1953), 197–200.

"Letters From Frank Fuller," *The Twainian,* The Fifteenth Year, No. 4 (July-August, 1956), 1–3.

Lillard, Richard G. "Studies in Washoe Journalism and Humor." Unpublished Ph.D. dissertation, University of Iowa, 1943.

Lorch, Fred W. "Cable and His Reading Tour With Mark Twain, 1884–1885," *American Literature,* 23, No. 4 (January, 1952), 471–86.

——. "Mark Twain in Iowa," *The Iowa Journal of History and Politics,* 27, No. 3 (July, 1929), 408–56.

——. "Lecture Trips and Visits of Mark Twain in Iowa," *The Iowa Journal of History and Politics,* 27, No. 4 (October, 1929), 507–47.

——. "Mark Twain's 'Artemus Ward' Lecture on the Tour of 1871–1872," *New England Quarterly,* 25, No. 3 (September, 1952), 327–43.

——. "Mark Twain's Lecture From *Roughing It,*" *American Literature,* 22, No. 3 (November, 1950), 290–307.

——. "Mark Twain's Lecture Tour of 1868–1869; The American Vandal Abroad," *American Literature,* 26, No. 4 (January, 1955), 515–27.

——. "Mark Twain's 'Morals' Lecture During the American Phase of His World Tour in 1895–1896," *American Literature,* 26, No. 1 (March, 1954), 52–66.

——. "Mark Twain's Orphanage Lecture," *American Literature,* 7, No. 1 (January, 1936), 455.

——. "Mark Twain's Public Lectures in England in 1873," *American Literature,* 29, No. 3 (November, 1957), 297–304.

——. "Mark Twain's 'Sandwich Islands' Lecture and the Failure at Jamestown, New York," *American Literature,* 25, No. 3 (November, 1953), 314–25.

——. "Mark Twain's 'Sandwich Islands' Lecture at St. Louis," *American Literature,* 18, No. 4 (January, 1947), 299–307.

——. "Orion Clemens," *Palimpsest,* X, No. 10 (October, 1929), 353–88.

Mack, Effie Mona. *Mark Twain in Nevada.* New York, 1947.

"Mark Twain and the Pacific Slope," *Pacific Monthly,* XXIV (August, 1910), 115–32.

"Mark Twain in San Francisco," *Bookman,* 31 (June, 1910), 369–73.

"Mark Twain as a Reader," *Harper's Weekly,* LV, No. 2820 (January 7, 1911), 6.

Matthews, Brander. "Mark Twain Stands and Delivers," *The Literary Digest International Book Review,* I (August, 1923), 23–24.

——. "Mark Twain as a Speech Maker and Story Teller," *Mentor,* XII (May, 1924), 24–28.

Mead, David. *Yankee Eloquence in the Middle West.* East Lansing, Michigan, 1951.

Merrill, W. H. "When Mark Twain Lectured," *Harper's,* 50 (February, 1906), 199, 209.

Moffatt, Wallace B. "Mark Twain's Lansing Lecture on Roughing It," *Michigan History,* 34, No. 2 (June, 1950), 144–70.

Mark Twain's Notebooks. *The Mark Twain Papers,* University of California Library, Berkeley.

Pabody, E. P. "Mark Twain's Ghost Story," *Minnesota History,* XVIII (March, 1937), 28–35.

Paine, Albert Bigelow. *Mark Twain: A Biography.* 3 vols. New York, 1912. Passages reprinted by permission of Harper and Row, Publishers.

———. *Thomas Nast, His Period and His Pictures.* New York, 1904.

——— (ed.). *Mark Twain's Letters.* 2 vols. New York, 1917. Passages reprinted by permission of Harper and Row, Publishers.

——— (ed.). *Mark Twain's Notebook.* New York, 1935.

——— (ed.). *Mark Twain's Speeches.* New York, 1925. Copyright © 1923, 1951 by Mark Twain Company.

Pemberton, T. E. *The Life of Bret Harte.* London, 1903.

Pond, James B. *Eccentricities of Genius.* New York, 1900.

———. "Memories of the Lyceum," *Modern Eloquence,* Vol. 6, pp. 893–917.

Read, Opie. *Mark Twain and I.* Chicago, 1940.

Roberts, Harold. "Sam Clemens: Florida Days," *The Twainian,* I, No. 3, New Series (March, 1942), 4–7.

Rourke, Constance. *American Humor: A Study of the National Character.* New York, 1931.

Schultz, John Ritchie. "New Letters of Mark Twain," *American Literature,* 8 (March, 1936), 47–51.

Smith, Henry Nash, and Anderson, Frederick (eds.). *Mark Twain of the Enterprise.* Berkeley, 1957.

Smith, Henry Nash, and Gibson, William M. (eds.). *Mark Twain–Howells Letters.* 2 vols. Cambridge, 1960.

Smythe, Carlyle. "The Real Mark Twain," *Pall Mall Magazine,* XVI, No. 65 (September, 1898), 29.

Stewart, George R. "Bret Harte Upon Mark Twain in 1866," *American Literature,* 13 (March, 1941–January, 1942), 263–64.

Stewart, William Morris (George Rothwell Brown, ed.). *Reminiscences.* New York, 1908.

Tichnor, Caroline. *Glimpses of Authors.* New York, 1922.

Tinker, Edward L. "Cable and the Creoles," *American Literature,* 5 (January, 1934), 313–26.

Turner, Arlin. *George W. Cable.* Durham, North Carolina, 1956.

———. "Mark Twain, Cable, and 'A Professional Newspaper Liar,'" *New England Quarterly,* XXVIII, No. 1 (March, 1955), 18–33.

Twain, Mark. *The American Claimant.* New York, 1892.

————. *Following the Equator.* 2 vols. New York, 1897.
————. *How To Tell a Story, and Other Essays.* New York, 1902.
————. *Mark Twain's Autobiography.* 2 vols. New York, 1924. Passages reprinted by permission of Harper and Row, Publishers.
————. "My First Lecture," *American Publisher,* 1 (December, 1871), 4.
————. *Personal Recollections of Joan of Arc.* New York, 1896.
————. *Roughing It.* 2 vols. New York, 1871.
————. *What is Man? And Other Essays.* New York, 1917.
"Twain's Trip Around the World," *Current Literature,* 29 (December, 1900), 709.
Twichell, Joseph H. "Mark Twain," *Harper's,* XCII (May, 1896), 817–27.
Vale, Charles. "Mark Twain as an Orator," *The Forum,* XLIV (July, 1910), 1–13.
Vogelback, A. L. "The Publication and Reception of *Huckleberry Finn* in America," *American Literature,* XI (1939–40), 260–72.
Wagenknecht, Edward. *Mark Twain: The Man and His Work.* Norman, Oklahoma, 1961.
Walker, Franklin. *San Francisco's Literary Frontier.* New York, 1939.
————, and Dane, G. Ezra (eds.). *Mark Twain's Travels With Mr. Brown.* New York, 1940.
Webster, Samuel C. (ed.). *Mark Twain, Business Man.* Boston, 1946.
Wecter, Dixon. *Sam Clemens of Hannibal.* Boston, 1952.
———— (ed.). *The Love Letters of Mark Twain.* New York, 1949. Copyright © 1947, 1949 by the Mark Twain Company.
———— (ed.). *Mark Twain in Three Moods.* San Marino, California, 1948.
———— (ed.). *Mark Twain to Mrs. Fairbanks.* San Marino, California, 1949. Passages reprinted by permission of the Henry E. Huntington Library and Art Gallery. Copyright © 1949 by the Mark Twain Company.
"When Mark Twain Petrified the Brahmins," *Literary Digest,* LXII, No. 2 (July 12, 1919), 28–29.
Wind, Herbert Warren. "Circuit Rider," *The New Yorker,* 29 (October 25, 1952), 39–68.

INDEX